Vision & Place

The publisher and the University of California Press Foundation gratefully acknowledge the generous support of the Peter Booth Wiley Endowment Fund in History.

Vision & Place

John Wesley Powell & Reimagining the Colorado River Basin

EDITED BY
Jason Robison, Daniel McCool, and Thomas Minckley

UNIVERSITY OF CALIFORNIA PRESS

University of California Press
Oakland, California

© 2020 by The Regents of The University of California

Library of Congress Cataloging-in-Publication Data

Names: Robison, Jason, 1975- editor. | McCool, Daniel,
 1950- editor. | Minckley, Thomas, 1966- editor.
Title: Vision & place : John Wesley Powell and
 reimagining the Colorado River basin / edited by Jason
 Robison, Daniel McCool, Thomas Minckley.
Description: Oakland : University of California Press,
 [2020] | Includes bibliographical references and index.
Identifiers: LCCN 2020007539 (print) | LCCN 2020007540
 (ebook) | ISBN 9780520375789 (cloth) | ISBN
 9780520375796 (paperback) | ISBN 9780520976238
 (ebook)
Subjects: LCSH: Powell, John Wesley, 1834–1902. |
 Colorado River Watershed (Colo.-Mexico)—History.
Classification: LCC F788 .V57 2020 (print) | LCC F788
 (ebook) | DDC 978.8—dc23
LC record available at https://lccn.loc.gov/2020007539
LC ebook record available at https://lccn.loc
 .gov/2020007540

29 28 27 26 25 24 23 22 21 20
10 9 8 7 6 5 4 3 2 1

To the Sesquicentennial Colorado River
Exploring Expedition participants, and to
Jonathan Bowler for helping spark the entire
SCREE project.
—The Editors

To my old friend Rani.
—J. A. R.

To the Old River Dog, R.I.P.
—D. C. M.

To JJ, for all of the support and patience through
the years.
—T. A. M.

Contents

List of Figures and Maps ... ix
Foreword ... xi
Charles Wilkinson

Introduction: The "Great Unknown" ... xix

PART I: WATER ... 1

1. Strange Resurrection: The Fall and Rise of John Wesley Powell ... 11
   Louis S. Warren and Rachel St. John

2. Communitarianism in Western Water Law and Policy: Was Powell's Vision Lost? ... 28
   Robert W. Adler

3. Common Water Commonwealth: The Paradox of a Shared Resource ... 54
   Amorina Lee-Martinez and Patricia Limerick

4. Powell's Legacy—The Bureau of Reclamation and the Contemporary West: Water Exchanges ... 76
   Robert Glennon

PART II: PUBLIC LANDS — 95

5. John Wesley Powell and the National Park Idea: Preserving Colorado River Basin Public Lands — 105
   Robert B. Keiter

6. Who Is the "Public" on the Colorado River Basin's Public Lands? — 125
   Paul Hirt

7. Powell as Unwitting Godfather of Outdoor Recreation in the Great Unknown — 148
   Emilene Ostlind

8. Stewart Udall, John Wesley Powell, and the Emergence of a National American Commons — 167
   William deBuys

PART III: NATIVE AMERICANS — 191

9. "We Must Either Protect Him or Destroy Him" — 201
   Weston C. McCool and Daniel C. McCool

10. "Pastoral and Civilized": Water, Land, and Tribes in the Colorado River Basin — 220
    Autumn L. Bernhardt

11. Civilizing Public Land Management in the Colorado River Basin — 242
    Daniel Cordalis and Amy Cordalis

12. John Wesley Powell's Land and Water Policies and Southwestern Native American Agricultural Practices — 265
    William J. Gribb

Afterword — 290
John C. Schmidt

References — 297
Contributors — 301
Index — 303

List of Figures and Maps

FIGURES

1. Bailey Russel, *View of Green River Lakes* (2016) / 6
2. Bailey Russel, *View of Flaming Gorge* (2017) / 7
3. Kate Aitchison, *Glen Canyon Dam* (2016) / 8
4. Bailey Russel, *View of Marble Canyon at Soap Creek* (2018) / 9
5. Erika Osborne, *Hoover Gates* (2011) / 10
6. Colorado River Basin Historical Water Supply and Use and Projected Future Water Supply and Demand (2012) / 83
7. David Jones, *Subterranean BTUs* (2010) / 99
8. Kate Aitchison, *The Hull 1* (2017) / 100
9. Kate Aitchison, *The Hull 2* (2017) / 100
10. Kate Aitchison, *Katie Lee* (2017) / 101
11. Erika Osborne, *Looking for Moran* (2012) / 102
12. Brandon Gellis, *Uncharted 1–3* (2018) / 102
13. Patrick Kikut, *Powell Point* (2018) / 104
14. Chip Thomas, *free yo mind + yo ass will follow* (2013) / 195
15. Will Wilson, *Auto Immune Response: Confluence of 3 Generations* (2015) / 196
16. Will Wilson, *Melissa Pochoema, Insurgent Hopi Maiden* (2015) / 198

17. Chip Thomas, *step in cow springs, navajo nation on the colorado plateau* (2014) / *199*
18. Patrick Kikut, *Dream Catcher* (2017) / *200*

MAPS

1. John Wesley Powell's Colorado River Exploring Expedition (1869) / *xxv*
2. Dams and Diversions, Colorado River Basin (2019) / *5*
3. Land Ownership, Colorado River Basin (2019) / *98*
4. Native American Reservations, Colorado River Basin (2019) / *194*
5. Distribution of Major Tribes in and around Colorado River Basin (c. 1860) / *267*
6. Major Military Posts and Transportation Networks in Southwest (1846–60) / *268*
7. Southwestern Reservations (1883) / *272*

Foreword

CHARLES WILKINSON

When Bruce Babbitt grew up in Flagstaff, Arizona, it was still an archetypal Western town dominated by logging, mining, and ranching. He liked and respected the people and the way of life but, at the same time, he was deeply intellectual, even as a boy. In 1954, at sixteen years old, he heard of Wallace Stegner's book and promptly bought a copy of *Beyond the Hundredth Meridian: John Wesley Powell and the Second Opening of the West*. For Bruce, reading it was "as though someone had thrown a rock through the window." Years later, as Secretary of the Interior, referring to Powell by his military title, Babbitt would say of difficult decisions: "I often ask myself, what would the Major do?"

Powell influenced another great Secretary of the Interior in much the same way. Stewart Udall also had grown up in multiple-use Arizona, and when he became Secretary in 1961 he lacked a larger, national perspective. Knowing of Stegner and his Powell book, Stewart called Stegner back to Washington to serve as a special advisor. Stegner presented the Secretary with a unique way to learn about the great ideas of the American West: write a book about them. Before long, Stegner offered an outline. John Wesley Powell was prominently featured. The result was a collaboration—Stewart had help, some from Stegner, some from a staff assistant and others—but he wrote most of *The Quiet Crisis* himself.

And, of course, it worked. Udall regularly acknowledged lessons that the writing process had imbued, and *The Quiet Crisis* and Rachel Carson's *Silent Spring*, published in 1963 and 1962, respectively, have become known as the intellectual foundation of the ideals held by the modern conservation movement.

By the mid-1960s, Westerners had launched an informal but wide-ranging examination of the West. What has happened? What is happening now? What should happen next? Stegner called it "agonizing about the West."

The timeline for this modern re-examination went back to the very beginning with the Native experience, and proceeded with the likes of Henry David Thoreau, Powell, John Muir, Theodore Roosevelt, and Aldo Leopold. This comprehensive assessment of the West also encompassed events bursting out day-by-day: Earth Day, the Sagebrush Rebellion, the rise of environmental law, the "discovery" of the science of ecology, conservative resource economics, climate change, the pushback on environmental policies in the Reagan, Bush Second, and Trump administrations, and the Clinton and Obama national monuments. The extraordinary population growth affected everything: the Southwest, fueled by the "Big Build-up," has exploded from eight million people in 1945 to almost forty million today.

The modern re-examination of the West has led to or influenced sturdy advances. The amount of first-rate research and literature from different disciplines and points of view is astonishing. Examples include Stegner himself, Richard White, John McPhee, Louise Erdrich, Edward Abbey, Vine Deloria, Jr., Edward O. Wilson, Terry Tempest Williams, and several contributors to this book. Pathbreaking scholarship in history, science, economics, and law has been put forth. Indian Country has achieved an historic and ongoing revival in culture and nation-building. Many universities have developed significant programs directed to understanding the West. Numerous national, regional, and local conservation groups have been established to protect land, water, and other natural resources. Congress has been active, and most of the work has been positive. The greatest steps forward were taken from the late 1960s through the early 1980s, when Congress created a raft of public land, wildlife, and environmental statutes, including the Clean Air Act and Clean Water Act, which remain in place today.

Needless to say, the foreboding matter of climate change is now at a perilous point for the Southwest, United States, and world. For generations, American scientists and policymakers have been prominent world leaders. As of this moment, those efforts have been blunted at the national level, but there is much still to be told. We can reasonably hope, and do our best to ensure, that the modern consensus about the reality and causes of climate change will hold and allow those scientists and policymakers to resume contributing the full range of their abilities in the future.

It is, then, a fair question whether there is a need for a book like this one. We have agonized over the Colorado River Basin and the West since John Wesley Powell began the practice. The agonizing has expanded and intensified over the past half-century. To top it off, Powell has already inspired impressive biographies by Wallace Stegner, William deBuys, and Donald Worster. Why do we need another Powell book? Why do we need this one?

For me, it has to do with the sesquicentennial. Powell took his first journey down the Green and Colorado rivers in 1869. Sesquicentennials (like centennials) of major events offer opportunities. They can refresh our thoughts or teach us about a past that we were previously unaware of. They can cause us to engage in critical thinking. What were the circumstances and ideas surrounding that event? Have we made progress since then? How could we have done better? And, critically, how can we do better in the future?

Powell's life, work and attitudes, and philosophies are fertile terrain for this kind of exploration. Even when deep in the Grand Canyon, Powell's mind fanned out to the landscape beyond. On his second expedition, two years later, he went on top and visited the Mormon town of Kanab. Later he visited Mormon homes in Sevier Valley. He loved the dancing and sense of family and community. Focusing on water, he learned that Mormon water rights were held by the community as a whole. This was in sharp contrast to the legal rule that water rights were owned by individual water developers, a notion already sweeping the West. In his *Arid Lands Report,* he drew upon the Mormon communitarian system and envisioned bona fide settlers creating irrigation districts—democratic organizations capable of locally managing water.

Powell also saw wisdom in the practices of Hispanic irrigators and proposed federal adoption of the land pattern of those communities: homesteads would not be square 160-acre parcels, but rather narrow and deep parcels with one end adjacent to the stream. He admired Spanish and Mexican *ejidos,* community collaboratives that held farming and ranching lands, instead of those lands being in individual ownership. In the *Arid Lands Report,* Powell, flying in the face of Western senators' rigid individualism, recommended that future homesteading proceed on the basis of these kinds of communal systems.

Powell's thinking evolved over the next decade. He expanded his notion of local democratic organizations, the irrigation districts, by urging the creation of larger watershed commonwealths throughout the region. They would have responsibility for decision-making over water and the public timber and grazing lands—the majority of all land in the West at that time. As shown in *Vision & Place,* watershed governance has continued to be a main theme for the Colorado River Basin's future.

Throughout all of his work, Powell drew upon his belief, gained through a better understanding of the West than any other non-Native person at the time, that this was dry country where aridity had to be considered in virtually all land and water decisions. Powell believed that water must be conserved, not wasted. He saw that homesteading amounted to fraud against prospective settlers. There was no information given about the key fact: how much available water was there in far-away valleys that homesteaders were heading for? Homesteaders weren't being told the truth. Big land interests were preying on that.

Powell dared to take action to address this fundamental flaw in the homesteading program at the height of his powers. By the 1880s, he had become famous and influential from the publicity surrounding his daring expeditions, having been named head of both the Bureau of Ethnology and the US Geological Survey.

In 1889, Powell, skillfully working the levers of the Interior Department, obtained a dramatic departmental order banning issuance of land patents to homesteaders for two years, and perhaps longer. The idea was that homesteaders were being duped into believing that settling the West was easy, when it was nothing of the sort. While homesteading was stayed, Powell would do a comprehensive survey of Western lands, identifying soil conditions and, most importantly, access to water. Then homesteading could proceed, watershed by watershed, with settlers having full and accurate information. Finally, Powell's vision of a West anchored on democracy and community would become a reality.

"Big Bill" Stewart and other Western senators rose up in fury, shouting that the survey would take countless years, while the westward movement would stagnate. Congress overrode the ban within a year. By 1894, Powell had been effectively blackballed and run out of office.

We can, then, use the sesquicentennial to revisit the times and proposals of a man whose contemporary vision of the West was broader-gauged than anyone else's. The *Arid Lands Report* and Powell's articles were more comprehensive, perceptive, and daring than any published in the nineteenth century. His homesteading ban was by any standard one of the most explosive actions in the history of federal public lands. Perhaps surprisingly, since so much has been written about Powell, *Vision & Place* offers numerous new takes, brightly written, on the Major and his times.

In an even larger sense, we can be inspired and informed by the creative, courageous, and energetic way Powell threw himself into imagining and creating the entire region's future. He knew the specifics cold, the on-the-ground details. He built upon them to boldly suggest unique policies and societal institutions for local communities. Then, beyond that, he dared to advocate systems for the whole West, more than half of the nation's land base. We cannot be sure that this country today is capable of building ideas of such reach. But perhaps we have to. How else can we address the existential threat of climate change, which, we should note, is hand in glove with Powell's breakthrough identification of aridity as the West's distinguishing characteristic?

Yet we need to acknowledge that Powell had one glaring blind spot: the place of Native Americans in this landscape that he dreamed would one day become a model of vibrant local and regional communities.

Powell liked Indian people individually. He admired their ability to see the details of the land while he saw broad landscapes and watersheds. Otherwise, he refused to give dignity to Native worldviews and institutions. He demeaned what he called "Indian theology." He failed to acknowledge tribes' ability to govern, ignoring their well-functioning justice systems for internal matters and ways of relating with other Indian governments. He never gave credence to the elaborate traditional knowledge that made them such dedicated, effective stewards of land and water.

While Powell's attitudes toward Native values and institutions were widely held, it may seem surprising that he did not rise above prevailing stereotypes. After all, he traveled extensively in Indian Country and held arguably the highest Indian affairs office in the United States. He wrote "expert" accounts of the ethnology and societies of tribes. He was looked to by presidents, senators, and scholars as the nation's leading authority on Native Americans. Nonetheless, in spite of all his experience, responsibilities, and stature, his views and actions significantly harmed Indian peoples.

Powell's vision was a middle-ground view that Native people should be moved off reservations over time and assimilated into majority society. Only by opening up large amounts of Indian land for settlement, the reasoning went, could Indian people be "saved" from extinction. This brand of thinking was employed to justify the raw, discredited General Allotment Act of 1887, which led to the loss of ninety million acres of Indian land. Powell was a principal, and influential, supporter of that statute.

Powell's lack of attention to key Indian concerns led to grievous lost opportunities and damage in addition to pulverization of the tribal land base through the General Allotment Act. In all of his proposals, there was not a single protection for Indian land or water rights, which he knew to be critical to people living in the West. In spite of his insistence on local democracy, he put forth no guidance on, much less affirmative protections for, tribal governance.

Now, 150 years later, as explored in several places in this volume, tribes are reclaiming land, water rights, and sovereign authority in impressive fashion. That is fair and good, but it has been accomplished in spite of, not because of, John Wesley Powell.

I am delighted to see *Vision & Place* come to fruition. It is blessed with chapters from eminent experts, as well as younger, diverse, and creative scholars and writers. Their words and ideas harness the past but continually push toward the horizon. What about the tomorrows?

I'd like to offer just one example.

The public lands are such a gift. They are one of the main prerogatives of citizenship in the nation and the West. Although we have made mistakes, we have protected them through inventing and employing categories such as "wilderness," and drawing upon the knowledge of western sciences.

But what kinds of knowledge have we omitted or slighted in our management of the peoples' lands? How could we expand our protection of these wondrous places and deepen our understanding and appreciation of them? How could we revere and love them even more?

Several authors in this volume mention Bears Ears National Monument, proclaimed by President Obama in December 2016. At 1.35 million acres, it was one of the country's largest monuments. (A year later, President Trump dramatically reduced the monument's size and altered President Obama's proclamation in several ways. The Trump action may well be legally invalid and is being challenged in court by tribes and conservation groups.) The Obama Bears Ears National Monument proclamation is a remarkable document. Whether or not its full vitality is restored by the courts, Obama's work is rich with new ways that the public lands can come to mean even more to us.

The Bears Ears Inter-Tribal Coalition—comprising the Hopi, Navajo, Ute Indian, Ute Mountain Ute, and Pueblo of Zuni tribes—was the lead organization proposing the monument, which lies in redrock glory country in southern Utah, homeland to these tribes. It was the first time tribes had ever taken the lead in creating a national monument.

The Obama monument will proceed on the basis of "collaborative management" between the five Coalition tribes and two federal agencies, the Bureau of Land Management (BLM) and the Forest Service. The core idea is to integrate traditional knowledge into decision-making at Bears Ears. Managing federal lands on a collaborative basis with tribes had never been tried before.

The Obama proclamation is a distinctive document honoring the land, the tribes, and the tribes' relationship to the land. The beginning pages are dedicated to an accurate, unadorned description of the robust and admirable tribal existence before non-Indians arrived. That description set the foundation for provisions involving traditional knowledge and collaborative management that would be, along with the cultural landscape preserved, the most exceptional aspects of the proclamation.

The Obama proclamation set forth the philosophical basis for infusing monument management with traditional knowledge in words of profound substance and literary power worthy of Muir, Leopold, or Stegner:

> The traditional ecological knowledge amassed by the Native Americans whose ancestors inhabited this region, passed down from generation to generation, offers critical insight into the historic and scientific significance of the area. Such knowledge is, itself, a resource to be protected and used in understanding and managing this landscape sustainably for generations to come.

Tribal people are quick to acknowledge that western sciences, such as ecology, are valuable and useful. Rather, traditional knowledge is "another way of knowing," a distinct voice that should be heard, respected, and used in federal land management when appropriate.

The Obama proclamation called for traditional knowledge to be used in collaborative management between the tribes, the BLM, and the Forest Service to develop comprehensive information about tribal relationships with places, animal and plant species, minerals, and water. Information about plants, for instance, would include names, locations, habitats, uses, harvesting methods, practices to protect and increase numbers, and threats. In addition to such on-the-ground data, traditional knowledge about species would also be articulated through, and embodied in, stories, songs, dances, art, sacred sites, and religious ceremonies.

Obviously, one issue is how exactly traditional knowledge should be embedded in monument land management to shape activities and development. If a particular plant—a medicine, let's say—needs rest, should its habitat be off-limits to roads? To mineral development? Closed to the general public? Like the demands of defining traditional knowledge for species, establishing processes for incorporating it into real-world management will be time-consuming and mature only after much elbow grease.

While tribes will consider some information confidential, there will be many ways to provide, usually through Native people, this new, yet so ancient, knowledge to the public, including exhibits, demonstrations, lectures, books, and displays. Out on the land, people who have learned of traditional knowledge will experience the joy of discovery in nature. Land management will protect plants and animals not previously appreciated or known. And overall land health will improve as attention and care are given to previously ignored species.

These initiatives continue to gain traction. In 2016, Secretary of the Interior Sally Jewell issued an order outlining a process for tribes to establish collaborative management with federal agencies. There is widespread interest across Indian Country in using this order, or other authorities, for collaborative management of parks, monuments, forests, and wildlife refuges. Traditional knowledge is receiving considerable attention in domestic and international universities. Articles are steadily coming out. These kinds of ideas can inflame a person.

Collaborative management and traditional knowledge are just two topics in *Vision & Place* that will spark peoples' minds and imaginations. "The Great Unknown." "A dryland democracy." Watershed governance. Ethnic diversity in public land and water decision-making. Climate change. The Colorado River Basin's future. Democratic Western communities. The fate of our public lands and rivers. We can imagine young Westerners learning about these ideas and finding one of them was the rock that came through the window.

Introduction

The "Great Unknown"

It has been 150 years since John Wesley Powell's famous voyage down the Green and Colorado rivers, yet he is still an icon. Why? The answer to that question, as this volume makes clear, depends upon whom you ask. Some would say it is because Powell was the first person to run the Grand Canyon's world-class rapids. Others might mention that he made the US Geological Survey into a modern, effective agency. Still others would point to Powell's groundbreaking ideas on water and land policy, or his prodigious work in ethnology and anthropology. A few academics might recognize that he was an industrious researcher, and arguably an even more influential supervisor of others' research, during the latter part of the nineteenth century. And, finally, some might draw attention to the fact that, by any reasonable contemporary standard, Powell would be considered an overt racist. Indeed, one would be hard-pressed to find a more complex, varied, and eclectic individual in the annals of US history than John Wesley Powell. In this volume, we delve deeply into the man, his time and ours, and the relative value of his ideas in guiding us into a future that will be markedly different from our past.

On May 24, 1869, Major Powell's Colorado River Exploring Expedition stood along the banks of the Green River in Wyoming Territory. Powell, his right arm missing from a wound received seven years earlier at Shiloh, launched four clumsy wooden boats into the current and entered *terra incognita*. As he subsequently described it, Powell and his crew had begun a journey down the "Great Unknown." Roughly three months later—after extraordinary challenges not to be recounted here—the expedition arrived at the Virgin River's mouth in southern Nevada, having run not only the Grand Canyon (and affixing its name en route) but several hundred miles of the Green and Colorado rivers in Utah and Colorado territories. A landmark event in US history had taken place, a journey comparable in import to the Lewis and Clark Expedition that would capture our collective imagination for the next 150 years.

Yet Powell was far more than an adventurous explorer and wounded Civil War veteran. He played a pivotal role in the intellectual and scientific development of the United States. A "man of letters" in the finest sense of the term, Powell authored more than 250 articles, monographs, and books during his lifetime, though he never quite adapted to writing with his left hand and had to dictate most of his work. As reflected in his voluminous publications, not only did Powell master multiple scientific disciplines over his career, he contributed significantly to the creation of several of them. Franz Boas worked for Powell during his formative years, for example, later moving on to a prestigious position at Columbia University where he founded the discipline of anthropology. Powell similarly employed and provided training to Lester Frank Ward, who later established the discipline of sociology. In addition, Powell helped leading universities such as Harvard, Yale, and the University of Wisconsin establish cutting-edge science programs.

Powell also created a host of enduring institutions. He started the Cosmos Club in 1878—an exclusive organization based on intellectual accomplishment. One year later, Powell organized the National Geographic Society with a small group of friends and simultaneously helped create the Anthropological Society of Washington, predecessor of the world's largest anthropological organization, the American Anthropological Association. In a similar fashion, Powell was instrumental in establishing the Smithsonian Institution's Bureau of Ethnology—later renamed the Bureau of American Ethnology—including serving as its first director (1879–1902). This directorship preceded, and for thirteen years ran concurrently with, Powell's position as second director of the US Geological Survey (1881–94), which he molded into the scientific bastion it is today.

These and other intellectual achievements garnered Powell national and international recognition. He was awarded an honorary law degree from Harvard University, an honorary doctorate from Illinois Wesleyan, a "doctor of laws" from George Washington University, and a

Ph.D. *in absentia* from Heidelberg University in Germany. Powell likewise accepted France's Cuvier Prize on behalf of the US Geological Survey. All told, John Wesley Powell was a giant in late-nineteenth-century intellectual endeavors, with an enduring legacy that still shapes contemporary pursuits. Not bad for a one-armed college dropout.

Notwithstanding his robust career and scientific accomplishments, Powell is most famous today for the 1869 Expedition, an enterprise so hazardous it is properly characterized as a dangerous stunt. He organized a "scientific" expedition to descend the Colorado River Basin's wild, often tempestuous canyons, yet none of his crew had scientific expertise. Nor did they have experience rowing boats through rapids. With characteristic perseverance and force of personality, however, Powell completed this pathbreaking adventure successfully, and all crew members who obeyed his orders and stuck with him survived. Unfortunately, that was not the fate of the expedition's full complement of ten men, but those who remained steadfast emerged from the Grand Canyon as national heroes. And Powell's entrepreneurialism and leadership propelled him through an illustrious career of public service and government science.

Powell's place in American history and culture has eclipsed most of his contemporaries. Other leading voices on water resources and geography at that time—W. J. McGee, Grove Karl Gilbert, Clarence Dutton, John Strong Newberry—have been largely forgotten. Powell's competitors in the post-Civil War surveys of the West—George Wheeler, Ferdinand Hayden, and Clarence King—generally live on only as place names on maps. Similarly, Powell's political nemeses—Senator William Stewart of Nevada, Congressman Hilary Herbert from Alabama, and irrigation booster William Smythe—are the stuff of historical trivia. But Powell rose to the status of icon.

Powell left a lasting legacy for water and land management in the Colorado River Basin and broader region. His *Arid Lands Report* has been described as prophetic, prescient, revolutionary, and visionary. But Powell's other field of study, anthropology, has virtually disowned him. His work is regarded today as ethnocentric claptrap. Why? How could a single individual have such dramatic success and failure in so many fields of academic study and public policy? This volume sheds light.

In an age of social media, it is perhaps difficult to conceive of a "media star" in the age of telegraphs. But John Wesley Powell was precisely that. His stardom partly explains why today there is something of a "Powell cult" among river runners, scholars, and water and land managers. Yet Powell's most enduring legacy is in public policy and academia. Powell reinvented himself over and over again, usually excelling at whatever new task he adopted. He set a new standard for being an eclectic polymath. That is why his life and work are the subject of so many writings, why he is still regarded as a major figure in US history, and why it is fitting upon the 1869 Expedition's sesquicentennial to delve into his ideas and proposals for their relevance to the past, present, and future of the Colorado River Basin.

Yet, although *Vision & Place* grows out of the sesquicentennial, it does not heavily emphasize Powell's river adventures. A large body of work already exists on the 1869 Expedition (and a subsequent 1871–72 Expedition) as well as on Powell's other exploits across the West. His most important contributions were not in running rapids, but rather in the two areas just noted: public policy and academia. The goal of this volume is to explore all facets of the man, not just those that are thrilling or involve the more attractive aspects of his ideology and actions. In short, it aims to see John Wesley Powell as a whole.

The cast of contributors serves this goal. Contributing authors consist of sixteen scholars with deep-rooted connections to the Colorado River Basin. They represent diverse fields such as American studies, anthropology, environmental studies, geography, history, law, Native American and Indigenous studies, political science, and watershed management. Accompanying these authors are eight visual artists whose images—coupled with maps produced by two cartographers—complement the volume's text.

This rich content is divided into three parts, on water, public lands, and Native Americans. Powell's opus revolved around these subjects, and they are unmistakable in contemporary discourse about the Colorado River Basin. For example, consider that roughly 40 million people now rely on the basin for water, including major population centers like Los Angeles, San Diego, Phoenix, Tucson, Las Vegas, Denver, Salt Lake City, and Albuquerque. This dependence belies climate change's impacts on the basin's hydrology and a two-decade drought that has depleted the basin's reservoirs by half. In a similar vein, the basin's abundant national parks and other public lands have been a powder keg for decades, most recently lit by a US President's attempt to invoke the Antiquities Act to reduce Bears Ears and Grand Staircase-Escalante national monuments. This attempt is being litigated in federal court. Finally, no study of Powell and the Colorado River Basin would be complete, credible, or fair without including the twenty-nine Native American tribes residing on reservations throughout the basin, including the largest tribe in the United States, the Navajo Nation. These Indigenous Peoples have survived over four hundred years of Euro-American attempts at colonization. It is impossible to capture the vexing, unresolved issues of cultural integrity, economic inequality, and social injustice facing the basin's tribes. But that is precisely what this volume attempts.

Each chapter has standardized elements. The first element is historical and concerns Powell's vision of water, public lands, and Native Americans in the Colorado River Basin and broader arid region. The second element, in turn, consists of contemporary material assessing the relative influence of Powell's vision on the physical and cultural landscape of the basin in modern times. Finally, the third element is prospective and prescriptive. It focuses on the basin's future, including authors' visions of water, public lands, and Native Americans going forward, as well as the relationship between these visions and Powell's own. This three-part format offers a unique combination of retrospective and prospective angles.

Our unifying theme is Powell's famous reference to the "Great Unknown." Powell penned this phrase on August 13, 1869, while at the confluence of the Colorado River and Little Colorado River in the Grand Canyon. "We are now ready to start on our way down the Great Unknown," he wrote. "We have an unknown distance yet to run; an unknown river yet to explore. What falls there are, we know not; what rocks beset the channel, we know not; what walls rise over the river, we know not. Ah, well! We may conjecture many things." Powell's "Great Unknown" phrase is apropos to the Colorado River Basin today. There is no precedent for how the basin is being inhabited and utilized. Again, roughly 40 million people rely on its water in an era of anthropogenic climate change. Tourism and recreation on the basin's public lands are at unprecedented levels. And we relish in stating the obvious: the basin's tribes have *not* vanished. They have persisted through Euro-American colonization and now hold significant claims to both water and land—claims with profound implications for human rights, postcolonialism, and multilevel governance in our constitutional democracy.

From this vantage point, *now* is the time we collectively launch into the "Great Unknown." How should we envision the Colorado River Basin's future? What would we like to see the basin become as a place?

Commemorating the historic 1869 Expedition's sesquicentennial, and revisiting John Wesley Powell's tremendous body of work for grounding, *Vision & Place* is rooted in these foundational questions. Our aim is to foster awareness and promote dialogue about the new "Great Unknown." Ultimately, it is this essential theme, and the love of place and sense of stewardship tied to it, that unify the volume.

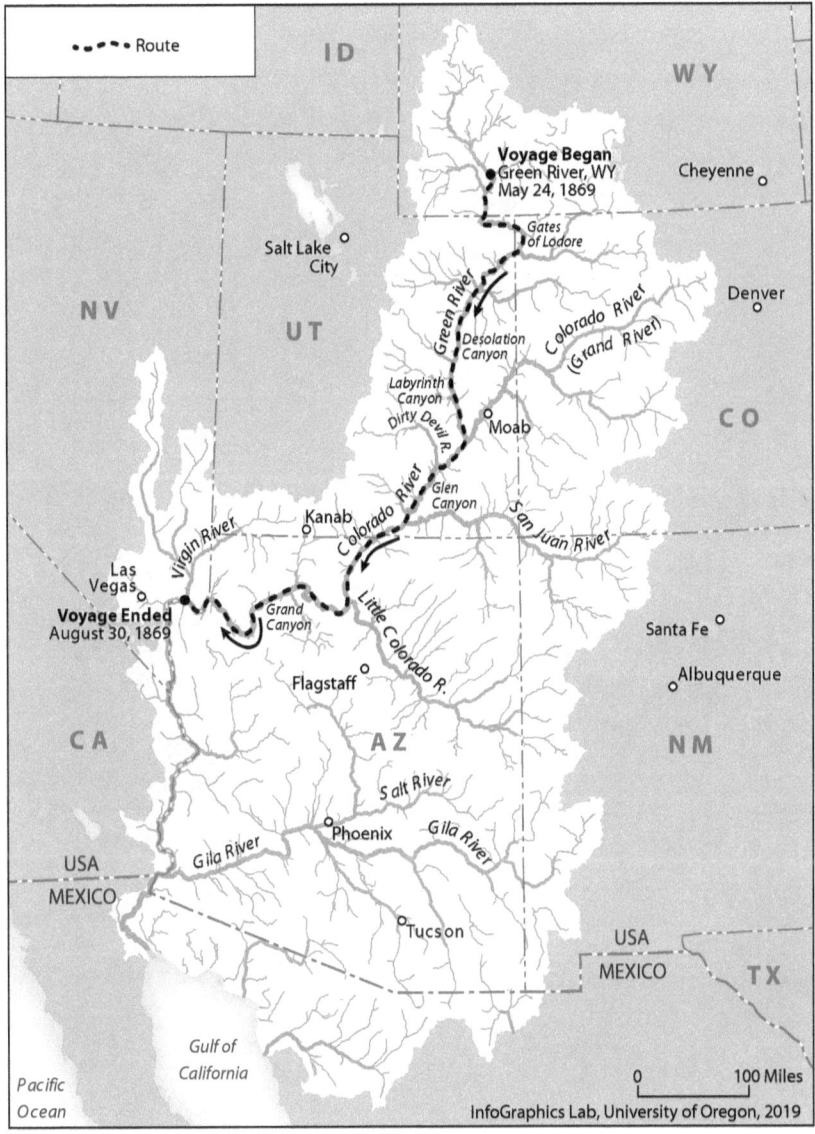

MAP 1. John Wesley Powell's Colorado River Exploring Expedition, May 24—August 30, 1869. Cartography: P. William Limpisathian and James Meacham, InfoGraphics Lab, University of Oregon, 2019.

PART ONE

Water

Mark Twain's biting though apocryphal saying, "Whiskey is for drinking and water is for fighting," is perhaps the most succinct characterization of Western water politics ever penned. It pairs well with John Wesley Powell's famous warning of a "heritage of conflict" over water rights. Aridity has defined the Colorado River Basin and broader West from the time when the Great Plains were known as the "Great American Desert" up to the two-decade drought currently vexing the basin. Responses to aridity have included hucksterism, deception, and delusion. Powell saw aridity and the myth that "rain follows the plow" for what they were. Today, we need to follow Powell's lead, solving the basin's water problems by facing reality.

Powell's relationship with the Colorado River system was dichotomous and paradoxical. On the one hand, he came to know the waterways intimately through the 1869 Expedition and other explorations, conveying in his writings a profound sense of adventure and deep appreciation for the basin's aesthetic beauty. On the other hand, Powell fervently sought to develop the river system. Powell's vision entailed Euro-American settlers engaging in scientific planning, utilitarianism, and communitarian, watershed-based governance. We ended up with something a bit different.

Today the Colorado River Basin exhibits all the symptoms of an overstressed system. Aridity has grown more pronounced due to anthropogenic climate change, resulting in increased temperatures and reduced streamflow. Yet despite sobering statistics on future water supplies, populations in and around the basin are booming. Water means many different things to these people, and the institutions allocating and managing the basin's flows are experiencing difficulty responding to these diverse values and needs. All told, there are more demands than there is water, and the future promises to expand this gap.

Louis Warren and Rachel St. John begin our foray into the Colorado River Basin's waterscape in chapter 1 by tracing the nuanced arc of John Wesley Powell's posthumous fame. Perhaps unsurprisingly to Powell devotees, the chapter flags Wallace Stegner's publication of *Beyond the Hundredth Meridian* in 1954 as the event that made the difference. Stegner's biography did more than any other work to bring Powell "out of obscurity and onto a pedestal," explain the authors, with Stegner proclaiming Powell the *"genius loci"* or guardian spirit of "all the canyons of the Green and Colorado." Can this characterization be reconciled with Powell's vision for Western water? If the Colorado River Basin had taken shape as Powell imagined, "there would not only have been no wild rivers . . . there would have been no rivers at all." These contradictions offer valuable lessons from his life and work, especially in regards to the timely topics of climate science, pragmatism and civic discourse, and social justice.

Chapter 2, by Robert Adler, wades further into the relational dimension of John Wesley Powell's vision for water in the Colorado River Basin and broader arid region—specifically, his controversial advocacy for communitarian water governance or "watershed democracy." "The classic story is that Powell's plan died on the vine," Adler writes. "The reality, however, is not so simple." While Powell's proposals "ran perpendicular" to contemporary economic, political, and social trends, Adler demonstrates how many proposals eventually seeped into Western water law, particularly allocation rules and water organizations prevalent throughout the basin states. The move toward more collective, holistic, watershed-based approaches today may well reflect Powell's idea of "seeing things whole." In this spirit, Adler suggests it is time to revisit the notion of a comprehensive, basinwide water governance structure for the Colorado River Basin.

Amorina Lee-Martinez and Patricia Limerick pick up a similar thread in chapter 3, describing how "[t]he complexity of multiple values, competing for a common water source that becomes more uncertain over time, is a hallmark of our era." This sentiment reveals the common ground with chapter 2: communitarianism. Yet there is a difference of scale. Chapter 3 pans down to a Colorado River tributary called the

Dolores River in southwestern Colorado. Paradox surrounds this river—the Paradox Valley through which it flows, the paradoxical nature of its governance, and the paradoxes of John Wesley Powell's character as they relate to collaborative efforts aimed at navigating the river's future. Describing Powell's conspicuous silence about the details of communal governance within his proposed "watershed commonwealths," the authors fill in some of these proverbial blank spots on the Dolores River Basin's map.

Finally, climate change takes center stage in chapter 4 by Robert Glennon. It is of crucial importance for the maze of laws and policies known as the "Law of the River." While Powell advocated for measures to address water conflicts along interstate and international rivers, he would find the Law of the River's modern complexity dizzying. Glennon sheds light on the imbalance between water supply and demand now confronting the Colorado River Basin after two decades of drought. Climate projections suggest the situation will worsen. Powell anticipated such a "heritage of conflict," and his example of foresight and creativity is helpful to water managers as they navigate the Law of the River through the new "Great Unknown." Water exchanges are one useful tool within this evolution. They could prove instrumental for meeting the needs of growing cities and a diversified economy without significantly jeopardizing the agricultural communities at the heart of Powell's vision for the basin and arid region.

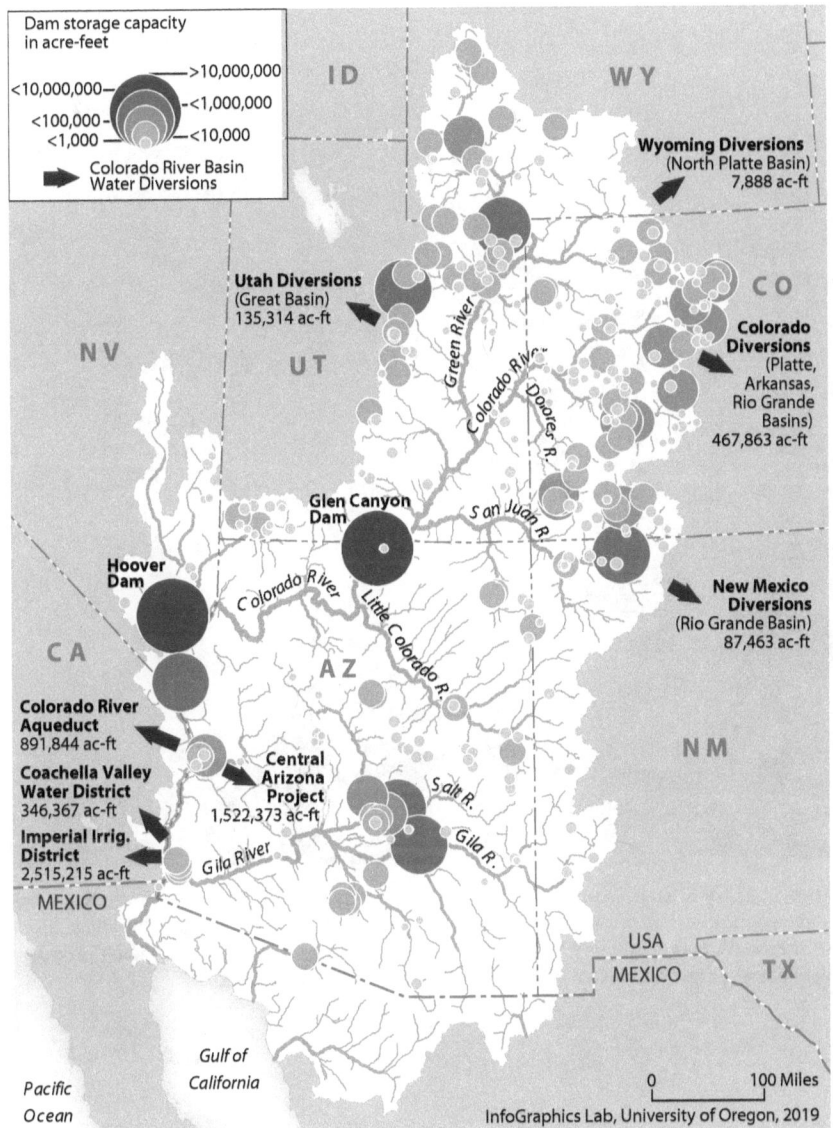

MAP 2. Dams and Diversions, Colorado River Basin. Cartography: P. William Limpisathian and James Meacham, InfoGraphics Lab, University of Oregon, 2019.

FIGURE 1. Bailey Russel, *View of Green River Lakes* (tintype, 4" × 5," 2016). Green River Lakes is the remote headwaters of the Green River in Wyoming's Wind River Range. This image, like those of Powell's photographer J. K. Hillers, was created using the wet-plate collodion process. Unlike Hillers's, however, this image is made on metal and thus is a tintype.

FIGURE 2. Bailey Russel, *View of Flaming Gorge* (tintype, 4"x 5," 2017). This image depicts the Green River as it enters Flaming Gorge. The tintype is made by coating a plate of blackened metal with collodion, a liquid traditionally used as a bandage. It serves as an emulsion and a necessary organic compound to bond with silver nitrate and make a light-sensitive surface.

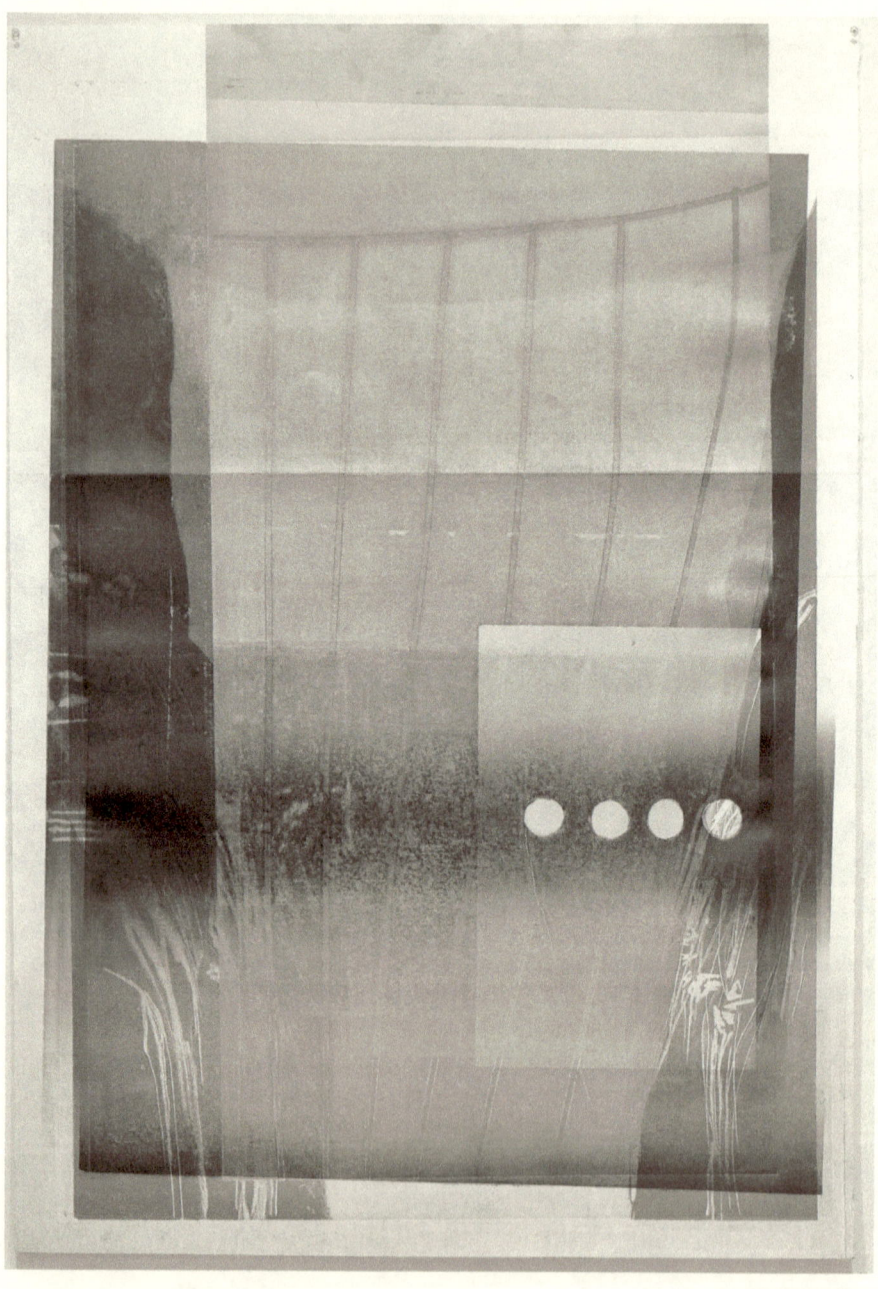

FIGURE 3. Kate Aitchison, *Glen Canyon Dam* (monotype, 36" × 50," 2016). Glen Canyon Dam impounds the Colorado River into a reservoir named after John Wesley Powell—Lake Powell. This image is part of a series of monotypes exploring visual and ecological changes resulting from dam construction.

FIGURE 4. Bailey Russel, *View of Marble Canyon at Soap Creek* (tintype, 8" × 6," 2018). Relying on an 8" × 10" camera, a portable wet-plate darkroom, and a very short time window for production, this tintype was made while floating the length of Grand Canyon during summer 2018. The image depicts an historic part of the upper canyon, Marble Canyon, at Soap Creek.

FIGURE 5. Erika Osborne, *Hoover Gates* (oil on canvas, 42" × 30," 2011). This painting references the wood engraving *Gate of Lodore*, created by Thomas Moran after he had participated in the Powell Survey during 1873. The piece plays with Moran's visual language to comment on the Colorado River's contemporary state: dammed and controlled—a product of "progress."

CHAPTER 1

Strange Resurrection

The Fall and Rise of John Wesley Powell

LOUIS S. WARREN AND RACHEL ST. JOHN

In 2001, Donald Worster highlighted the heroic stature that John Wesley Powell had attained: "And everywhere they go the tourist hordes encounter the name and image of John Wesley Powell. He has been canonized by the National Park Service and by the Bureau of Reclamation, by outdoor writers and boatmen, as one of the greatest pathfinders in American history and as a prophet of what the West might still become."[1]

Of course, in his own time, Powell was a justly renowned figure. His 1869 Expedition down the Green and Colorado rivers earned him nationwide acclaim. He utilized that fame to become one of the most effective institution builders in the federal government's history, playing a formative role in the creation of the US Geological Survey and the Bureau of American Ethnology in 1879. From 1888 to 1894, he simultaneously directed both agencies. He was the first surveyor to systematically analyze and explain the ramifications of Western aridity and to propose corresponding reforms to public lands policy. He published seminal works on geology and was a pre-eminent influence in the making of modern anthropology, a field in which he published myriad articles and served as patron and mentor to a cadre of acolytes.

But most of that was forgotten upon Powell's death in 1902. Indeed, between his contemporary fame and the reputation he holds today, there was a long period of obscurity. After his death, Powell would be remembered primarily in Washington, DC, where he was a legend. Among a nascent group of "river runners" in the first two decades of the twentieth century, his exploits on the Colorado River became a subject of debate, with many questioning his leadership and the cumbersome design of his boats (which Powell had supervised), and some alleging he had inflated his accomplishments. Elsewhere, his star simply faded. Some of his associates compiled a memorial volume on his death, and some of his social theories retained attraction for a few scholars. But by the mid-twentieth century he was largely forgotten. Unlike other major figures of Western history like Lewis and Clark, Daniel Boone, or George Custer, no biographers took up Powell's story. Midway through the twentieth century, few historians knew who he was, and the public had largely forgotten him.[2]

And yet, as Worster points out, today Powell looms large among diverse admirers, from Western historians to environmental advocates to public land managers. Although fame can be lasting, it is unusual, indeed, for anyone to renew it after falling into posthumous obscurity. What accounts for this strange resurrection? How was it that Powell became such a compelling figure, and remains one, more than a century after dying and being forgotten? This chapter engages these questions upon the 1869 Expedition's sesquicentennial. In offering answers, we are not only able to weigh Powell's formidable reputation against his actual achievements, we may also begin to ascertain what he has to offer scholars and citizens interested in water and public lands in today's arid West.

THE FALL AND RISE OF JOHN WESLEY POWELL

Consigned to the ash heap of late exploration after his 1902 death, Powell's reputation began to re-emerge during Franklin Roosevelt's administration, when ambitious New Dealers found themselves struggling against a stiff headwind of Western myth. The West had long been a realm of imagined self-sufficiency, and by the 1930s that was especially so. Republicans had invoked "rugged individualism"[3] as the guiding ethos of American government since 1928, when Herbert Hoover invented it as a rallying cry to shrink the federal government, which had grown prodigiously during World War I. Although Hoover presented rugged individualism as a generic American trait, it came to be associated particularly with pioneers and their frontier exploits, as a kind of quintessential Americanness that rejected government assistance.

In contrast, Roosevelt's administration needed a new frontier mythology to justify a much bigger government, one active and technocratic enough to resolve the Great Depression and its attendant Western challenges, including drought, Dust Bowl, and social collapse. Applied social sciences—including economics, sociology, and political science—were among the administration's most powerful tools for these problems. But it was regional planning, especially, that attracted New Dealers. Technocrats who sought to forestall social inequity and ecological catastrophe by managing and rationalizing vast landscapes, regional planners achieved new authority in the 1930s. The Tennessee Valley Authority was the showcase of New Deal regional planning. In the Colorado River Basin and other parts of the West, however, regional planners also shaped huge new projects, including the Hoover and Grand Coulee dams, and they helped inspire new agencies such as the Soil Conservation Service and the Resettlement Administration.[4]

A hallmark of regional planning was (and is) to adapt landscape development to ecological constraints: to avoid importing practices or institutions from one region into another without being sure the natural environment can support them. Its champions began to find a technocratic visionary in Powell. As they reformed the public lands system, New Dealers hailed him for his proposals, with one federal study in 1936 summarizing Powell's *Arid Lands Report* as a "classic report presenting a thoughtful and coherent program for the proper utilization of the Great Plains which recognized the necessity of adjusting to the natural environment."[5]

Such thinking shaped New Deal policy in powerful ways. In 1934, FDR signed the Taylor Grazing Act, which forbade individual claims under the Homestead Act and implemented federal supervision of grazing, mining, and lumbering on public lands. The law somewhat fulfilled Powell's prescriptions for the arid lands, and supporters of this new form of land management thus burnished his reputation.[6]

The New Deal signified the federal government's commitment not only to planning, but also to social science and scientific analysis, as engineering projects and university extension programs proliferated. Federally sponsored science continued to expand dramatically during World War II and the beginning of the Cold War, so that by the late 1940s Powell was a heroic figure not only in regional planning circles, but more broadly to a growing cadre of government scientists in places like the US Geological Survey and the Bureau of Reclamation.[7]

Thus, Powell's fame continued to rise through the 1940s. In 1951 came the first book-length biography, *Powell of the Colorado,* in which William Culp Darrah, a historian of science, celebrated Powell's intellectual contributions to natural science and his physical courage in river exploration.[8] But it was the next biography that made the difference.

REMAKING POWELL'S IMAGE FOR ENVIRONMENTAL POLITICS

In 1954 came Wallace Stegner's *Beyond the Hundredth Meridian: John Wesley Powell and the Second Opening of the West*, which outstripped all predecessors both in literary quality and in its compelling arguments for Powell's outsize contribution to the history of the Colorado Plateau and broader region.[9] Already a Western writer of considerable stature, Stegner had written the book under the auspices of a Guggenheim Fellowship. By profession neither a river runner nor a government official, but a professor at Stanford (where he founded the creative writing program), Stegner was drawn to Powell for a host of reasons outlined in his Guggenheim application in 1948. According to Stegner, Powell's *Arid Lands Report* had "laid down a program of land and water development that was a half century ahead of its time." His "revolutionary proposals for the handling of the public lands and his insistence that large parts of the West could be plowed only at the risk of erosion, soil loss, and depletion of the water tables and timber reserves" had become "the backbone of our conservation program." Stegner hewed to the New Deal line—"the Dust Bowl of the Thirties was the crucial demonstration of the rightness of Powell's stand"—and hailed his fight for conservation "through a long and active career as a government scientist."[10]

Attracting Stegner's interest might have been the best thing Powell could have done posthumously for his historical reputation. Stegner had spent formative years of his adolescence in Salt Lake City and graduated from the University of Utah before going on to the University of Iowa to take a Ph.D. in English. It was during this period that he began to interpret the reports of southwestern exploration, including Powell's, as a form of regional literature.[11]

But by the late 1940s, Stegner had developed other concerns that led him to see Powell's story as particularly relevant to mid-century Americans. The Red Scare emanating from the House Un-American Activities Committee fanned the flames of anti-intellectualism, "the dark suspicion," Stegner wrote to his literary agent, "that intelligence and subversion go hand in hand."[12] The anti-Communist movement harrowed the ranks of New Deal bureaucrats from the State Department to Interior, driving many into early retirement under a cloud of suspicion. To Stegner, Powell represented a useful figure for contemporary American intellectuals: a reformer in government service who dedicated his vast intelligence to pursuing the public good in Western water and land management. He anchored what Stegner saw as a tradition of forward-thinking reformers whose loyalties could not be impugned by even the most zealous anti-Communist.

Perhaps strategically, Stegner kept these latter concerns out of his Guggenheim materials, focusing instead on Powell's virtues as a proto-conservationist. On March 31, 1948, the Guggenheim Foundation wrote Stegner to inform him they were awarding him a fellowship to carry out his proposal.[13] Written over the next four years, *Beyond the Hundredth Meridian* did more than any other work to bring Powell out of obscurity and onto a pedestal.

But the book, of course, could not have achieved such influence without readers. And among a new generation of recreationists, there was a prospective public eager to read about John Wesley Powell, or at least Wallace Stegner's version of him. The interwar period saw a rise in outdoor recreation, followed by a veritable boom in camping and hiking after World War II. Rising wages and leisure time among the middle class, and the invention of new lightweight, durable gear, brought about rapid growth in outdoor recreation, including river rafting. As early as 1938, tourists rode even the most remote rivers on inflatable rubber rafts. By 1955, outboard motors and war-surplus neoprene rafts had turned river running into safe, middle-class recreation for greenhorns, and wild rivers suddenly became popular. As one old hand put it that year: "Everybody runs the river now."[14]

It was this democratization of recreation and river running that helped sell Stegner's biography of Powell, while simultaneously spurring a new movement for wilderness and especially wild river protections. New outdoors enthusiasts swelled the Sierra Club's ranks as they took on the Bureau of Reclamation over the Colorado River Basin's future in the very moment that *Beyond the Hundredth Meridian* appeared, with its gripping account of Powell's 1869 descent of the roaring, untamed river. Indeed, in 1954, the year Stegner's book was published, the US Congress convened hearings on what became a notorious proposal to dam Echo Canyon and thus inundate Dinosaur National Monument, a 200,000-acre stretch of canyon and plateau between the Green and Yampa rivers.[15]

Stegner paid close attention to those hearings and soon inserted himself into the fight. Dinosaur was so remote that few Americans had heard of it, and even fewer had seen it. How to get them to value a place they did not know? In 1955, in support of the Sierra Club, Stegner agreed to produce a book to introduce the Echo Park country to the public and hopefully persuade them to defend it: *This Is Dinosaur*. Stegner edited this essay collection and contributed his own chapter, aiming to familiarize readers with Dinosaur's beauty and recreational opportunities. The book was a kind of warning, Stegner wrote, about what Americans "would be giving up" if they acceded to proposals to dam this stretch of wild river.[16]

Stegner's lyrical writing invited readers to imagine the wild river as a respite from modernity. "It is a better world with some buffalo left in it, a richer world with some gorgeous canyons unmarred by signboards, hot-dog stands, super highways, or high-tension lines, undrowned by power or irrigation reservoirs." In the decades to come, he warned, "it will not only be the buffalo and the trumpeter swan who need sanctuaries. Our own species is going to need them too. It needs them now."[17]

This is Dinosaur reflected the burgeoning environmental movement's values in the postwar period, articulating beautifully the popular desire to save wild spaces from commercial development. And as if to found this movement on a heroic forebear, Stegner also invoked the name of John Wesley Powell, whom he now proclaimed the "*genius loci*," or guardian spirit, of Dinosaur and indeed "all the canyons of the Green and Colorado."[18] In Stegner's hands, Powell became not just the first American scientist to descend the Colorado, but a kind of patron saint of wild river preservation.

And in keeping with this image, subsequent celebrations of Powell connected strongly with wild rivers and people who run them. In 1969, on the centenary of the 1869 Expedition, Walt Disney Corporation released a heavily fictionalized, wholly celebratory account of the voyage called "Ten Who Dared." That same year, the US Postal Service unveiled a postage stamp commemorating Powell's journey, depicting two expedition members in a boat being steered through swirling rapids by the courageous one-armed explorer.

ASSESSING STEGNER'S POWELL, AND OUR OWN

Of all the rhetorical moves Stegner made to bring Powell out of historical obscurity, making him into a partisan for wild rivers was the most dubious. In fact, it verged on the preposterous. Powell was indeed visionary; he did propose transformations in Western land and water policy that he hoped would alter Western development.[19] But in the future Colorado River Basin as he imagined it, there would not only have been no wild rivers, but, had his proposals come to fruition, there would have been no rivers at all.

For, while Powell twice rode the turgid Colorado, he never hoped to keep it wild, or even to keep it flowing. As most people who know of Powell's plan are aware, his vision was to remove water from rivers and spread it over land. On the face of it, this seems perfectly reasonable in historical context. But most Powell admirers seem blind to his true intentions, which were to take *all* water out of Western rivers. Of course, the sheer canyons of the Colorado would be too deep to plumb for irrigation, and he did not foresee the engineering feats of the twentieth century, with its massive concrete dams and titanic reservoirs. But his proposed legislation called for irrigation districts to remove water high up in basins like the Colorado, and he predicted that, as a result, the lower reaches of Stegner's beloved river would one day run dry. "All the waters of all the arid lands will eventually be taken from their natural channels," he wrote in his famed *Arid Lands Report,* "and they can be utilized only to the extent to which they are thus removed."[20]

A land of small farm communities and desiccated, empty riverbeds: this was the future Powell hoped to see. He did not shy away from it. Indeed, he readily acknowledged his plan would have drained Western rivers completely—making him anything but their guardian spirit—and his vision extended far beyond the Colorado River Basin. "The time must come soon when all the waters of the Missouri will be spread over the great plains, and the bed of the river will be dry," Powell predicted.[21] On occasion, he even invoked this imagined future to correct the excesses of irrigation enthusiasts. In 1893, after listening to particularly grandiose exclamations on the potential for greening the West at the International Irrigation Congress in Los Angeles, Powell rose to the lectern and warned:

> When all the rivers are used, when all the creeks in all the ravines, when all the brooks, when all the springs are used, when all the reservoirs along the springs are used, when all the canyon waters are taken up, when all the artesian waters are taken up, when all the wells are sunk or dug that can be dug in this arid region, there is still not sufficient water to irrigate all this arid region.[22]

Historians and biographers, among them Wallace Stegner, have preferred to highlight Powell's wisdom in proclaiming Western water's relative scarcity, rightly hailing him for his declaration of limits in an age of imagined cornucopias. We may commend Powell for being correct—and brave—in describing those limits. But we should also note his unequivocal acceptance of the cost he was willing to impose. He did not warn *against* draining rivers. Rather, in the Colorado River Basin and elsewhere, he labored to call into being a West that would remain largely dry even after rivers had been entirely drained. Thus his construction of the warning not as an "if," but a "when": "*When all the rivers are used . . . when all the canyon waters are taken up.*"[23] Stegner's *genius loci* of wild rivers joined his contemporaries in planning the destruction of wild rivers in ways far more total than even modern dams have inflicted.

This may run against the image of Powell we know from our own culture and time. But it is unsurprising. For, despite the many encomiums Powell has earned from historians and other scholars proclaiming him "ahead of his time,"[24] Powell was actually, like everyone in history, very much of his time. Again: he was visionary; he was prescient. But his views on Western water and other aspects of regional development were far more in keeping with his peers than our more hagiographic accounts would have us believe.

Many of the virtues ascribed to Powell, explicitly or implicitly, are conceptions of a much later period. Thus, Powell had no understanding of rivers as ecologically necessary, or as having rights to exist. He expressed no concern about the survival of fish, waterfowl, or other creatures who depend on free-flowing water. He could not connect the flow of the Missouri to the health of the Mississippi, into which it flows, and he could link neither to the larger health of the aquatic systems of the Gulf of Mexico, into which their waters drain, precisely because the notion of a "healthy" river system derives from the concept of the ecosystem itself, and "ecosystem" as a term did not even enter the English language until 1935.[25]

Moreover, if he valued nature as retreat from modernity, his need for that retreat was much less urgent than for Stegner's readers. Powell mused on Grand Canyon's "sublime beauty" in particular, hailing "the music of waters" resonating from its cliffs, while at the same time dreaming of removing those very waters. His notions of natural beauty were heavily informed by Romanticism and a sense of nature's glory as transient and bound to vanish before the advance of Progress.[26]

It took a longer experience of industrialism and urbanization, and a heightened sense of earth's fragility in the atomic age, to birth Stegner's conception of wilderness, a vision that saw remote country simultaneously as a legacy of the past, a trust for the future, and worthy of preservation. Stegner's conjuring of a world being "richer" for having "gorgeous canyons unmarred by signboards, hot-dog stands, super highways, or high-tension lines," and for being "undrowned by power or irrigation reservoirs," was beyond Powell's ken.

The limitations of Powell's vision shaped all of his proposals and writing, but they were nowhere more openly displayed than in his most famous publication: the *Arid Lands Report*. Stegner called it "one of the most important books ever written about the West," and "the classic statement of the terms on which the West could be peopled." Following Stegner (and New Dealers before him), scholars and writers have praised the *Report* for how it anticipated the conservation movement.[27] And yet, as a plan for environmental management, its shortcomings are profound. For all its virtues, it contains a great deal of misinformation and wishful thinking, all of which reflects how much even a brilliant mind like Powell's was burdened by the assumptions and technological limitations of his day.[28]

Powell's optimism about Western irrigation was vast. Farms in the arid lands would "perennially yield bountiful crops," because, he believed, irrigation water from Western rivers and streams would deposit silt on fields much like the Nile once fertilized Egypt. "It is probable," he projected, "that the benefits derived from this source alone will be full compensation for the cost of the process."[29]

While his understanding of irrigation was encumbered by this overly optimistic view of Western hydrology and sediment flows, for a man who supposedly first envisioned "the backbone of our conservation program," Powell's grasp of forestry was surprisingly blinkered. Even many of his contemporaries were mystified. After 1864, when George Perkins Marsh first sounded the alarm about losses to the nation's forests, fear of overcutting trees and denuding mountainsides began to spread. Although there was little hard evidence to support the theory, most early conservationists took the view that forests were key to preventing erosion and sedimentation of rivers, and indeed that forest health was what kept mountain streams flowing. Without forests, there would be no rivers.[30]

But at least through the 1870s, Powell took a contrary view, in which forests soaked up water that could be used by irrigators. He may or may not have told Secretary of Interior John Noble in an 1890 meeting, as one irate forester recounted, "the best thing to do with the Rocky Mountain forests was to burn them down."[31] But in his *Arid Lands Report* he did urge that Western forests be sold to private owners, and for years after, perhaps until 1890, he seems to have agreed with others in his US Geological Survey advocating for removal of Western forests to facilitate irrigation (and to reduce spending on the Bureau of Forestry in favor of the US Geological Survey).[32]

Such ideas about forests were widely held at the time; the dispute over the relation between streamflow and forestry would not be settled for years. But Powell's *Arid Lands Report* helps to explain his early ambivalence about forest conservation. There he reported that because white settlers had cut down forests and grazed alpine meadows, "the streams have steadily increased in volume,"[33] and projected that further alteration of land and forest would "increase the supply of water."[34]

Ultimately, Powell modified these views, and beginning in 1890 called for forest preservation to maintain streamflow. But he never accepted the emergence of a federal bureaucracy committed to forest protection. In his view, local settlers should protect the forests themselves, through "local self-government by hydrographic basins," the communitarian system of governance he envisioned for the arid region.[35]

Localized communitarianism is the characteristic that most separates Powell from both his contemporaries and more recent policy approaches. Most conservationists, then and now, have favored public ownership of forests, with centralized government regulation and supervision to save them and other public lands from destruction. Powell, in contrast, sought to extend community self-regulation not only to forests, but to irrigation and pasturage districts, where settlers could make by-laws to regulate themselves, so long as their rules did not conflict with larger guidelines for the districts' formation laid out in bills proposed by Powell.[36]

In defense of this approach, Powell hearkened to historical precedent. As he saw it, his communitarian settlements had precursors in "the district or colony system," which was "essentially the basis of all the mining district organizations of the West. Under it the local rules and regulations for the division of mining lands, the use of water, timber, etc., are managed better than they could possibly be under specific statutes of the United States."[37] As Powell saw it, communal regulations would prevent resource monopolization. "The association of a number of people prevents single individuals from having undue control of nature privileges," he claimed, "and secures an equitable distribution of mineral lands; and all this is secured in obedience to statutes of the United States providing general regulations."[38]

And yet, some of the very monopolistic institutions that Powell abhorred and sought to contain with reforms had grown precisely out of these self-regulating mining camps. Chief among these were private water companies. Powell excoriated water companies for separating water rights from land and for their "monopoly of water rights," which he predicted would one day "be an intolerable burden to the people."[39] But he left unstated the genesis of these companies in the local, communal rule-making that he esteemed.[40] During the Gold Rush, it became a custom in California mining camps that anyone could divert water so long as they put it to beneficial use and nobody else had established a claim to it. This "right" to prior appropriation, wielded by individuals, was rapidly claimed by corporations, who captured water across the West and sold it to other users on contract. The problem of water monopoly did not originate in state or federal law; it was the unintended result of a communitarian practice, invented in western mining camps where miners themselves believed that such arrangements were fair.

THE LESSONS OF JOHN WESLEY POWELL

Assessing Powell's arguments, one has to ask how closely his greatest admirers have actually read his proposals. If Powell's ideas really had become, as Wallace Stegner claimed, "the backbone" of America's conservation program, and if he remains, as others have claimed, "the prophet of what the West might still become," then the Colorado River Basin and other parts of the region would have remained thinly populated, overwhelmingly agrarian, and communal in governance. The public lands would be greatly diminished, for vast acres would be privately held in the many irrigation districts that Powell proposed. Millions of acres today supervised by federal agencies—national forests and other public lands—would be governed primarily by local communities. It seems unlikely there would be a US Forest Service. And every Western river would vanish between headwaters and mouth, spread over miles of farm fields. There would be no rafting or kayaking on the Green, the Yampa, the Colorado, or other Western rivers. There would be no fishing, and far fewer wild animals, from bald eagles to grizzly bears. A river would not run through it.

Powell's shortcomings remind us how dangerous it is to rely on nineteenth-century proposals to remedy today's problems. For Powell's failings are perfectly comprehensible given his context, the state of the natural sciences, and the limited knowledge of Western lands and waters that prevailed in the United States.

But for all Powell's limitations, there are still things he can teach us, lessons we can take into our own battles over water and public lands. Regardless of the substance of his policy prescriptions, his method in reaching those prescriptions remains valuable, and in fact indispensable.

In this sense, Powell's primary lesson might be intellectual. For Powell's primary contributions to his age were less in the realm of policy—most of his prescriptions were rejected, after all—than in the use of science as a tool for creating new institutions for modern conditions and the development of scientific approaches that allowed for venturing and testing of hypotheses and vigorous scientific debate.

In this respect, Powell was at the forefront of post-Civil War intellectual developments. The historian Louis Menand has argued that the Civil War proved once and for all the futility of older ways of thinking, and opened a door to a much more pragmatic and experiential kind of intellectualism, expressed by the likes of Oliver Wendell Holmes, Jr., William James, and others.[41] To this list we might add John Wesley Powell. Like Holmes and James, Powell reveled in the advancement and testing of hypotheses through intellectual exchange. In 1885, he organized and began service as the first president of the Cosmos Club, the first society in Washington, DC, devoted to literature and the arts, and in 1888 he helped found the National Geographic Society. He believed fundamentally in free exchange of knowledge among specialists and the public as a means for conceptualizing problems and advancing solutions. We can see this characteristic in his leadership of the Bureau of American Ethnology, where he hired researchers with whom he often disagreed, but whose work he supported and published nonetheless as contributions to a larger body of scholarship.[42]

Powell's commitment to pragmatism and experimentalism is perhaps most evident in his resort to science to understand pressing social and environmental problems, and the need to test proposals against experience. The *Arid Lands Report* should be understood in this light: as a scientifically informed proposal for settlement of arid lands that should be tested and amended as needed. Indeed, by 1890, when Powell published a series of articles in *Century* magazine,[43] he had updated his ideas, acknowledging that forests could not be sold, but instead would need some form of protection to guarantee irrigation water. Powell's proposals were prescriptive, but they were also prospective. The laws he drew up were recommendations and as such, he admitted, subject to change. Settlers' experiences would necessarily reshape laws going forward. It was partly for this reason that he wanted settlers to retain powers to regulate their own communities, which he trusted more than federal or even state governments.[44]

In other words, the *Report* and subsequent proposals were not dogmatic. They were a framework for a grand experiment in communal self-regulation, through which settlers could make their own laws, test them against experience, and adapt them to the new country as needed. Powell acknowledged his proposals' prospective nature, issuing a caveat about the irrigation- and pasturage-district bills he had drafted. "It is not supposed that these forms are the best that could be adopted; perhaps they could be greatly improved."[45] To refer to Powell's report as "prophecy," as Bernard DeVoto once did, is to miss the spirit of the thing.[46] It was, rather, meant to be a field test. It was meant not to end discussion about the arid lands, but to initiate a wider trial that could result in still more advancement in knowledge and technology and the creation of more durable institutions.

Durability, though, was not the only test of institutional viability for Powell. Justice, too, was required. Powell took a dim view of Gilded Age excess, and during the latter decades of his life, he was an ever-sterner critic of corporate power and monopoly. He was sympathetic to Populists, and his communitarianism represented, perhaps more than anything else, an effort to reconnect Americans with small-scale government and to protect them from the railroads, steel corporations, and investment banks increasingly dominating the country. A classic illustration appears in Powell's remarks at the 1893 International Irrigation Congress:

> [M]y prime interest is not in great enterprises—these great railroads—these great progressive enterprises. My prime interest is in such a system as will develop the greatest number of cottage homes for the people. I am more interested in the home and the cradle than I am in the bank counter.[47]

If his proposals could not, in the end, rise to that challenge, the sentiment behind them—individuals and communities need a resort and a redoubt from corporate power—is hard to fault.

It is in his scientific method and his pursuit of justice that Powell still holds lessons for us. In an age of warming temperatures and radically changing climate, Powell's example should inspire us to adapt both our policies towards water and public lands, and our expectations for them. And this returns us to one of Stegner's central concerns in writing *Beyond the Hundredth Meridian*. Stegner presented Powell as a heroic figure, a rigorous thinker who could not be shaken from his dedication to scientific inquiry, despite powerful corporate interests that sought to destroy him. To Stegner, Powell was a model of public service and intellectual integrity who, in withstanding the red-baiters of his day, could also serve as a model for public-spirited professionals accused of being communists.

Red-baiting remains with us in the twenty-first century. It rears its head often in right-wing opposition to government science, particularly environmental science and especially science on climate change. Since 1988, climate scientists at NASA, the EPA, and elsewhere have become targets of conservative critics seeking to block or undermine proposals to regulate greenhouse gases. In many cases, these critics have taken the position that the climate is not changing, or that its changes are insignificant, or that they are unrelated to human activity. This consistently negative stance has earned them the name "climate deniers."[48]

Powell paid a heavy price for confronting his era's climate deniers, the "rain follows the plow" enthusiasts, land boomers, and railroad promoters who encouraged Americans to ignore warnings about limits on farming in the arid West, and who instructed them to turn a blind eye to science and experience, and to trust in Providence.[49] He watched as they persuaded thousands to risk their savings and short lives in the marginal lands of Kansas, South Dakota, and other places where rainfall was slight, only to be broken and dispossessed by aridity's hard hand. His efforts at reform, to create a new process of dry land settlement, ultimately failed, in part because of a wave of corporate opposition. Nonetheless, he bore witness to the advancing scientific knowledge of his time and to the injustice done to the masses in ignoring it.

We need not elevate Powell to the status of prophet or hero to follow his example, in confronting the fact of aridity and seeking sound, pragmatic solutions that might, on occasion, threaten conventional wisdom and tired platitudes. We could do much worse than to follow Powell, and look aridity in the face. Like him, we might try to imagine, as best we can, the world that science tells us is coming—and then seek modes of adaptation. And like Powell, we might make social justice a priority as we try to envision a new future for the Colorado River Basin and broader West.

In seeking a heroic Powell, scholars have too often emphasized his exceptional ideas and activities—the ways in which he broke with his contemporaries—and downplayed the ways in which he was one of them. Powell's awareness of the limitations of irrigated agriculture in the arid West, and his belief that the federal government could deploy scientific expertise to better manage land and water, might be said to presage modern conservation. But he was also, of course, a man of his time and place, constrained by the biases and beliefs of a culture that assumed natural resources could best be used to promote agrarian development, that presumed the dominion of white men over Native people and the natural world alike, and that imbibed a blind faith in progress that would lead mostly to intense disappointment.

But for all that, Powell's virtues endure. In his commitment to the scientific method, pragmatism, open debate, and social justice, Powell provides an example that we might follow as we map a new route through the canyons of the Southwest and the changing globe.

NOTES

1. Donald Worster, *A River Running West: The Life of John Wesley Powell* (New York: Oxford University Press, 2001), xi.

2. Emery Kolb and Ellsworth Kolb, *Through the Grand Canyon from Wyoming to Mexico* (New York: MacMillan, 1914); Clyde Eddy, *Down the World's Most Dangerous River* (New York: A. Stokes Co., 1929); Grove Karl Gilbert, ed., *John Wesley Powell: A Memorial to An American Explorer and Scholar* (Chicago: Open Court Publishing, 1903); William Morris Davis, *Biographical Memoir of John Wesley Powell, 1834–1902* (Washington, DC: National Academy of Sciences, 1915); Bernard DeVoto, "Introduction," Wallace Stegner, *Beyond the Hundredth Meridian: John Wesley Powell and the Second Opening of the West* (Boston: Houghton, Mifflin, 1954), xvi.

3. Herbert Hoover, "Rugged Individualism Campaign Speech," *Digital History*, accessed November 26, 2019, http://www.digitalhistory.uh.edu/disp_textbook.cfm?smtID=3&psid=1334.

4. Otis L. Graham, *Toward a Planned Society: From Roosevelt to Nixon* (New York: Oxford University Press, 1976); Patrick D. Reagan, *Designing America: The Origins of New Deal Planning, 1890–1943* (Amherst: University of Massachusetts Press, 2000).

5. *The Future of the Great Plains: Report of the Great Plains Committee* (Washington, DC: Government Printing Office, 1936), 193. Powell was restored to some of his fame in the widely influential work of Walter Prescott Webb, *The Great Plains* (New York: Ginn and Company, 1931), 353–54.

6. H. H. Dunham, *Government Handout: A Study in the Administration of Public Lands, 1875–1891* (Ann Arbor, MI: Edward Brothers, 1941), 35–36, 42, 66–67, 81; E. Louise Peffer, *The Closing of the Public Domain: Disposal and Reservation Policies, 1900–1950* (Stanford, CA: Stanford University Press, 1951), 24–25; R. M. Robbins, *Our Landed Heritage: The Public Domain, 1776–1936* (Princeton, NJ: Princeton University Press, 1942), 327.

7. E.g., Mary C. Rabbit, "John Wesley Powell: Pioneer Statesman of Federal Science," *Geological Survey Professional Paper 669-A* (1969), https://pubs.usgs.gov/pp/0669/report.pdf#page = 8.

8. William Culp Darrah, *Powell of the Colorado* (Princeton, NJ: Princeton University Press, 1951). See also Paul Meadows, *John Wesley Powell: Frontiersman of Science* (Lincoln: University of Nebraska Press, 1952).

9. Stegner, *Beyond the Hundredth Meridian*.

10. Proposal, undated, included as an enclosure with a letter dated November 10, 1948, from Wallace Stegner to Henry Allen Moe, John Simon Guggenheim Memorial Foundation, in Wallace Earle Stegner papers, Ms 676, Box 6, Folder 6, Special Collections and Archives, University of Utah, J. Willard Marriott Library, Salt Lake City, Utah (hereafter, Stegner papers).

11. Wallace Stegner, "Clarence Dutton: Geologist and Man of Letters" (Ph.D. diss., University of Iowa, 1935). See also Phillip L. Fradkin, *Wallace Stegner and the American West* (Berkeley: University of California Press, 2009).

12. Wallace Stegner to Brandt, May 27, 1953, Box 24, Folder 4, Stegner papers.

13. March 31, 1948, Henry Allen Moe to Wallace Stegner, Stegner papers.

14. Otis "Dock" Marston, "Fast Water," in Wallace Stegner ed., *This is Dinosaur* (New York: Alfred A. Knopf, 1955), 67. For the history of outdoor recreation, see Terence Young, *Heading Out: A History of American Camping* (New York: Cornell University Press, 2017), especially 248–50, and Silas Chamberlain, *On the Trail: A History of American Hiking* (New Haven: Yale University Press, 2016).

15. Mark W.T. Harvey, *A Symbol of Wilderness: Echo Park and the American Conservation Movement* (Seattle: University of Washington Press, 1994).

16. Stegner to Brandt, January 20, 1954, Box 24, Folder 6, Stegner papers; Stegner, *This is Dinosaur*, vi.

17. Stegner, "The Marks of Human Passage," in Stegner, *This is Dinosaur*, 17.

18. Ibid., 12.

19. John Wesley Powell, "Institutions for the Arid Lands," *Century* 40 (1890); John Wesley Powell, *Report on the Lands of the Arid Region of the United States, with a More Detailed Account of the Lands of Utah*, 45 Congr., 2 Sess., H.R. Exec. Doc. 73, 1878.

20. Powell, *Arid Lands Report*, 54.

21. Worster, *A River Running West*, 362 (citing "Surveys of the Territories," 45 Cong., 3 Sess., House Misc. Doc. 17).

22. Ibid., 529.

23. Ibid.

24. "[E]vents have proved that [Powell] was not visionary but merely in advance of his time" (G.K. Gilbert, "John Wesley Powell," *Science* 16 (1902): 567).

25. Pierre Dansereau, "Ecosystem," *The Canadian Encyclopedia*, accessed November 26, 2019, https://www.thecanadianencyclopedia.ca/en/article/ecosystem.

26. John Wesley Powell, *Canyons of the Colorado* (1898), 394, http://www.gutenberg.org/files/8082/8082-h/8082-h.htm.

27. Wallace Stegner, "Introduction," in Wallace Stegner, ed., *The Arid Lands* by John Wesley Powell (Cambridge, MA: Belknap Press of Harvard University, 1962), vii, xxiv. See also Webb, *The Great Plains*, 422.

28. For a more critical appreciation of Powell, see Worster, *A River Running West*, especially xii.

29. Powell, *Arid Lands Report*, viii, 10; also 8, 14.

30. Gordon B. Dodds, "The Stream-flow Controversy: A Conservation Turning Point," *Journal of American History* 56, no. 1 (1969): 59–69; Donald J. Pisani, "Forestry and Reclamation, 1891–1911," *Forest & Conservation History* 37, no. 2 (1993): 68–79.
31. Pisani, "Forestry and Reclamation," 70.
32. Powell, *Arid Lands Report*, 27–28; Pisani, "Forestry and Reclamation," 70.
33. Powell, *Arid Lands Report*, 90.
34. Ibid., 92.
35. Powell, "Institutions for the Arid Lands," 114.
36. Ibid.
37. Powell, *Arid Lands Report*, 29.
38. Ibid.
39. Ibid., 51–53.
40. Robert G. Dunbar, *Forging New Rights in Western Waters* (Lincoln: University of Nebraska Press, 1983).
41. Louis Menand, *The Metaphysical Club: A Story of Ideas in America* (New York: Farrar, Straus & Giroux, 2001).
42. Louis S. Warren, *God's Red Son: The Ghost Dance Religion and the Making of Modern America* (New York: Basic, 2017), 362–63.
43. Powell, "Institutions for the Arid Lands"; John Wesley Powell, "The Irrigable Lands of the Arid Region," *Century* 39 (1890): 766–76; John Wesley Powell, "The Non-Irrigable Lands of the Arid Region," *Century* 39 (1890): 915–22.
44. Powell, "Institutions for the Arid Lands," 114; Powell, *Arid Lands Report*, 29.
45. Powell, *Arid Lands Report*, 30.
46. DeVoto, "Introduction," xxii.
47. John Wesley Powell, "Address and Comments," *International Irrigation Congress Official Proceedings* 2 (1893): 108.
48. Brian Brettschneider, "Climate Change Skeptic or Denier?," *Forbes*, Aug. 3, 2018, https://www.forbes.com/sites/brianbrettschneider/2018/08/03/climate-change-skeptic-or-denier/#c4ebbd6e8c2c.
49. John Wesley Powell, "Address to the North Dakota Constitutional Convention, August 5, 1889" *Reclamation Era* 26 (1936): 201.

CHAPTER 2

Communitarianism in Western Water Law and Policy

Was Powell's Vision Lost?

ROBERT W. ADLER

John Wesley Powell championed communitarian water management, which Wallace Stegner labeled a "blueprint for a dryland democracy."[1] We might reframe it a blueprint for a watershed democracy. Powell's proposals, however, reflected inconsistencies between his personal attributes and his philosophy that paralleled similar contradictions in Western water law and policy.

Powell was a stereotypical rugged individualist who headed westward in the late-nineteenth century.[2] In government, he was an intellectual nonconformist facing political opposition from Washington officialdom.[3] As a leader, reflecting his military experience, Powell was authoritarian. Regarding Powell's 1869 Expedition, William deBuys wrote: "He was in charge, they were to work for him, and he left things at that ... [but] a more democratically-organized expedition might have abandoned the canyon and failed to achieve as much."[4] Powell's individualism and authoritarian leadership, however, contrasted with his egalitarian philosophy and commitment to democratic governance. He responded to President Lincoln's call for Civil War recruits because of his belief in the Union cause and his faith in the nation's democratic ideals.[5] His sociological writings countered the contemporaneous philosophy of individualism and laissez-faire capitalism.[6]

In Powell's best-known writing, his 1878 *Arid Lands Report,*[7] and later pieces in which the report's ideas evolved,[8] he outlined a broad vision of a communitarian West. Yet those texts were prescriptive and ambiguous about his assessment of human nature. Powell knew what was good for the West and its inhabitants. He derided individualism and the capitalistic quest for profit, but lacked faith that individuals would "do the right thing" absent guidance from scientific experts. His communitarian plan for Western settlement, however, relied on collaborative human endeavor, if properly organized.

The classic story is that Powell's plan died on the vine.[9] The reality is not so simple. Western water law and institutions include some aspects of Powell's vision,[10] with potential for more in the future. Over the past several decades, Powell's "watershed blueprint" has been analyzed for its potential to foster bioregional and ecological approaches to watershed management.[11] Environmental interpretation of Powell's watershed proposal is appropriate today. The latter half of the twentieth century brought an experimental amalgam of watershed programs around the country, with diverse scales, formats, and governance structures.[12]

In the late nineteenth century, however, Powell was not motivated by ecological concerns. He promoted maximum use of water and land from a scientifically informed perspective but with utilitarian goals, urging the construction of reservoirs "until all of the streams of the arid region are wholly utilized . . . so that no water runs to the sea."[13] Given the contemporaneous debate over laissez-faire capitalism, however, Powell proposed local, communitarian governance emphasizing democracy and equity, to protect small farmers against monopolistic corporate power. Questions remain about the extent to which this communitarianism has been revived, and the desirability of additional use of those ideas.

This chapter begins by outlining the ways Powell promoted egalitarian water allocation and democratic water governance in the West. Next, the chapter analyzes the extent to which Western water law and institutions in the Colorado River Basin and elsewhere evolved to reflect Powell's ideas, but through a more flexible and organic process. Finally, the chapter closes with an assessment of the potential for further evolution of water law and policy in the basin and elsewhere to further embrace Powell's communitarian vision.

THE VISION: POWELL'S PROPOSAL FOR WATERSHED DEMOCRACY

Beginning with the *Arid Lands Report,* Powell set out a broad vision of how Western states and territories should allocate and use finite water resources, and how their water and land should be governed. He recognized more clearly than many contemporaries that water scarcity should dictate land use: "Thus, practically, all values inhere in the water, and an equitable division of the waters can be made only by a wise system of parceling the lands. . . . "[14] In addition to tomes of scientific data and analysis, the report included precise recommendations for irrigation and water policy, and accompanying proposals for land disposal, settlement, organization, and governance.

Powell sought to maximize water use for irrigation and other utilitarian purposes, while democratizing water governance and preventing concentration of economic power. Although he admired the "individual enterprise" of water diversions, he disapproved of inefficiencies resulting from haphazard diversions.[15] Physical challenges plagued irrigation systems when individuals diverted water from smaller streams for use on preferred lands, foreclosing or limiting larger diversions from mainstem streams. The evolving prior appropriation system, with its "first in time, first in right" rule for water rights, caused a race to the diversion point.[16] Inefficient prior appropriators gained seniority over more efficient and economically beneficial future diversions.

Yet Powell recognized the need for cooperative labor and capital to build and operate larger and more efficient water projects. Examples of cooperation included Mormon Church-controlled settlements in Utah, community irrigation by Pueblo Indians, and Hispanic *acequia* systems created under Spanish colonial and Mexican rule.[17] A distinctly different model involved Eastern and European capital investments, with concentrated control over land or water by corporations or wealthy individuals. A third option, which ultimately dominated Western water development, involved government investment in water infrastructure. Powell embraced the collaborative model to achieve both efficiency and equity in water allocation and use, arguing that "the people in organized bodies can well be trusted with this right, while individuals could not be trusted."[18] He believed the capitalist model posed grave threats to equity. He initially rejected the government model, possibly because it was impracticable politically, but more likely because he favored local citizen control. To implement his vision, Powell suggested that the federal government use his comprehensive topographic surveys and mapping to classify public lands into those suitable for irrigation, pasturage, and timber, with less extensive land for mineral and coal extraction. The plan assumed that centralized, scientific decisions were more efficient than individual enterprise.

Powell offered two bills in the *Arid Lands Report* to implement his vision: one authorizing "irrigation districts,"[19] the other "pasturage districts."[20] Nine or more people could settle and organize an irrigation district, and each could acquire title to appropriately sized parcels of irrigable land. Members of each district could adopt by-laws "as they may deem wise for the use of waters in such districts for irrigation and other purposes. . . . " Water rights to each parcel would "inhere in the land," passing to subsequent owners with title, but those rights would lapse on failure to irrigate. Subsequent water rights could be obtained only in amounts needed to irrigate the particular parcel, and only "by priority of utilization." Latecomers could join an irrigation district, with identically defined water rights, if they caused no injury to existing users.[21] The pasturage district bill was conceptually identical in all key respects.

Powell was equally prescriptive in his recommendations for water infrastructure. To minimize water loss through seepage and evaporation, Powell proposed siting reservoirs in headwaters where temperatures are cooler, and where possible off stream channels, or expanding natural lakes rather than building reservoirs. He preferred natural stream channels to artificial canals for conveyance. Upstream storage would maximize reliance by downstream users on return flows from upstream users. Had this system been adopted exclusively, huge reservoirs such as Lake Mead and Lake Powell may not have been built.

Congress did not adopt Powell's legislative proposals.[22] Not known for quitting, however, he tried again a decade later after becoming the second director of the US Geological Survey. The core components of his vision remained,[23] as did the key provisions of the proposed legislation.[24] Indeed, he became even more strident in his view that private, capitalistic control of water and irrigation would lead to monopolies and "despotism," which "cannot obtain in the United States, where the love of liberty is universal."[25] He warned: "wherever a company owns the water it practically owns the land; that is, it owns all the agriculture."[26]

Powell's thinking evolved, however, based on new topographic surveys. He articulated more clearly that Western states' geopolitical organization should follow watershed boundaries,[27] and he broadened the size of his proposed water institutions to defined watersheds.[28] That would facilitate his resource allocation process, with organized water courts, water masters, and local self-government within logical boundaries. Powell also recognized that the West's major stream systems were too large for management within one district, and modified his earlier proposal to account for different districts for headwaters, storage basins, and mainstem river segments.[29] Prophetically, while maintaining his preference for upstream storage, Powell acknowledged that some downstream storage would be needed, including "great reservoirs or artificial lakes."[30] Likewise, although he continued to oppose government-funded projects as late as 1890,[31] he partially retreated from that position two years later, asserting that the only solution to major disputes on larger interstate river systems was for the national government to build dams and assign water among states.[32]

Although some politicians embraced Powell's views, his proposals ran perpendicular to social and political trends that favored individualism over collectivism, private property and capitalism over a water commons, entrepreneurship over government planning, states' rights over federal oversight, and the perception of a West devoid of any limits.[33] Each of those dichotomies would have profound implications for water and water rights in the Colorado River Basin and elsewhere across the arid region.

THE VISION IN HISTORICAL PERSPECTIVE

Prior appropriation was evolving but uncertain when Powell developed his water law proposals. Although its origins are often attributed to customary rules developed in mining camps dating to the 1849 California Gold Rush,[34] formal confirmation and precise delineation of the doctrine, especially its relationship to the common law doctrine of riparian rights, came later. The California Supreme Court accepted prior appropriation in 1855,[35] but also recognized the continuing status of riparian rights two years later.[36] It did not address the relationship between the two doctrines until 1886 in *Lux v. Haggin*.[37] The Colorado Supreme Court decided the seminal case of *Coffin v. Left Hand Ditch* in 1882, although it referred to provisions of the 1876 Colorado Constitution.[38] The US Supreme Court did not determine the relative roles and authority of the state and federal governments in Western water law until 1935, in *California Oregon Power v. Beaver Portland Cement*.[39]

Powell correctly predicted some aspects of Western water law, but he did not know, and could not have foreseen, the manner in which that law would develop. Ironically, however, to navigate many of the concerns Powell sought to address, Western water law would develop its own solutions through the usual process by which law evolves in the United States—a combination of common law, legislative, and regulatory decisions.

Allocation Versus Appropriation

Powell proposed that the government *assign* water rights within irrigation and pasturage districts to each landowner based on need, rather than allowing each user to *appropriate* water with subsequent governmental recognition and protection as a property right. He agreed that temporal priority should play a role in water allocation, but only consistent with his other proposals.[40] The prior appropriation doctrine reflected the Lockean notion that property rights are justified when someone diverts a resource and puts it to beneficial use through application of labor and capital, thus generating economic benefits for the individual and for society.[41] In its pure form, however, prior appropriation does not involve collective societal decisions about maximum resource use. It assumed that individual appropriation decisions would promote efficiency.

Notwithstanding its focus on private decisions, prior appropriation considers water a public resource. Appropriative rights are usufructuary, but government owns the water, or holds it in public trust. Moreover, as the doctrine evolved in most states, appropriation requires a governmental "public interest" determination and other conditions. Those include beneficial use, abandonment or forfeiture for non-use, and prohibitions against waste and speculation. Courts in some Western states restrict water uses that violate the state's version of the public trust doctrine.[42]

Thus, prior appropriation evolved in theory to safeguard public values in water use, but in different ways than Powell proposed. Powell envisioned comprehensive planning to allocate water. Prior appropriation relies instead on individual economic decisions, but with government checks to safeguard public welfare. That system suffers in application due to the reluctance of courts and state officials to enforce rules against waste and other protections.[43] It does, however, consider a broader range of public uses and values than Powell's approach included.

Land-tied Versus Severed Water Rights

The original "natural flow" version of riparian rights protected the use and enjoyment of streams unimpaired in quality or quantity, and water could not be diverted to non-riparian lands, or beyond the watershed. Riparian rights inhered in land ownership. For most purposes, they could not be severed from that title, and could be conveyed only by selling the land,[44] although states modified those limitations to facilitate municipal, industrial, and other uses.

Powell disfavored one of these riparian rights rules but supported the other. He recognized that arid conditions, and the location and topography of irrigable lands relative to the dispersed water bodies in the West, required that "water rights must of necessity be severed from the natural stream channels." The riparian rule would "practically prohibit the growth of [the West's] most important industries." This rule was being modified by "custom," but Powell was uncertain about the degree to which it had "color of authority in statutory or common law."[45] Although early prior appropriation doctrine required appurtenance,[46] it ultimately rejected the principle that water must be used on adjacent lands.[47]

Powell viewed the second limitation of riparian law, that water rights inhere in land, as essential to protect small farmers and other landowners. This provision would "give settlers on pasturage or irrigation farms the assurance that their lands would not be made worthless by taking away the water to other lands by persons settling subsequently in other portions of the country." He also feared that priority rules would disfavor "men of few means," who could not quickly build the works necessary to put water to beneficial use. They needed reasonable time to perfect those rights either individually or cooperatively.[48]

Powell's concerns that prior appropriation afforded fragile protection did not materialize. The priority rule protected early settlers from subsequent claims. Because farmers were among the earliest users throughout the Colorado River Basin and the entire West, agriculture enjoys some of the most senior water rights, in ways that critics have argued lock in outdated economic and other values.[49] As just one example, farmers in California's Imperial Valley enjoy some of the most senior—and hence the most secure—water rights in the the Colorado River Basin.

Powell's proposal that water rights inhere in the land was inconsistent with prior appropriation, but for a different reason. His method of providing security to landowners would have prevented transfers of water for uses that he did not anticipate or encourage. Powell feared that alienability of water independent of land would result in water monopoly and oppression, similar to what he saw elsewhere in American industry. He promoted the Jeffersonian ideal of a largely rural West inhabited by small farmers and ranchers, supported by small associated communities, timber from the mountains, and a small mining economy. Particularly for someone who was brilliantly prophetic in other ways, it was an unrealistically static vision of Western society. Unlike his contemporary Clarence King,[50] Powell did not predict the rise of industry.

He did not foresee that the West would become more urban than rural in its population distribution and economic structure, and that so many citizens would value water as part of natural ecosystems and recreational playgrounds. Despite his extensive study of Native American languages and cultures, he also did not anticipate that the Supreme Court would later recognize tribal water rights.[51]

Powell's plan would have doled out every drop of water so that none would "run to waste," in ways that would have locked in fixed uses on specified land parcels. It would have prevented water transfers for other uses and to other locations in ways that ultimately rendered Western water law more flexible to meet changing needs by a wider range of users. It would have prohibited rural-to-urban transfers to satisfy municipal needs, and water banks and instream flow rights to protect aquatic ecosystems and recreation.

Capitalism Versus Communalism in Water Management

Powell's concept of democratically governed irrigation and pasturage districts within watershed boundaries diverged from Western water law's initial trajectory. Water institutions later incorporated some of the collaborative governance Powell envisioned, however. Although the watershed aspect of Powell's proposal is not the main focus here, Western water law and policy borrowed that idea to some extent. Colorado organizes its water courts around the state's river basins;[52] other states administer water planning and management within watershed boundaries;[53] and general stream adjudications determine water rights within hydrological boundaries.[54]

Modern water governance addresses many of the same concerns Powell identified, but in different ways. Powell feared concentration of wealth and power by those who controlled water:

> But if in the eagerness for present development a land and water system shall grow up in which the practical control of agriculture shall fall into the hands of water companies, evils will result therefrom that generations may not be able to correct, and the very men who are now lauded as benefactors to the country will, in the ungovernable reaction which is sure to come, be denounced as oppressors of the people.[55]

Corporations and outside capital were beginning to control water, threatening equitable wealth distribution and the viability of small farms and ranches.[56]

Corporate water development did not succeed on a wide scale—not because it was undemocratic, but because water infrastructure was a poor investment with significant risk. For-profit irrigation companies were sometimes undercapitalized and sometimes overcapitalized, leading to bankruptcy and bond default.[57] In his fear of monopoly, Powell did not realize that the threat was bidirectional; according to some economists, monopsonistic power by organized water users doomed many early commercial water companies.[58] By the end of the twentieth century, for-profit companies served only a tiny percent of Western irrigated acreage.[59]

Notwithstanding the decline of for-profit water wholesalers, individuals or businesses still made water diversion decisions to benefit entrepreneurial interests. Powell was correct, however, that expensive water storage and conveyance systems required aggregated labor and capital. Ultimately, two alternatives emerged to serve that need. The first was not-for-profit or local governmental water institutions. The second was a much larger federal role in water project financing, construction, and management. Both entail a greater extent of democratic governance than reflected in the laissez-faire approach. Both focus on protecting the collective welfare. Neither is as utopian as Powell envisioned, but both avoid the unchecked water "despotism" he feared.

Diversity of Western Water Institutions

As highlighted earlier, at the time of the 1878 *Arid Lands Report,* there was precedent for communal water use and allocation in the Colorado River Basin and across the West, including the Mormon tradition of institutional decision-making and the Hispanic *acequia* systems under Spanish colonial and Mexican rule.[60] Some commentators question whether Mormon water law was egalitarian in practice, alleging that Church control served as "engines of oppression" to consolidate power and exclude non-Church members from water ownership, and that Church officials received preference.[61] Spanish rulers likewise used water for political and military power, to control the Indians and maintain social and economic hierarchy.[62] Thus, although those precedents influenced Powell as he formulated his communal water governance proposal,[63] they suggest caution. Whenever exclusive resource control is vested in a discrete group, others may be excluded intentionally or overlooked due to lack of participation.

The first alternative to the capitalist model includes a range of nonprofit water institutions, from unincorporated mutual water districts to formal mutual water companies, water districts, and irrigation districts.[64] Mutual water companies and irrigation districts arose in part out of the Mormon experience in Utah. California encouraged cooperative irrigation districts through the 1887 Wright Act, designed to offset the lack of security appropriators experienced in the wake of *Lux v. Haggin*.[65] Every Western state adopted similar legislation.[66]

Local water institutions now control about half of the water used in the West.[67] These institutions solved the problem of monopoly and monopsony through vertical integration, in which end users control nonprofit wholesale and retail water entities. That provides water users with the economic protection Powell sought, but through different structures. Vertical integration was simpler and more efficient than governmental utility regulation developed for industries such as electric power and telecommunications, and overcame the economies of scale and other problems that beset for-profit companies.[68] Institutions can resolve water management problems by creatively reconfiguring water rights, and by adapting to changing conditions. They can devise *pro rata* or other water allocation systems during shortages and facilitate collaborative conservation measures.[69] Those strategies will become increasingly important in the Colorado River Basin as climate change threatens water supplies. They can also overcome barriers to water markets, including the high transaction costs that render trades by small users difficult.

A more profound explanation for user-controlled water institutions tracks Powell's aspirations for community governance. "Most Westerners historically have viewed water as a crucial necessity, central to life, livelihood, and community. As a result, they long for some personal control over distribution of the resource—no matter how attenuated—and often fear turning decisions concerning water over to the marketplace."[70] Western water institutions developed through bottom-up experimentation[71] rather than Powell's singular system. This allowed states and communities to devise solutions deemed most appropriate to their circumstances. That process, however, did not always result in democratic governance—for example, unelected leaders with taxation powers. While organizations lack the breadth of government authority Powell recommended for his watershed districts, they are recognized legal entities with some governance authority, including eminent domain, taxing and bonding, and tax exemptions.[72] That suggests concern about voices and interests that may be ignored.

For-profit water corporations and nonprofit mutual companies are governed for their shareholders' benefit. Absent a specific directive to consider broader concerns, such as environmental protection, recreation, or other instream uses and values, they are likely to maximize the interests of irrigators or other shareholders. Where agricultural and municipal interests conflict, single-purpose entities are less likely to safeguard public welfare. In many regions, a patchwork of local and regional entities serve water to different end users, sometimes with overlapping jurisdictions that ignore watershed boundaries. Given those limitations, the state's regulatory apparatus, including the public-interest test and the public trust doctrine discussed above, is needed to consider broader public welfare in water use and management decisions. Unlike the watershed democracy Powell envisioned, water users are more likely to challenge than to embrace regulatory constraints.

Irrigation districts have greater potential to consider the public interest because they require a majority vote of area residents to be formed,[73] and are governed by democratically elected boards that operate "much like local governments,"[74] similar to Powell's vision. Even these democratically governed institutions, however, have incentives to act only in their members' interests. In some districts, voting is weighted by land ownership or water rights rather than "one person, one vote." Those measures can be less than egalitarian.[75] Citizens have unsuccessfully challenged the fact that district voting rights can be allocated according to property ownership, allegedly in violation of the "one person, one vote" principle guaranteed by the Fourteenth Amendment.[76] Such institutions can "parochially ignore outside interests and use their insulation and considerable political power to thwart broader community goals," including efforts to impede external water markets they perceive as harmful to their members.[77] A key example has been litigation by the Imperial Irrigation District to thwart market-based efforts to address California's overuse of its allocation of Colorado River water.[78]

The Federal Role in Western Water

Just as Powell incompletely predicted the evolution of Western state water law, he only partially anticipated the eventual roles of the federal and state governments in water law and management. Those developments had profound implications for water project financing and operation, as well as watershed governance, in the Colorado River Basin and elsewhere.

Particularly given legal and political disputes over federalism in the wake of the Civil War, Powell seemed somewhat tone deaf regarding the relative authority of the states and the federal government to control water. In the *Arid Lands Report,* Powell suggested federal legislation to validate "the legality of the practices of the people in the arid country relating to water and land rights,"[79] referring to the still largely customary prior appropriation doctrine. Much of the region remained in territorial status, suggesting more federal authority than might exist in admitted states. The majority of Western land was federally owned. Had riparian rights law continued, the federal government would have owned and controlled all water on federal land. The Supreme Court had upheld significant federal control over navigable waters under the Commerce Clause,[80] supporting federal legal authority to resolve interstate water disputes.[81]

Despite this potential for significant federal authority over water, in statutes governing mineral rights, Congress protected pre-existing appropriative rights to water and related rights-of-way.[82] Indeed, nearly six decades later the Supreme Court held that Congress, in the Desert Land Act of 1877, had severed all water from the public domain, leaving its allocation and use to state discretion.[83]

Powell also underestimated the federal government's role in water infrastructure, an issue about which his own thinking evolved over time. In the *Arid Lands Report,* he envisioned that settlers would construct and operate communal irrigation systems by combining their own labor or by pooling capital and contracting with private businesses. Aside from legislation authorizing irrigation and pasturage districts, he envisioned no federal role in project design, financing, construction, or operation. Powell later concluded that control should remain with the local population and not the federal government:

> I demand that the laborers shall employ themselves; that the enterprise shall be controlled by the men who have the genius to organize, and whose homes are in the lands developed, and that the money shall be furnished by the people; and I say to the Government: Hands off! Furnish the people with institutions of justice, and let them do the work for themselves.[84]

In his congressional testimony, however, Powell's views were ambiguous. In 1888, he maintained his view that irrigation districts should develop projects themselves.[85] But based on more recent topographic and hydrologic surveys, he acknowledged that while reservoirs were still preferable in upper watershed reaches, some would be needed below, including (as noted earlier) "great reservoirs or artificial lakes." In his 1890 testimony, frustrated by the degree to which interstate conflict in basins such as the Rio Grande impeded his vision of orderly water allocation and management, Powell argued that the only solution was for the federal government to build dams, from which it would allocate water to states.[86]

Powell could not have envisioned the massive federal role in later water project development, operation, and governance. A little over a decade after his showdown with the Senate Special Committee on Irrigation and Reclamation of Arid Lands, Congress passed the Reclamation Act of 1902[87] and created its implementing institution, the Bureau of Reclamation. What Congress intended as a modest startup for a reclamation revolving fund became the largest water development program in the world. Federal reclamation projects became the dominant source of irrigation water within the Colorado River Basin and across the West.[88]

The growing federal role in water project development also shifted the balance in Western water governance, certainly compared to the "build it and get out" role Powell envisioned. The Bureau of Reclamation must comply with state water law and obtain state water rights in operating its projects, but specific provisions of the Reclamation Act preempt inconsistent requirements of state law.[89] The Bureau sells federal reclamation water to local irrigation districts and other end users. That confers considerable influence, though not plenary authority, over water management. In the Colorado River Basin, the Bureau was almost singlehandedly responsible for the massive complex of dams and diversion works that dominate water storage and distribution, and that have reshaped the hydrology and ecology of natural river systems. Statutes authorizing those projects included more detailed operating criteria than the Reclamation Act itself,[90] augmented by federal administrative decisions.[91] That imposed significant federal constraints on how water is used and managed in the region.

Powell saw more clearly that however democratic and rational water allocation might be at the small watershed level, local irrigation districts could not resolve larger interstate disputes.[92] The states were "almost at war" over water allocation, and no clear dispute resolution system had yet developed. His solution to transboundary allocation was simple and logical, but naïve and incomplete in the interests it would protect. It was also confused and inconsistent. At times, Powell argued that the federal government should settle all interstate problems, while still leaving control of water within each district to its members and respecting state water law.[93] At other times, he asserted that Congress should adopt legislation to establish "the means and authority" by which interstate waters would be divided, without identifying how or by which levels or branches of government.[94] In 1890 congressional testimony, Powell clarified that Congress should divide water among states directly. He dodged a query on the constitutional source of that authority, saying that his view was one of policy, not law.[95]

Powell did not, however, anticipate the Supreme Court's role in defining and resolving transboundary water conflicts within the Colorado River Basin and elsewhere. Testifying before the 1890 Senate Committee, he discussed conflicts between Colorado and Kansas over the Arkansas River and between New Mexico and Texas on the Pecos River and Rio Grande.[96] But the Supreme Court did not confirm its original jurisdiction to resolve interstate water disputes until 1907, in the conflict between Kansas and Colorado.[97] A year later, in *Winters v. United States*,[98] the Supreme Court added another complexity Powell would not have predicted. The Court declared that the federal government, in reserving lands for Indian tribes (and in later cases, for other federal purposes such as parks and wildlife refuges), implicitly reserved sufficient water to meet the needs of the particular reservation. Throughout the West, that added another set of water interests to consider and further complicated the relationship between the states and the federal government, which has an independent trust duty to protect tribes. The Supreme Court recognized and quantified these reserved water rights for several Colorado River tribes in its pivotal decision *Arizona v. California*.[99]

Likewise, although Powell identified allocation of the Colorado as a "problem of great importance," he lacked faith in the states' ability to resolve it on their own. He was only partially correct. States recognized the potential to use the Compact Clause of the Constitution to resolve water disputes by mutual agreement in the 1922 Colorado River Compact.[100] But Congress did not exercise its legislative authority to resolve interstate water disputes until 1928, also regarding the Colorado River, in the Boulder Canyon Project Act.[101] In this statute, Congress took the constitutionally necessary step of ratifying the Compact. The Supreme Court, however, later ruled that the Act also authorized the Secretary of the Interior to serve as "water master" for the Lower Colorado River.[102] Subsequent federal legislation strengthened that authority, leaving the secretary with overriding authority over the most significant water management decisions in the region.

Yet neither the Compact nor other federal or state measures resulted in "peace" in the basin, leading to a long series of management disputes that continue today. Disputes over the Colorado River went to the Supreme Court four separate times, and in *Arizona v. California* the Court decided some of the issues presented.[103] More recently, the states and the federal government have interpreted the Compact flexibly enough to avoid interstate litigation.

Two other factors reinforced the federal role in Colorado River water management. First, the Lower Colorado River flows through Mexico to the Sea of Cortez, and the Colorado River Compact only included a placeholder to account for any future agreement with Mexico. The United States negotiated such an agreement in 1944.[104] As with the Compact, the treaty did not permanently resolve all disputes between the two countries regarding the Colorado River. Through the International Boundary and Water Commission, the federal government continues to reach key decisions about water quantity and quality in ways that affect other aspects of Colorado River governance. Second, despite the emergence of a national conservation movement contemporaneous with his work,[105] Powell could not anticipate the role that aquatic ecosystem protection and restoration, or other values such as public recreation, would play in the ensuing century. A wide range of federal environmental statutes, implemented by a bevy of federal agencies, further complicated water governance but invited a new set of interests to engage in the discourse.[106]

Powell's vision for democratic watershed governance was logical and orderly from a scientific perspective, and included important interests that existed at the time. It did not, however, account for subsequent changes and the much wider range of interests that would materialize. The strong but complex federal role in Western water law and management—particularly within the Colorado River Basin—is justified in part by massive federal financial investment in reclamation projects as a matter of national policy. It also makes sense given the much broader range of interests and values now recognized regarding water and ecosystems, which federal agencies can address through regulatory statutes that provide for public participation and judicial review. The complex governance process that resulted, however, is a far cry from the local watershed democracy Powell sought. The key prospective governance question is the extent to which the noblest aspects of Powell's vision for watershed democracy remain possible, even if his specific plan was too one-dimensional for the modern world.

TOWARD MORE INCLUSIVE COLORADO RIVER GOVERNANCE

Powell's idea of a system of small communities of land and water users reaching collective decisions absent a strong federal presence is no longer feasible. A wide range of water governance institutions and processes has developed throughout the West, suited to the particular needs of different states and localities. That institutional diversity is not likely to be dismantled in favor of a single federally devised system. Nor is such unification necessarily preferable to a process through which we continuously explore new approaches to evolving problems and circumstances. This practice may better effectuate Powell's philosophy that those who use or manage resources within a local area are best positioned to devise appropriate solutions. Nor is it feasible to effectuate a radical shift in the region's geopolitical boundaries, to organize water and land governance within watershed boundaries.

Powell's concept of a limited federal role in Colorado River or other Western water governance is also unlikely. Despite recent but quixotic efforts to divest federal lands to the states,[107] the federal presence in Western water law and management is unlikely to disappear. Federal investment in water infrastructure is too large; the national interest in tribal water rights, environmental protection, and interstate and international relations is too profound; federal ownership and management of land in the basin is too substantial; and the federal statutory and administrative process is too entrenched for such a shift to materialize.

Nevertheless, more collective, watershed-based approaches to decision-making in the Colorado River Basin are possible. This effort, however, must take into account the manner in which Western water law developed in the decades after Powell's proposals, and the evolution of federal law and its relationship to state water management. It must consider significant ways that the basin and other parts of the West have changed since Powell's time, from environmental, socioeconomic, hydrologic, and other perspectives, and the even greater volatility generated by climate change.[108] Although Powell would have discouraged major transbasin diversions of water,[109] they are a reality, the implications of which must be considered in basinwide governance.

Processes have already evolved to achieve some of these goals. The Colorado River Compact, the Upper Colorado River Basin Compact (which established the Upper Colorado River Commission),[110] and other documents comprising the "Law of the River" reflect significant collaboration between the basin states. Most of those legal authorities, however, do not include direct representation of Indian tribes, Mexico, environmental or recreation groups, or water users. The federal government, under the Endangered Species Act[111] and the Grand Canyon Protection Act,[112] operates four collaborative restoration programs along discrete stretches of the river, in an effort to reconcile environmental values with water and power uses. Those efforts, however, focus on limited objectives dictated by specific statutory goals.[113] They include no process by which actions in one stretch are evaluated or modified to address impacts upstream, downstream, or along tributaries. Thus, existing efforts to achieve progress through consensus rather than litigation are laudable but fall short of Powell's overall vision.[114]

Comprehensive, Inclusive Watershed Governance

Public officials in other large, complex interjurisdictional watersheds, with equally challenging problems, have devised institutions to govern basinwide rather than piecemeal.[115] Prominent examples include the Chesapeake Bay Program, Great Lakes Program, Delta Stewardship Program, and Everglades Restoration Program, but similar efforts exist at diverse scales.[116] These programs consider connections throughout the watershed and across issues (such as water quality and quantity, or land use and water use). None of these programs are perfect, and they are routinely critiqued, given the massively complex and challenging problems they face. But they approach problems from a comprehensive, holistic perspective. In William deBuys's words, that is consistent with Powell's approach of "seeing things whole."[117]

Over twenty years ago, David Getches proposed a comprehensive approach to Colorado River governance through a Colorado River Commission, acknowledging that the idea was not original. Some Colorado River Compact negotiators had favored such a mechanism in 1922. Getches suggested that the idea was not politically feasible, and that incremental approaches would be more promising, potentially by delegating some authority Congress confers on federal agencies as an incentive for collaboration by basin states and others.[118]

Getches was correct that additional opportunities for collaboration were possible short of a basinwide commission. Thorny water management problems have been resolved in the basin through informally negotiated agreements, using what John Fleck refers to as "social capital."[119] Examples include the Interim Surplus Guidelines that reigned in California's over-use of its Colorado River apportionment;[120] the 2007 Interim Shortage Guidelines to conserve and store water to mitigate drought-related shortages, and to pre-negotiate responses to declines in Lake Powell and Lake Mead;[121] and minutes to the US-Mexico Treaty that facilitated environmental restoration experiments for the Colorado

River Delta.[122] Yet those laudable efforts have not resolved all tensions and uncertainties about long-term management. The basin states continue to quarrel over implementation of the 2007 guidelines.[123] Tensions may heighten if drought continues, or if it becomes, as some scientists predict, aridification rather than time-limited drought.[124] Some tribes are entitled to unresolved federal reserved water rights. Environmental restoration programs have shown only limited success, and endangered species remain a long way from recovery.

It is time to revisit the concept of basinwide governance. Perhaps the new challenges facing the basin provide sufficient incentive to overcome the political obstacles previously identified by Getches. Despite those challenges, some form of basinwide governance may provide the best way to make significant further progress based on collective values.

Including all Watershed Interests

One objection to a new Colorado River Commission is that so many existing institutions are already involved in Colorado River governance. That proliferation of institutions, however, with different, conflicting, or overlapping roles, is the best reason to consider consolidation of functions, or a process by which they can be better coordinated. More importantly, no existing institution includes a voice for all interests affected by basin governance.

Another objection to the idea is that existing interests, including the basin states, water users, and federal agencies already have a sufficient voice in basin governance. That may be true, but it proves the point by whom it excludes. Powerful basin interests often resolve disputes behind closed doors, excluding other important interests. The federal government has a trust responsibility to protect tribal water interests, for example, but tribes often have no direct seat at the bargaining table, despite their status as independent sovereigns. Several federal processes involve diverse stakeholders to address environmental restoration, recreational uses, or protection of cultural resources. Those decisions, however, are isolated from other river decisions. A restoration program, for example, may not succeed if water needed to implement it is allocated elsewhere. The United States consults with Mexico on transboundary issues,[125] but that consultation should not be isolated from other river decisions.

Comprehensive governance also allows for consideration of a more diverse range of ideas and perspectives. This diversity can stimulate more collaborative and effective solutions. And that can frighten those in power. But collaborative governance need not demand that existing interests lose control of their institutions and decisions, and the resulting ideas could improve rather than impede existing processes.

There is no single "best" model for collaboration, but several exist, and the most appropriate structure can be tailored to the Colorado River Basin. The formal decision-making entity in the Chesapeake Bay Program, for example, involves only representatives of the core political jurisdictions (each watershed state, the District of Columbia, and the Environmental Protection Agency). But other interest groups participate through advisory committees.[126]

Nested Watersheds

A collaborative decision-making process embracing the entire Colorado River Basin differs from Powell's vision of watershed democracy. Despite his realization that river systems are connected, he advocated for local governance. Once the federal government divided the watershed into irrigation and pasturage districts, and the federal and state governments allocated water among them, Powell would have vested governance in those districts, with state legal oversight. Conflicts between districts could be resolved judicially.[127]

Powell's understanding of Western hydrology, however, although impressive for its time, was static and incomplete. He assumed that water supplies, once controlled through storage facilities, would be relatively stable. He could not have foreseen that anthropogenic climate change would exacerbate natural hydrologic variability.[128] He did not understand the impact of his proposals on environmental systems, or that society would value these systems in addition to diversionary water uses. He did not foresee the complexity of interstate and international river management, or massive social and economic changes in the basin. Those issues require regional governance, with involvement at the federal, state, tribal, and local levels.

Regional governance does not necessarily foreclose the local watershed democracy Powell envisioned. It must, however, be consistent with the federal presence in the Colorado River Basin and similar Western river systems, via federal water project management and interaction between federal regulatory statutes and state water law. Emulating the Chesapeake Bay Program, local governments, water institutions, and other interest groups could provide input through advisory committees. Alternatively, the overall program could nest organized local or regional collaborative bodies within a basinwide process. The Great Lakes Program facilitates individual lake restoration plans within its overall umbrella.[129] That would parallel Powell's vision of local watershed democracy.

CONCLUSION

It is too late to implement Powell's late-nineteenth-century proposals for watershed democracy. Some of his ideas, however, were embedded in evolving institutions and other aspects of Western water law. Looking more broadly at his philosophy and intent suggests ways to further effectuate Powell's vision in the twenty-first century. Challenges facing the Colorado River Basin—and other parts of the West—are more complex and unpredictable than Powell imagined. They require more broadly conceived institutions than Powell advocated, but those institutions can and should be designed with his view toward democratic governance.

Bernard DeVoto wrote that "irreversible events went on out west and what we did in error will forever prevent us from catching up with [Powell's vision] altogether."[130] Donald Worster disagreed. Some viewed Powell's ideas as "backward-looking" even at the time, but the problem was not in Powell's ideas; it was in politicians who resisted change.[131] If we embrace appropriate change, achieving more of Powell's vision may be possible.

NOTES

1. Wallace Stegner, *Beyond the Hundredth Meridian: John Wesley Powell and the Second Opening of the West* (New York: Penguin Books, 1992), 202–38.

2. William deBuys, ed., *Seeing Things Whole: The Essential John Wesley Powell* (Washington, DC: Island Press, 2001), 12.

3. Donald Worster, *A River Running West: The Life of John Wesley Powell* (New York: Oxford University Press, 2001), 472–94.

4. deBuys, *Seeing Things Whole*, 54–55.

5. Worster, *A River Running West*, 85, 96.

6. deBuys, *Seeing Things Whole*, 320–23; Worster, *A River Running West*, 442–49.

7. H.R. Exec. Doc. No. 73 (1878): John Wesley Powell, "Report on the Lands of the Arid Region of the United States," in deBuys, *Seeing Things Whole*, 149–208.

8. John Wesley Powell, "The Irrigable Lands of the Arid Region," *Century* 39 (1890): 766–76; Powell, "The Non-Irrigable Lands of the Arid Region," *Century* 39 (1890): 915–22; Powell, "Institutions for the Arid Lands," *Century* 40 (1890): 111–16.

9. Stegner, *Beyond the Hundredth Meridian;* Worster, *A River Running West;* deBuys, *Seeing Things Whole;* Bernard DeVoto, "Introduction," in Stegner, *Beyond the Hundredth Meridian.*

10. deBuys, *Seeing Things Whole,* 5.

11. Janet Neuman, "Dusting Off the Blueprint for a Dryland Democracy: Incorporating Watershed Integrity and Water Availability Into Land Use Decisions," in *Wet Growth: Should Water Law Control Land Use?,* ed. Craig Anthony (Tony) Arnold (Washington, DC: Environmental Law Institute, 2005), 119–70.

12. Keith H. Hirokawa, "Driving Local Governments to Watershed Governance," *Environmental Law* 42 (2012): 157; A. Dan Tarlock, "Putting Rivers Back in the Landscape: The Revival of Watershed Management in the United States," *Hastings West-Northwest Journal of Environmental Law & Policy* 14 (2008): 1059; Robert W. Adler, "Addressing Barriers to Watershed Protection," *Environmental Law* 25 (1995): 974.

13. John Wesley Powell, "The Lesson of Conemaugh," *The North American Review* 149, no. 393 (1889): 150–56.

14. H.R. Exec. Doc. No. 73 (1878).

15. Ibid., 150, 167.

16. Worster, *A River Running West,* 494.

17. deBuys, *Seeing Things Whole,* 142.

18. H.R. Exec. Doc. No. 73 (1878).

19. John Wesley Powell, "A Bill to Authorize the Organization of Irrigation Districts by Homestead Settlements Upon the Public Lands Requiring Irrigation for Agricultural Purposes," in deBuys, *Seeing Things Whole,* 190–95 (hereafter "Irrigation District Bill").

20. John Wesley Powell, "A Bill to Authorize the Organization of Pasturage Districts by Homestead Settlements on the Public Lands Which Are of Value for Pasturage Purposes Only," in deBuys, *Seeing Things Whole,* 195–99.

21. Irrigation District Bill, §10.

22. Worster, *A River Running West,* 385.

23. *Letter From the Secretary of the Interior, Transmitting, in Response to Senate Resolution of Feb. 13, 1888, Report Concerning the Irrigation of Certain Lands,* 50th Cong., 1st Sess. (1888), 3–6 (hereafter "*Secretary's Report*").

24. *Report to the Special Committee of the United States Senate on the Irrigation and Reclamation of Arid Lands,* 51st Cong., 1st Sess. (1890), 67–68 (statement of John Wesley Powell, Director, US Geological Survey) (hereafter "*Special Committee Report*").

25. Powell, "Institutions for the Arid Lands," 111.

26. *The Geological Survey, Statements Before the Subcommittee on the Sundry Civil Bill,* 50th Cong., 1st Sess., 114–15 (1888) (statement of John Wesley Powell, Director, US Geological Survey) (hereafter "*Subcommittee Statement*").

27. John Wesley Powell, "Address to the Montana Constitutional Convention," in deBuys, *Seeing Things Whole,* 240–42.

28. deBuys, *Seeing Things Whole,* 250.

29. *Special Committee Report,* 67–68.

30. *Letter From the Secretary of the Interior, Transmitting, in Pursuance of Law, Report of the Geological Survey on the Subject of Irrigation*, 50th Cong., 2nd Sess. (1889), 7–9.
31. Powell, "Institutions for Arid Lands," 113.
32. *Special Committee Report*, 27–28.
33. Worster, *A River Running West*, 472–94.
34. See, e.g., Maynard v. Watkins, 55 Mont. 54, 173 P. 551 (1918).
35. Irwin v. Phillips, 5 Cal. 140 (1855).
36. Crandall v. Woods, 8 Cal. 136 (1857).
37. Lux v. Haggin, 69 Cal. 255, 10 P. 674 (1886).
38. Coffin v. Left Hand Ditch Co., 6 Colo. 443 (1882).
39. California Oregon Power Co. v. Beaver Portland Cement Co., 292 U.S. 142 (1935).
40. H.R. Exec. Doc. No. 73 (1878).
41. Robert W. Adler, "Natural Resources and Natural Law Part I: Prior Appropriation," *William & Mary L. Rev* 60 (2019): 739–808.
42. Robert Adler et al., *Modern Water Law, Private Property, Public Rights, and Environmental Protections*, 2nd edition (St. Paul, MN: Foundation Press, 2018), 1, 155–62, 192, 314–21, 401–62.
43. Janet C. Neuman, "Beneficial Use, Waste, and Forfeiture: The Inefficient Search for Efficiency in Western Water Use," *Environmental Law* 28 (1998): 919.
44. Adler et al., *Modern Water Law*, 48–54, 81–82.
45. H.R. Exec. Doc. No. 73 (1878).
46. Steven J. Shupe et al., "Western Water Rights: The Era of Reallocation," *Natural Resources Journal* 29 (1989): 413, 422.
47. Adler et al., *Modern Water Law*, 192–202.
48. H.R. Exec. Doc. No. 73 (1878).
49. Charles F. Wilkinson, *Crossing the Next Meridian: Land, Water, and the Future of the West*. (Washington, DC: Island Press, 1992); Donald Worster, *Rivers of Empire: Water, Aridity, and the Growth of the American West* (New York: Oxford University Press, 1985); Marc Reisner, *Cadillac Desert: The American West and its Disappearing Water*, revised edition (New York: Penguin Books, 1993).
50. Worster, *A River Running West*, 411.
51. Winters v. United States, 207 U.S. 564 (1908).
52. Colo. Rev. Stat. Ann. §37-92-203 (West).
53. Adler et al., *Modern Water Law*, 332–42; Utah Code Ann. §73-4-1 (West); Cal. Water Code §34150 (West).
54. In re Gen. Adjudication of All Rights to Use Water in Gila River Sys. & Source, 201 Ariz. 307 (2001); In re Gen. Adjudication of All Rights to Use Water in the Big Horn River Sys., 753 P.2d 76 (Wyo. 1988), aff'd sub nom. Wyoming v. United States, 492 U.S. 406 (1989), and abrogated by Vaughn v. State, 962 P.2d 149 (Wyo. 1998).
55. H.R. Exec. Doc. No. 73 (1878).
56. *Special Committee Report*, 18.

57. Stephen N. Bretsen & Peter J. Hill, "Irrigation Institutions in the American West," *UCLA Journal of Environmental Law & Policy* 25 (2006–07): 283, 297.

58. Barton H. Thompson, Jr., "Institutional Perspectives on Water Policy and Markets," *California Law Review* 81 (1993): 671, 691; Bretsen & Hill, "Irrigation Institutions in the American West," 298.

59. Thompson, Jr., "Institutional Perspectives on Water Policy and Markets," 690.

60. For a history of this tradition in water law, see Michael C. Meyer, *Water in the Hispanic Southwest: A Social and Legal History 1550–1850* (Tucson: University of Arizona Press, 1984).

61. Worster, *Rivers of Empire*, 74–83; Worster, *A River Running West*, 351.

62. Meyer, *Water in the Hispanic Southwest*, 21, 101.

63. Worster, *A River Running West*.

64. Bretsen & Hill, "Irrigation Institutions in the American West," 285.

65. Ibid., 305; Barton H. Thompson, Jr. et al., *Legal Control of Water Resources: Cases and Materials*, 4th edition (St. Paul, MN: Thomson/West, 2006), 684.

66. Bretsen & Hill, "Irrigation Institutions in the American West," 312–19.

67. Thompson, "Institutional Perspectives on Water Policy and Markets," 674.

68. Bretson and Hill, "Irrigation Institutions in the American West," 299–302.

69. Thompson, "Institutional Perspectives on Water Policy and Markets," 696–98.

70. Ibid, 694.

71. Bretson and Hill, "Irrigation Institutions in the American West," 285.

72. Thompson, "Institutional Perspectives on Water Policy and Markets," 689. For an overview of private water organizations, see Elizabeth Burleson, "Private Organizations," in *Waters and Water Rights*, 3rd edition, ed. Robert E. Beck & Amy K. Kelley (New Providence: LexisNexis 2009), chapter 26. For a similar discussion of quasi-public water organizations, see Elizabeth Burleson, "Public Water Districts," in Beck & Kelley, *Waters and Water Rights*, chapter 27.

73. Bretson and Hill, "Irrigation Institutions in the American West," 321.

74. Thompson, "Institutional Perspectives on Water Policy and Markets," 687–88.

75. Bretson and Hill, "Irrigation Institutions in the American West," 321–22.

76. Falbrook Irrig. Dist. v. Bradley, 164 U.S. 112 (1896); Ball v. James, 451 U.S. 355 (1981).

77. Thompson, "Institutional Perspectives on Water Policy and Markets," 675–77.

78. John Fleck, *Water is for Fighting Over and Other Myths About Water in the West* (Washington, DC: Island Press, 2016).

79. H.R. Exec. Doc. No. 73 (1878).

80. Gibbons v. Ogden, 22 U.S. 1 (1824); *The Genesee Chief*, 53 U.S. 443 (1851); *The Daniel Ball*, 77 U.S. 557 (1870).

81. Martin v. Waddell's Lessee, 41 U.S. 367 (1842); Pollard v. Hagan, 44 U.S. 212 (1845).
82. Broder v. Natoma Water & Mining Co., 101 U.S. 274 (1879).
83. California Oregon Power Co. v. Beaver Portland Cement Co., 295 U.S. 142 (1935).
84. Powell, "Institutions for the Arid Lands," 113.
85. *Secretary's Report*, 125–26.
86. *Special Committee Report*, 7–9, 27–28.
87. Reclamation Act of 1902, 43 U.S.C. § 372 et seq.
88. Worster, *Rivers of Empire;* Reisner, *Cadillac Desert*.
89. California v. United States, 438 U.S. 645 (1978).
90. Boulder Canyon Project Act, Pub. L. No. 642–70 (1928); Colorado River Storage Project Act, Pub. L. No. 485, ch. 203 (1956); Colorado River Basin Project Act, Pub. L. No. 90–537, 82 Stat. 886 (1968).
91. Colorado River Reservoirs: Coordinated Long-Range Operation, 35 Fed. Reg. 8951 (June 10, 1970); Annual Operating Criteria (AOCs), e.g., Annual Operating Plan for Colorado River Reservoirs 2018, https://www.usbr.gov/uc/water/rsvrs/ops/aop/AOP18.pdf; Colorado River Interim Surplus Guidelines, 66 Fed. Reg. 7772 (Jan. 25, 2001); Colorado River Interim Guidelines for Lower Basin Shortages and Coordinated Operations for Lake Powell and Lake Mead, Bureau of Reclamation, last modified June 5, 2015, https://www.usbr.gov/lc/region/programs/strategies.html.
92. *Special Committee Report*, 63.
93. Ibid., 66.
94. Powell, "Institutions for the Arid Lands," 115.
95. *Special Committee Report*, 65.
96. Ibid., 16–17.
97. State of Kansas v. State of Colorado, 206 U.S. 46 (1907).
98. Winters v. United States, 207 U.S. 564 (1908).
99. Arizona v. California, 373 U.S. 546 (1963).
100. Colorado River Compact, 1922 (codified in Colorado at Colo. Rev. Stat. §37–61–101 [2012]).
101. Boulder Canyon Project Act, Pub. L. No. 642–70 (1928).
102. Arizona v. California, 373 U.S. 546 (1963).
103. Ibid.
104. Treaty Between the United States of America & Mexico Respecting Utilization of Waters of the Colorado & Tijuana Rivers & of the Rio Grande, 59 Stat. 1219 (Nov. 8, 1945) (hereafter "United States-Mexico Treaty").
105. Worster, *A River Running West;* deBuys, *Seeing Things Whole*.
106. Robert W. Adler, *Restoring Colorado River Ecosystems: A Troubled Sense of Immensity* (Washington, DC: Island Press, 2007).
107. Donald J. Kochan, "Public Lands and the Federal Government's Compact-Based 'Duty to Dispose': A Case Study of Utah's H.B.148–The Transfer of Public Lands Act," *BYU Law Review* 2013 (2014): 1133.
108. Jason Robison & Lawrence MacDonnell, "*Arizona v. California* & the Colorado River Compact: Fifty Years Ago, Fifty Years Ahead," *Arizona Journal of Environmental Law & Policy* 4 (2014): 130.

109. *Subcommittee Statement,* 114–15.

110. Upper Colorado River Basin Compact, 1948. For more information on the Upper Colorado River Commission, see http://www.ucrcommission.com.

111. Endangered Species Act of 1973, 16 U.S.C. §§ 1531–1599 (1973).

112. Grand Canyon Protection Act of 1992, Pub. L. No. 102–575, 106 Stat. 4669 (1992).

113. Adler, *Restoring Colorado River Ecosystems.*

114. Fleck, *Water is for Fighting Over.*

115. Adler, "Addressing Barriers to Watershed Protection"; Adler et al., *Modern Water Law,* 793n5.

116. See US Environmental Protection Agency, "Healthy Watersheds Protection," last updated Aug. 8, 2019, https://www.epa.gov/hwp. See also Chesapeake Bay Program, "Healthy Watersheds," accessed November 28, 2019, https://www.chesapeakebay.net/what/goals/healthy_watersheds; US Environmental Protection Agency, "The Great Lakes," last updated May 15, 2019, https://www.epa.gov/greatlakes; Delta Stewardship Council, "Delta Science Program," accessed November 28, 2019, https://www.deltacouncil.ca.gov/delta-science-program; South Florida Water Management District, "Everglades," accessed November 28, 2019, https://www.sfwmd.gov/our-work/everglades.

117. deBuys, *Seeing Things Whole.*

118. David H. Getches, "Colorado River Governance: Sharing Federal Authority as an Incentive to Create a New Institution," *Univ. of Colorado Law Review* 68 (1997): 573.

119. Fleck, *Water is for Fighting Over,* 156.

120. Colorado River Interim Surplus Guidelines, 66 Fed. Reg. 7772 (Jan. 25, 2001).

121. Bureau of Reclamation, "Colorado River Interim Guidelines for Lower Basin Shortages and Coordinated Operations for Lake Powell and Lake Mead," last updated June 5, 2015, https://www.usbr.gov/lc/region/programs/strategies.html.

122. Extension of Cooperative Measures and Adoption of the Binational Water Scarcity Contingency Plan in the Colorado River Basin, International Boundary and Water Commission, Minute 323, Sept. 21, 2017, https://www.ibwc.gov/Files/Minutes/Min323.pdf.

123. Board Members of the Upper Colorado River Commission to Tom Buschatzke, Director of the Arizona Department of Water Resources, April 13, 2018, https://tucson.com/upper-colorado-river-commission-letter/pdf_dd60eab9-1752-536a-9a0a-c14400a397c6.html.

124. Bradley Udall and Jonathan Overpeck, "The Twenty-First Century Colorado River Hot Drought and Implications for the Future," *Water Resources Research* 53, no. 3 (2017), 2404–18.

125. See United States-Mexico Treaty.

126. See Chesapeake Bay Program, "How We're Organized," accessed November 28, 2019, https://www.chesapeakebay.net/who/how_we_are_organized.

127. Powell, "Institutions for the Arid Lands," 114–15.

128. P.C.D. Milly et al., "Stationarity is Dead: Whither Water Management?," *Science* 319 (2008): 573–74.
129. See US Environmental Protection Agency, "The Great Lakes."
130. DeVoto, "Introduction," *Beyond the Hundredth Meridian.*
131. Worster, *A River Running West,* 359–60.

CHAPTER 3

Common Water Commonwealth

The Paradox of a Shared Resource

AMORINA LEE-MARTINEZ AND PATRICIA LIMERICK

The Colorado Plateau's landscapes have long functioned as a social psychology experiment on a cosmic scale. For Euro-Americans accustomed to an abundance of bright-green vegetation and a far more moderate juxtaposition of heights and depths, the plateau's dramatic spires and canyons have shattered conventional expectations formed in very different geophysical circumstances. This chapter's aim is to track Euro-American understandings of, and adaptations to, Western American settings. By connecting the historic ideas of John Wesley Powell to the current circumstances of the Dolores River, a tributary of the Colorado River, we chart a route to an improved understanding of the relationship between the Western past and present.

The Dolores watershed is a direct challenge to conventional expectation. The river, "coursing roughly northward, cuts 'across the grain' of a series of alternate uplifts and valleys which lie perpendicular to the River's path."[1] This landscape originated as an ancient salty seabed overtopped by sandstone. Because it is more buoyant than solid rock, the salt eventually rose up through weak points of sedimentary layers that separated from each other like a giant accordion. The salt then dissolved, leaving behind a series of chasms. The Dolores River cut through these uplifts, maintaining its original path as the land changed around it. Paradox Valley is one aptly named canyon the Dolores River cuts *across*, rather than flowing through.

The quality of paradox is not confined to geomorphology. Residents in proximity to the Dolores exist between two opposed convictions, one supporting diversion of water from the river, and the other supporting protection of the river's flows. In a paradoxical feature of history, John Wesley Powell's life history serves as a launching point for both convictions. Powell was an adventurer who explored the West's wild rivers and landscapes. He was also a utilitarian who encouraged his fellow citizens to tame and develop the resources of Western landscapes to provide maximum human benefit. Powell's paradoxes extend to his recommendations for Western settlement: he advocated for both federal oversight and localized control, two arenas for decision-making that have often collided.

In the Dolores River Basin, what we might christen the "Powell Paradoxes"—navigating between recreational adventure and irrigated agriculture as well as federal authority and local governance—set the framework for efforts at problem-solving and reconciling civic disagreement. The custom of separating different parts of Powell's legacy from its entirety reflects stakeholders' tendencies to cast only one aspect of their river system and its values as true, stopping short of seeing the system (both natural and anthropogenic) as a whole. Powell's paradoxical roles and ideas, and the conflicting positions taken by people in disputes over the Dolores River, present compelling patterns of complexity. These patterns provide opportunities to examine and rethink historic traditions of thought and conduct in order to improve our ability to negotiate the future.

We begin our exploration of the connections between Powell and the Dolores River community by discussing Powell's ideas for settlement, development, and governance of Western watersheds. Against this backdrop, we utilize the Dolores River as a case study of the continued relevance of the Powell Paradoxes. To make this relevance unmistakable, we appraise an attempt by stakeholders living within the watershed to develop a river management plan and policy that meets the divergent needs of water withdrawals and instream protections. Finally, we conclude with an inventory of insights gathered from our attempt to connect the Western past to its present.

For appraising his legacy, we should note that Powell had a deep faith in the power of reason to analyze natural conditions and to direct the governance of complex watersheds. Embracing reason, he moved ahead of nearly all his contemporaries in recommending that Western Americans should manage water resources based on watershed boundaries and the constraints of water's limits. As configurations of water and land, watersheds turned out to be less clearly bounded than Powell had thought. Deciding, for instance, which streams constitute the true headwaters of a major river was a matter shaped as much by political maneuverings as by the findings of hydrologists.

The far-from-linear changes that delivered us to our current circumstances make it irresponsible to evaluate Powell's ideas for their power to withstand the test of time and to match up with contemporary scientific research. We can most productively honor Powell's vision of watershed commonwealths 150 years after the 1869 Expedition by carefully thinking about his framework of rational governance, as well as his comfortable sense that watersheds—complex networks of streams that converge to form a river's mainstem—could be easily identified and serve as domains of local governance. With this in mind, we set off on our own venture into another "Great Unknown": the economic and ecologic sustainability of the Colorado River, and one of its tributaries, the Dolores River, in the twenty-first century.

POWELL'S VISION OF WATERSHED COMMONWEALTHS

In his essay "Institutions for the Arid Lands," John Wesley Powell declared that Euro-Americans should conduct their settlement of the arid region—the Colorado River Basin and elsewhere—with a foundation of respect for the boundaries of watersheds, or as he called them, "hydrographic basins."[2] Exploring the interior of the American West, he realized the arid climate required migrants to settle and manage the land in a different way than in the East. The aridity and semi-aridity of the West would require people to manage water as a limited resource. Powell's solution was to understand the land as an arrangement of hydrographic basins. These basins offered Americans a suitable and even necessary way to define regions of management because, as he said confidently, "hydraulic basin is segregated from hydraulic basin by nature itself, and the landmarks are practically perpetual."[3]

To Powell, this strategy of organization made sense because each hydrographic basin is a "unit of country well defined in nature," and as such, "a district of country is a commonwealth by itself. The people who live therein are interdependent in all their industries. Every man [and woman] is interested in the conservation and management of the water supply, for all the waters are needed within the district."[4] By designating basins as boundaries for governmental units, Powell's faith in the power of reason to decipher nature's meanings reached its peak. And yet this confident declaration also came with a cautionary exhortation: "With wisdom you may prosper," Powell said memorably, "but with folly you must fail."[5]

"Wisdom" for Powell meant citizens in each hydrographic district would work communally to conserve their water resources and to distribute them equitably. "The people in such a district have common interests, common rights, and common duties," he insisted, "and must necessarily work together for common purposes."[6] Communal "conservation" of water meant that people would store river water to utilize it fully for agriculture. "[T]he waters of the non-irrigating season will run to waste," he wrote, "unless they are stored in reservoirs."[7]

Celebrating a vision of the "interdependence" of people within the same watershed, Powell believed that irrigation infrastructure, called into being by local control of water, would provide the essential foundation for the arid region's settlement. Powell thus wrote a romantic dream of a Western future that hinged on "irrigation," a term and a practice not instantly associated with romance. Let the American people who would settle the arid West "organize, under national and State laws, a great irrigation district, including an entire hydrographic basin," Powell proclaimed, "and let them make their own laws for the division of the waters."[8]

Aspiration and imagination were not the sole sources for his vision. Powell gathered ideas about local irrigation governance by observing practices of the Mormon Church in Utah. The Church communally built infrastructure for diverting water and designed towns so all members would have access to irrigation and make their livings off the land. The Mormons learned this cooperative approach from the *acequias*, or community ditches, of Hispanic communities in the Rio Grande Valley.[9]

Irrigation districts, Powell thought, should be designated under the duties of the "general government," his term for the federal government. He believed the general government, as the owner of the greatest share of Western lands, had responsibility for "the establishment of the institutions for the arid region." Putting this responsibility into action, the general government would survey its lands and "segregate" them as "the irrigable lands, the timber lands, the pasturage lands, and the mining lands."[10] By a series of statutes, the general government would give irrigable lands to individual homesteaders and "retain possession"[11] of all other categories as public lands. For irrigable lands, the leaders of each district would have the right to distribute water among the people as they saw fit by building their own water system. Powell wrote that "the authorities of each district" would be formed within the constraints of "state and national laws,"[12] a division of governmental powers known as "federalism."[13]

After taking an inventory of its lands, the general government would establish rights for the people of each district to create their own authority for distributing and using their resources. The "institutions of justice"[14] at the federal level would give people rights to use resources and provide protections from the "evil" of land speculation and monopolization of "lands and waters" at the "hands of a comparatively few persons."[15] Powell clearly favored hardworking people living off the land over corporate owners making large profits at the expense of the many. At the state and district levels, "institutions of justice" would include courts that would "adjudicate questions" over resources.[16]

Powell charged people within each hydrographic district to use organized labor and capital to control their own "enterprise" of land development. But if the people did not manage water carefully by pooling local funds and labor to store it, the failure would be theirs to bear. On the subject of how communities should carry out district self-regulation, Powell was conspicuously silent, leaving citizens to create their own plans and processes for sharing the duties of developing local resources for communal economic and social benefit. In his support for general, state, and district responsibilities, Powell visualized nested and interconnected scales of governance to manage land and water resources.

After Powell's time, the damming of rivers so that "no waste water runs to the sea"[17] acquired the status of a norm in the Colorado River Basin. On this count, his legacy for the West is unmistakable and omnipresent. But another dimension of that legacy, communal local management of distinct watershed units with minimal federal presence, has not characterized the Colorado River system's infrastructure. The past century of piecemeal management by an increasing multitude of government agencies has benefitted irrigators and municipalities, and simultaneously resulted in the degradation of land and over-allocation of water. These consequences have made Powell's ideas about communal management increasingly relevant to resource users and managers today. In a wide range of Western locales, residents have formed local initiatives to deal with the complexities of watershed health, while working to include the needs of local stakeholders who are affected by river management changes. Communities living around the Dolores River provide an example of Westerners' management efforts.

THE DOLORES PROJECT: MANY ENTITIES, ONE RIVER

There are compelling reasons to focus on McPhee Reservoir, located on the Dolores River's mainstem in southwestern Colorado, and to ask: *To what degree does this project align with Powell's ideas about locally controlled water management?* Built by the Bureau of Reclamation in the 1980s, the Dolores River Project stores water behind McPhee Dam and delivers it, via a series of long-range canals and pipes, to the neighboring San Juan River Basin. Three municipalities and the farmers of over 70,000 acres of agriculture, including enterprises on the Ute Mountain Ute Reservation, depend on these deliveries.[18]

A tributary of the Colorado River, the Dolores River (see map 2) flows southwest from the western side of the San Juan Mountains in the Four Corners region of Colorado. It then leaves the mountains, cuts a canyon and turns north, flowing about 150 miles through canyon country, including Paradox Valley, before its confluence with the Colorado River near Moab, Utah. The big bend in the river where it turns north is the site of McPhee Reservoir, in the north-central part of Montezuma County. To the south and west of the Dolores River Canyon lies a large expanse of relatively gentle landscape called the Montezuma Valley that drains into the adjacent San Juan River Basin. The narrow canyon of the Dolores River provides limited land for farming or pasturage, which has influenced how people have developed the river.

The region of the Dolores River has a long history of human occupation dating back to 1 CE.[19] The Ancestral Puebloans, well known for their cliff dwellings at Mesa Verde National Park and the surrounding region, utilized small-scale water storage and diversion to support agriculture and domestic needs. Long before Powell's time, they left the area and moved south into present-day New Mexico and Arizona. These peoples are the ancestors of today's Pueblo communities in New Mexico as well as the Hopi in Arizona.[20] Extended drought and competition with hunter-gatherer peoples, including the Ute, were possible motivations for their departure.[21] Ute people lived semi-nomadically in the Four Corners region from about the time of the Ancestral Puebloan departure.[22] Pre-European settlement in this region demonstrates that limited water availability created the need to either store water, live nomadically, or move away from competition because of limited resources.

Four years after Powell's 1869 Expedition, in 1873, prospectors discovered gold and silver in the San Juan Mountains.[23] In a familiar pattern of Western history, the influx of population for extractive enterprises forced

Indigenous people (the Ute in this case) onto reservations, and created a market for the products of farms and ranches, leading to early Euro-American settlements in southwestern Colorado. In the Montezuma Valley, the newcomers initially tried to farm by drawing from natural springs near present-day Cortez, Colorado, but demand soon outstripped supply. These immigrants looked north to the Dolores River's relatively abundant water. But it was not easily diverted because canyon walls separated it from Montezuma Valley. They made the choice to stay in Montezuma Valley for its favorable agricultural landscape and to undertake huge investments of capital and labor to divert water from the river.

From 1878 to 1920, seven different ventures sprouted and withered in an attempt to build infrastructure to divert, store, and channel Dolores River water for use in Montezuma Valley. The first company to begin building a tunnel was unable to complete the project because the "undeveloped area could not fiscally support such a venture." The second company, Montezuma Valley Water Supply Company, founded by the well-connected James W. Hanna, had help from wealthy investors from Boston. Hanna also owned the Cortez Land and Investment Company and was strategic in selling land that would soon have access to water via his infrastructure. With the direction of Montezuma Valley Water Supply Company, local ranchers and transient workers of German and Russian descent used imported air compressor-powered drills from Connecticut to construct the first interbasin transfer from the Dolores Canyon to Montezuma Valley. Begun in 1886, the diversion was a mile-long tunnel that took three years to complete. A separate company constructed a forty-foot-deep canal called the "Great Cut" through the ridge to deliver water north of Cortez for irrigation and domestic uses.[24]

Despite financial troubles, by 1890 both the tunnel and the Great Cut were diverting Dolores River water into the San Juan River Basin through a hundred miles of distribution canals that reached farmlands and the city of Cortez. Sparse population and financial mismanagement plagued subsequent companies for decades. The arrangement called "mutual liability" caused trouble, since it set terms by which "each member" would be "held in debt . . . as long as the district as a whole remained in debt." Locals distrusted reliance on a water company that held every individual responsible for the entire company's shortfalls.[25]

In 1920, forty-two years after the first diversion attempts, the Montezuma Valley Irrigation Company (MVIC) consolidated ownership and operation of the existing water projects and associated senior Dolores River water rights. By this time, the population depending on

Dolores River irrigation had grown, and consequently carried more financial power. MVIC changed its terms so that each individual only held liability for her or his own property, which motivated users to invest in the company. Money from selling shares of water to irrigators kept (and keeps) the company in operation.[26]

These projects moving water from the Dolores River Basin to the San Juan River Basin were among the first interbasin transfer works in the West.[27] But the diversions directly challenged Powell's ideas about hydrographic basins as distinct boundaries for water districts. At the least, interbasin transfers showed that engineering projects posed a challenge to natural boundaries, as well as to the integrity of local control. Outside capital and corporate ownership were initially required to build this water infrastructure, which further challenged Powell's ideal of locally funded and constructed water works. As financial management improved and population grew, local investment stabilized under the operation of MVIC, demonstrating a shift closer to Powell's ideal.

While the Dolores River diversions brought water to the desired location, the people using that water still faced the problem of inconsistent supply. In the spring, snowmelt runoff brought plenty of water to the Dolores. As runoff slowed in summer, the entire river was often completely diverted into canals, going dry downstream. Even with all available water from the stream fully used, there was not enough to meet agricultural and municipal needs. For the river to support the late-summer growing season, and municipal and industrial use, large-scale storage was necessary.[28] Motivation for building a dam came from the goal Powell had articulated: preventing water from being "wasted."[29]

In the 1950s, citizens in the Montezuma Valley founded a "volunteer economic committee" called the "Cortez Bootstraps" to advocate for more water storage. To receive federal funding from the Bureau of Reclamation for large-scale storage, then Chairman of the House Interior Committee Wayne Aspinall advised the Bootstraps to form a water district under Colorado law. Following Aspinall's advice, the Dolores Water Conservancy District (DWCD) was established in 1961 "to support, organize, and manage the nascent [Dolores River] Project, and to contract with the Bureau of Reclamation as a public entity under the Colorado Water Conservancy District Act."[30] In 1979, the Bureau began construction of the Dolores River Project, which included McPhee Dam and associated delivery systems, and later completed the dam in 1986. The project became fully operational in 1999 once all delivery systems were constructed. This dynamic, where local citizens relied on a federally funded dam project, demonstrates how water management in the twentieth century was much more reliant on federal investment than Powell had thought necessary. Additionally, the dam's array of duties extend far beyond Powell's single objective of preventing water waste.

Three factors besides irrigation are important to McPhee Dam's management. First, a stretch of the Lower Dolores River was listed as "suitable" for the National Wild and Scenic Rivers System, reflecting the "outstandingly remarkable . . . recreational, scenic, and wilderness qualities" of the river.[31] An "outstandingly remarkable value . . . must be a river-related value that is [a] rare, unique, or exemplary feature at a regional or national scale."[32] This listing means the river segment is managed by the Bureau of Land Management (BLM) to preserve its outstandingly remarkable values so that it could be included in the Wild and Scenic Rivers System if the National Park Service recommends it to Congress.[33] Second, the DWCD has allocated part of the reservoir pool for annual releases downstream to support a non-native rainbow and brown trout fishery. Just below the dam, the cold water coming from the reservoir's bottom is ideal for trout. Several miles downstream, the water warms enough to support native fish populations (roundtail chub, flannelmouth sucker, and bluehead sucker). Third, during years when there is more than enough water for the DWCD to meet all its obligations, it will plan managed releases for whitewater recreation.[34]

The Dolores Project expanded the pre-existing water delivery system and increased storage for agricultural and municipal needs, contingent upon annual precipitation rates and snowpack levels. Since the project's substantial completion in the 1980s, allocations of water have supported a near doubling in irrigated acreage within Montezuma Valley, from 37,500 to 73,600 acres. Municipalities in Montezuma and Dolores counties now have a more reliable supply of water, including piped deliveries to the town of Towaoc on the Ute Mountain Ute Reservation, which formerly trucked in water.[35]

While aiding farmers and town-dwellers, the Dolores Project has had negative impacts on recreation downstream of McPhee Reservoir. Construction of the reservoir all but eliminated the recreational boating economy that depended on the Dolores River's natural flows. Before the Dolores Project went fully online in 1999, more than twenty commercial outfitters were running the Dolores. Today there are two or three commercial permit holders who attempt trips during managed releases from the reservoir when there is enough water.[36] Since the 1990s, only one in every three years has had enough water to boat the Lower Dolores.[37]

The river's ecology has also declined because of the conditions created by the dam. Non-native tamarisk has taken the place of native flora in long reaches of the Lower Dolores channel, though local efforts are underway to reverse this pattern. Native fish compete with invasive fish species. Brown trout are predatory, though interactions with natives are minimal, but smallmouth bass—accidentally released into the Lower Dolores River from McPhee Reservoir—have had a greater impact than brown trout, eating the eggs and larvae of native species. Changes in the timing and magnitude of floods below the reservoir have also impacted the chub and suckers. Native fish adapted to a river that is warm, laden with sediment, and floods annually in spring with low flows the remainder of the year. Modifications to the river's flow began with the first interbasin transfer in the 1880s, but the spring floods stopped after McPhee Dam was built in the 1980s.

Since McPhee Dam was completed, local people, government agencies, and non-governmental organizations have been attempting to address the Lower Dolores's ecology while honoring water rights that depend on the reservoir—the Powellian paradox common throughout the Colorado River Basin. Attempts to embrace paradox and reconcile all the needs of the varied entities that depend on Dolores River water have led to disputes over conflicting priorities.

PATTERNS OF DISPUTE AND ALIGNMENT IN THE DOLORES RIVER COMMUNITY

The dynamics of the Dolores Project on this single tributary of the Colorado River offer insight into basinwide changes in attitudes, values, and needs associated with water. Therefore, there is broad relevance to the political and ideological alliances that underpin controversies in the Dolores River community. Dolores Project stakeholders have aligned into at least two major coalitions based on their rights, occupations, perceived economic interests, and values.[38] One coalition of ranchers and farmers prioritizes diverting Dolores water from McPhee Reservoir into the Montezuma Valley—the "Montezuma Valley coalition." Another coalition of boaters and river ecology advocates prioritizes maintaining flows in the Lower Dolores River downstream of McPhee Dam—the "Lower Dolores coalition." Although these broad categorizations downplay the diversity within these communities, they generally describe the boundaries and sources of conflict between them.

Two major patterns reflect the coalitions' respective interests. The first addresses the legal allocation of water: having versus not having water rights. The second addresses economic interests and associated values: being a user of irrigation water in the Montezuma Valley versus being an environmentalist/recreationalist in relation to the Lower Dolores River.

One community member from the Montezuma Valley coalition described the first pattern in this way:

> I've always thought that really the contention between water is the contention between the haves—'we have a senior water right, and, boy, we're not gonna let it go and to heck with you guys,'—and the have-nots, which are the ones that want some of that water.[39]

Another, equally quotable member of the community from the Lower Dolores coalition talked about the general nature of the second pattern. While there are farmers and boaters in the middle of the spectrum that are "amenable to each other," there is polarization of values between these two groups:

> There's an extreme group of boaters and there's an extreme group of farmers. There's a lot of boaters and a lot of farmers who are very amenable to each other and want to talk and want to get along. But there are some boaters who are really far out there who think that there should be a lot more water released [below McPhee Dam] and there's farmers who don't think there should be any released.[40]

These patterns of opposition make it challenging for stakeholders to negotiate common solutions for water management. One stakeholder stated: "any kind of water-related problem solving is most difficult."[41] Another put it this way: "If there was lots of water, it'd be pretty easy to collaborate."[42] These statements suggest there is not enough water to satisfy every need and value, and therefore collaboration is difficult. And yet, there are points of agreement across the coalitions.

Community members commonly agree that water should not be wasted. There are different ideas about what constitutes "waste": farmers don't want water released downstream when it can be put to use in Montezuma Valley, which is related to Powell's ideas about preventing "waste." Boaters and environmentalists don't want unplanned releases when there is more water than the reservoir can hold. There are few instances of high flows downstream since McPhee Dam was completed, so if the DWCD releases a spill without warning to prevent the reservoir from overflowing, rafters and scientists are unable to take advantage of the recreational and ecological research opportunities offered by that water. Even with different meanings of "waste," both groups similarly value making the most of available water.

Community members also agree that a strong economy is important: boaters want a strong recreational economy supported by consistent, predictable flows in the Lower Dolores, while irrigators want a strong agricultural economy supported by damming and diversion of the Dolores River. Though there are different ideas about what is economically important, both groups agree that agricultural use is desirable for the region, and some community members value both agricultural land and recreational open space. As one described it: "We must protect agricultural land and open space. I don't want to see agricultural land be sacrificed for [urban and industrial purposes]. We value these working lands, rural lifestyle, and open space that we moved here for."[43] Love for the open landscape is important common ground for people in this distinct part of the Colorado River Basin.

EFFORTS TO ADDRESS LOWER DOLORES RIVER CONDITIONS AND DIVERGENT VALUES

One hundred and thirty years after Powell wrote his recommendations in "Institutions for the Arid Lands," we are still trying to find the best process for community decision-making for water resources. Since McPhee Dam's completion in 1986, several initiatives have been convened by local stakeholders to reconcile values associated with the Lower Dolores coalition and those associated with the Montezuma Valley coalition. We focus on the Lower Dolores Plan Working Group (LDPWG), which initiated legislation for protecting natural conditions in the Lower Dolores River to replace federal designations.

In 2010, the LDPWG addressed concerns about the Wild and Scenic River suitability of the Dolores River, as well as concerns about the Endangered Species Act. The group was "made up of about 50 people representing a broad spectrum of interests including counties, water boards, agriculture, private landowners, conservation groups, and recreational users. . . ."[44] If Congress were to designate the Lower Dolores as Wild and Scenic, this designation would come with a federal reserved water right that the federal government could, in certain circumstances, rely on to protect outstandingly remarkable values. Additionally, "[i]f any of the three native fish species [were] listed in the future as 'threatened' or 'endangered' by the U.S. Fish and Wildlife Service, under the provisions of the Endangered Species Act," irrigation deliveries from the Dolores Project could be reduced by federal intervention.

The LDPWG agreed that a National Conservation Area (NCA) designation along the Lower Dolores would be the best alternative to a Wild and Scenic designation. Provisions in federal NCA legislation that "conserve, protect, and enhance" resources, including native fish, recreation, and ecology, could fulfill the expectations of a Wild and Scenic River without the potential threat to existing water rights posed by a federal reserved right associated with Wild and Scenic designation.[45] If passed, the NCA designation would protect 100,000 acres of BLM land on both sides of the river along a reach that crosses three counties downstream from McPhee Reservoir.

In April 2015, the LDPWG's Legislative Subcommittee publicly released a draft NCA bill. Montezuma Valley coalition representatives, including MVIC and the Montezuma County Commissioners, criticized the draft. They claimed that water managers could interpret the bill as allocating more water for native fish and other downstream needs, which is a threat to water rights in Montezuma Valley. Over the next two years, representatives from both MVIC and Montezuma County stopped participating because they felt their voices were disregarded in the NCA drafting process. As a result, the NCA bill negotiations reached an impasse.

In spring 2018, commissioners and other representatives from Montezuma and Dolores counties held a public meeting to once again debate the NCA bill. This was an attempt by Dolores County to bring Montezuma County back into the conversation and process. Dolores County representatives expressed that they prefer the NCA legislation to Wild and Scenic designation because the NCA language is more "flexible" and does not entail a federal reserved water right. Conversely, Montezuma County representatives are not comfortable with the federal nature of the NCA designation, and do not agree with language in the bill that calls for "enhancing" resources in the river, which water managers could interpret as allocating more water for fish to the detriment of water rights holders dependent on McPhee storage. Montezuma County representatives do not oppose the potential Wild and Scenic designation because they believe the Dolores River is not in a condition for the National Park Service to recommend its inclusion in the Wild and Scenic Rivers System.[46]

Representatives of these two counties do not agree about what is a potential threat to their way of life, and, therefore, cannot agree on a potential solution. These recent attempts to find common ground about water rights protections and Dolores River protections have resulted in a stalemate, demonstrating the challenge of local water governance among stakeholders with contrasting water rights and values.

POWELL'S VISION AND TODAY'S REALITY

In the twenty-first century, Powell's template of rationality rests uneasily on the configurations of natural settings and human communities. Many water projects, including the Dolores Project, move water across borders of hydrological basins to satisfy agricultural and domestic demands. Powell knew that agricultural and municipal water needs require projects to store and deliver water, but he did not anticipate that Westerners would respond to those needs by relocating water across watershed boundaries. Created by human design, political boundaries rarely defer to the outlines of hydrological basins. Federal public lands, lands under state administration, irrigation and conservancy districts, and private landholdings have fragmented watersheds, resulting in a patchwork of land and water management units that are a world apart from Powell's vision of unified watershed commonwealths.

In the late 1800s and early 1900s, the resource-based livelihoods of mining, logging, farming, and ranching brought the Dolores River communities into being. In his *Arid Lands Report* and related writings, Powell categorized and mapped the arid region's lands based on these uses.[47] People with these livelihoods in the late 1800s had a common interest in enhancing their economies by developing the land and creating irrigation infrastructure. Celebrating local self-determination, Powell assumed rural Westerners would provide their own labor and build their own capital. In contrast, the first projects on the Dolores River required corporate investment and imported labor. And yet, once these projects were in place, an element of community-funded management came into play, bearing a closer resemblance to Powell's conception of irrigation districts.

McPhee Dam exhibits a connection to Powell's understanding of the value of water. But his concept of damming rivers "so that no waste water runs to the sea"[48] is no longer the sole priority of water management. Driven by motives distant from Powell's assumptions, the DWCD conducts managed releases from McPhee Reservoir to maintain non-native and native fish in the Lower Dolores. Today's dam operations have been significantly modified to support river ecology. Reservoir managers shift between the resource-development values that led to the dam's construction *and* environmental conservation values. In his time, Powell could not have anticipated the emergence of environmental values, currently prominent in the West, and their connection to livelihoods other than harvesting and marketing of natural resources.

As the founder of the Bureau of Ethnology, Powell was very interested in Indian peoples, and yet that interest did not lead him to contemplate the future roles of tribes in Western society. Tribal sovereignty's bearing on water allocations did not enter his mind. In contrast, the Dolores Project's construction was contingent upon ensured water deliveries to the Ute Mountain Ute Reservation, whose rights to water stem from the 1908 *Winters* Doctrine. Tribal water rights with priority dates based on the establishment of reservations did not come into being until after Powell's death in 1902. Tribes were a major omission in the range of participants in local decision-making that he supported.

Powell's expectation—of a West dotted with homogeneous commonwealths centered on common interests and common rights—has collided with the emergence of a huge diversity in livelihoods, values, and changing allocations of rights and duties. Today in the Dolores community, some residents have water rights, and others do not. Some hold authority to manage irrigation infrastructure, and others do not. Some value the preservation of native fish, and others do not. All these differences in rights and values dramatically alter the dynamic process of a "commonwealth," from embracing what people have in common, to pursuing reconciliation of their differences.

And yet the desire to work communally continues to mobilize people tied to the Dolores River. Historically, citizens worked together to develop the river. And, in the present, with a different but intense vigor, they explore the conflict between—and the possible resolution of—the best interests of the Montezuma Valley and the Lower Dolores. In Powell's mind, the contest over water management hinged on a tension between economic privatization and public provision of water. Today, that contest still plays out in the West, especially as the tension between economic and ecological needs complicates the relationship between private and public interests. Unmistakably, Powell's advocacy for communal watershed management still provides a point of orientation in reckoning with this complexity.

In the last century and a half, governmental agencies, non-governmental entities, and regulations have proliferated in the Dolores River Basin and every other area of the West. Powell would likely be shocked by the range of individuals and groups who manage, regulate, and advocate for land and water in the region. With an enviable clarity and simplicity, he saw three tiers of governance: federal, state, and local, with local districts having primacy over decisions about their land and water. Today, multiple entities at federal, state, district, and local levels regulate resources at multiple scales. This interconnected, enmeshed, and sometimes clashing arrangement of authorities exhibits how Western water policy has dynamically reconfigured federalism.

Powell's assessments call our attention to three core elements of undiminished relevance to our times.

First, he invited us to keep our attention on the limited water of the arid West, and on the importance of responding to that scarcity by thinking deliberately about the units of land affected by our water management decisions. Our hodgepodge of political boundaries and institutions often do not align with watersheds and hydrologic basins. Powell's ideas can give us bearing as we coordinate human-imposed boundaries in ways that enhance the integrity and resilience of particular landscapes.

Second, Powell's focus on the value of local engagement in resource management has steadily acquired relevance. For the Dolores River today, local deliberation and decision-making, and the livelihoods and values of residents, necessarily means engagement with federal, state, and non-governmental institutions.

Third, with his high-impact statement—"with wisdom you may prosper, but with folly you must fail"—Powell still exhorts us to appraise our own conduct by those two key words, "wisdom" and "folly." Wisdom, for Powell, meant restricting waste by damming and diverting water for maximum human benefit. Reckoning with his legacy, we have the opportunity to expand upon what wisdom might mean in our contested times. This opportunity requires us to think in terms more complex than the watershed boundaries and simple tiers of governance that held Powell's belief. These webs of paradoxical institutions and values present a stiff challenge to defining a form of wisdom that can hold its own in the twenty-first century. Even though Powell asked his contemporaries to manage resources within their limits, and to work together to live within those limits, he provided no formula or specific ideas about how to initiate and conduct communal management. In innumerable efforts throughout the region, Westerners today are trying to figure this out by trial and error.

The current impasse between the Montezuma Valley coalition and the Lower Dolores coalition over the NCA bill is a useful focal point as we ask ourselves how Westerners might carry on where Powell's observations and recommendations left off. Recent precipitation patterns draw our attention to uncertainty: 2017 was a year of abundant water, making it possible to release surplus flows from McPhee Reservoir into the Lower Dolores, benefiting fish and boaters but still retaining a full supply in the reservoir. As encouraging as we may find a year of abundance, we cannot assume that such abundant precipitation will prevail in the future. Dramatic water shortages in 2018 are a testament. The concatenation of causes and effects often labeled "climate change" throws into relief the invitation that Powell offered Westerners: manage resources carefully with their limits in mind so that the water—and your communities—will be sustained into the future.

WISDOM AND FOLLY ON THE EDGE OF THE GREAT UNKNOWN

In the post-Powellian world, Peter Gleick and Todd Bryan are carrying on the tradition of thinking deeply about Western resource management. Consider, for instance, Gleick's valuable working definition for "water sustainability": "the use of water that supports the ability of human society to endure and flourish into the indefinite future without undermining the integrity of the hydrological cycle or the ecological systems that depend on it."[49] What decision-making processes will permit citizens and officials to put this definition into operation? How are Westerners to sustain human society and river ecology equally and simultaneously?

Returning to the idea of paradox offers a key step toward finding answers. It is within the reach of imagination that Dolores River Basin residents—and Westerners in many other locales—could experiment with envisioning aspirations for the well-being of communities and rivers as parts of a whole, rather than as separate, disconnected concerns. They could seize opportunities for face-to-face discussion at regular intervals, invoking a commitment to honor divergent needs for sustaining the Dolores River into the future.

Joining Peter Gleick in thinking on a post-Powellian track about improving relations between water and Westerners, Todd Bryan has coined a term as promising as it is clunky in artful expression: "a multiple-value commons dilemma."⁵⁰ A recognition of paradox, which Bryan defines as seemingly self-contradicting elements that each express truth and are parts of a whole, provides the key to dealing with this dilemma.⁵¹ "Paradoxical tensions," Bryan declares, are "inherent in balancing economic development and resource protection."⁵² Balance, though, cannot come into play if stakeholders choose to regard only one side of the paradox as valid and "disown" the other.⁵³ Offering a prime example of what Bryan calls "splitting," the Montezuma Valley coalition insists, "the NCA bill threatens our water rights," while the Lower Dolores coalition insists, "the NCA protects our water rights."

"Since the contradictions are usually more salient than the connections," Bryan writes, "our response is to sever the connections, thereby splitting the contradictory forces." "Splitting" exaggerates an intractable conflict where "[t]he parties then endlessly debate the contradictions, without discovering the interconnected problem."⁵⁴ This description maps nearly perfectly onto debates over the NCA legislation. Splitting also compartmentalizes and maintains roles and responsibilities that stakeholders associate with their identities and therefore "fiercely maintain," posing yet another obstacle to forging solutions. "[W]e are unable to focus on the larger problem precisely because it contains a paradoxical tension that we wish to avoid. Splitting, therefore, prevents shared ownership of complex social and environmental problems from emerging."⁵⁵

Is there an alternative to splitting? Creating a shared sense of ownership marks an essential move toward productive outcomes. Collaborative processes, Bryan argues, have the capacity to restore paradox. "Because of our tendency to own parts of the paradox, while disowning other parts, it makes sense to bring people together who individually carry the various parts."⁵⁶ Bryan provides us with a vision for local decision-making without offering a clear, concrete strategy for achieving that goal, a problem that has persisted since Powell wrote about communal management of resources. Both Bryan's and Powell's lack of specific strategies highlight the challenge of applying singular solutions to unique resource-use contexts.⁵⁷

In the stalemated NCA negotiations, Montezuma Valley participants have felt unrepresented or even threatened, though they have a place at the table. These feelings hinder movement toward shared ownership of the problem and keep participants engaged in splitting. Water rights holders can't be guaranteed that they won't experience water scarcity if they agree to a compromise. They have not been persuaded thus far to put their rights at risk to redirect water to the Lower Dolores when water scarcity will rob them of their ability to make a living. With that view entrenched, stepping away from the table makes far more sense than "negotiating their rights away."[58] Without an incentive to compromise, the status quo prevails.

The complexity of multiple values, competing for a common water source that becomes more uncertain over time, is a hallmark of our era. This circumstance seems certain to persist far into the future. Thus it is in our interest today—and in the interest of posterity—to choose wisdom over folly. As twenty-first century Westerners reckon with Powell's heritage, the desire to be guided by wisdom may well require making peace with paradox and embracing the convergence of many needs and values on one, limited resource. This acceptance would make it imaginable to diversify our practices so that one failure will not cause failure of the entire system. Avoiding such risk and vulnerability inherently requires working with a network of local stakeholders *and* federal agencies and officials, given the unavoidable reality of federal oversight of major dams and reservoirs like McPhee. The wisdom of working with this network requires recognizing the legitimacy of perspectives and truths other than our own. Moreover, that wisdom rests on a willingness to compromise, rather than allowing that some will receive coveted water, while others go dry.

On the other hand, folly in the context of the Dolores River disputes could be defined as the choice to remain in conflict rather than to embrace paradox. The people of the present and the future have a wide range of choice, and folly would consist of dismissing that power of choice and adopting unrealistic assumptions of inevitability and fatalism. Folly would also mean ignoring the preciousness and precariousness of water, as well as discounting the value of honoring all precious life, whether it is a healthy crop or a healthy fish, that thrives on this essential element. Folly would entail refusing to pay attention and not respond to needs other than one's own.

Human minds can conjure up far more illuminating, productive foundations for decision-making than pitting the Lower Dolores and Montezuma Valley coalitions against each other. Rather than rigid polarization, we can seize the opportunity presented by this paradoxical place to experiment with ways of thinking that might produce more wisdom than folly. Montezuma Valley and the Lower Dolores are, after all, deeply connected. By respecting the limits of our water resources and choosing communication and cooperation in the face of uncertainty, we stand a far better chance of sustaining our communities and passing on our learning to the people who, 150 years from now, will live in the Colorado River Basin. While we can steer our course by various calculations of wisdom, we have every reason to follow Powell's example and to look out for the interests of those distant figures whom we call "posterity," thereby doing our part to build foundations for a healthy environment that supports robust economies and connected, interdependent communities.

When John Wesley Powell stood on the banks of the Green River in 1869 he could not see—but he could imagine!—the rapids ahead. With equal bravery and daring, he stood on the edge of time. Unable to see where that river would lead, Powell put into the current, charting a course with an intense vision that maintains its force. Today, standing on the edge of our "Great Unknown," we can enlist Powell to our cause and, pushing off from shore, plot our course with forethought and care, hoping that posterity will receive the benefits.

NOTES

1. Bureau of Land Management, "Dolores River Colorado———River of Sorrows: Recommendation for Inclusion Under Section 5(d) of the Wild and Scenic Rivers Act" (1971): 4, http://npshistory.com/publications/nwsr/co-dolores.pdf.
2. William deBuys, ed., *Seeing Things Whole: The Essential John Wesley Powell* (Washington, DC: Island Press, 2001), 306.
3. Ibid.
4. Ibid.
5. Ibid., 311.
6. Ibid., 308.
7. John Wesley Powell, "The Lesson of Conemaugh," *North American Review* 149 (1889): 152.
8. deBuys, *Seeing Things Whole*, 308.
9. Donald Worster, *A River Running West: The Life of John Wesley Powell* (Oxford: Oxford University Press, 2001), 351–52.
10. deBuys, *Seeing Things Whole*, 309.
11. Ibid.
12. Ibid., 310.
13. Editors of the Encyclopedia Britannica, "Federalism: Political Science," *Encyclopedia Britannica*, accessed November 27, 2019, https://www.britannica.com/topic/federalism.
14. deBuys, *Seeing Things Whole*, 306.
15. Ibid., 304.
16. Ibid., 308.
17. Powell, "The Lesson of Conemaugh," 152.
18. Dolores Water Conservancy District, Draft Dolores Project Drought Contingency Plan (2017): 6, 36–41, http://doloreswater.com/wp-content

/uploads/2017/05/Draft-Dolores-Project-Drought-Contingency-Plan-.pdf; Dolores Water Conservancy District, Lower Dolores River Implementation, Monitoring & Evaluation Plan Overview (2012): 3, http://ocs.fortlewis.edu /drd/pdf/IP-Brochure-Final_090412_small.pdf.

19. Marsha Porter-Norton and Dolores River Dialogue, Appendix 2 : History of Dolores River Water Use, the Dolores Project, the Rise of Environmental Consciousness Nationally and Locally, and Stakeholder Collaboration to Promote Conservation of Lower Dolores River Natural Resources (2013): 1, http:// ocs.fortlewis.edu/drd/pdf/Dolores-Watershed-Plan-Appendix-2.pdf.

20. National Park Service, "Science of the American Southwest: Ancestral Puebloan," last updated December 7, 2015, https://www.nps.gov/subjects /swscience/ancestral-puebloan.htm.

21. Ibid.

22. University of Utah, Utah American Indian Digital Archive, "History: The Northern Utes," accessed November 27, 2019, http://utahindians.org /archives/ute/history.html.

23. Porter-Norton and Dolores River Dialogue, Appendix 2, 3.

24. Maureen Gerhold, "Eastern Capital and the Frontier Initiative: The History of the Montezuma Valley Irrigation System," in *The River of Sorrows: The History of the Lower Dolores River Valley*, ed. Gregory D. Kendrick (Rocky Mountain Regional Office: US National Park Service, 1981), https://www.nps .gov/parkhistory/online_books/rmr/river_of_sorrows/chap3.htm.

25. Dolores Water Conservancy District, Drought Contingency Plan, 18–19.

26. Ibid.; Gerhold, "Eastern Capital."

27. Dolores Water Conservancy District, Drought Contingency Plan, 18–19.

28. Ibid., 19.

29. Powell, "The Lesson of Conemaugh," 152.

30. Dolores Water Conservancy District, Drought Contingency Plan, 20.

31. Ibid., 10.

32. National Park Service, "Wild and Scenic River Program, Fact Sheet: Outstandingly Remarkable Values," last modified September 2011, https://www .nps.gov/orgs/1912/upload/ORV_9_2011.pdf.

33. National Park Service, "Wild and Scenic Rivers Program: Eligible and Suitable," last modified September 17, 2018, https://www.nps.gov/orgs/1912 /eligible-and-suitable.htm.

34. Dolores Water Conservancy District, Drought Contingency Plan, 7.

35. Dolores Water Conservancy District, Plan Overview, 3.

36. Ralph DeVries and Stephen G. Maurer, *Dolores River Guide* (Albuquerque, NM: Southwest Natural and Cultural Heritage Association, 1997), 87–88; Amorina Lee-Martinez, "What Helps and Hinders Collaboration in Watershed Negotiation? An Analysis of Four Case Studies on the Dolores River" (M.S. Thesis, University of Colorado, Boulder, 2017), 17.

37. Lee-Martinez, "Collaboration in Watershed Negotiation," 17.

38. Christopher M. Weible and Paul A. Sabatier, "A Guide to the Advocacy Coalition Framework," in *Handbook of Public Policy Analysis: Theory, Politics, and Methods*, ed. Frank Fischer et al. (Boca Raton, FL: CRC Press, 2006), chapter 9.

39. Lee-Martinez, "Collaboration in Watershed Negotiation," 65.
40. Ibid., 66.
41. Ibid.
42. Ibid.
43. Ibid., 66–67.
44. Amber Clark and Marsha Porter-Norton, "Proposed Dolores River Canyon National Conservation Area: Questions and Answers" (2015): 1.
45. Dolores Drafting Committee, "To establish the Dolores River National Conservation Area and the Dolores River Special Management Area in the State of Colorado, to designate the Dolores River Canyon Wilderness in the State, to protect private water rights in the State, and for other purposes (Discussion Draft)," October 3, 2016, 3.
46. Jim Mimiaga, "Two counties renew debate over conservation status for Dolores River," *The Journal,* March 22, 2018, https://the-journal.com/articles/89839#slide = 2.
47. John Wesley Powell, *The Arid Lands,* ed. Wallace Stegner (Lincoln: University of Nebraska Press, 1962).
48. Powell, "The Lesson of Conemaugh," 152.
49. Peter Gleick, "The Changing Water Paradigm: A Look at Twenty-first Century Water Resources Development," *International Water Resource Association* 25, no. 1 (2000): 131.
50. Todd A. Bryan, "Tragedy Averted: The Promise of Collaboration," *Society & Natural Resources* 17, no. 10 (2004): 886.
51. Ibid., 888.
52. Ibid.
53. Ibid., 887.
54. Ibid.
55. Ibid., 888.
56. Ibid., 889.
57. Lucy Moore, *Common Ground on Hostile Turf: Stories from an Environmental Mediator* (Washington DC: Island Press, 2013), 180.
58. Lee-Martinez, "Collaboration in Watershed Negotiation," 59.

CHAPTER 4

Powell's Legacy—The Bureau of Reclamation and the Contemporary West

Water Exchanges

ROBERT GLENNON

River runners across the globe revere John Wesley Powell for his skill, bravery, and fortitude as the first person to explore the Colorado River through the Grand Canyon. Would Powell be horrified to know that the reservoir behind Glen Canyon Dam, which regulates the wild river in the canyon, is called Lake Powell? Not at all.

Powell's legacy includes his 1878 *Arid Lands Report,* researched and written while Powell was head of the Rocky Mountain Region of the US Geographical and Geological Survey, now called the US Geological Survey, an agency within the Department of the Interior.[1] In this seminal work, Powell sketched a pattern of development of Western lands controlled by the federal government that conflicted with the Homestead Act's commitment of 160 acres to virtually anyone who wanted land.

Powell focused his report on the hydrological character of the federal lands. He argued, correctly, that 160 acres was not enough land for pasturage, which would require 2,560 acres for a family to survive, but it was more than enough if the land had irrigation potential. He tried to prevent surveyors in Washington, DC, who were ignorant of the West's topography, from taking maps and drawing rectangular lines to set boundaries for many Western states. He lost that battle. The political power of those who advocated for, and would benefit from, rapid uncontrolled growth overwhelmed his proposal for a planned agricultural economy. And the land grab set off.

Powell's report also advocated for federal lands to be used for different purposes, depending upon their elevation. High-elevation land should be used for timber, medium-elevation land for pasturage, and low-elevation land for irrigated agriculture. He thought that the government should determine where dams would be built. It made the most sense, Powell believed, for "great reservoirs" to be constructed at higher elevations.

Powell's concept of a government-planned and -controlled water supply profoundly impacted another Department of the Interior agency, the Bureau of Reclamation, which was created in 1902—the year that Powell died. Reflecting "the essential pattern for scientific government bureaus" exemplified by Powell's Irrigation Survey and associated work,[2] Reclamation's mission was to construct irrigation systems, from storage reservoirs to distribution canals. Benefitted farmers would reimburse the federal government for some of the costs incurred. Powell favored the creation of irrigation districts, authorized under state law but controlled by local farmers.[3]

In the twentieth century, Reclamation became the world's greatest dam-building agency.[4] It remade the American West as it constructed enormous dams, from Hoover to Glen Canyon, on the region's major rivers, and engineered massive distribution systems, from the Central Valley Project to the Central Arizona Project, to provide water largely to farmers. Reclamation followed Powell's ideas: most of the "great reservoirs" are located at higher elevations, and most farms are located at low elevations.

Reclamation's engineers realized that Powell's report was spot on. It made sense to grow crops in areas where the growing season is year-round rather than those with a growing season of a couple months. The massive irrigation projects that spread across California's central and southern valleys and Arizona's deserts are so productive because they are located at lower elevations. During Powell's lifetime, the federal government rejected the essence of his report but, in the twentieth century, built a hydraulic society that embraced it. Powell's influence was so profound that Wallace Stegner described him as Reclamation's "spiritual father."[5]

This chapter reexamines the legal system that allocates rights to use the waters of the Colorado River Basin. By the 1960s, various federal statutes, compacts, and judicial decisions had allocated 16.5 million acre-feet of water. However, tree-ring scientists subsequently determined that the river's annual flow is only 14 million acre-feet. Climate change is making things worse.

The Colorado River Basin states were slow to recognize that the river carries less water than they once thought. In the early twenty-first century, after the current drought began, the states acted collaboratively to build resilience into the allocation system. John Wesley Powell would have approved. By 2012, even the Bureau of Reclamation realized that the era of great dams and canals was over.

The essential problem that the basin states confront is simple: demand exceeds supply. By a lot. Even in the face of dwindling resources, several states are proposing new dams and diversions.

Despite these challenging problems, there is no need to despair. There are solutions available, ones that even Powell would endorse. A combination of conservation, reuse, desalination, price signals, and market forces provide tools for the basin states to control their own destinies. What is needed is the political will and moral courage to act. The time may be propitious to emulate Powell's leadership. Recent, creative efforts by the states, federal government, and tribes, working within the Law of the River, have developed programs to foster water exchanges, which encourage users to use less or which substitute one source of water for another. The reallocation of water poses significant hurdles. The reallocated water is coming mostly from agricultural users. The challenge is how to encourage water exchanges without harming the future of rural agricultural communities.

THE IRONIC LOSS OF "A SMASHING VICTORY"

The legal regime that controls the water of the Colorado River system consists of international law, Mexican domestic law, and US domestic law, mixed with a blend of statutes, treaties, contracts, court decisions and decrees, administrative rules and regulations, and interstate compacts. This complicated regime is collectively known as the "Law of the River," with uppercase L and R and no need to mention the name of the river involved. Powell would be amazed at the Law of the River's modern complexity, even though he predicted future national and international tensions over water in the arid region. As described in Powell's seminal 1890 article "Institutions for the Arid Lands": "The waters must be divided among the States, and as yet there is no law for it, and the States are now in conflict."[6]

Given the age of the Colorado River system, the Law of the River consists of surprisingly recent developments, because human beings did not begin to make substantial use of the system's flows until the early twentieth century. Robust development in Imperial Valley, California and Yuma, Arizona during the early years of the century prompted the seven basin states to convene at Bishop's Lodge near Santa Fe, New Mexico under the leadership of Herbert Hoover, then US Secretary of Commerce.[7] The group drafted the 1922 Colorado River Compact, which divvied up the system's water by allocating 7.5 million acre-feet (maf) per year to the Upper Basin, another 7.5 maf to the Lower Basin, an additional 1.0 maf to the Lower Basin, and promised a future allocation to Mexico. The Compact also obligated the Upper Basin states to deliver 75.0 maf to Lee Ferry, Arizona over a rolling ten-year average.[8] All states, except Arizona, quickly ratified the Compact, and Congress gave its blessing. Arizona resisted because it feared that, under the prior appropriation "first in time, first in right" doctrine, California would get the lion's share of the Lower Basin's allocation.

In 1928, Congress passed the Boulder Canyon Project Act, which authorized California, Arizona, and Nevada to enter into a compact that divided up the Lower Basin's allocation, with California getting 4.4 maf, Arizona 2.8 maf, and Nevada 0.3 maf.[9] The Act also authorized the construction of Hoover Dam, which would provide hydroelectric power to fuel the growth of Southwestern cities, and the All-American Canal, which would prevent Mexican farmers from diverting Colorado River water that farmers in the Imperial Irrigation District considered theirs.

The Republic of Mexico finally received rights to Colorado River water in 1944 when the United States and Mexico ratified a treaty that allocated 1.5 maf to Mexico.[10] The treaty finally prompted Arizona to ratify the 1922 Colorado River Compact. But Arizona still had no specific allocation of the Lower Basin's share. That changed dramatically and surprisingly.

After several failed attempts by Arizona to get the Supreme Court to rule on the rights of the Lower Basin states, the Court finally decided *Arizona v. California* in 1963.[11] The Court held that Congress, in the 1928 Boulder Canyon Project Act, had itself made a binding allocation of the Lower Basin's rights. This came as quite a shock to the states, given that they had interpreted the Act as merely allowing the Lower Basin states to enter into a compact—which never happened. For thirty-five years, the states had acted as though their rights were unsettled, only to find out that Congress had settled them decades earlier.

Arizona was jubilant, and the *Arizona Republic* crowed about the state's "smashing victory."[12] The Court held that prior appropriation did not govern the interstate allocation among the Lower Basin states.

Instead, under the Boulder Canyon Project Act, Arizona received 2.8 maf *and* complete control over water from the Gila River, which California had argued should be deemed part of the Lower Basin allocation. But Arizona's glee did not last long. The state now had rights to a considerable amount of water, but lacked a conveyance system for transporting it to Phoenix and Tucson.

Arizona politicians had long advocated for Congress to fund construction of the Central Arizona Project (CAP), a canal that would pump Colorado River water 330 miles and almost 2,900 feet up in elevation for distribution across Arizona. Stung by its loss in *Arizona v. California*, California's congressional delegation refused to support any appropriation for construction. The two states reached an accommodation in 1968 in the Colorado River Basin Project Act, when California agreed to support the authorization and appropriation for the CAP in exchange for Arizona agreeing to accept the lowest priority of water among the Lower Basin states in case of shortages.[13] Under the Act, California's 4.4 maf receives the highest priority; the second priority goes to Nevada's 0.3 maf and Arizona's on-stream users' rights to 1.4 maf; and the lowest priority is for Arizona's 1.4 maf for the CAP.

At the time, Arizona's low priority didn't appear troublesome because the Colorado River system seemed to have plenty of water. Remember, the drafters of the Colorado River Compact had doled out 15.0 maf—expecting to make additional allocations in the future—and the United States-Mexico treaty had followed suit with another 1.5 maf for Mexico.

THE SCIENCE OF DENDROCHRONOLOGY

In the 1960s and 1970s, scientists at the University of Arizona Tree-Ring Laboratory made path-breaking discoveries that elevated a once obscure and imprecise discipline into a cutting-edge science: dendrochronology. Tree rings vary in thickness directly proportionate to precipitation patterns: wetter years produce wider rings than drier years. Tree rings are like barcodes on consumer products. The unique characteristics allow tree-ring scientists to move backward through time. By sophisticated and clever comparisons of core samples from trees, scientists take current, accurate knowledge of precipitation levels and river flows and overlay them with cuttings from increasingly older trees.

Beginning in the 1970s, the University of Arizona Tree-Ring Laboratory released studies of flow patterns in the Colorado River that sent shock waves around the West. Instead of the river annually carrying 18 or 20 maf, as drafters of the 1922 Colorado River Compact had thought, scientists at the tree-ring lab found that over the last 500 years, the river annually carried only 14 maf.[14]

Powell recognized that aridity was the defining feature of the West. How prescient he was. Over the latter half of the twentieth century, population growth transformed the West, as urban centers, such as Los Angeles, Phoenix, Denver, Salt Lake City, and Las Vegas, ballooned beyond anyone's expectations and rampant development overwhelmed water supplies. The Colorado River, once thought to have abundant water when the basin states fought over how to divide the system's flows, now appeared vulnerable and finite.

FROM SURPLUS TO SHORTAGE

Even as late as the year 2000, the basin states were asking the secretary of the interior to promulgate rules that would allow states to divert more water than allowed by the Law of the River.[15] In a fitting lesson in the hubris of ignorance, Mother Nature began a drought that year that has not ended. Within a few years, all seven basin states came to understand that they needed to confront a different reality: shortage.

The year 2007 was remarkable for the states' approach to the Law of the River. They spent most of the twentieth century battling each other in bitter litigation and hardnosed scrambles in the halls of Congress. Given the high stakes, it's rather surprising that the states have not resorted to litigation, which, as their twentieth-century experience with *Arizona v. California* demonstrates, is contentious, expensive, and protracted. That case, stretching over a half century, taught the states a powerful lesson: litigation is a painful process that can consume immense emotional energy and deplete state budgets. Perhaps the states should try to work together to find mutually satisfying solutions to collective water shortages.

In the twenty-first century, cooler heads have prevailed thus far, and the states have been as diplomatic as seasoned representatives at the United Nations. The new century ushered in a different approach: negotiation and conciliation. Negotiation proved successful as the states reached consensus on principles of shortage, which the Secretary of the Interior approved in 2007 as the "Interim Guidelines."[16]

The Interim Guidelines established standards for releasing water from Hoover and Glen Canyon dams when their reservoirs, Lakes Mead and Powell, are at specified low levels. The agreement also established rules for shortage allocations along the Lower Colorado River, which are triggered by Lake Mead's elevation.

To try to ward off shortage allocations, the Interim Guidelines allow water users in Lower Basin states to generate Intentionally Created Surplus water through measures such as lining canals and fallowing land. The conserved water is stored in Lake Mead for delivery at a later date. The program aims to keep Lake Mead's elevation higher and thus potentially to avoid or stave off initiation of shortage allocations. This program is a step in the direction of creating a market for water because it allows entities to pay existing users to refrain from using water, and the entity financing the fallowing gets water rights to that water, which is temporarily stored in Lake Mead.

THE END OF THE RECLAMATION ERA

In 2012, shortly after the developments above had taken place, the Bureau of Reclamation released a remarkable report, the *Colorado River Basin Water Supply and Demand Study* (the Basin Study), which signaled the end of the Reclamation Era of building massive dams and canal systems. The Basin Study analyzed current and future imbalances in water supply and demand, and developed adaptation and mitigation strategies to address the imbalances. The results are sobering. By 2060, Reclamation projects that demand will exceed supply by 3.2 maf in the basin (figure 6).[17]

To identify potential solutions to the imbalance between supply and demand, Reclamation invited suggestions from both stakeholders and the general public, receiving more than 150 ideas. Some, such as towing icebergs from the Arctic, were laughable. I think John Wesley Powell would have smiled at these proposals. But instead of dismissing ideas out of hand, Reclamation took all at face value and subjected them to rigorous comparative analysis. In the end, the dreams of icebergs and pipelines over mountains failed to stack up. None of the options involving major construction projects, whether dams or pipelines, fared well under scrutiny. Two of the most cost-effective options turned out to be conservation and reuse.

The 2012 Basin Study is an exceptional document. In deciding that the better options rely on policy tools rather than massive construction projects that import water from other basins, Reclamation put an exclamation point on the idea that the era of massive dams and canals is over. The most important dam-building agency in the history of the world

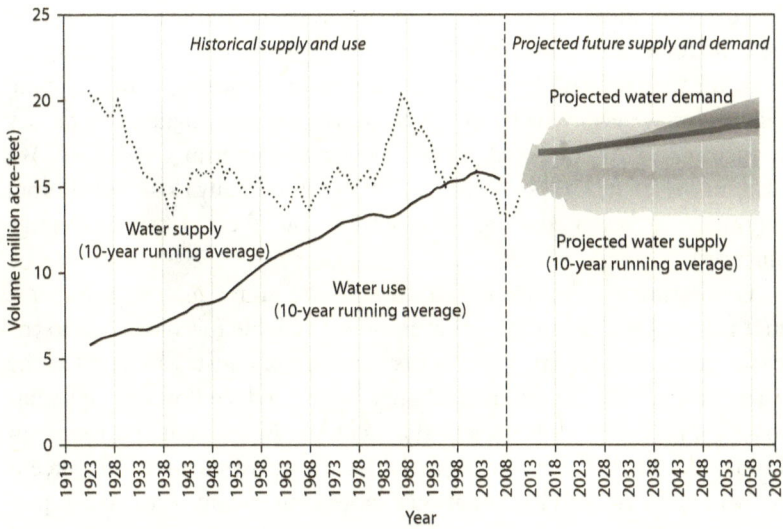

FIGURE 6. Colorado River Basin Historical Water Supply and Use and Projected Future Water Supply and Demand. Source: US Bureau of Reclamation, *Colorado River Basin Water Supply and Demand Study* (2012).

acknowledged that the best path forward lies in using wisely the water we already have rather than in augmenting the available supply.

A MATH PROBLEM

As mentioned above, the essential problem the basin states face is clear: demand exceeds supply.[18]

Let's walk through the numbers. The 1922 Colorado River Compact allocated 7.5 maf to the Upper Basin and another 7.5 maf to the Lower Basin, for a total of 15.0 maf, with an expectation of additional allocations. The United States-Mexico Treaty of 1944, in turn, recognized that the Republic of Mexico has rights to 1.5 maf, bringing the new allocated total to 16.5 maf. But the tree-ring scientists at the University of Arizona have calculated that the mean annual flow of the Colorado River over the last 1,000 years is only about 14.6 maf. Things get worse.

The current drought in the basin began in 2000. No one knows whether we're in the twentieth year of a twenty-year drought or the twentieth year of a fifty-year drought. "The period from 2000 to 2015 was the lowest 16-year period for natural flow in the last century.

Paleorecords indicate that this period was also one of the lowest 16-year periods for natural flow in the past 1,200 years...."[19] We do know that, for the last few years, Lake Mead has been flirting with dropping below 1,075 feet, which, as noted above, would trigger mandatory reductions to Arizona and Nevada under the Interim Guidelines. We also know that Lakes Mead and Powell annually lose substantial amounts of water due to evaporation off these reservoirs' huge surfaces.

One estimate pegs this evaporation figure at 1.1 maf.[20] Deduct 1.1 maf from 14.6 maf, and the new amount available for allocation to the basin states is 13.5 maf. In turn, Reclamation scientists estimated in the 2012 Basin Study that climate change would reduce flows by approximately 9 percent.[21] Other scientists, including Brad Udall and Jonathan Overpeck, predict a grimmer future, with upwards of a 20 percent reduction.[22] Let's use Reclamation's more conservative estimate: 9 percent of 14.6 is 1.3 maf, deducted from 13.5 maf, leaves 12.2 maf.

Next, consider the impact of climate change on farmers, who consume between 70 to 80 percent of the Colorado River Basin's water. Reclamation has calculated that for each degree of temperature increase, these farmers would need to increase their water use by 5 percent to grow the same amount of product.[23]

In other words, there are more paper rights to use water than there is "wet" water in the Colorado River system, to the tune of almost 5.0 maf per year. The basin states are playing an adult version of musical chairs. The light at the end of the tunnel is an oncoming train. Why, then, hasn't the wreck already occurred? For two reasons.

First, the two large reservoirs, Lakes Mead and Powell, store about 56.0 maf when full, or roughly four years of typical river flow. This storage system has buffered the states from shortages. As recently as 1999, both reservoirs were close to full. But as the ongoing drought has continued, the reservoirs' levels have declined. In late 2019, the level in Lake Mead was at roughly 39 percent of capacity, and Lake Powell at 53 percent.[24]

And here is a sobering fact: things could get worse very quickly. Colorado River water wonks have begun to refer to "the Lake Mead teacup," which is an allusion to the shape of Lake Mead below the surface. Historically, Mead filled up Boulder Canyon and Powell filled up Glen Canyon. Western canyons are narrower at the bottom than at the rim. The reservoirs will decline faster in the future because each foot of elevation in the lower parts of the canyons holds less water in the reservoirs. At some point, both reservoirs could reach dead pool levels, which means there wouldn't be enough water in them to get through the lowest outlets and spill out into the rivers below. Should this happen, the Lower Basin states would not get even one gallon of water. An equally ominous effect: the hydroelectric power generated by Hoover and Glen Canyon dams would cease, throwing the Western power grid into turmoil, and diminishing hydropower revenues historically used to fund a host of important programs in the basin.[25] Replacing this power would require generation from other power plants, which use large quantities of water in their cooling towers, thus creating additional stress on other Western rivers.

The second reason why the wreck hasn't occurred is that the Upper Basin states have not used all the water they are entitled to under the Colorado River Compact. In many years, the Upper Basin states have used only about 4.5 maf of their 7.5 entitlement.[26] But that may not last much longer. Wyoming, Utah, and Colorado are all planning new dams and diversions that would draw water from the system.[27]

The combination of a disparity of almost 5.0 maf between supply and demand, a historic drought that shows no signs of ending after two decades, the amount of water stored in Lakes Mead and Powell rapidly declining, and new diversions on the drawing board in the Upper Basin creates formidable challenges for the basin states and the Bureau of Reclamation. The basin states, federal and state water agencies, tribes, water users, and the environmental community will need the foresight and creativity of John Wesley Powell to find solutions to the looming water crisis. Powell anticipated what we are now witnessing: "Now, I want to say to you as years go by . . . the interests in these water rights will swiftly increase; that you are piling up a heritage of conflict of all the waters; that is what you are doing. What matters it whether I am popular or unpopular? I tell you, gentlemen, you are piling up a heritage of conflict and litigation over water rights, for there is not sufficient water to supply these lands."[28]

A MENU OF OPTIONS

Despite the enormous challenges, there is no need to despair. A menu of options exists to make headway in addressing the imbalance between supply and demand, and in keeping Lake Mead above elevations that would trigger shortages. None of the options alone will solve the challenges, but collectively there is room for optimism.[29]

Let's start with the low-hanging fruit: conservation. Some cities in and around the Colorado River Basin have done remarkably well at water conservation, including Albuquerque, El Paso, and Tucson. Others, such as Phoenix and Las Vegas, have cut water use below where it was decades ago, even though their populations have surged in the interim.[30] But others—well, let's just say some cities could do better.

A second option is to become more serious about reusing water we already have.[31] Most municipal water gets used once, treated, and then dumped into a nearby river or the ocean. That water is no longer available for reuse until the hydrologic cycle completes another circle, which may take decades or even generations. Phoenix and Tucson are among the nation's leaders in reusing water, which is put toward agricultural irrigation, water parks, golf courses, cemeteries, highway medians, and cooling water for the Palo Verde Nuclear Generating Station.[32] The Orange County Water District has taken reuse further by developing an indirect potable reuse project, which takes treated water, stores it in a recharge basin, then pumps it out and delivers it to customers.[33] The final step, now being pioneered by El Paso, bypasses the recharge segment and immediately uses reclaimed water as drinking water (known as direct potable reuse).[34] Reclaimed water has its own set of challenges, including the need for a separate system of pipes and pumps, which does drive up cost. Still, it is water the city already has, which is often cheaper than having to go to the market for new water supplies. Scarcity is prompting cities to take a closer look at the reuse option. Los Angeles's Hyperion Treatment Plant treats a volume of water equal to the annual flow of the seventh largest river in the United States, but, until recently, every drop of it was dumped into the Pacific Ocean. Los Angeles has now taken steps to reuse that water.[35]

Because science has developed technologies for taking salt out of ocean water or brackish groundwater, desalination offers a third option. Desalination is not a silver bullet because it faces three hurdles. First, it's very expensive. The membranes used in reverse osmosis are very high tech, prone to fouling, and costly to replace. Second, the high-pressure removal system is extremely energy consumptive. The nexus between water and energy results in substantial water use to produce the energy required for the desal process. Finally, the process distills the salts into one very briny concoction, which creates a disposal problem. Simply dumping brine into the ocean would be convenient and inexpensive, but the location of disposal may create gnarly environmental problems for species that live in the interface between fresh and salt water. A big slug of briny water would degrade many estuaries, which often are habitat for threatened or endangered species. Still, for cities in and around the Colorado River Basin with high-value uses for new water supplies and few other options, desal offers another item on the menu.[36]

A fourth policy tool is to price water to encourage conservation. We Americans are spoiled. We can turn on the tap and get virtually a limitless supply of clean water for less than we pay for cell phone service or cable television. In fact, there is no charge for water. Not a penny. When consumers get bills from water providers, the rates are set to recapture the expenses incurred by the utility in providing the water service. In the utility world, this is known as "cost of service" rates. There is no commodity charge for water. Elsewhere, I have argued for recognizing a human right to water for basic needs and then using a system of tiered rates that rise progressively at specified levels of use. It makes sense to give guidance to consumers so that they can decide whether to curtail discretionary uses such as lush gardens or swimming pools.[37]

These options collectively offer tools to help the basin states adjust to a new era in the history of the Colorado River system. But more must be done, and the states have recently developed an innovative tool to build adaptability into water management: water exchanges.

WATER MARKETS AND WATER EXCHANGES

Moving water from one user to another presents a critical tool for addressing the imbalance between supply and demand in the Colorado River Basin. Think of our water supply as a giant milkshake glass, and each demand for water as a straw in the glass. Many states have permitted limitless straws. This tragedy of the commons needs to end. As Powell urged, the nation needs to come to terms with aridity as a limiting factor in human habitation of the West. First, we need to halt more straws from sucking on our finite supply. Second, we need to protect those who have existing straws because, well, there is no other way and it's the right thing to do. And third, we need to allow those who have new and valuable uses for water to get the water they need. How do we do that? By encouraging or requiring new users to compensate existing users for taking their straws out of the glass.

Water marketing offers an underused tool for addressing water shortages. For present purposes, we need to acknowledge the elephant in the room. Farmers consume between 70 to 80 percent of the Colorado River system's water,[38] much of it for low-value crops such as alfalfa, by using the often-inefficient flood irrigation method. Water marketing presents an opportunity to secure water for growing cities and to protect rural areas by securing needed funds to modernize agricultural infrastructure. This is a sensitive topic, and farmers rightly bristle when they read pious attacks on their way of using water by city dwellers with lawns. Yet cities and farmers in the basin states have found novel ways to bridge the divide.

Over the last generation, the basin states and Reclamation have developed, fostered, and funded various types of water exchanges, which encourage some users to use less water to allow other users to use that water or to leave the unused water in Lake Mead to avoid triggering shortage conditions. Water exchanges may also substitute one source of water for another—for example, surface water for groundwater—thus saving the groundwater for future use. The key conceptual point is that these innovations build resilience into water management by creating incentives to use less water.[39]

Water transfers take many forms as water lawyers create instruments that vary with each state's law.[40] Consider a few examples. Forbearance agreements typically involve a payment to a water user not to use a portion of her water right, leaving the water in place to benefit instream flows for fish or to support Lake Mead's elevation. Rotational fallowing keeps a farm in active cultivation but systematically fallows some land each year. Dry-year leases, or interruptible supply agreements, usually give a municipal provider the right to call on a farmer not to use water in a particular year, in exchange for an annual premium and a payment of substantial money if the option is exercised. Deficit irrigation, which entails watering crops intermittently, frees up water for municipal purposes and generates an income stream for the farmer.

Three other exchanges deserve greater attention.

The first is the Tucson/Phoenix CAP Exchange. In 2017, the cities of Phoenix and Tucson agreed to the Exchange and the System Use Agreement, which is a nice example of using creative lawyering to solve a water storage problem.[41] Phoenix currently has unused CAP water but no place to store it. Tucson, in contrast, has more capacity to store water in its wellfields than it needs. The cities agreed that Tucson would store Phoenix's CAP water. When Phoenix needs that water, it will divert some of Tucson's CAP water from the canal in Phoenix; in turn, Tucson will get rights to the Phoenix CAP water stored in Tucson. This exchange financially benefits both cities and secures a supply for the future.

The second exchange involves federal Indian reserved rights. Arizona has twenty-two federally recognized tribes with claims to surface water from rivers running through reservations. Under the prior appropriation doctrine, non-Indians currently use most of this water. When the tribal rights are quantified, court decrees would effectively require the non-Indians to stop using water that they had been using for, in some cases, several generations. Water transfers have been a powerful vehicle for achieving settlements of tribal rights without harming existing non-Indian users. For example, in 2004, Congress enacted the Arizona Water Settlements Act, which settled the rights of the Gila River Indian Community (GRIC) by providing GRIC with rights to Colorado River water delivered through the CAP in exchange for GRIC waiving its rights to surface water from the Gila River. Congress also appropriated funds to enable GRIC to modernize its irrigation infrastructure. This water exchange substituted surface water from the CAP for surface water from the Gila River and succeeded in benefiting both GRIC and non-Indian users.[42]

In the years since, GRIC has actively engaged water providers in Maricopa County, especially the Salt River Project, in mutually beneficial agreements. Under a 2013 agreement, GRIC agreed to store two million acre-feet of its CAP rights in Salt River Project aquifers.[43] Rights to use this water have been a powerful factor in allowing recent growth in Maricopa County. According to Patrick Sigl, a lawyer with the Salt River Project, seven tribes have leased 182,000 acre-feet to cities in the county. That's 8 percent of the water used in Maricopa County. Eight percent of Maricopa County's gross domestic product is $19 billion.[44]

Finally, the most ambitious proposal for water exchanges is the Lower Basin Drought Contingency Plan (DCP) recently adopted by the Lower Basin states and Reclamation.[45] Although the details are complex, the essence of the DCP is to substantially reduce the risk that Lake Mead will fall below an elevation of 1,025 feet—the level where the wheels come off the Law of the River. Achieving this goal will require leadership from Reclamation and substantial reductions in water use by Arizona, California, and Nevada. The DCP changes the 2007 Interim Guidelines by broadening opportunities for creating Intentionally Created Surplus by states and, notably, by Mexico and Indian tribes. The DCP aims to achieve its ambitious goal by providing local and federal funding for conservation efforts. The states and federal government will pay users to use less water. In sum, water exchanges in the form of water marketing will secure the needed quantities of water to insure shortage cutoffs do not occur.

A VISION OF HARMONY

In the twenty-first century, Reclamation and the Colorado River Basin states have embraced some remarkably innovative tools to address water shortages without driving a stake through the heart of any state or economic interest. Price signals, market forces, water exchanges, and sales and leases of water have enabled the states to address not only pressing urban demands for water, but also environmental interests in restoring river habitat degraded by water diversions. The challenge is how to accomplish these water transfers without putting at risk the rural agricultural communities at the core of Powell's vision of the arid region.

As the Earth's population surges from seven billion to more than nine billion by 2050,[46] how will farmers secure the water needed to provide food for another two billion inhabitants of our planet? As a matter of fundamental human rights, it is imperative that we ensure a bright future for our farmers, because they feed the rest of us. The moral burden rests on developed countries, especially the United States, which exports more food than any other country, to make sure farmers can produce enough food.

The challenge of feeding the world is under threat from many socioeconomic forces. In the United States, water need not be one of them. A small reduction in the percentage of water consumed by farmers translates into a large percentage of the water consumed by the municipal and industrial sectors. A 4 percent reduction in agricultural consumption would produce an almost 50 percent increase in the water available for municipal and industrial users.[47]

In the context of the Colorado River Basin and more broadly, the question becomes: how can farmers achieve this reduction without undermining their capacity to feed the world? The answer turns on recognizing that almost half the irrigated acres in the West are watered with flood irrigation. More efficient methods are available, but they are quite costly. For example, subsurface drip irrigation produces much higher efficiencies, but it's expensive to install. Systems run $1,800 or more per acre—way beyond the financial means of many farmers who are land-wealthy and cashflow-poor. But it's not beyond the means of Western cities.

Peter Culp, Gary Libecap, and I have proposed a municipal program to underwrite the cost of modernizing farm infrastructure.[48] Enabling farmers to become more efficient with systems paid for by cities is a win-win solution. Farmers continue to produce as much product but with slightly less water, and cities get water they need. It's also a program consistent with John Wesley Powell's vision of hydrological basins in the arid region having sensible irrigation systems. Wallace Stegner's biography of Powell, *Beyond the Hundredth Meridian,* optimistically ends with a prophesy that a thinker ahead of his time, such as Powell, could "contemplate the truly vortical, corkscrew path of human motion and with some confidence wait for the future to catch up with him."[49] The basin states have moved into an era of surprising cooperation and unparalleled creativity as they have recognized that demand exceeds supply. The "Great Unknown" for the states is whether they will find creative ways to fundamentally rework the Law of the River. If they do, maybe, just maybe, they will catch up with Powell.

Acknowledgments

I am grateful to Jennifer Wendel, University of Arizona College of Law Class of 2019, for her careful edit of an earlier draft. To the volume editors, I am indebted for contributions going well beyond their usual roles. They kept me from numerous mistakes, suggested more felicitous phrases, offered transitions where needed, and even provided me with references for endnotes. Most of all, they used their immense knowledge of Powell, his writings, and the secondary literature to help me create a more nuanced narrative. They epitomize the best in collegiality. It has been a pleasure to work with them.

NOTES

1. John Wesley Powell, *The Arid Lands,* ed. Wallace Stegner (Lincoln: University of Nebraska Press, 2004 [1878]).
2. Ibid., 23n3.
3. John Wesley Powell, "Institutions for the Arid Lands," *Century* 40 (1890): 113–14.
4. Marc Reisner, *Cadillac Desert: the American West and its Disappearing Water* (New York: Penguin Books, 1986).
5. Powell, *The Arid Lands,* 23n3.
6. Powell, "Institutions for the Arid Lands," 113.
7. Norris Hundley, Jr., *Water and the West: The Colorado River Compact and the Politics of Water in the American West* (Berkeley: University of California Press, 2009).
8. 70 Cong. Rec. 324 (1928). See Hundley, *Water and the West.*
9. 43 U.S.C. §617 et seq. (1928).

10. Treaty Between the United States and Mexico, Treaty Series 944, 59 Stat. 1219 (1944).

11. Arizona v. California, 373 U.S. 546 (1963).

12. Robert Glennon and Jacob Kavkewitz, "A Smashing Victory? Was *Arizona v. California* a Victory for the State of Arizona?," *Arizona Journal of Environmental Law & Policy* 4 (2013): 1–38.

13. 43 U.S.C. §1501 et seq. (1968).

14. Charles W. Stockton and Gordon C. Jacoby, Jr., "*Long-Term Surface-Water Supply and Streamflow Trends in the Upper Colorado River Basin Based on Tree-Ring Analyses,*" Lake Powell Research Project, Bulletin No. 18 (1976).

15. Robert Glennon and Peter Culp, "The Last Green Lagoon: How and Why the Bush Administration Should Save the Colorado River Delta," *Ecology Law Quarterly* 28 (2002): 945–50.

16. Colorado River Interim Guidelines for Lower Basin Shortages and Coordinated Operations for Lake Powell and Lake Mead, 72 Fed. Reg. 9026 (2007), https://www.usbr.gov/lc/region/programs/strategies/RecordofDecision.pdf.

17. Bureau of Reclamation, *Colorado River Basin Water Supply and Demand Study, Study Report* (2012), SR-34, https://www.usbr.gov/lc/region/programs/crbstudy/finalreport/Study%20Report/CRBS_Study_Report_FINAL.pdf.

18. Grand Canyon Trust, "A Problem of Math" (2016), accessed November 24, 2019, www.grandcanyontrust.org/advocatemag/spring-summer-2016/problem-math.

19. Bureau of Reclamation, *SECURE Water Act Section 9503(c)—Reclamation Climate Change and Water 2016* (2016), 3–6, www.usbr.gov/climate/secure/docs/2016secure/2016SECUREReport.pdf.

20. Trevor Carey, "Comprehensive Review of the Fill Lake Mead First Initiative" (2018), 5, https://watershed.ucdavis.edu/education/classes/files/content/page/T.CareyFinalFLMFforWebsite.pdf.

21. Bureau of Reclamation, Study Report, SR-19, SR-21.

22. Bradley Udall & Jonathan Overpeck, "The Twenty-First Century Colorado River Hot Drought and Implications for the Future," *Water Resources Research* 53 (2017): 1763–66, agupubs.onlinelibrary.wiley.com/doi/abs/10.1002/2016WR019638.

23. Bureau of Reclamation, *Study Report*, SR-26. See also Bureau of Reclamation, *Colorado River Basin Water Supply and Demand Study, Technical Report C—Water Demand Assessment, Appendix C-10 Historical Consumptive Use and Loss Detail by State* (2012), https://www.usbr.gov/lc/region/programs/crbstudy/finalreport/Technical%20Report%20C%20-%20Water%20Demand%20Assessment/TR-C_Appendix10_FINAL.pdf.

24. "Lake Powell Water Database," accessed November 24, 2019, http://lakepowell.water-data.com/?ct = t(October_Lowdown10_20_2016_COPY_01); "Lake Mead Water Database," accessed November 24, 2019, http://lakemead.water-data.com/?ct = t(October_Lowdown10_20_2016_COPY_01).

25. Glen Canyon Dam Adaptive Management Program, "Frequently Asked Questions," https://perma.cc/DL4G-9W3C.

26. The Bureau produces Upper Basin consumptive uses and losses reports in five-year increments. The most recent complete report contains provisional data for 2011–15, during which annual consumptive uses and losses averaged 4.062 maf. See Bureau of Reclamation, *Upper Colorado River Basin Consumptive Uses and Losses Report 2011–2015*, (2019), v, https://www.usbr.gov/uc/envdocs/reports/ColoradoRiverSystemConsumptiveUsesandLossesReports/20191000-ProvisionalUpperColoradoRiverBasin2011–2015-CULReport-508-UCRO.pdf.

27. Eric Balken, "Utah Is Headed into a Water Battle It Can't Win," *High Country News*, January 23, 2018, www.hcn.org/articles/opinion-utah-tries-to-put-another-straw-in-the-colorado-before-it-runs-dry; Keith Schneider, "A County in Utah Wants to Suck 77 Million Gallons a Day out of Lake Powell," *Los Angeles Times*, December 3, 2017, www.latimes.com/nation/la-na-lake-powell-pipeline-20171203-htmlstory.html; Melodie Edwards, "Lawmakers Move Forward Dam Project On Colorado River System," *Wyoming Public Media*, January 23, 2018, www.wyomingpublicmedia.org/post/lawmakers-move-forward-dam-project-colorado-river-system#stream/0; Governor Matthew H. Mead, "Leading the Charge: Wyoming Water Strategy" (2015), 37, http://waterplan.state.wy.us/plan/statewide/govstrategy/20150115-GovWaterStrategy.pdf; Matt Weiser, "Its Population Booming, Colorado Ponders New Water Diversions and Dams," *News Deeply*, March 26, 2018, www.newsdeeply.com/water/articles/2018/03/27/its-population-booming-colorado-ponders-new-water-diversions-and-dams. See Colorado Water Conservation Board, "Colorado's Water Plan: The Plan" (2016), accessed November 24, 2019, https://www.colorado.gov/pacific/cowaterplan/plan.

28. John Wesley Powell, "Address and Comments," *International Irrigation Congress Official Proceedings* 2 (1893): 111–12.

29. Robert Glennon, *Unquenchable: America's Water Crisis and What to Do About It* (Washington, DC: Island Press, 2009), chapter 18; Peter W. Culp et al., *Shopping for Water: How the Market Can Mitigate Water Shortages in the American West* (2014), http://www.hamiltonproject.org/assets/files/how_the_market_can_mitigate_water_shortage_in_west.pdf.

30. Cheryl A. Dieter et al., US Geological Survey, *Estimated Use of Water in the United States in 2015* (2018), pubs.er.usgs.gov/publication/cir1441.

31. Glennon, *Unquenchable*, part III.

32. Chuck Graf, "Reclaimed Water: A Growing Component of Arizona's Water Supply" (2018), https://west.arizona.edu/sites/default/files/Reclaimed%20Water%20Presentation_Chuck%20Graf%20Aug%202018.pdf.

33. Glennon, *Unquenchable*, chapter 4.

34. Zoë Schlanger, "El Paso Is on the Cutting Edge of Water Conservation. It Really Has No Choice," *The Texas Observer*, August 23, 2018, www.texasobserver.org/el-paso-is-on-the-cutting-edge-of-water-conservation-it-really-has-no-choice.

35. Robert Glennon, "The Genius of Toilet to Tap," *Los Angeles Times*, March 5, 2019.

36. Glennon, *Unquenchable*, chapter 8.

37. Ibid., part III.

38. Bureau of Reclamation, *Study Report*, SR-26. See also Bureau of Reclamation, *Appendix C-10*.

39. Robert Glennon, "Water Exchanges: Arizona's Most Recent Innovation in Water Law and Policy," *Arizona Journal of Environmental Law & Policy* 8 (2018): 1–21, https://docs.wixstatic.com/ugd/952fod_686c057c3ba2458ea9eaba571384ac5a.pdf.

40. Jonathan King and James Ecklund, "Water Transfer Options," *The Water Report* 172 (2018): 1.

41. Christopher Avery, "New Flexibility on the Central Arizona Project Canal: The Tucson/Phoenix Exchange and the System Use Agreement," *Arizona Journal of Environmental Law & Policy* 8 (2018): 89–100, https://docs.wixstatic.com/ugd/952fod_92a761ba6bec47eab1d2aa59ac3d36ed.pdf.

42. Glennon, "Water Exchanges," 12.

43. Ibid.; Susanna Eden et al., "The Business of Water," *The Water Report* 173 (2018).

44. Patrick Sigl, unpublished manuscript, available in the Archives of the *Arizona Journal of Environmental Law & Policy* website, https://www.ajelp.com/archives; Glennon, "Water Exchanges."

45. Thomas Buschatzke & Nicole Klobas, "Ensuring Arizona's Future Today: The Lower Basin Drought Contingency Plan and the Its Implementation in Arizona," *Arizona Journal of Environmental Law & Policy* 8 (2018): 29–52, https://docs.wixstatic.com/ugd/952fod_72f4b994dc384444b70c4dbdab584f57.pdf.

46. "World Population Prospects: The 2017 Revisions," United Nations Department of Economic and Social Affairs, accessed November 24, 2019, https://www.un.org/development/desa/publications/world-population-prospects-the-2017-revision.html.

47. Culp et al., *Shopping for Water*, 12, 34n3.

48. Culp et al., *Shopping for Water*.

49. Wallace Stegner, *Beyond the Hundredth Meridian: John Wesley Powell and the Second Opening of the West* (New York: Penguin Books, 1954).

PART TWO

Public Lands

Western politicians often decry "rule from Washington," claiming people back East cannot possibly understand issues rooted in the wide swaths of public lands that distinguish the Western landscape. That notion is certainly debatable in the twenty-first century—an age of easy travel and instant communication—but it undoubtedly held merit at the time of John Wesley Powell's 1869 Expedition. Native Americans understood the arid region's remarkably diverse landscape in a deep, visceral way. But such knowledge was rare in the nation's capital—a gap especially pronounced for the last area of the lower forty-eight to be explored and mapped: the Colorado River Basin. Thus, it is unsurprising that Congress supported public land laws conceived in the verdant, flat expanses east of the Hundredth Meridian.

Powell devoted much of his life's work to this incongruity. He opposed superimposing the land grid system of sections and townships on the mountainous West—a schema that fit the arid region like a prom dress on a lumberjack. In his seminal *Arid Lands Report*, he outlined a public-lands classification scheme embodying utilitarian and populist elements, challenging the acreage allotments of disposal-era statutes such as the Homestead Act. Powell consistently advocated for local primacy in public lands governance, an idea that evolved over time into his innovative yet ultimately doomed proposal for watershed commonwealths.

The eventual organizational scheme for the arid region's landscape largely deviated from Powell's vision. Much of the Colorado River

Basin and other parts of the Interior West would become national parks and monuments, national forests, national wildlife refuges, and federally designated wilderness areas. At the same time, roughly 1.3 billion acres of the nation's public domain would be sold or given away to individuals and enterprises under disposal-era legislation. The residual public domain—land that was not privatized or withdrawn for federal reservations—is today some of the most contested in the West. All of these diverse types of lands, and associated conflicts, can be found throughout the basin.

What traction does Powell's vision hold for the future of this landscape? As the authors in this part of the volume make clear, public lands policy has profound implications for the Colorado River Basin's cultural, ecological, economic, political, and social character.

Robert Keiter begins in chapter 5 by focusing on the basin's "crown jewels": the national park units along the Colorado River and its tributaries. These parks embody the preservationist ethic of one of Powell's most notable contemporaries, John Muir. In contrast, other classes of lands within the basin, both public and private, track Powell's recurring emphasis on utilitarian conservation. In modern times, these bodies of thought, preservationism and conservationism, wield "co-equal status," as Keiter describes, with national parks and other preserved lands defining the basin's character as much as "the precious water sources that Powell sought to harness in his day." Keiter illuminates how navigating the "Great Unknown" across this one-of-a-kind landscape entails formidable challenges involving climate change, unprecedented visitation and recreational demands, and numerous other stressors.

In chapter 6, Paul Hirt turns to the longstanding, often polarized debate about private versus public property and optimal public land management. "That debate is the price of democracy," explains Hirt, shedding light not only on Powell's utilitarianism and idealized "nineteenth-century vision of human-scaled, self-governing island communities," but also the disconnect between that vision and the West's transformation after Powell's death. Public lands are now a cherished "birthright" of all Americans, and we do not have the luxury of antiquated, simplistic modes of public land management. Rather, as outlined in Hirt's chapter, careful attention must be paid in the "Great Unknown" to democratic processes, science-based decision-making, and collaboration as key features of public lands governance.

While its predecessors emphasize Powell's utilitarianism, chapter 7, by Emilene Ostlind, takes a different tack. Drawing attention to

Powell's adventure stories like *The Exploration of the Colorado River and Its Canyons,* the chapter ordains Powell the "unwitting godfather of outdoor recreation in the Colorado River Basin." As reflected in the *Arid Lands Report* and other writings, recreation was plainly not what Powell had in mind when developing his public-lands classification scheme. Equally clear, however, is the prominence recreation has attained across the basin's public lands since Powell's time—a point emphasized by all authors in this part. Ostlind's chapter explores aspects of Powell's vision for the public lands that might serve as guides to land managers muddling through this dimension of the "Great Unknown."

Finally, bringing to a close this part's dialogue about the Colorado River Basin's public lands, William deBuys, editor of *Seeing Things Whole: The Essential John Wesley Powell,* authors chapter 8. The intellectual genealogy between Powell and former Interior Secretary Stewart Udall marks its focus. DeBuys describes both as prey to the "constant pull of the Colorado River and its canyons," taking as his subject the historic figures' respective contributions to the creation of a "national American commons." Powell's vision for the arid region's public lands, including his watershed commonwealths proposal, intersects in this space with Udall's advocacy for federal reservations as Interior Secretary and his publication of *The Quiet Crisis*. Yet nothing about deBuys's connecting of these dots foreordains the fate of the basin's public lands—except that it "may well prove to be a bellwether for the nation." Love of place, personified by Powell and Udall, is the medicine prescribed for the "Great Unknown."

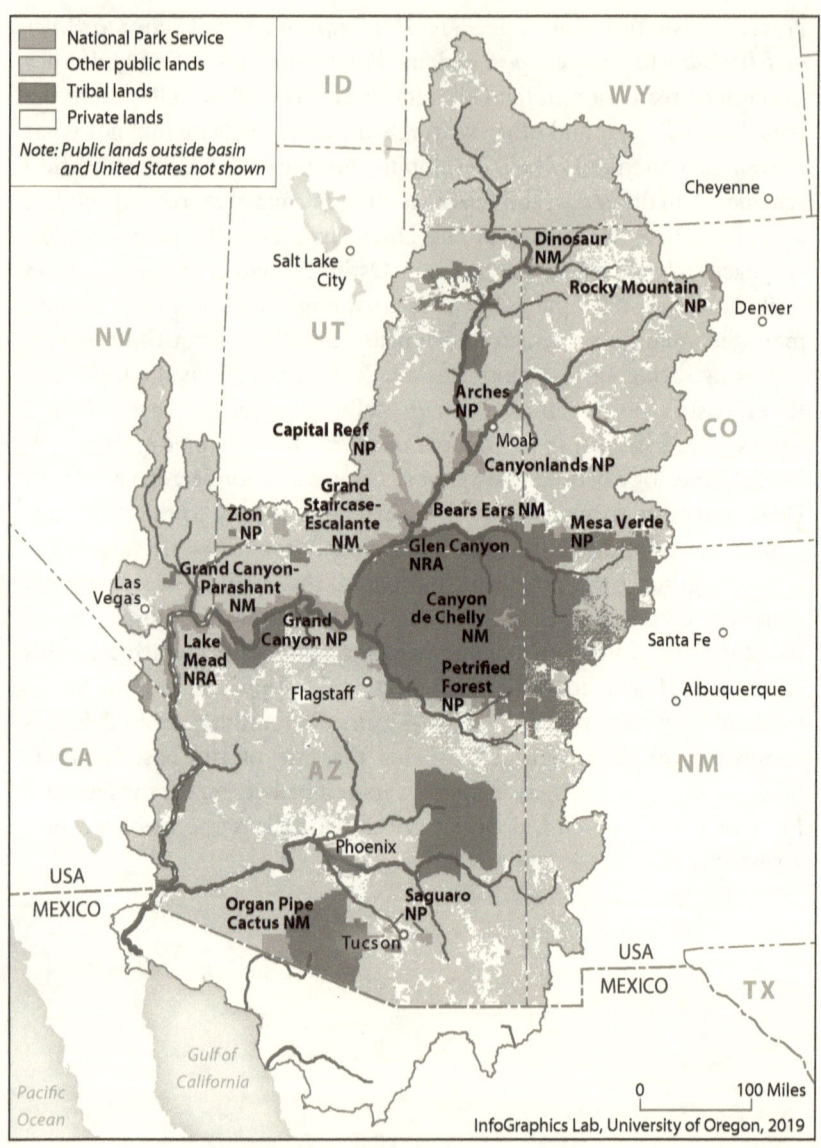

MAP 3. Land Ownership, Colorado River Basin. Cartography: P. William Limpisathian and James Meacham, InfoGraphics Lab, University of Oregon, 2019.

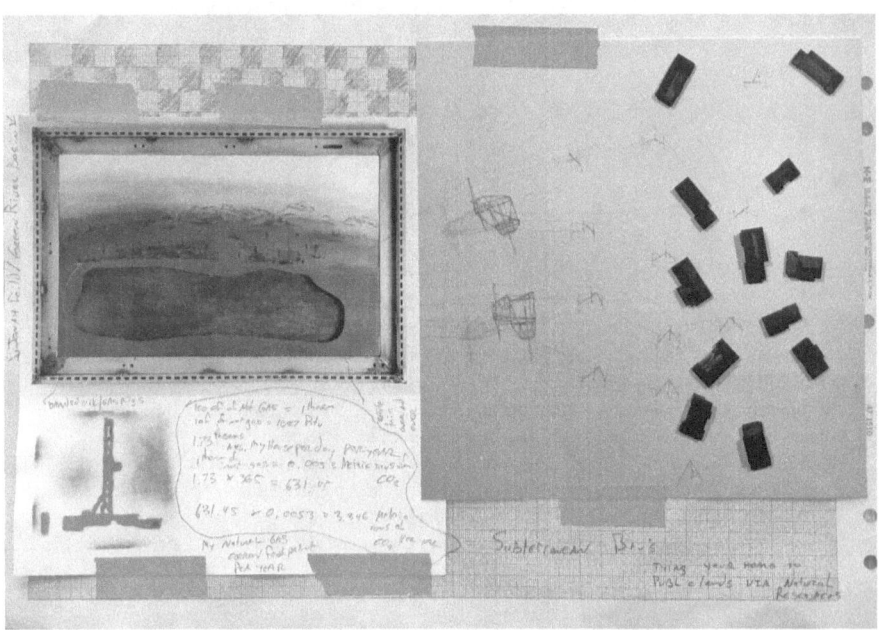

FIGURE 7. David Jones, *Subterranean BTUs* (acrylic and graphite on panel, pyro branding, thread, wood, and found objects, 11" × 5," 2010). This piece highlights the literal physical connections between households in and around the Colorado River Basin and natural gas extraction on public lands within the Green River Basin. The drawing depicts the piece *Subterranean BTUs* as installed and the thought processes involved in developing its conceptual blueprint.

FIGURES 8, 9, AND 10. Kate Aitchison, *The Hull 1 & 2* and *Katie Lee* (wooden drift boat + relief prints, 24" × 192," 2017). The *Katie Lee* drift boat is constructed as a visual journey through the contemporary landscape of the San Juan River Basin and Bears Ears National Monument. The boat's hull and its journeys became the visual representation of those places. *The Hull 1* and *The Hull 2* are woodcuts that exist on paper simultaneously as part map, part landscape, and part calendar. Marking time and space, this combination of print and boat will continue to change as new journeys are made and new viewpoints are discovered. Like the landscape, it is a living project.

FIGURE 11. Erika Osborne, *Looking For Moran* (oil on linen, 48" × 96," 2012). Thomas Moran's painting *Chasm of the Colorado* has become a cultural access point for experiencing the Grand Canyon. The vistas Moran looked upon have become a commodity since his participation in the Powell Survey during 1873. *Looking for Moran* reflects on landscape commodification as an artifact of Moran's era—the era of Manifest Destiny.

FIGURE 12. BRANDON GELLIS, *Uncharted 1–3* (laser etching and cutting, clear acrylic, 2018). *Uncharted 1–3* consists of three digital reconstructions of cartographer renderings and drawings in Clarence Dutton's famous book *Tertiary History of the Grand Cañon District* (1882). The first piece (left center, below) is a reconstruction of William H. Holmes's drawing "Panoramic View of the Temples and Towers of the Virgen." The second piece (right center, below) is a reconstruction of Thomas Moran's drawing "Transept at Kaibab Division, The Grand Cañon." The third piece (above) is a reconstruction of William H. Holmes's drawing, "The Panorama from Point Sublime."

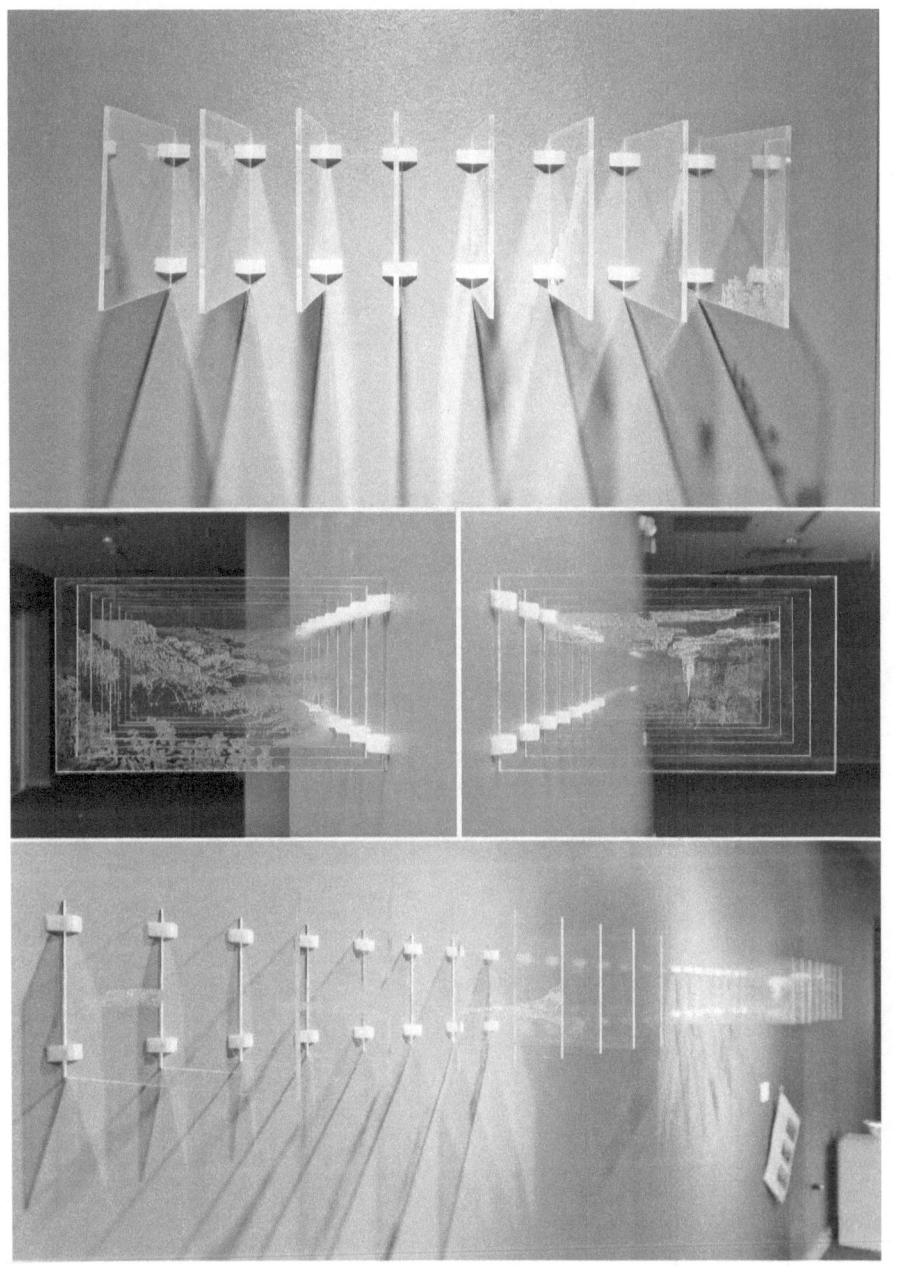

FIGURE 13. Patrick Kikut, *Powell Point* (oil on canvas, 22" × 30," 2018). Deep in the Grand Canyon a letter "P" was inscribed on the cliffs to honor John Wesley Powell. Behind the letter, two airliners have streaked a vapor-trail cross resembling Thomas Moran's painting *Mount Holy Cross*. The imagery poses rich questions about moving forward from Manifest Destiny in the Colorado River Basin.

CHAPTER 5

John Wesley Powell and the National Park Idea

Preserving Colorado River Basin Public Lands

ROBERT B. KEITER

John Wesley Powell, a visionary as well as a man of his times, viewed the vast Western landscape in largely utilitarian terms. Intent on promoting orderly settlement and development of the West, Powell conceived of the region's natural resources—its waters, forests, grasses, and minerals—as a means to support a growing populace and local economy. He envisioned small privately owned farms, communal pastures, and regulated forests, enriched by reclaimed waters to support agricultural activities, and overseen mainly by benevolent local governmental institutions. Although Powell regularly described the region's stunning landscapes in majestic terms, he did not seek to protect these lands, nor did he endorse the then-nascent national park idea until late in his life. Indeed, Powell's views on the West's lands stood in stark contrast to those of his contemporary, John Muir, who feared despoliation of the region's natural beauty and called upon the national government to retain and protect its special places.

Both men, as it turned out, made profound contributions to the public land laws and policies that define the Colorado River Basin and the broader American West. Trained in science, Powell recognized the interconnectedness of the region's mountains, valleys, and waters, and argued for a governance structure based on hydrographic basins to promote orderly management of the region's resources. Trusting early settlers, Powell endorsed local institutions to oversee resource use and development. In contrast, Muir extolled the region's breathtaking scenery, decried early settlers' destructive impulses, and promoted national park designations. Although both men lost major battles, their ideas are nonetheless evident today across the basin, where myriad dams disrupt natural river flows while major national park units line the river corridors.

This chapter explores another dimension of the "Great Unknown": the Colorado River Basin's national parks. It first examines Powell's prolific writings, extracting his views about nature conservation and contrasting them with Muir's. It then explores the evolution of the national park idea, the role of national parks in the basin, and related management challenges. Finally, the discussion concludes by drawing upon Powell's and Muir's key ideas to offer park-related policy proposals designed to meet looming challenges of the next century. Neither man could foresee the enormous changes that have occurred during the past 150 years, but both would take heart in the valuable role national parks have assumed in today's world.

POWELL, MUIR, AND THEIR COMPETING VISIONS
Powell's View: Putting Nature to Work

John Wesley Powell's lifetime spanned the era of Western expansion and settlement, shaping his views on land and water policy. A wounded Civil War veteran, Powell displayed great courage as the first person to navigate the Colorado River on his perilous 1869 Expedition.[1] He likewise exhibited enormous knowledge and wisdom, parlaying his Western explorations into seminal reports and other writings describing the little-known region and policies necessary to ensure its orderly settlement and development. He placed great faith in science as well as the good character and fundamental fairness of settlers rapidly populating the West. Recognizing the region's aridity and primary resources, he promoted policies designed to capture surface waters in reservoirs to support agriculture, which he viewed as the foundation of a prosperous society. His science-based vision promoted utilitarian resource management, with privately owned agricultural lands flanked by federal forests and pasturage areas controlled by locally governed commonwealths.

Powell's vision for Western settlement focused on four resources—water, forests, grass, and minerals—all of which he viewed as essential for regional development. He explained his views on these resources, and the institutions necessary to develop them, in an 1890 article entitled "Institutions for the Arid Lands,"[2] which reflects a deep understanding of the

West and its evolving society. Displaying a keen grasp of the natural world, Powell described the interconnectedness of forests, climate, streamflow, and wildfire, presaging insights the emerging science of ecology would later confirm. He observed, for example, "climate would cover the earth with trees, wherever there is more than ten inches of rain . . . [so] [r]ainfall, then furnishes the potential limit to forest growth, fire the actual limit."[3] Recognizing these connections, he understood, would ensure the West's resources were appropriately managed for productive purposes—to produce timber, grass, and minerals for consumptive use. The value of these resources, he believed, was purely economic and tangible.

Powell foresaw only a limited federal role in the region. In his view, the national government was too distant from the land and people to understand the importance of the region's natural resources in the daily lives of inhabitants.[4] He supported private ownership of irrigated agricultural lands, but he thought the federal government should retain the region's timber and forage lands subject to local management of these resources. Consistent with existing federal law, he also endorsed continued federal retention of underlying minerals.[5] Understanding nature, Powell argued that governmental units in the arid West should be organized to conform to hydrographic basins. Local governmental institutions organized to fit the landscape, he was convinced, would responsibly manage the region's water, timber, and grass. In his words, the people "may be entrusted with their own interests."[6]

Powell's writings were almost uniformly bereft of references to national parks, wilderness, wildlife conservation, recreation, or the like. His utilitarian instincts generally did not countenance these concepts in this time of settlement, when the West seemed a wilderness-like frontier that needed taming, not preservation. For Powell, according to historian Donald Worster, "wilderness . . . was like savagery, a condition to be overcome."[7] Of course, the national park concept was still nascent, having only surfaced in 1872 when Congress established Yellowstone to protect the area's unique natural features.[8] Powell regularly rhapsodized, however, about the West's beauty:

> The lofty peaks of the land are silvered with eternal rime; the slopes of the mountains and the great plateaus are covered with forest groves; the hills billow in beauty, the valleys are parks of delight, and the deep cañons thrill with the music of laughing waters. . . . Clouds rarely mask the skies, but come at times like hosts of winged beauty floating past. . . . The soul must worship these glories.[9]

And Powell extolled the Grand Canyon, referring to it as "the most sublime spectacle on the earth."[10] Yet he did not translate these musings into formal recognition of related, less tangible values—tranquility, spiritual refreshment, or recreation—or policy prescriptions designed to safeguard the region's stunning settings.

Muir's View: Preserving Nature

John Muir, in contrast, wholeheartedly endorsed the national park idea and campaigned tirelessly to protect the West's special places. Following the Yellowstone model, Muir pressed relentlessly to protect Yosemite and other scenic Sierra Nevada locations as national parks. Although not trained in science, Muir, like Powell, was a keen observer of the natural world and understood the connections within it, memorably observing: "When we try to pick out anything by itself, we find it hitched to everything else in the Universe."[11] Muir lamented that early miners and settlers were fast destroying the Western landscape, cutting over the region's timber, diverting its streams, and overgrazing mountain meadows. Not trusting local citizens to rise above self-interest, Muir advocated to retain public lands in federal ownership and to establish national parks to safeguard nature's beauty. He heralded the intangible values of personal renewal and peaceful contemplation to support national park designations—an antidote to the hurly-burly of civilized life in the nation's growing cities.

Rather than viewing the natural world in human-plunder terms, Muir believed society was obliged to preserve major portions of it for future generations. In a letter to President Roosevelt, he wrote: "These sacred mountain temples are the holiest ground that the heart of man has consecrated, and it behooves us all faithfully to do our part in seeing that our wild mountain parks are passed on unspoiled to those who come after us, for they are national properties in which every man has a right and interest."[12] Unlike Powell, who pushed for new dams, Muir fought dam proposals—most famously the O'Shaughnessy Dam on the Tuolomne River inside Yosemite National Park's Hetch Hetchy Valley. And he founded the Sierra Club to bring his preservation campaigns into the political arena.[13] In sum, Muir's legacy embodies the related concepts of nature preservation and the national park idea.

Although Powell was not an outright advocate of national parks or land preservation, he was aware of Muir's views and the emergent popular interest in protecting special places. In 1890, Powell and Muir both published seminal articles in *Century* magazine, setting forth their contrasting visions for Western public lands.[14] Earlier, Powell encouraged Arnold Hague, one of his trusted US Geological Survey scientists, to pen articles supporting the creation of Yellowstone National Park and adjacent forest reserves.[15] Even earlier, fearing imminent damage to his treasured Grand Canyon country, Powell publicly endorsed the idea of a Grand Canyon National Park, asserting that the "herding of sheep and cattle would be incompatible with the purposes of a National Park."[16] In 1893, at Muir's invitation, Powell spoke at the second annual Sierra Club meeting, where he recounted his Grand Canyon adventures.[17] By then, Powell's watershed commonwealth idea had fallen by the wayside in a resistant Congress, and he would have witnessed mounting damage inflicted on the West's precious resources from wanton development. Moreover, both men were plainly enamored with the West's rugged beauty. Powell's vivid descriptions of the Grand Canyon closely mirror Muir's colorful prose: "The gorge is black and narrow below, red and gray and flaring above, with crags and angular projections on the walls, which, cut in many places by side canyons, seem to be a vast wilderness of rocks."[18] Though Powell remained an advocate for utilitarian public land policies throughout his lifetime, he also came to appreciate the national parks.

THE COLORADO RIVER BASIN: A CHANGED LANDSCAPE

Evolving Federal Policies

During their coinciding lifetimes, Powell and Muir witnessed profound changes in public land law and policy. By 1890, while both men were busy promoting contrasting visions for Western public lands, historian Frederick Jackson Turner proclaimed the frontier closed and the nation settled.[19] In the same year, Congress established Yosemite and Sequoia national parks,[20] taking initial steps toward what eventually became the national park system.[21] In 1891, responding to the rapid destruction of the West's forests, Congress vested the President with authority to designate forest reserves that were placed in permanent federal ownership.[22] Congress followed with the Organic Administration Act of 1897, explicitly devoting the new forest reserves to timber management and watershed protection.[23] In 1900, faced with the near-extinction of once-abundant bison through overhunting, Congress adopted the Lacey Act to halt the wanton destruction of the nation's wildlife.[24] In 1906,

Congress adopted the Antiquities Act,[25] giving the President authority to designate national monuments to protect scientific and historic objects. These measures fundamentally reshaped Western public land policy, incorporating the related principles of federal retention, active management, and nature conservation into law. To be sure, Powell's private ownership and resource development notions remained elements of federal policy, but Muir's preservation ideas had attained legitimacy.

As the twentieth century unfolded, federal policy underwent even more profound changes that have elevated conservation and environmental values. In brief, the United States retains more than 630 million acres in federal ownership and manages these lands through four federal land management agencies.[26] The US Forest Service manages the 190-million-acre national forest system for multiple-use purposes, though wildlife conservation and recreation have become ever-more important priorities.[27] The Bureau of Land Management (BLM) administers 247 million acres under a multiple-use policy that today includes burgeoning wilderness preservation and recreational management responsibilities.[28] The National Park Service oversees 85 million acres under a legal mandate to conserve these lands in an unimpaired condition.[29] The US Fish and Wildlife Service administers the 89-million-acre national wildlife refuge system, which is devoted to wildlife conservation and related recreation.[30] During the 1970s, Congress passed an array of environmental laws, including the Endangered Species Act, National Environmental Policy Act, Wild and Scenic Rivers Act, Clean Air Act, Clean Water Act, and Land and Water Conservation Fund Act, as well as the National Forest Management Act and Federal Land Policy and Management Act, which have collectively enshrined environmental protection as a primary federal responsibility.[31] This remarkable evolution in public land law and policy reflects broader social and economic changes that have reduced the allure of Powell's strictly utilitarian values.

Preserving the Basin's Landscape

The Colorado River Basin exemplifies these profound changes in public land policy since Powell's day. The basin's land ownership pattern is mixed, though more acreage has been retained in federal ownership than is privately owned. Most private lands are situated near water sources or benefit from federal reclamation policies that promoted dam construction across the basin.[32] The regional populace primarily lives in a few major cities dependent on the basin's water—Salt Lake City,

Denver, Los Angeles, Phoenix, Las Vegas, Tucson, and Albuquerque—while numerous smaller towns dot the region. The basin's forested mountainsides are largely in federal ownership and managed by the US Forest Service for multiple use, which today encompasses recreation, wildlife, and wilderness, along with a dwindling level of extractive activities. The BLM administers the largest amount of federal land in the basin, namely the lower-elevation, mostly arid lands. Other landowners include the US Fish and Wildlife Service, which oversees the basin's national wildlife refuges, Native American tribes, whose reservation lands extend across broad expanses, and the basin states, which oversee school trust lands acquired at statehood to support public education.[33]

The "crown jewels" of the Colorado River Basin are its national park units along the river corridors. These units, working roughly downriver, include Rocky Mountain National Park; Dinosaur National Monument; Black Canyon of the Gunnison National Park; Curecanti National Recreation Area; Arches National Park; Canyonlands National Park; Glen Canyon National Recreation Area; Rainbow Bridge National Monument; Capitol Reef National Park; Bryce Canyon National Park; Zion National Park; Saguaro National Park; Grand Canyon National Park; and Lake Mead National Recreation Area. Other units outside the river corridors include Mesa Verde National Park, Petrified Forest National Park, Canyon de Chelly National Monument, and Hovenweep National Monument. Collectively, these National Park Service-administered sites protect more than six million acres and host more than 35 million visitors annually, offering diverse recreational, cultural, and educational experiences.[34] In most instances, the units' scenic and natural characteristics, as well as associated recreational opportunities, have some connection to the river system. The Grand Canyon has been carved over eons by Colorado River flows, and the river is regularly characterized as the national park's heart and soul. The same is true for the Black Canyon of the Gunnison, which has been shaped by Gunnison River flows.

The basin's national parks are flanked by other federally protected lands, reflecting widespread acceptance of John Muir's preservation ethic. The idea of preserving large swathes of public land in largely undeveloped condition has taken several forms, including wilderness, wildlife refuge, and national monument designations. In fact, nearly 40 percent of federal acreage in the lower 48 states is protected by law or rule,[35] representing a significant national commitment to nature conservation. In many locations, these diverse protective designations form a de facto network of protected lands safeguarding large landscapes.[36] In the Colorado River Basin, Grand Canyon National Park is bordered by Grand Canyon-Parashant National Monument and Vermillion Cliffs National Monument, and connected upstream to Glen Canyon National Recreation Area and downstream to Lake Mead National Recreation Area—creating an expansive protected landscape along the river corridor.[37] In southeastern Utah, Canyonlands National Park, Glen Canyon National Recreation Area, Dark Canyon Wilderness Area, and the revised Bears Ears National Monument create another expansive, legally protected landscape. In southern Nevada, Lake Mead National Recreation Area conjoins Grand Canyon National Park, Gold Butte National Monument, BLM-managed wilderness areas, and a large state park. And in the Colorado River's headwaters, Rocky Mountain National Park abuts four federally designated wilderness areas. All of this reflects a deep federal commitment to preservation within the basin, as well as the need to manage these interconnected complexes on a landscape scale to maximize their conservation value.

Several national parks in the Colorado River Basin also adjoin Native American reservations, making tribes an increasingly important force in public land matters.[38] Because most of the basin's reservations are lightly populated, reservation lands adjacent to parks often provide a de facto buffer protecting sensitive park resources. That is not always true, however. Activities on nearby reservation lands can adversely impact park resources and visitor experiences. On the Navajo reservation, the coal-burning Navajo Generating Station has long polluted Southwestern skies, though the plant recently shut down.[39] On the Hualapai reservation, helicopters removing Colorado River rafters at Grand Canyon National Park's western end significantly disrupt the natural quietude. At the same time, tribes have sought to safeguard sacred places and cultural sites, a goal shared with southwestern national park units. The Navajo Tribal Council recently rejected a proposal to construct a tramway and resort just outside Grand Canyon National Park that would have permanently marred the landscape and damaged an area regarded as sacred by tribal members. An intertribal group also spearheaded the original Bears Ears National Monument proposal, convincing President Obama to protect more than 1.35 million acres adjacent to the Canyonlands and Glen Canyon park units.[40] President Trump has since radically reduced the monument's size, but tribes and other parties have challenged this action in federal court.[41] In short, the basin's park managers cannot ignore tribal interests and concerns—a point explored further in Part III of this volume.

National Park Policy: An Emergent Ecological Perspective

The Colorado River Basin's national parks are managed for preservation rather than Powell's utilitarian purposes. In 1916, just fourteen years after Powell's death, Congress adopted the National Park Service Organic Act,[42] establishing the national park system and the Park Service. The legislation instructed the Park Service to manage the national parks "to conserve the scenery and the natural and historic objects and the wild life therein, and to provide for the enjoyment of the same . . . by such means as will leave them unimpaired for the enjoyment of future generations."[43] Early Park Service management policies sought to protect scenery and promote visitation. The agency largely ignored science to ensure attractive venues for visitors—basically engaging in "facade" management.[44] In the 1960s, however, the Park Service changed direction and began emphasizing science-based management, incorporating ecological insights into management policies. To meet its statutory obligation to conserve park resources in an "unimpaired" condition, the Park Service and the federal courts have concluded that resource protection and environmental values take priority over visitor services or activities that might harm these resources.[45]

Ecological science has demonstrated how interconnected the national parks are to each other and surrounding landscapes. Echoing John Muir's insight that everything in the universe is "hitched" together, ecologists have shown how watersheds are really one functioning unit, how wildlife habitat and migration corridors span multiple jurisdictional venues, and how pollution sources impact distant lands and resources. Powell understood such connections too, as reflected in his admonishments to employ scientific principles and to establish "watershed commonwealths" to manage the West's waters wisely as the lifeblood of downstream forests and grasses essential to early settlers.[46] Scientists have translated the dynamic relationship between species, processes, and functions into the ecosystem concept,[47] which is generally accepted as the defining basis for federal policy.

The federal land management agencies, acknowledging that artificial boundary lines do not conform to natural conditions, have each endorsed some form of ecosystem management.[48] The agencies have recognized the need to coordinate planning and management decisions to better account for climate change, wildlife movement, fire events, water flows, and transient pollution. The Park Service manages its lands "to preserve fundamental physical and biological processes, as well as individual species, features, and plant and animal communities," understanding that "park units must be managed in the context of their larger ecosystems."[49] The Forest Service instructs managers to prepare landscape-level assessments at the outset of forest-planning processes to account for watersheds, ecological processes, climate change, wildland fire, and the like.[50] These ecosystem management approaches place national parks at the core of larger ecosystems, making them central factors in resource planning and management decisions. Faced with climate change, scientists and land managers have embraced the related notion of landscape-scale conservation, effectively expanding ecosystem management to an even larger scale.[51]

The Colorado River Basin's national parks plainly demonstrate regional ecological and other interconnections. Maps show the basin's national parks forming an almost unbroken chain running down the Colorado River and its tributaries across Utah, Arizona, and Nevada, with additional units further upstream in Colorado (see map 3). Multiple dams impact these park units, including the Aspinall Unit, Flaming Gorge, Glen Canyon, and Hoover dams (see map 2). The dams have altered the flow regime, affecting the ecological composition of river corridors, primarily by alleviating springtime flooding, reducing sediment load, and changing water temperature, which has altered riverbanks, nutrient flows, and habitat. Several warm-water fish species are imperiled, while non-native, cold-water fish species have taken over river stretches below dams. Tamarisk and other non-native vegetation have invaded river corridors. Similarly, with population growth in and around the basin, the increased human presence—off-road vehicle use, livestock grazing, road construction, etc.—has negatively affected national park resources by increasing erosion, water pollution, and wildlife habitat destruction. Resource development on nearby federal and state lands, such as oil and gas exploration or uranium mining, has also adversely affected park wildlife and viewsheds, as well as air and water quality. This fragmented landscape calls out for better-coordinated management processes that take full account of science and the region's ecological and cultural values.

Parks, People, and Commerce

The Park Service's non-impairment mandate presents difficult management dilemmas as more and more people seek the national park experience. In the Colorado River Basin, park visitation numbers and recreational pressures have escalated dramatically in recent years—something

Powell could not have imagined. In Grand Canyon, Zion, and Bryce Canyon national parks, the agency has imposed limits on visitors and automobiles. Zion and Bryce Canyon have established shuttle systems to eliminate auto congestion and exhaust pollution, while Grand Canyon has experimented with a railroad to limit congestion on the popular South Rim. The Grand Canyon rafting experience is so popular that the Park Service has long limited daily launches to protect fragile beaches and maintain a quality experience. But these limits have repeatedly generated conflict between commercial outfitters and individual boaters, prompting a series of river management plans and related lawsuits.[52] At Canyonlands National Park, the Park Service found itself entangled in litigation when it closed the Salt Creek drainage to off-road vehicles to protect the stream and adjacent soils.[53] While these controversies appear to pit different recreationists against one another, underlying economic concerns often bring powerful commercial interests—park concessionaires, the Outdoor Industry Association, and gear manufacturing companies—into the fray.

Although national parks do not support the extractive activities Powell championed, the parks have come to play vital roles in state and local economies. This is certainly true within the Colorado River Basin. In 2017, 331 million park visitors spent an estimated $18.2 billion in local gateway regions across the country, which supported 306,000 jobs.[54] That same year, the basin's national parks attracted more than 35 million visitors, who spent in excess of $2.5 billion in local communities and supported 34,000 jobs.[55] The economic significance of the region's national parks now outstrips that of traditional natural resource industries, such as mining, ranching, or oil and gas development.[56]

Contemporary economic realities associated with national park tourism and recreation illustrate how much the basin state economies have evolved. Utah, for example, is aggressively promoting its national parks as the "Mighty Five" in a worldwide advertising campaign bringing record visitation to Zion, Arches, and the state's other national parks. The town of Moab, situated on the doorstep of Arches and Canyonlands national parks, rebranded itself during the 1980s, shifting from the "Uranium Capital of the World" to the "Mountain Biking Capital of the World," dramatically enhancing its economic fortunes.[57] Grand Canyon National Park continues to attract visitors from around the world, while international visitation has soared across the basin's national parks. Economic studies report similar positive returns for Western towns and counties situated near national parks or other federally protected lands, bringing benefits in the form of recreation-related employment, new affluent residents, footloose entrepreneurs, and available capital.[58] Unsurprisingly, economic pressures associated with the basin's rapidly growing tourism and recreation economy have created new tensions for the Park Service in meeting its non-impairment responsibility.

CONTEMPLATING THE FUTURE: INTO THE UNKNOWN AGAIN

As the twenty-first century unfolds, the Colorado River Basin's national parks will continue playing a prominent role within the region. The fundamental idea of preserving public land in a near-natural condition—as a national park or other protective designation—is now entrenched in public land policy. For the basin, with its unique natural and cultural features as well as evolving economic realities, this national commitment to nature preservation presages additional park designations or expansions. As steward of these special places, the National Park Service's commitment to scientific management is only likely to deepen. As it does, the Park Service and its sister federal land management agencies will be compelled to embrace the notion of landscape-scale management to address the basin's ever-changing environment, including the effects of climate change and growing human pressures.[59] Of course, controversy will continue to dog the basin's parks and other public lands, but ongoing social and economic changes virtually ensure that the conservation impulses behind the national park idea will grow in importance. Although John Wesley Powell would not recognize the basin's landscape today, he might take heart that several of his fundamental ideas lie beneath the shape it has taken.

An Enduring Commitment to Nature Conservation

The nation's early-twentieth-century turn toward preservation is today reflected in our extensive national park system.[60] Focused on resource use and development, Powell could not have anticipated the evolution of such an expansive system. Yet, Powell recognized the extraordinary character of the Grand Canyon and, late in life, endorsed protecting it as a national park. Since then, that same impulse has taken hold across the basin. During the past century, both Congress and presidents have protected the region's special places as new national parks, national monuments, wilderness areas, and the like. In several cases, Congress has expanded basin parks to protect their special features or values.[61] In other cases, after the President—often over local objection—has designated a new national monument, Congress has converted the area into a national park.[62] This was true for Grand Canyon, Zion, Bryce Canyon, and Arches national monuments. These developments testify to the strong, ongoing national commitment to preserving the basin's special federal lands—a sentiment that bodes well for new protective designations in coming years. Today, the basin's preserved lands are as integral and valuable to the basin as were the precious water sources that Powell sought to harness in his day.

National parks are so integral to the basin that their presence is prompting new landscape conservation initiatives that will only strengthen in the years ahead. Powell, who invoked science to promote watershed-based management policies, would recognize the parallels between his proposals and today's landscape management concepts—both designed to sustain critical resources. With the Colorado River and its tributaries connected to many of the basin's national parks, broad-scale planning and decision-making are imperative to preserve important natural values. In fact, the responsible federal agencies and the basin states are currently engaged in several coordinated management efforts involving Colorado River flows and endemic species,[63] which suggests that inter-jurisdictional coordination arrangements involving the region's public lands are tenable. Because the basin's parks generally conjoin other public lands, there is an obvious need—and opportunity—to coordinate management efforts for such shared resources as wildlife, water, and airsheds. Contemporary ecosystem and climate science not only supports landscape-level management policies, but also helps to define the scale for such planning efforts. As a person committed to science-based management, Powell would understand the rationale for managing the basin's federal lands at a landscape scale, and he might also confirm the wisdom of viewing the basin's national parks as central to this effort.

The centrality of national parks to federal land management in the Colorado River Basin is bolstered by social, cultural, and economic changes that will only accelerate during the twenty-first century. With increasing urbanization, population growth, and economic prosperity, people are traveling to national parks in record numbers, seeking quietude and outdoor experiences similar to those John Muir extolled in his writings. Nature conservation and environmental values continue to rank high in public opinion polls,[64] and that is unlikely to change in the years ahead. As tourism and recreation assume an ever-greater role on public lands, national parks have become "cash cows" for nearby communities,[65] enhancing the parks' economic value and fostering important local support. The basin states are no exception. They promote national parks, seeking to draw more visitors and capture additional revenue at both the state and local levels. Meanwhile, extractive activities on the region's public lands have declined during the past several decades, with the exception of energy development,[66] though even this industry is evolving toward solar and wind power. Simply put, the economic and social importance of the basin's national parks will only increase over time, lending momentum to efforts to safeguard and expand these special places.

The Controversies Ahead

The Colorado River Basin's national parks will doubtless continue to evoke controversy. Dramatic increases in park visitation already confront park officials with difficult choices for managing crowds without impairing park resources or diminishing the visitor experience. One option the Park Service has long resisted is limiting access to popular parks, such as Grand Canyon, Zion, and Arches, during peak times. Restrictions are in place for automobiles at several parks and for whitewater rafting and backcountry camping in others.[67] Outside the parks, new federal Master Lease Planning policies were recently implemented—though now reversed—to limit mining and fossil fuel leasing on public lands adjacent to parks.[68] The pressure to reinstitute similar policies is unlikely to abate, just as the public interest in protecting additional federal acreage will not soon subside, renewing the age-old preservation versus development debate. This debate underlies the controversy over the expansive Bears Ears and Grand Staircase-Escalante national monument designations respectively decreed by Presidents Obama and Clinton. These designations had important implications for the basin's national parks, because several parks abutted the original monument boundaries and were thereby buffered from new industrial and other threatening activities. The same debate continues over proposed wilderness designations on the basin's undisturbed public lands,[69] many of which border national parks and would lend additional protection.

These controversies will ultimately be resolved either in a political or judicial forum. Both Congress and the president are involved with these manifold land-designation and resource-management issues, highlighting the political nature of public land policy. This reality is illustrated by varied legislative proposals to accelerate energy development on the basin's federal lands and by President Trump's order, noted above, attempting to dramatically revise the Bears Ears and Grand Staircase-Escalante national monument boundaries. This order and similar actions have prompted litigation, making federal courts an increasingly important institution for resolving public land and national park conflicts. Powell, whose own policy proposals prompted congressional backlash, would recognize the inherently political nature of these controversies, and the reality that new public land policies will inevitably require time before gaining acceptance. And Powell, who also envisioned a role for courts in resolving controversies within his watershed commonwealths,[70] would not be disturbed to learn that the federal judiciary has assumed a key role in resolving today's natural resource controversies.

Future Reforms

Moving forward, legal and institutional reforms are essential to sustain and enhance the important role national parks play in the Colorado River Basin. These reforms must reflect ongoing scientific insights regarding climate change, the region's growing populace, mounting visitation, and shifting economic realities. Because science-driven, landscape-level conservation has gained acceptance within the Park Service and other land management agencies, Congress should consider legislation endorsing landscape-scale planning in agency decision-making processes. Congress should also strengthen current statutory coordination mandates to ensure national park concerns are fully considered in management decisions on adjacent federal lands. Coordinated interagency planning could help shift park crowds and certain recreational activities outside parks onto nearby public lands better-suited to accommodate them. A clear congressional statement empowering park managers to regulate (and even limit) visitation and recreation would clarify their authority in dealing with these mounting problems. To address damage on the basin's public lands from industrial activity and unregulated recreation, congressional support for ecological restoration would help improve the health of these lands for conservation-related purposes. As the pace of change quickens within the basin, legislation legitimizing adaptive management strategies would help to address climate change and other environmental problems.

The Colorado River Basin is a better-known and different place today than in Powell's time. Much of the basin remains in federal hands, and its national parks have come to occupy a central position within the region. Preservation ideas have attained co-equal status with Powell's utilitarian, resource-development ideas. A science-based approach to resource management is now widely practiced in national parks and elsewhere on the public lands, though political considerations continue to muddle agency priorities. Landscape-scale management has secured a foothold within the Park Service and other agencies—a development mirroring Powell's call for watershed-based management. With climate change and population growth portending dramatic changes, a coordinated, landscape-level planning approach is more important than ever to sustain the basin's national parks in an unimpaired condition for future generations to enjoy. These challenges are no less daunting than those confronting Powell in the era of Western settlement. Drawing upon his wisdom as well as our own hard-earned knowledge, and acknowledging the important role national parks now occupy in the basin, these public land management challenges should prove surmountable in the years ahead.

NOTES

1. Wallace Stegner, *Beyond the Hundredth Meridian: John Wesley Powell and the Second Opening of the West* (Boston: Houghton Mifflin, 1954), 54–115.

2. John Wesley Powell, "Institutions for the Arid Lands," *Century* 40 (1890). See also Select Committee on Irrigation of Arid Lands, Ceding the Arid Lands to the States and Territories, H.R. Rep. No. 3767, serial 2888 (1891).

3. John Wesley Powell, "The Non-Irrigable Lands of the Arid Region," *Century* 39 (1890): 916.

4. Powell, "Institutions for the Arid Lands," 114.

5. Ibid., 115.

6. Ibid.

7. Donald Worster, *A River Running West: The Life of John Wesley Powell* (New York: Oxford University Press, 2002), 471.

8. Yellowstone National Park Protection Act, 17 Stat. 32 (1872). See Alfred Runte, *National Parks: The American Experience,* 4th ed. (Lanham: Rowman and Littlefield, 2010), 33–41.

9. Powell, "Institutions for the Arid Lands," 116.

10. John Wesley Powell, *Canyons of the Colorado* (1895), 390, https://www.gutenberg.org/files/8082/8082-h/8082-h.htm.

11. John Muir, *My First Summer in the Sierra* (Boston: Houghton Mifflin, 1911), 110.

12. John Muir to Theodore Roosevelt, April 21, 1908, in *The Life and Letters of John Muir,* ed. William Badè (Boston: Houghton Mifflin, 1924), chapter

18, https://vault.sierraclub.org/john_muir_exhibit/life/life_and_letters/chapter_18.aspx.

13. Robert W. Righter, *The Battle over Hetch Hetchy: America's Most Controversial Dam and the Birth of Modern Environmentalism* (New York: Oxford University Press, 2005).

14. Powell, "Institutions for the Arid Lands"; John Muir, "Treasures of the Yosemite," *Century* 40, no. 4 (1890).

15. Worster, *A River Running West*, 471.

16. Ibid.

17. Donald Worster, *A Passion for Nature: The Life of John Muir* (New York: Oxford University Press, 2008), 329.

18. Powell, *Canyons of the Colorado*, 251.

19. Frederick Jackson Turner, "The Significance of the Frontier in American History (a paper read at the American Historical Society meeting, July 12, 1893)," accessed June 20, 2018, http://nationalhumanitiescenter.org/pds/gilded/empire/text1/turner.pdf. Between 1889 and 1890, Congress granted six Western territories statehood, demonstrating the level of settlement and development achieved across the West by 1890 (Amy Bridges, *Democratic Beginnings: Founding the Western States* [Lawrence: University Press of Kansas, 2015], 137–56).

20. Runte, *National Parks*, 50–55.

21. National Park Service Organic Act, 39 Stat. 535 (1916).

22. Forest Reserve Act of 1891, 26 Stat. 1103 (1891), repealed Pub. L. 94-579, 90 Stat. 2792 (1976).

23. Organic Administration Act, 16 U.S.C. § 473 (1897) et seq.

24. Lacey Act, 31 Stat. 187 (1900), modified and recodified as 16 U.S.C. §§ 3371–3378 (1981).

25. Antiquities Act, 16 U.S.C. § 431–433 (1906), recodified as 54 U.S.C. §§ 320301–320303 (2014).

26. Carol Hardy Vincent, US Library of Congress, Congressional Research Service, *Federal Land Ownership: Overview and Data*, R42346 (2017).

27. Samuel P. Hays, *The American People and the National Forests: The First Century of the U.S. Forest Service* (Pittsburgh: University of Pittsburgh Press, 2009).

28. James R. Skillen, *The Nation's Largest Landlord: The Bureau of Land Management in the American West* (Lawrence: University Press of Kansas, 2009).

29. National Park Service Organic Act, 16 U.S.C. § 1 (1916), recodified as 54 U.S.C. § 100101 (2014); Robert B. Keiter, *To Conserve Unimpaired: The Evolution of the National Park Idea* (Washington, DC: Island Press, 2013), 14–15.

30. Robert L. Fischman, *The National Wildlife Refuges: Coordinating a Conservation System through Law* (Washington, DC: Island Press, 2003).

31. Robert B. Keiter, *Keeping Faith with Nature: Ecosystems, Democracy, and America's Public Lands* (New Haven: Yale University Press, 2003), 22–25.

32. George Cameron Coggins et al., *Federal Public Land and Resources Law*, 7th ed. (New York: Foundation Press, 2014), 733–37.

33. On state trust lands, see Jon A. Souder and Sally K. Fairfax, *State Trust Lands: History, Management, and Sustainable Use* (Lawrence: University Press of Kansas, 1996).

34. These figures are compiled from several sources, including National Park Service Visitor Use Statistics, at https://irma.nps.gov/Stats/.

35. Robert B. Keiter, "Toward a National Conservation Network Act: Transforming Landscape Conservation on the Public Lands into Law," *Harvard Environmental Law Review* 42 (2018): 65–85.

36. Ibid., 111–27.

37. Grand Canyon National Park also lies adjacent to or nearby the Grand Staircase-Escalante National Monument in southern Utah, several Indian reservations, and the undeveloped Kaibab National Forest.

38. To illustrate tribal political clout, the Havasupai Tribe, advancing historical dispossession claims, convinced Congress to grant it 185,000 acres of national park and national forest lands as part of the 1975 Grand Canyon National Park Enlargement Act. Keiter, *To Conserve Unimpaired*, 126–28.

39. Dylan Brown, "Navajo plant shutdown marks end of an era," *Greenwire*, November 19, 2019, https://www.eenews.net/greenwire/2019/11/19/stories/1061592567.

40. President Barack Obama, Establishment of the Bears Ears National Monument, Proclamation No. 9558, 82 Fed. Reg. 1139 (January 5, 2017).

41. President Donald Trump, Modifying the Bears Ears National Monument, Proclamation No. 9681, 82 Fed. Reg. 58081 (December 8, 2017).

42. National Park Service Organic Act, 16 U.S.C. § 1 et seq., recodified as 54 U.S.C. § 100100 et seq. On the adoption of the 1916 organic act, see Robin Winks, "The National Park Service Act of 1916: 'A Contradictory Mandate'?," *Denver University Law Review* 74 (1997).

43. National Park Service Organic Act, 16 U.S.C. § 1, recodified as 54 U.S.C. § 100100.

44. Richard West Sellars, *Preserving Nature in the National Parks: A History* (New Haven: Yale University Press, 1997), 4–5.

45. National Park Service, *Management Policies* (Washington, DC: US Dept. of Interior, 2006), 11–13; Bicycle Trails Council of Marin v. Babbitt, 82 F.3d 1445, 1448 (9th Cir. 1996); Mausolf v. Babbitt, 125 F.3d 661, 668–669 (8th Cir. 1997).

46. John Wesley Powell, "The Irrigable Lands of the Arid Region," *Century* 39 (1890): 766–76.

47. Frank B. Golley, *A History of the Ecosystem Concept in Ecology: More than the Sum of Its Parts* (New Haven: Yale University Press, 1993); Daniel B. Botkin, *Discordant Harmonies: A New Ecology for the Twenty-first Century* (New York: Oxford University Press, 1990).

48. Keiter, *Keeping Faith with Nature*; James R. Skillen, *Federal Ecosystem Management: Its Rise, Fall, and Afterlife* (Lawrence: University Press of Kansas, 2015); Robert B. Keiter, "Public Lands and Law Reform: Putting Theory, Policy, and Practice in Perspective," *Utah Law Review* 4 (2005): 1192–1202.

49. National Park Service, *Management Policies*, 36.

50. 36 C.F.R. § 219.5 (2018).

51. On landscape conservation, see National Academies of Sciences, Engineering, and Medicine, *A Review of the Landscape Conservation Cooperatives* (Washington, DC: National Academies Press, 2016), https://doi.org/10.17226/21829; Matthew McKinney et al., *Large Landscape Conservation: A Strategic Framework for Policy and Action* (Cambridge, MA: Lincoln Institute of Land Policy, 2010).

52. National Park Service, "Colorado River Management Plan Record of Decision," February 17, 2006, https://www.nps.gov/grca/learn/management/upload/CRMP_ROD_2006.pdf; National Park Service, "Colorado River Management Plan Final Environmental Impact Statement," November 2005, https://www.nps.gov/grca/learn/management/upload/CRMP-Volume-One.pdf; River Runners for Wilderness v. Martin, 593 F.3d 1064 (9th Cir. 2010).

53. Southern Utah Wilderness Alliance v. National Park Service, 387 F. Supp. 2d 1178 (D. Utah 2005).

54. In addition, the national parks generated $11.9 billion in labor income, $20.3 billion in value added, and $35.8 billion in economic output in the national economy. See National Park Service, "2017 National Park Visitor Spending Effects: Economic Contributions to Local Communities, States, and the Nation" (2018), https://www.nps.gov/nature/customcf/NPS_Data_Visualization/docs/NPS_2017_Visitor_Spending_Effects.pdf.

55. Ibid.

56. Headwaters Economics, "The Value of Public Lands" (2017), https://headwaterseconomics.org/public-lands/public-lands-research.

57. Keiter, *Keeping Faith with Nature*, 222–27.

58. Ray Rasker et al., "The Effect of Protected Federal Lands on Economic Prosperity in the Non-metropolitan West," *Journal of Regional Analysis & Policy* 43, no. 2 (2013): 110.

59. Patrick Gonzalez et al., *Disproportionate Magnitude of Climate Change in United States National Parks*, Environ. Res. Lett. 13 (2018), http://iopscience.iop.org/article/10.1088/1748-9326/aade09/pdf.

60. "National Park Service Overview," National Park Service, accessed July 3, 2018, https://www.nps.gov/aboutus/upload/NPS-Overview-07-03-18.pdf.

61. For example, Congress expanded Grand Canyon National Park in 1975 by 400,000 acres. Grand Canyon National Park Enlargement Act, Pub. L. 93-620, 88 Stat. 2089 (1975). On several occasions, Congress has enlarged Rocky Mountain National Park. 16 U.S.C. § 192 (1917); 16 U.S.C. § 192b (1930); 16 U.S.C. § 192b-1 (1945).

62. Mark Squillace, "The Monumental Legacy of the Antiquities Act of 1906," *Georgia Law Review* 37 (2003): 476–514.

63. Robert W. Adler, *Restoring Colorado River Ecosystems: A Troubled Sense of Immensity* (Washington, DC: Island Press, 2007), 19–23. The Colorado River coordination efforts have been driven by several forces: litigation, drought, practical realities, and sheer necessity. Although similar forces are not yet as evident on the basin's public lands, the experiences gleaned from river coordination efforts should encourage similar efforts on these lands, where many of the same agencies and players are involved.

64. Pennsylvania Land Trust Association, "National Poll Results: How Americans View Conservation," 2017, https://conservationtools.org/guides/111-national-poll-results; Colorado College, State of the Rockies Project, "The 2018 Conservation in the West Poll," January 25, 2018, https://www.coloradocollege.edu/stateoftherockies/conservationinthewest.

65. Keiter, *To Conserve Unimpaired*, 103–5.

66. Keiter, *Keeping Faith with Nature*, 258–72; Jan G. Laitos and Thomas A. Carr, "The Transformation on Public Lands," *Ecology Law Quarterly* 26 (1999).

67. Keiter, *To Conserve Unimpaired*, 54–59, 70–72.

68. Elena Connolly, "BLM Eliminates Master Leasing Plans, Simplifies O&G Leasing," *Western Wire,* February 2, 2018, http://westernwire.net/blm-eliminates-master-leasing-plans-simplifies-og-leasing.

69. Jedediah S. Rogers, *Roads in the Wilderness: Conflict in Canyon Country* (Salt Lake City: University of Utah Press, 2013); Doug Goodman and Daniel McCool, *Contested Landscape: The Politics of Wilderness in Utah and the West* (Salt Lake City: University of Utah Press, 1999).

70. Powell, "Institutions for the Arid Lands," 114–15.

CHAPTER 6

Who Is the "Public" on the Colorado River Basin's Public Lands?

PAUL HIRT

In a nation so enthusiastically committed to private property, it is easy to think of public lands as a historical anomaly in America's political economy. Indeed, many conservative economists and policymakers interpret public ownership as aberrant to our nation's traditions and core values. Nothing could be further from the truth. Both private *and* public property have been fundamental components of America's institutional landscape from the nation's founding. Even in the colonial era, Americans created and defended—at least for certain privileged races—public access to community woodlots, grazing commons, public roads, urban parks, commercial harbors, navigable waters, schools, hospitals . . . the list goes on and on. These public properties and institutions are so ubiquitous and so embedded that we rarely stop to think about how important they are to civic order, equity, and quality of life; or how different—and diminished—our lives would be without them.

The federal land estate is one of the most important institutions of public ownership in America. Not surprisingly, it is also one of the region's most volatile topics of political debate. The US government's long history of acquiring the region's lands and resources over the last two centuries, and its policies for privatizing or reserving them for specific purposes, have repeatedly brought this public versus private debate into sharp relief. Between 1803 and 1853, the federal government acquired the entire western two-thirds of what is now the United States through warfare (for example, the Mexican-American War); treaties (including the Louisiana Purchase, the Oregon Treaty, and the Gadsden Purchase); and brute dispossession of the Indigenous inhabitants.[1] During this brief half century, the federal government acquired legal title, vis-à-vis other nation-states, to virtually everything from the Mississippi River to the Pacific Coast. It acquired most of the lands and waters of the Colorado River Basin in what is often called the "Mexican Cession" that ended the Mexican-American War in 1848. Small areas encompassing several basin tributaries were also acquired in the Texas Annexation of 1845 and the Gadsden Purchase of 1853, both of which were similarly arm-twisted from Mexico. Since the US government has constitutional authority to declare war and make treaties, it was the only institution capable of acquiring these vast lands intended for the nation's expansion at the expense of Indigenous peoples who saw their lands and sovereignty commensurately diminished.

In the nineteenth century, the US government sought to privatize most of this acquired land to stimulate Euro-American colonization. At first, land sales were the primary means for privatizing what was referred to as the "public domain." But during and after the Civil War, the federal government adopted a series of laws and land grants designed to get Western lands more quickly into the hands of homesteaders, railroad corporations, miners, farmers, ranchers, timber companies, and real estate developers.[2]

While the federal government embraced a policy of "disposal" of federal lands into private hands throughout the nineteenth century, it did not intend to dispose of *all* the lands it owned. Privatization was accompanied by a parallel policy of "reservation"—lands reserved for specific purposes or granted to states to use for revenue, education, and other public goods. These lands included reservations for military bases and later for tribes, as well as reservations for national parks (starting with Yellowstone in 1872), national forests (after 1891), irrigation projects (after 1902), and national wildlife refuges (after 1903).[3] Land ownership maps reveal that the federal government ultimately retained a very large percentage of the Colorado River Basin's lands and that Native American tribes, especially the Navajo, secured large reservations (see maps 3 and 4). The economies, cultures, and community life of the basin states are intricately tied to these public and reserved lands that make up four-fifths of the landscape.

Private property owners had virtual carte blanche to do as they pleased with their land during the nineteenth century, so long as they didn't cause major nuisances or significantly harm neighboring property values. This laissez-faire attitude modified quite a bit during the twentieth century, leading to more restrictions on what property owners could do on their land. These restrictions on individual liberty were designed to protect against harms to others and to the public welfare, such as property damage, pollution, exploitation of commons, and other injustices. Such public interventions have generated much hue and cry about losses of liberty and overbearing regulators. This is not new. The debate about restraints on the liberty of property owners was fundamental to the debate over slavery that led up to the Civil War.[4] Finding a balance between personal liberty and public order and justice remains one of the key features of American democratic deliberation.

The debate over private versus public is often messy and contentious. While decision-making for private property is still largely a matter for the owner to consider, decision-making for public properties must respond to interests and values of entire communities and states, as well as the nation as a whole. Some people think there is too much federal ownership in the West, while others believe privatization policies went too far, and some lands should be returned to the public domain. That debate is the price of democracy. As Winston Churchill wisely observed after World War Two: "No one pretends that democracy is perfect or all-wise. Indeed it has been said that democracy is the worst form of Government, except for all those other forms that have been tried."[5] Negotiating the cacophony of private and public interests to arrive at desirable regionwide ownership and management regimes is the great opportunity *and* great burden of those living in the Colorado River Basin. The path forward is indeed a "Great Unknown," but we do have wise, experienced guides whom we can consult for our journey.

POWELL'S GUIDANCE IN THE LATE NINETEENTH CENTURY

John Wesley Powell's life and work for the federal government came at a critical time of transition in the debate over public land policy. Powell came to adulthood during the Civil War, rising up the ranks to become a major in the Union Army, where he lost an arm in battle. Despite this extraordinary setback, after the war Powell led various government agencies as a geologist, ethnologist, explorer, and advisor to Congress and the executive branch on Western land development.[6] Before the war, the federal government had a fairly simple land policy: get the public domain surveyed as quickly as feasible and open it up for entry.

Unsurprisingly, there were numerous examples of graft and corruption in the process.[7]

By the 1860s, many members of Congress had grown concerned that a simple land-sale policy was both inefficiently slow and inequitable to rank-and-file homeseekers who could rarely outbid or outsmart wealthy land speculators and corporations. Passage of the Homestead Act in 1862 marked one of the first important departures in public land policy. A person with modest financial means could stake a claim to up to 160 acres of public land and get virtually free title after five years by making "improvements" and filing the proper paperwork. In 1862, Congress also passed the first of several Pacific Railway Acts that granted tens of millions of acres of public lands in the West to the Union Pacific, Northern Pacific, and other railroad companies to use as collateral for building transcontinental railways. The federal government eventually transferred 131 million acres to railroads.[8] In the three decades following the Civil War, Congress passed numerous additional laws providing a variety of grants of public lands for a multitude of purposes to a wide array of citizens and businesses. Though many laws were ill-designed and poorly implemented, they nevertheless met the broad goal of getting public lands and natural resources rapidly into private hands to promote settlement and economic development.[9]

The next important stage in land policy came in 1891 with the General Revision Act,[10] crafted to address well-publicized failures, frauds, and inefficiencies of the land laws. Essentially, Congress sought to limit the ability of the landed class to monopolize land acquisition, and to systematize and reduce some of the chaos in homesteading on the public domain. The act barred land auctions, which wealthy speculators had dominated, and repealed preemption laws that had benefited and encouraged squatters. It also sought to put land laws on a firmer scientific foundation. For example, it repealed the 1873 Timber Culture Act, which was based on the flawed assumption that planting trees would increase rainfall on the arid plains. Powell himself sought to debunk that assumption.[11]

Regardless of the degree to which the intended goals of the 1891 General Revision Act were achieved, they were arguably laudable policies. Moreover, they were central to John Wesley Powell's vision of orderly, planned, and scientifically-based community development in the arid region, which posited that a frontier free-for-all approach would be doomed to failure. For example, in his 1878 *Arid Lands Report,* Powell stated: "To a great extent, the redemption of all these lands will require extensive and comprehensive plans, for the execution of which aggregated capital and cooperative labor will be necessary."[12]

Consistent with the goals of the Homestead Act and General Revision Act, Powell felt strongly that rank-and-file householders and small businesses should be protected from unfair competition by wealthy corporations that held advantages far beyond the means of the middle class. In an 1893 speech to the International Irrigation Congress, Powell admitted: "My prime interest is in such a system as will develop the greatest number of cottage homes for the people. I am more interested in the home and the cradle than I am in the bank counter."[13]

Tucked into the 1891 General Revision Act was a little-noticed provision—Section 24—that proved extremely consequential for America's public lands. It stated that "the President of the United States may, from time to time, set apart and reserve . . . any part of the public lands wholly or in part covered in timber or undergrowth, whether of commercial value or not, as public reservations."[14] Over the next seven years, presidents Harrison and Cleveland proclaimed nearly 40 million acres of forest reserves, which became the foundation of the national forest system during Teddy Roosevelt's administration. By the end of Roosevelt's second term in 1909, the newly established Forest Service administered approximately 150 million acres of national forests.[15] Congress articulated the purpose of the forest reservations in the Pettigrew Act of 1897: "To improve and protect the forest within the reservation, or for the purpose of securing favorable conditions of water flows, and to furnish a continuous supply of timber for the use and necessities of citizens of the United States." Here, the core values of Progressive Era conservation policy are on display: the federal government should use its landed assets to provide and protect public values that might be harmed by uncoordinated and potentially short-sighted private development.

This was the origin of the conservation movement and the start of an irreversible trend toward the federal government retaining most of its remaining land holdings in the West rather than continuing to aggressively dispose of them.[16] From the 1890s through the 1930s, the US government developed an extraordinary public estate of national forests, national parks, national wildlife refuges, national recreation areas, military reservations, flood control projects, irrigation projects, and more. Powell would not live to see all this unfold, but he witnessed its origins during his last productive decade in the 1890s.

Surprisingly, Powell's writings from the 1870s to the 1890s do not reveal him as being in the vanguard of this trend toward federal land retention and conservation. Instead, he seems to have remained a product of the previous generation that embraced privatization and a laissez-faire policy out of Washington, DC. Consistently, he advocated for local control and local/regional decision-making, being equally skeptical of the ability of national wealth-seeking corporations and national governing institutions to properly direct economic development in the Colorado River Basin and the broader West. One of the best examples of this perspective comes from Powell's 1890 essay "Institutions for the Arid Lands":

> [I]n the name of the men who labor I demand that the laborers shall employ themselves; that the enterprise shall be controlled by the men who have the genius to organize, and whose homes are in the lands developed; and that the money shall be furnished by the people; and I say to the Government: Hands off! Furnish the people with institutions of justice, and let them do the work for themselves.[17]

The narrative throughout Powell's famous 1878 *Arid Lands Report* exhibits the same laissez-faire and utilitarian perspective. Chapter 1 elaborates Powell's land classification scheme, in which all lands in the arid West are divided into three simple categories: irrigable, pasturage, and timber. Note that the terms do not actually describe a land type but rather its utility—farming, grazing, and lumbering. Lands without such utility were virtually absent from his discourse, except on occasion when he refers to them as "wastes." In chapter 2, Powell alludes to two additional classifications, mineral and coal lands, once again privileging utility. In this report, he characterized forests as so abundant that regulation of their use was unnecessary: "In general it may be stated that the timber regions are fully adequate to the growth of all the forests which the industrial interests of the country will require if they can be protected from desolation by fire. No limitation to the use of the forests need be made."[18]

Even as late as 1890, the year before Congress passed the General Revision Act authorizing the president to create forest reservations, Powell criticized growing calls for federal management of public forest lands. In his 1890 *Century* article "The Non-Irrigable Lands of the Arid Region," Powell repeated his opposition to federal management of Western forests, acknowledging that there was great interest in this idea, but judging many of the arguments favoring it as "factitious."[19] In his counterpart essay on "Institutions for the Arid Lands," he further explained his reasoning: "If the forests are to be guarded, the people directly interested should perform the task.... [A] forestry organization under the hands of the General Government would become a hotbed of corruption."[20]

While Powell agreed that care must go into deciding which lands should be "denuded" of forest, he fervently advocated for those decisions to remain with the people living in the particular watershed, as they would presumably know the land and be forced to live with the consequences—"with wisdom you may prosper, but with folly you must fail."[21] This was definitely out of sync with the opinions of a growing cadre of professional foresters in the United States, most notably Gifford Pinchot, who by the 1890s was vigorously advocating for retention of federal forestlands and their scientific management by a professional agency to protect watersheds and provide a sustained yield of timber.[22]

For grasslands, or "pasturage" in Powell's terminology, he recommended a land tenure system of mid-sized ranches with property boundaries drawn so each family had access to water. Grazing would take place in unfenced commons.[23] This vision not only reflected the late-nineteenth-century utilitarian view of land, but also Powell's appreciation for Jeffersonian agrarianism—a preference for distributed land ownership and a recognition of the value of smallholdings in a democracy. Interestingly, while Powell felt irrigable land should be privately owned "in severalty," meaning a collection of individually owned parcels, he also embraced the idea of commons for both pasturage land and forested uplands. Powell felt strongly that rangelands and forests should be collectively managed by locals. For example, in Powell's testimony to the Montana Constitutional Convention of 1889, he forcefully argued that all land in a watershed should be controlled by the people who live there:

> [T]he government of the United States should cede all of the lands of that drainage basin to the people who live in that basin. . . . I believe that the people of the drainage basin themselves are more interested than any other people can be in that particular drainage basin—that they are the only people who can properly administer that trust, and I believe that the people who live along every valley in this country should be the people who control three things besides the land on which they live: they should have the control of the water; they should have the control of the common or pasturage lands, and they should have the control of the timber lands.[24]

While Powell was wary of wealthy interstate corporations, he was not opposed to corporate enterprise per se. Indeed, he thought corporate or collective endeavor was absolutely necessary to develop the arid region, but he worried about the risks of absentee ownership, water rights monopolies, and the potential loss of local self-reliance. Powell wanted financing, governance, and management regimes to be homegrown and rooted in the watersheds where people lived. Even for very large rivers like the Green and Colorado, Powell insisted regional cooperation was the answer, and resisted the siren call of federal involvement. But conventional wisdom was changing in the 1890s, just as Powell's influence as a policy advisor was waning. In 1902, the year Powell died, Congress passed the Newlands Reclamation Act, creating the dam-building agency that quickly morphed into the Bureau of Reclamation. It immediately launched five major reclamation projects across the West in 1903, including two within the Colorado River Basin: the Uncompahgre (Gunnison) project in Colorado and the Salt River Project in Arizona.

Powell remained so committed to local control that in only one of his published writings did he ever suggest that the federal government should retain ownership of public lands. In his essay "Institutions for the Arid Lands," Powell stated: "[T]he General Government must bear its part in the establishment of the institutions for the arid region. It is now the owner of most of the lands, and it must provide for the distribution of these lands to the people in part, and in part it must retain possession of them and hold them in trust for the districts." Lest anyone mistake his meaning, however, Powell immediately qualified this statement as follows: "Then let the General Government declare and provide by statute that the people of each district may control and use the timber, the pasturage, and the water powers, under specific laws enacted by themselves and by the States to which they belong."[25] The federal government might possess the land, but it would not control its use.

POWELL IN PERSPECTIVE

An old but influential 1966 monograph by historian Robert Wiebe, *The Search for Order—1877–1920*,[26] provides some clues as to why Powell may have resisted the trend toward an increasingly activist federal government and increasing attention to national interests in public land management. Wiebe argued that prior to industrialization, before the rise of urbanism and the transportation and communication revolutions, Americans mostly lived in "island communities," relatively independent and somewhat isolated human-scaled villages and towns where people knew their neighbors and had a significant degree of control over forces that shaped their lives. Social and cultural identity was anchored in localities and regions, not at the national level. Washington, DC was distant, weak, abstract, and mostly irrelevant to daily life.

With the rise of industrialization came the advent of national corporations that began affecting people and their communities in novel, often uncomfortable ways.[27] Transcontinental railroads connected far-flung towns, opened new markets, and launched new industries and manufacturing at scales unimaginable just a few decades earlier. The telegraph and telephone provided nearly instantaneous communication across distances that formerly required weeks or months of shipping for letters and newspapers to reach readers. The miraculous technology of electricity lit interiors and thoroughfares, vastly increased mechanization and productivity in factories, and sent trains and trolleys down urban and interurban tracks. More people moved to cities and cities sprawled ever larger. Assembly lines increasingly replaced skilled craftwork. The gap between rich and poor widened. Immigrants flooded the borders. Communities were transformed.

Many people were thrilled at this "modernization," but many were estranged and distrustful. Moreover, the changes and disruptions came at an ever-accelerating pace, engendering conversations in communities all across the nation about how change should be managed. Some sought to embrace and unfetter industrial capitalism and this so-called modernization. Some sought to channel it and ameliorate its negative consequences, such as labor exploitation and environmental pollution. Others sought to stymie the transformations and hold fast to the old order. All of this, in Wiebe's memorable words, represented a profound national search for order.

Order might come from many sources.

Some thought leaders hoped industrial capitalists would use their considerable organizational genius to design, from the top down, a more efficient, prosperous, and stable economic order that would lift all boats. Those hopes, however, rarely materialized, as the Gilded Age economy proved extraordinarily volatile, with hundreds of communities suffering booms and busts and wage laborers often working themselves to an early death without ever getting ahead.

Other thought leaders hoped organized labor might replace industrial capitalism as a ruling force in economic life, distributing America's wealth more broadly and ensuring the health and welfare of workers creating that wealth. But this dream, too, never gained much traction in nineteenth-century America.

A third and ultimately more successful approach to seeking order was to expand the power and reach of the national government to balance the power and reach of national corporations. That was the main strategy of Progressives from the 1890s through Teddy Roosevelt's administration.[28] And it was foundational to the Progressive Conservation movement led by Pinchot, Roosevelt, and others. This strategy had flaws and limitations, like any other, but it got results. By the turn of the twentieth century, some monopolies were being restrained, workers received protections, cities became cleaner, food and drugs got safer, health and education advanced, government bureaus grew more professional, and a new philosophy of wise, sustainable use of natural resources disseminated into popular culture and influenced many state and federal policymakers and business leaders alike.

Communities, then states, then the national government slowly but steadily expanded both citizen-empowerment measures (such as initiative, referendum, and recall) and government resources and regulatory power to promote responsible development, rein in abusive and damaging practices, increase transparency and accountability, and invest in public infrastructure and institutions. The national government, of course, had more financial resources than the states for this new role and increasingly became the only governing institution capable of going head to head with the likes of Rockefeller's Standard Oil, Carnegie Steel, Edison Electric, and J. P. Morgan Bank. Powell, up to his death, remained peculiarly unwilling to embrace this new powerful tool for social and economic betterment.

In his search for order, Powell remained staunchly committed to the island-community model of social and economic organization, as revealed in this quote from 1890 describing his ideal watershed commonwealth: "Thus it is that there is a body of interdependent and unified interests and values, all collected in one hydrographic basin, and all segregated by well-defined boundary lines from the rest of the world. The people in such a district have common interests, common rights, and common duties, and must necessarily work together for common purposes."[29] In light of how diverse and divided American society has always been, one might consider this vision of all people in a watershed sharing common interests and working toward common purposes unrealistic at best. Nevertheless, it still carries today a powerful magnetism: the idea that some force of nature, like a shared geography, might draw people together into a cooperative commonwealth. Ernest Callenbach's 1975 novel *Ecotopia* offers a twentieth-century version of this vision.[30]

Powell's equal resistance to the rising power of national corporations *and* the rising power of the national government positioned him in a limited intellectual space where he idealized a nineteenth-century vision of human-scaled, self-governing island communities that became increasingly anachronistic in the urban, industrial, and globalized twentieth century. Likewise, his view that federal lands should be controlled and managed by locals to serve their needs faded as a viable option in the face of the power of interstate and international timber and mining corporations seeking access to public lands. Was Powell being woefully naïve, or laudably idealistic? Whichever the case, his was not the path America took in the Colorado River Basin, or elsewhere, in the twentieth century.

Despite Powell's limited foresight about the role of national governing institutions in twentieth-century American land and water policy, he nevertheless embraced a forward-thinking brand of modernization that informed the Progressive Conservation movement: a commitment to rational, coordinated resource development governed by democratic institutions responsive to the people and mindful of the capabilities and limits of the local environment, particularly aridity. Powell never let go of his commitment to intelligent social design. He sought and fought for a republic that understood the interdependence of public and private enterprise, the combined value of both private ownership and the commons. He was a fierce defender of property rights, but also an articulate champion of collective enterprise, collaborative decision-making, and community-governed commons. He recognized that people living in a watershed do indeed have common interests and that social organization might be improved by coordinating our lives and economies around those interests.

THE NATION-CENTRIC POLITICAL ECONOMY OF THE TWENTIETH-CENTURY WEST

While Powell and many others worried about the increasing centralization of power in both the business sector and government, the trend seemed unavoidable. Indeed, it greatly accelerated during the first half of the twentieth century. The two world wars bound Americans to a single cause and forged a new kind of patriotic national identity that had largely eluded American culture in the nineteenth century. Earlier wars, like the War for Independence and the Civil War, pitted Americans against Americans. Even the Mexican-American War sharply divided the country North, South, and West. In contrast, World Wars I and II forged greater unity of purpose and a stronger national identity.

Importantly, they also propelled the federal government into the role of financier and orchestrator of the nation's manufacturing. The government raised taxes, provided loans, grants, and contracts to industry, incentivized factories to convert to military production, directed employment, provided housing for workers, rationed goods, etc. The federal government even briefly nationalized the railways during World War I. In all manner of ways, the American public learned from the two world wars how the federal government could use its authority, treasury, and expertise to mobilize the nation, restructure its economy, and accomplish extraordinary goals in the national interest.

The Depression between the wars taught Americans a few additional lessons about national power and responsibilities. The collapse of capitalism in 1929 and the following ten years of deep economic depression increased the public's sense that the federal government ought to be responsible for creating a social safety net, reducing risk in the business sector, protecting workers and the middle class, investing in infrastructure (public works), and providing many kinds of social goods that the private sector provided poorly or not at all.[31]

Public lands ranked high among the many resources available to the federal government for these endeavors. Public lands held large amounts of critical minerals like copper and energy resources like coal and oil. Public lands contained important rivers, hydroelectric dam sites, and reservoir locations that the Army Corps of Engineers and Bureau of Reclamation vigorously developed on behalf of the nation. Public lands provided large amounts of timber for the war effort in World War II, especially in California and the Pacific Northwest. Public lands were a location where unemployed young men could find work and skills during the Depression (the Civilian Conservation Corps) and where the government could stimulate the lagging economy by building roads, bridges, fire lookouts, and public facilities.

Increasingly, over the course of the twentieth century, the responsibilities and reach of federal agencies extended more and more deeply into people's lives and the broader economy. National programs sought to implement national aims to serve a national public. By the 1950s, the era of island communities, so formative of Powell's vision for the arid lands, had essentially vanished, with the exception of a few remote rural regions. Public lands could no longer be seen as an exclusive resource for local communities, nor would local interests completely control the use of those lands. They came to be cherished as an asset, a birthright, of all Americans.

THE COLORADO RIVER BASIN'S PUBLIC LAND ESTATE IN THE TWENTY-FIRST CENTURY

The US government's decision to retain a large, complex estate led to the creation of a fascinating patchwork of federal, tribal, state, and private landholdings in the West—a complexity that brings benefits as well as challenges to the sustainable management of lands in the Colorado River Basin. The vast majority of basin lands are federally owned and managed (see map 3). As described earlier, these lands were nearly all held for disposal by the General Land Office until 1891. A few military and Indian reservations had been carved out of this public domain land, but the rest were simply awaiting privatization. Then, over the next half century, wide swaths of the remaining public domain lands were transformed into national forests, national parks, national monuments, national wildlife refuges, and national recreation areas. A Grazing Service was created in 1939 to oversee federally owned grasslands of the arid West, and that agency was then merged with the General Land Office in 1946 to create the last of the great federal land agencies: the Bureau of Land Management (BLM).[32]

It is hard to overstate the complexity and significance of public lands in the Colorado River Basin. Take just the state of Colorado, for example. While its eastern half is largely state and private land, the western half is about 80 percent federal and Indian land.[33] It contains the headwaters of the Colorado River, the Rocky Mountains, and the high-elevation valleys and desert canyons of the Colorado Plateau. There are four national parks and eight national monuments, including 265,000-acre Rocky Mountain National Park. Surrounding these protected lands are 13 million acres of national forest, some of it protected as wilderness but most dedicated to multiple use. In addition, there are eight million acres of BLM lands, some protected but most dedicated to multiple use, plus four national wildlife refuges. There are also a handful of military reservations plus two Ute Indian reservations in the southwest part of the state.

Each category of public lands has a federal agency responsible for management that has accumulated a unique mission and mandate over the years. For example, the national forests are managed by the US Forest Service, and at least since 1960 they have been dedicated to "multiple use" and "sustained yield."[34] BLM lands have a similar mandate codified in the Federal Land Policy and Management Act of 1976.[35] The wildlife refuges are managed by the US Fish and Wildlife Service, which also implements the Endangered Species Act. They are dedicated to fish and wildlife conservation but also generally open to hunting, fishing, bird-watching, and other recreation. Wildlife refuges often include intensively managed environments, such as artificially constructed and maintained wetlands. National Recreation Areas can be overseen by a variety of federal agencies such as the Park Service, Forest Service, and Bureau of Reclamation. The upshot of this tremendous diversity of land designations and federal agencies is to ensure a wide diversity of values and uses for the public lands.

THE CHALLENGE OF PUBLIC LAND MANAGEMENT IN A COMPLEX, INTERCONNECTED WORLD

Because it's impossible for every acre to serve every purpose simultaneously, public lands are essentially "zoned" to emphasize certain resources and values. For example, while most lands in the national forest system support a variety of compatible uses simultaneously, the Forest Service nevertheless identifies priority uses for many areas of national forests. Some are dedicated primarily to commercial logging, others to livestock grazing, and still others to camping, fishing, hunting, and hiking.[36] On many areas of public land, mining is allowed and even encouraged. In the Colorado River Basin, dam and reservoir development most often occur on public lands. They also include wilderness areas where roads are not allowed as well as off-road vehicle playgrounds and ski resorts where motorized recreation is encouraged. Some areas have protected archeological or historic resources, others have protected biological resources. It is a remarkably complex task for even one federal land agency to translate these diverse priorities into a comprehensive, landscape-level management plan, let alone to coordinate management across jurisdictional boundaries.

Controversies over public land management are most often disagreements over which uses should have priority in which areas. Virtually everyone agrees that some lands deserve heightened protections while others can be dedicated to more intensive uses. The disagreement comes over how to manage specific areas, and the degree to which one particular use should dominate others. Southeastern Utah, for example, has long been rife with land use conflicts over where uranium mining should be allowed, where off-road vehicles should be allowed, how archeological sites should be protected, how much wilderness should be designated, how many cattle should be permitted to graze and in what seasons, where to build water impoundments, where to allow mountain bikes on trails, etc.

Occasionally, the rhetoric in these debates paints the issue as one of "locals" versus "outsiders." But this is often disingenuous. Locals themselves are usually divided, and there are always outside interests at play on every side of public land debates, whether it is a national environmental group advocating for wilderness or a multinational mining company advocating for mineral access. Claims about who is an outsider and who is local are rhetorical efforts to legitimize or delegitimize the groups. Moreover, this brand of rhetoric privileges a questionable logic: that "local" means legitimate, knowledgeable, and responsible while "outsider" means the opposite. Surely, this is a gross oversimplification. Even the concept of "local" raises troubling questions of definition. What geography of residence makes one local? Does one have to live in a specific community? Or, like Powell suggested, a specific watershed? How long must one live in that locality to be considered a local? The average American moves their residence every eleven or so years.[37] Can one become "local" in eleven years? If not, most Americans will forever be excluded from that category. Finally, does length of tenure in a place automatically translate into deep knowledge of and respect for it?

If only locals, by whatever definition, have legitimate claims in public land decision-making, then the public lands themselves can hardly be deemed a public asset. Far more workable is the concept of "stakeholder." Anyone with a verifiable stake in particular areas of public lands ought to be recognized as a legitimate participant in decision-making processes. Powell was not a proponent of this expanded definition of who constitutes a legitimate stakeholder, but again his world of island communities is no longer our world. Moreover, the categories of stakeholders and the spectrum of land values expressed in Powell's writings no longer fit our times. We can no longer classify lands into four simple categories: irrigable, pasturage, forest, and mineral. We can no longer focus land management only on farming, grazing, logging, and mining. We can no longer assume that productive lands will all be privatized or given to local communities to manage for their own purposes, though there are some interest groups in the West who still advocate for this. Instead, managers now appropriately recognize that land is not just a bank of extractable resources, but rather a complex web of ecological relations. Management itself is a complex web of socio-ecological interactions in an environment of profound uncertainty.[38]

Near the end of Powell's 1890 essay "Institutions for the Arid Lands," he stated: "Hard is the heart, dull is the mind and weak is the will of the [person] who does not strive to secure wise institutions for the developing world of America."[39] As Powell knew, progress does not just happen by inevitable natural forces. Wise institutions are necessary if Americans hope to achieve socially responsible, ecologically sustainable, scientifically informed, and publicly engaged management of the Colorado River Basin's public lands today and in the future.

WHITHER THE PUBLIC LANDS IN THE "GREAT UNKNOWN"?

In the Colorado River Basin, public lands provide an extraordinarily diverse and powerful tool for pursuing myriad personal and collective aims and experiences. Imagine how diminished life would be in the basin and beyond if all land were privately owned, replete with exclusionary fences and no-trespassing signs. Imagine how difficult it would be to pursue regional and national goals if all decisions were made locally and there were no public land base on which to pursue the broader public interest. No individual parcel of land, regardless of who owns it, is separate and independent of the lands surrounding it. Everything is connected to everything else, as John Muir was fond of saying. It is a great honor and privilege to have publicly owned parks, forests, deserts, canyons, mountains, rivers, fish, and wildlife in the Colorado River Basin, and to be able to work out through democratic institutions the collective purpose, use, and maintenance of those remarkable resources.

What institutions seem most appropriate and useful today for managing these federal commons? Powell offered a simplistic answer for the nineteenth century: turn them over to local watershed communities to manage as they see fit. He did not explain how competing interests should be negotiated, how marginalized people should gain a seat at the table, or how resource depletion and pollution should be remediated. He simply held faith that local communities would work these things out if given proper institutions of justice.[40] We no longer have the luxury of imagining that things will just work out. We need to think more wisely and systematically about what kinds of policies and practices facilitate things working out, particularly for the Colorado River Basin.

Three key characteristics of public land governance seem especially promising: (1) keep federal land management agencies open and accountable to the public; (2) ground decision-making in adaptive science; and (3) anchor decision-making in local communities but keep it responsive to regional affairs and national policies. Let me address each one separately.

The Colorado River Basin's sociocultural landscape is at least as diverse as its physical landscape. The mountains and valleys are united by one great river system, but divided by state boundaries and property boundaries, urban versus rural, diverse economies, political and cultural divisions, etc. The ever-proliferating array of federal land designations that evolved over the twentieth century resulted from the American people's demands for a more complex, responsive government to meet more complex public interests for an ecologically diverse landscape. Simplification of land ownership patterns and streamlining of land management goals would take us in the wrong direction, likely back to a time when only utilitarian values mattered and only a slice of the populace had a voice in determining how resources would be allocated. To develop the region in a sustainable and just manner while accommodating this great hodge-podge of societal interests will require maintaining or expanding the existing diversity of public lands and agencies. Those lands and agencies are the workshop of our democracy because they supply much of the region's water, energy, timber, forage, recreation, and mind-body rejuvenation, and because decision-making for those lands is now a profoundly public process.

In the past, land management agencies could be insular, narrow in their management focus, and unresponsive to changing public values. In response, the 1960s and 1970s saw a comprehensive reform of public land laws that greatly increased federal agency responsiveness, transparency, and citizen empowerment. Notable laws such as the National Environmental Policy Act (1969) (NEPA), National Forest Management Act (1976), and Federal Land Policy and Management Act (1976) broadened the management mandates of the public land agencies, required comprehensive integrated planning and environmental impact assessments, and opened decision-making to more democratic engagement.[41] In most ways, this was a successful reform era, although many observers lament how much time and effort it consumes to go through environmental impact assessments and to engage the public meaningfully. There is a legitimate call for some streamlining, but it should not undermine the critical reforms facilitating transparency, public engagement, and accountability. We have to tolerate some degree of inefficiency in exchange for ensuring decision-making is a truly democratic process responsive to diverse constituents and values.

Regarding the role of science, one of the great reforms of the late nineteenth century that John Wesley Powell himself helped instigate was to base government decision-making and natural resource management on sound scientific principles and empirical evidence, as mentioned earlier in the discussion of the 1891 General Revision Act. As a scientist working for a federal agency, Powell advocated brilliantly for a functional marriage of science and politics. He wanted the arid region comprehensively surveyed, property rights and land uses distributed according to the land's biological capabilities, and communities organized rationally by hydrographic basins. The early twentieth century Progressive Era famously enshrined this principle that the best political decisions about how to manage our modern world are founded on the best available science.[42] While it is critical to balance that scientific perspective with democratic responsiveness, the principle of using the best available science has only become more integrated into public land management. This is a laudable trend worth maintaining, but which occasionally requires vigorous defense by citizens when the inconvenient truths of science undermine partisan political agendas.

The third governance characteristic noted above refers to stakeholder legitimacy in public land decision-making. As mentioned earlier, Powell stated that only locals in a watershed are legitimate stakeholders. I depart from this viewpoint. Certainly, we can all agree that locals are essential stakeholders in decision-making for public lands. Perhaps their interests should even be afforded extra weight given that they will be most affected by management decisions. But local interests and perspectives need to be accompanied by larger regional and national counterparts.

Think about it: decisions regarding allocation of the Colorado River's waters are an international and interstate affair, rightly and necessarily. Imagine what it would be like if decisions about water management on every stream and tributary of the river system were determined only at the sub-basin level by local communities? Perhaps Powell could imagine that in 1890, but it seems entirely infeasible as well as inadvisable today.

The same is true for the basin's public lands. Management and protection of the values of Rocky Mountain National Park or Grand Canyon National Park, as just two examples, depend in large measure on how surrounding lands are managed. Many wildlife depend on habitat in multiple watersheds. People living in one community use and enjoy resources in neighboring communities and across state lines. Landscape-level resource management requires regional coordination. And that often requires federal engagement, investment, and authority to accomplish, as shown in the water context by the 1922 Colorado River Compact and recent efforts to negotiate drought contingency plans for the basin.[43] Stakeholders with interests in the basin's public lands are local, regional, and national, and all three levels must be involved if these lands are to be managed responsibly and sustainably.

One notable trend in public land management is the advent of multi-stakeholder, multi-jurisdictional collaborative approaches to resource management spanning many land ownership boundaries. An excellent example is the "Firescape" program in southeastern Arizona, on a distant edge of the Colorado River Basin.[44] Firescape is a collaboration between four federal land management agencies, four state agencies, one university, one county government, and at least ten nongovernmental organizations. The aim is to develop landscape-level fire management and ecological restoration plans for the basin and range ("sky island") region of southeastern Arizona. So far, six plans for six different mountain ranges have been completed. They all met NEPA requirements so that post-fire restoration efforts can be quickly implemented. Each plan required years of effort and dozens of stakeholder meetings, but resulted in substantial consensus regarding how to adapt to changing fire regimes in a warming and drying climate. The effort forged new relationships between local, state, and federal agencies, as well as stronger relationships between the public and private sectors. Hopefully, such collaborative efforts across land ownership boundaries are a harbinger of the future.

Another regional collaboration worth mentioning as a useful model for the Colorado River Basin's future is the Glen Canyon Dam Adaptive Management Program.[45] Launched in the 1990s, this program seeks to mitigate the dam's environmental impacts on downstream resources, particularly through the Grand Canyon. A large number of federal, tribal, state, and nongovernmental stakeholders from throughout the basin meet several times a year to address environmental and cultural resource issues, determine which scientific research to fund, recommend management actions to modify dam operations to achieve resource goals, and monitor results. The program was mandated by the Grand Canyon Protection Act of 1992 and has been funded by hydropower revenues from Glen Canyon Dam. It includes five federal agencies and is administered under the Secretary of the Interior's authority, so it has strong national components. Moreover, six tribes and all seven basin states have representatives on the Adaptive Management Work Group (AMWG). Various local, state, and regional stakeholders also have official representation on the AMWG.

These multi-stakeholder, collaborative management efforts, founded in both science and democracy, might be considered a more institutionally complex version of how Powell envisioned decision-making in his watershed commonwealths. Powell believed everyone with a stake in land management would somehow participate in local governance where competing interests would be balanced and tradeoffs negotiated. Firescape and the Glen Canyon Dam Adaptive Management Program approximate just such a negotiation of values, stakes, and tradeoffs as Powell imagined, except that local, regional, and national policies and perspectives are integrated.

Americans have a laudable history of progress and problem-solving, despite occasional backsliding and institutional failures. But the new challenges and uncertainties we face today and in the near future from climate change and population growth may be more difficult than any we have faced in the past. The recent increase in frequency and severity of wildfires, the decline in biodiversity, resource depletion, water scarcity, soil erosion . . . all are *our* problems to solve. The Colorado River Basin's public lands, and the federal, state, tribal, and other entities shaping management of those lands, are among our most important tools to address these extraordinary challenges. Heading into the "Great Unknown," we will likely continue to make progress toward sustainable and just resource management in the basin so long as we avoid, in Powell's inimitable phrasing, becoming hard of heart, dull of mind, and weak of will.

NOTES

1. Richard White, *"It's Your Misfortune and None of My Own": A New History of the American West* (Norman: University of Oklahoma Press, 1991), 61–84.

2. George C. Coggins et al., *Federal Public Land and Resources Law*, 7th ed. (St. Paul, MN: Foundation Press, 2014), 58–108.

3. Ibid., 108–29.

4. James L. Huston, *Calculating the Value of the Union: Slavery, Property Rights, and the Economic Origins of the Civil War* (Chapel Hill: University of North Carolina Press, 2003).

5. Winston Churchill, November 11, 1947. Quote taken from "The Worst Form of Government," International Churchill Society, accessed November 20, 2019, https://winstonchurchill.org/resources/quotes/the-worst-form-of-government.

6. The best recent biography of Powell is Donald Worster, *A River Running West: The Life of John Wesley Powell* (Oxford: Oxford University Press, 2001).

7. See the classic monograph by Stephen A. Douglas Puter, *Looters of the Public Domain* (Portland, OR: Portland Printing House, 1908). Puter was a land surveyor roped into a fraudulent scheme in Oregon and jailed in 1905. He wrote the book as a form of penance. See also Paul Wallace Gates, *A History of Public Land Law Development* (Washington, DC: US Government Printing Office, 1968), 463–94.

8. Primary source documents on the Pacific Railway Acts can be found at "Primary Documents in American History," Library of Congress, accessed November 20, 2019, https://www.loc.gov/rr/program/bib/ourdocs/pacificrail.html. On the total amount of land granted to railroads, see Richard White, *Railroaded: The Transcontinentals and the Making of Modern America* (New York: Norton, 2011), 24.

9. The classic and exhaustive monograph on this subject is Gates, *Public Land Law*. For a succinct survey of public land laws with citations to more contemporary scholarship, see Adam M. Sowards, "Public Lands and Their Administration," *Oxford Research Encyclopedia of American History* (2017), http://americanhistory.oxfordre.com/view/10.1093/acrefore/9780199329175.001.0001/acrefore-9780199329175-e-396. See especially the section titled "Obtaining and Disposing of the Public Lands," pp. 2–5.

10. On the General Revision Act of 1891, see Richard N. L. Andrews, *Managing the Environment, Managing Ourselves: A History of American Environmental Policy*, 2nd ed. (New Haven: Yale University Press, 2006), 104–6.

11. John Wesley Powell, "Trees on Arid Lands," *Science* 12 (1888): 170–71.

12. John Wesley Powell, *The Arid Lands*, ed. Wallace Stegner (Lincoln: University of Nebraska Press, 1962), 8. All page numbers in this chapter that refer to Powell's 1878 *Arid Lands Report* are cited from this edited version of the report.

13. Powell, "Address and Comments," *International Irrigation Congress Official Proceedings* (1893): 108.

14. General Revision Act of 1891, *Statutes at Large*, 1095–1103, section 24.

15. Gerald W. Williams, *The USDA Forest Service—The First* Century, FS-650 (Washington, DC: USDA Forest Service, 2005), 8, 25–26. See also "Theodore Roosevelt and Conservation," National Park Service, accessed October 19, 2018, https://www.nps.gov/thro/learn/historyculture/theodore-roosevelt-and-conservation.htm.

16. Samuel P. Hays, *Conservation and the Gospel of Efficiency: The Progressive Conservation Movement, 1890–1920* (Cambridge: Harvard University Press, 1959).

17. John Wesley Powell, "Institutions for the Arid Lands," *Century* 40 (1890), 113.

18. Powell, *The Arid Lands*, chapters 1 and 2. The quotation is from ibid., 27.

19. John Wesley Powell, "The Non-Irrigable Lands of the Arid Region," *Century* 39 (1890), 920.

20. Powell, "Institutions for the Arid Lands," 114.

21. Ibid., 115. Interestingly, when Powell talked about careful consideration of which forests to cut, he was referring to the tension between eliminating trees

to increase streamflow versus maintaining forest cover to protect reservoirs from sedimentation. He endorsed the idea that fewer trees meant more streamflow but acknowledged that forest cover is the best way to minimize erosion. So, the "care" in choosing where to "denude" a forest was based on assessing trade-offs between more water versus ruined water storage facilities. See Powell, "The Non-Irrigable Lands of the Arid Region," 920.

22. The best biography of Pinchot's life and work is Char Miller, *Gifford Pinchot and the Making of Modern Environmentalism* (Washington, DC: Island Press, 2004); see especially chapters 6 and 7.

23. Powell, *The Arid Lands,* 35–36.

24. John Wesley Powell, "Address to the Montana Constitutional Convention, August 9, 1889," in *Proceedings and Debates of the Constitutional Convention* (Helena: State Publishing Company, 1921), 823.

25. Powell, "Institutions for the Arid Lands," 115.

26. Robert Wiebe, *The Search for Order* (New York: Hill and Wang, 1966); see especially chapters 3–6.

27. On the general anxiety in America over urbanization, industrialization, and the nationalization of economic power in the 1880s, see ibid., chapter 3.

28. On the tools and means for creating new order during the industrial era, see ibid., chapter 7.

29. Powell, "Institutions for the Arid Lands," 114.

30. Ernest Callenbach, *Ecotopia* (New York: Bantam, 1975).

31. For an example of how the Great Depression affected one region of the United States and led to extensive federal involvement in social and economic planning and investment, see Paul W. Hirt, *The Wired Northwest: A History of Electric Power, 1870s–1970s* (Lawrence: University Press of Kansas, 2012), chapters 8–10.

32. White, *It's Your Misfortune,* 479, 531.

33. Free downloadable maps showing federal and Indian lands of the United States, with separate maps for each state, can be found at https://nationalmap.gov/small_scale/printable/fedlands.html. Acreage figures in this paragraph were extracted from various websites of the federal agencies managing these lands.

34. The 1960 Multiple-Use Sustained-Yield Act clarified and codified the management mandate for the US Forest Service, although it largely endorsed what had already been the agency's standard policy for decades. See Paul Hirt, *A Conspiracy of Optimism: Management of the National Forests Since World War Two* (Lincoln: University of Nebraska Press, 1994), chapter 8.

35. Bureau of Land Management, "The Federal Land Policy and Management Act of 1976 As Amended: Commemorating 25 Years" (2001), https://www.blm.gov/or/regulations/files/FLPMA.pdf.

36. On the practical application of zoning concepts to public land management in the post-war era, see Hirt, *A Conspiracy of Optimism,* chapters 7, 8, and 10, especially 229–33.

37. The US Census Bureau periodically estimates this measure of personal and family mobility. It last did so in 2007, estimating an average of 11.7 moves in a lifetime. The data organization FiveThirtyEight analyzed and updated

those estimates in 2015 and found the number similar at 11.4. See https://fivethirtyeight.com/features/how-many-times-the-average-person-moves.

38. For a broad array of perspectives on the shift from an emphasis on commodity extraction to ecosystem management, see Mark S. Boyce and Alan Haney, eds., *Ecosystem Management: Applications for Sustainable Forest and Wildlife Resources* (New Haven: Yale University Press, 1999).

39. Powell, "Institutions for the Arid Lands," 116.

40. Ibid., 113.

41. On reformations of public land law during the 1970s, see Samuel P. Hays, *Beauty, Health and Permanence: Environmental Politics in the United States, 1955–1985* (Cambridge: Cambridge University Press, 1987), especially chapters 10–12. On how these laws enabled greater democratic participation in decision-making, see Cody Ferguson and Paul Hirt, "Power to the People: Grassroots Advocacy for Environmental Protection and Democratic Governance," in *The Nature of Hope: Grassroots Organizing, Environmental Justice, and Political Change*, ed. Char Miller and Jeffrey Crane (Boulder: University Press of Colorado, 2019), 52–76.

42. The classic monograph that established this understanding of the Progressive Era is Hays, *Conservation*.

43. The seminal work on the Colorado River Compact is Norris Hundley, Jr., *Water and the West: The Colorado River Compact and the Politics of Water in the American West*, 2nd ed. (Berkeley: University of California Press, 2009). For information about drought contingency planning in the basin, see Bureau of Reclamation, "Colorado River Basin Drought Contingency Plans," accessed November 20, 2019, https://www.usbr.gov/dcp.

44. "Welcome to FireScape," accessed November 20, 2019, https://www.azfirescape.org.

45. Bureau of Reclamation, Upper Colorado Region, "Glen Canyon Dam Adaptive Management Program," accessed November 20, 2019, https://www.usbr.gov/uc/progact/amp/index.html.

CHAPTER 7

Powell as Unwitting Godfather of Outdoor Recreation in the Great Unknown

EMILENE OSTLIND

"We mount our horses at Flagstaff," John Wesley Powell described in 1890. "In ten minutes we are in the woods and out of sight of the railroad town. We ride for hours among the pines, and from time to time see San Francisco Mountain on our right." He goes on to unravel a multi-day expedition through northern Arizona. "[O]ur way is across glades carpeted with flowers, and through open forests where we now and then see a deer bounding on its way."[1]

Powell's purpose in describing this adventure was to emphasize the lack of water in the region. The trip was one of dozens Powell made throughout what he called the "arid lands" during his more than thirty-year career as an explorer and scientist. His mission was to fill in unknown places on the map of the growing country and to classify and quantify resources those lands could provide. He strove to convince the nation's leaders that the Colorado River Basin and surrounding region would not support the same density of agriculture or human civilization as the Midwest, simply because of the scarcity of water.

However, another unintended message comes through Powell's words as well. This horse-packing expedition was a venture anyone might long to experience: to travel for a couple weeks on horseback, to smell the clean forests, to sleep out under the stars, and even to view one of the world's great spectacles. Powell describes "wonder-seeing" at "the brink of the Grand Cañon of the Colorado."[2] Vivid depictions of beautiful, wild, wide-open country not only lured readers into writings where Powell could expose them to his pragmatic ideas for taming and industrializing the land, but also inspired adventurers to pursue their own exploratory travels through the Colorado River Basin.

Today, thanks in part to such tales of adventure, the Colorado River Basin's public lands support our Western communities in a way Powell didn't exactly anticipate—by providing opportunities for outdoor recreation, escape from the hubbub of everyday life, and a chance to experience remote, rugged landscapes free from development and civilization. As we consider the benefits and experiences these lands provide now and into the future, we must turn again to Powell's visionary ideas to better understand how we might address the challenges facing us.

HISTORICAL CONTEXT: POWELL'S TWO VOICES

John Wesley Powell—explorer, scientist, and philosopher of the late nineteenth and early twentieth centuries—left us with abundant texts that describe his vision for developing the West and reveal his populist interest in a society organized to benefit the common, hardworking, industrious person over the rich or powerful.

"If divisional surveys were extended over the pasturage lands," Powell writes in the *Arid Lands Report,* his 1878 manifesto outlining a strategy for making these lands productive to mainstream US society, "favorable sites at springs and along small streams would be rapidly taken under the homestead and preemption privileges for the nuclei of pasturage farms."[3] And thus unfolds his strategic scheming and careful argument for thoughtfully crafted systems of surveying, dividing up, and managing land and resources. Over the latter part of the nineteenth century, Powell compiled his ideas, research, and scholarship into hundreds of reports, maps, speeches, and other documents designed to provide sound, quantitative information about a misunderstood portion of the United States. In those pages, he described systems of governance, land and water management, and social structures that would enable enterprising citizens to settle and develop farms and communities in this land of scarcity.

Powell's approach was to survey and map the region and to quantify resources it could provide. To this end, he carried barometers and other cartographic tools on his explorations, continually diagramming lands, linking tributaries to rivers, and delineating forests and watersheds. He identified four main uses of the arid lands: farming, grazing, timber harvesting, and mining. As director of the US Geological Survey from 1881 to 1894, he measured, mapped, and described lands suitable for each purpose. He tried to convince the country's leaders and decision-makers, most of whom were stationed in the humid East, that Euro-American settlement of the arid lands would be strictly limited by water supply and impossible without irrigation systems and water sources.

Powell seemed to imagine a situation similar to what his parents had found in Illinois in 1851—where the hard-working individual could freely create a lovely home, plenty to eat, and a passel of children running through the farm. He envisioned a land where the West's streams and creeks were home to farms interspersed with industrious little towns made up of banks, businesses, and schools, with people mining mountainsides, damming reservoirs in upstream valleys, producing coal and oil from hills, grazing livestock over ranges, harvesting timber from forests, and growing crops in bottomlands. Citizens, mostly white people from the East, would busily transform and tame the land, converting it to their own needs.

Powell recognized that settlers would be completely interdependent, relying on one another to construct the dams, reservoirs, and canals necessary to move water from streams to farmlands. No individual would be able to develop such infrastructure alone. Powell suggested that the cost of irrigation infrastructure ran about $10 per acre, and thus the necessary investment to support a million acres would be $1 billion. He calculated the return in value to the country from such an investment would total $5 billion, and he implored the federal government to invest heavily in irrigation infrastructure for the arid lands.[4]

Powell described a system for divvying up Western lands that involved dispensing irrigable lands, those along streams, springs, and rivers, to settlers to work into productive farms. But not all lands should be privatized, he argued. He concluded that the federal government should retain ownership of uplands—higher-elevation areas either too dry or too rugged to farm but useful for grazing and timber harvest. The mining lands, meanwhile, should also remain in federal ownership until proven up, and then be transferred to miners who could extract the ores they had to offer.

Further, to ensure sustainable social and governmental structures for these lands, Powell suggested dividing the West by hydrographic basin. He thought people living within a watershed would make the best decisions for utilizing and sustaining rangelands, forests, and water. He suggested individuals working the land should make decisions about resource management, as they would have a genuine interest in ensuring rangelands were not overgrazed nor forests overharvested. Powell advocated to "allow the people to regulate their own affairs in their own way ... and to say to them 'with wisdom you may prosper, but with folly you must fail.'"[5] He promoted systems that would favor individual farmers or laborers and prevent putting too much power into the hands of banks, corporations, or government overlords.

All these ideas and arguments accumulated into a grand vision for the lands—mostly public, yet some private—of the arid region, including the Colorado River Basin. Yet, in the midst of his mapmaking and technical writing, another side of Powell came through, foreshadowing uses of public lands that he didn't formally recognize as valuable. His more emotional and dramatic voice emerged when he needed to sway hearts and minds. At such times, Powell diverged from his cool, scientific perspective to reveal a bit of wonder about the places he explored. When he switched to popular writing, he created stories that have captivated readers for the last 150 years.

Powell was not ignorant of the power of a well-crafted adventure story. To capture the interest of prospective funders in Congress, he swerved away from data explanation and toward storytelling. These writings reveal hints of Powell's love for the country and the pleasure of travelling through it. He describes delight in summiting a peak or finding a clear spring to camp near. "Wet, chilled, and tired to exhaustion, we stop at a cottonwood grove on the bank, build a huge fire, make a cup of coffee, and are soon refreshed and quite merry," Powell writes of one adventure, noting the thrill of making it through a difficult day in the backcountry.[6] He shares awe at encountering flower-filled meadows and snow-draped peaks. It's hard to imagine that Powell would have committed so many days of his life to exploring the West, and so many nights sleeping on the ground, if he did not, to some extent, thrill at the experience.

Powell is best remembered for the adventure at the center of this volume—his extremely dangerous and heroic exploration of the Green and Colorado rivers in 1869, which he published several years later as *The Exploration of the Colorado River of the West and Its Canyons*. In organizing, leading, and completing the 1869 Expedition, his reputation as an adventure hero overshadowed his reputation as a scientist. In that tale, along with national news reports celebrating the journey, Powell cemented himself into the public imagination as an explorer of the last "unknown" portions of the continental United States and an inspiration to free-spirited, adventure-seeking readers who lusted, also, to set foot atop unnamed peaks or venture into undeveloped lands.

How many citizens, even 150 years after Powell's expedition, gather around a fire pan deep inside the Grand Canyon on a summer night to read aloud of Powell's journey, while their rafts, tethered to sand-stakes, softly bump the shore? For a century and half, tales of Powell's adventures boating the death-defying, exhilarating white water of the Colorado, ascending high peaks in the Colorado Rockies, exploring Utah's labyrinthine canyon lands, travelling through Arizona's forests, and more have mesmerized and inspired readers. Sitting in their homes around the world, they take from Powell's writings an invitation to plan their own trips onto the Colorado River Basin's expansive public lands, to test their mettle against the elements, and to escape from industrialized society to that freer, wilder place Powell experienced yet obscured under his utilitarian vision.

What Powell could not foresee was that the wild, untrammeled land itself would one day become as coveted a resource as the irrigated agriculture, rangelands, minerals, and timber. He did not anticipate that people from across the globe would one day spend their hard-earned money to vacation to the West's awe-inspiring landscapes, much the way he carved out a few weeks for his horse-packing expedition to the Grand Canyon. Powell saw himself as a completely objective scientist, but he was in fact the unwitting godfather of outdoor recreation in the Colorado River Basin.

OUTDOOR RECREATION ON THE COLORADO RIVER BASIN'S PUBLIC LANDS

Today, countless people from around the world seek adventures similar to those Powell celebrated in his writings. Though few arrive by horseback, nearly six million people per year partake in "wonder-seeing" at the Grand Canyon, established as a national monument in 1908 and further protected as a national park in 1919.[7] Their experiences today are vastly different from Powell's. Most pay an entrance fee at the park gates and follow paved roads to fenced overlooks shared with thousands of other sightseers. They adhere to rules about safety and resource preservation enforced by park rangers. They partake in restaurants, souvenir stands, and toilets. And they come from all over the world, arriving in mere hours from once seemingly impossible distances.

The last document Powell published, a co-authored essay in a guidebook to *The Grand Canyon of Arizona*, described generations of explorers who had visited the region and laid the groundwork for a culture of outdoor recreation on lands he knew so well.[8] Around that time, a railroad began to carry tourists to the Grand Canyon, and the next year, 1902, just as the first automobile reached the canyon rim, Powell passed away in Maine at the age of 68.[9] In the decades following his death, America continued to shift. The population expanded. Wars came and went. The economy grew, collapsed, and grew again. Eventually the notion of leave from work for vacation took hold. An increasingly mobile population sought reprieve and solace from city life by venturing to wilder places, including the Colorado River Basin's arid, public lands.

In 1946, the National Park Service prepared *A Survey of the Recreational Resources of the Colorado River Basin.* This more than two-hundred-page report responded to a request from the Bureau of Reclamation to inform water development planning. "Here too, one may enjoy much sunshine and find perfect climates for outdoor recreation the year around," the document describes. "Hunting, fishing, photography, snow sports, boating, swimming, horseback riding, camping, mountain climbing, exploration—the entire realm of outdoor recreational activities may be enjoyed."[10]

The publication described a phenomenon taking hold in the country. "Now, with the Pacific Coast more fully developed, people seeking undeveloped, uncrowded areas are beginning to discover the basin. It is time for immediate action which will assure the preservation of its many and varied recreational features," the authors wrote. "It is also time to develop facilities which will enable people to see and enjoy the region."[11]

The report makes recommendations for preserving historic artifacts and recreation sites while laying out a strategy to develop dams to supply electric power and irrigation storage. It details recreational resources in the basin, most of which remain relevant today, such as alluring streams and lakes, historic cabins and mining towns, archaeological sites, wildlife, and even "the great open spaces and views without end; silence so complete the hum of a bee sounds like a distant airplane."[12]

The demand for such experiences has only increased with the passing decades. In 2016, 144.4 million Americans, or 48.8 percent of the population, participated in an outdoor activity at least once,[13] and federal public lands received 620 million recreational visits, more than half to national parks.[14] That same year, outdoor recreation contributed $373.7 billion to the US economy, about 2 percent of gross domestic product, and the outdoor industry employed 7.6 million people. Further, the outdoor recreation economy grew at 3.8 percent, compared to just 2.8 percent for the overall economy.[15]

The outdoor recreation industry is gaining national recognition. In 2016, the Bureau of Economic Analysis first recognized outdoor recreation as a contributor to the economy, adding credibility to the industry. The agency found economic contributions from outdoor recreation to be on par with industries Powell imagined as dominant uses of the arid lands. Agriculture, fishing, and forestry combined contributed $386 billion compared to outdoor recreation's $373 billion. Mining, including oil and gas as well as coal and ore minerals that Powell discussed, contributed $431 billion.[16] (These contributions are dwarfed by industries like manufacturing, transportation, and public utilities.)

And yet, outdoor recreation is not all about the money. Many people gravitate to outdoor recreation, especially on public lands, because it is inexpensive. Families fill campgrounds and hiking trails every weekend. Others camp at distributed sites without amenities or fees. Mountain bikers, boaters, and hikers enjoy public lands with modest or no trailhead fees, spending money only on gas to get to and from the location. Even pricier activities, such as reserving a group campsite or renting a cabin, tend to be less expensive than comparable in-town activities. As the Forest Service puts it in one report:

> Outdoor recreation plays a significant role in American lives. It provides physical challenges and a sense of well-being, helps develop lifelong skills, provokes interest and inquiry, inspires wonder and awe of the natural world, and often provides an alternative to daily routines. Recreation contributes greatly to the physical, mental, and spiritual health of individuals; bonds family and friends; and instills pride in natural and cultural heritage.[17]

Over the last 150 years, outdoor recreation has emerged as a top consideration on public lands throughout the Colorado River Basin for land management agencies, state economies, elected leaders, and individuals. Communities throughout the Colorado River Basin are defined by adjacent recreational public lands—Green River, Wyoming's Flaming Gorge Country; Vernal, Utah's Dinosaur National Monument; Moab, Utah's Arches and Canyonlands national parks; Escalante, Utah's Grand Staircase-Escalante National Monument; Bluff, Utah's Bears Ears National Monument; and Flagstaff, Arizona's Grand Canyon, to name but a few.

Public lands are central to outdoor recreation. As described by the Forest Service, "Federal lands contribute significantly, and in many cases uniquely, to the provision of nature-based outdoor recreation opportunities."[18] And according to the Outdoor Industry Association,

"Public lands and waters are the outdoor industry's basic infrastructure, and without them the industry cannot survive. Preserving access is imperative to enhancing the industry's economic and social impact. Access ensures every American's ability to get outside where jobs, health, and communities grow."[19]

The Colorado River Basin spans nearly a quarter of a million square miles, or about 8 percent of the continental United States.[20] About 156,000 square miles, or roughly 65 percent of the basin, is public land encompassing Bureau of Land Management lands, national forests, national parks, national monuments, national recreation areas, national wildlife refuges, and state lands, most of which are open to the public for outdoor recreation, among other uses (see map 3). Another 19 percent of the basin's lands belong to Native American tribes, portions of which are managed for public recreation as well, including parks, monuments, and other recreational sites. Some cater to visitors from elsewhere, and tribal members also enjoy outdoor recreation on those lands.

The public lands of each basin state have their own characteristics. For example, Colorado's public lands are dominated by high-elevation national forests spilling westward from the Continental Divide and harboring alpine snowpack that feeds tributaries to the Colorado River throughout summer. Utah is home to dry Bureau of Land Management lands and several extensive national parks and national monuments. Nearly the entire state of Arizona is within the basin. That state is home to large swaths of Indian country, including the 27,000-square mile Navajo Nation, as well as a matrix of state and national forest lands surrounding and north of Phoenix and Tucson, plus Grand Canyon National Park.

These public lands face enormous pressure from many directions, including an expanding human population and accompanying sprawling human footprint; a changing climate and diminishing water; development pressure for energy and other resources; threats to biodiversity such as exotic diseases and invasive species; hostility toward and defunding of public land management agencies; and more. Our challenge today, if we want the outdoor recreation opportunities these public lands provide to persist, is to define a vision for the future and to create systems of management and governance to sustain that vision. To ensure our children, their children, and many generations going forward continue to enjoy and benefit from resources and experiences these lands provide, including life-altering outdoor recreation, thoughtful, creative, and well-informed decisions about our priorities for the Colorado River Basin's public lands are needed. Powell can be our guide. His vision offers a model for how we can think about protecting and using these lands simultaneously as we launch into the next "Great Unknown."

SEEKING A GUIDE INTO THE FUTURE GREAT UNKNOWN

On August 13, 1869, Powell and his crew stood at the mouth of the Little Colorado River at what now marks the eastern boundary of Grand Canyon National Park, above more than 200 miles of unexplored river. "We are now ready to start on our way down the Great Unknown," Powell wrote.[21]

This moment—introduced at the outset of this volume—where Powell tried to make his best judgment of what the future would hold, offers an apt metaphor. Powell spent much of his career trying to divine and to mold what was to come. His ideas carried forward for a nearly unfathomable 150 years to where we stand today. And now we again peer into a future obscured by uncertainty, trying to pick a route. Will we let powerful currents sweep us along, or will we choose our own line? In another 150 years, the year 2169, will citizens of the West look back at our ideas with admiration or dismay?

When we think of the fate of outdoor recreation on our public lands, the Great Unknown we face in the Colorado River Basin is a mirror to the one Powell faced. Whereas his project was to fill in blank places on the map, ours is to escape to unknown places. Whereas his aim was to see the West developed and put to utilitarian use, ours is to keep a few places free from development. Whereas his objective was to outline a strategy for "civilizing" the West, ours is to offer relief from being over-civilized. And yet, despite the dramatically different circumstances in the Colorado River Basin today, might we nonetheless make use of Powell's ideas, reflecting them upon the region's current and potential future circumstances?

In addition to the threats to biodiversity and water supplies in the basin, major challenges overshadow the fate of recreation on public lands, including overpopulation and crowding, unequal access to outdoor recreation, and shortcomings with federal land management. In some ways, these challenges are so different from those Powell faced in the Colorado River Basin that his ideas feel irrelevant today.

Powell promoted population growth (with some limitations) on the arid lands, but cities in and around the Colorado River Basin now burst at their seams, spilling sprawl into surrounding lands and sucking up water. Whereas Powell invited development on the landscape, this agenda is arguably no longer relevant. Powell wanted to see growth fueled by immigration from white Easterners, but as today's population inside and adjacent to the basin becomes increasingly diverse, so must the population accessing outdoor recreation on public lands.

Powell also believed resource management decisions should be left exclusively to people living within watersheds. In an era when a resident of New York City can pop into Moab, Utah for the weekend, however, excluding the public land recreation interests of citizens from farther afield is untenable. The watershed is now too small in scale. Greatly increased mobility among outdoor recreationists mean that people from as far away as Anchorage, Alaska and Orlando, Florida, not to mention Sydney, Australia or Beijing, China, have a stake in public lands.

Further, Powell's focus on utilitarian and consumptive uses of resources within the basin, such as water for irrigation, rangelands for grazing, forests for timber harvest, and ore deposits for mining, are very different from today's non-consumptive uses of public lands, which include protection of wildlife habitat and scenic vistas, water conservation, and outdoor recreation. Translating Powell's detailed ideas for how to manage this landscape to our modern outdoor recreation challenges in the Great Unknown at first feels fruitless.

But despite the dramatically transformed population, technology, and culture since Powell's time, several aspects of his visionary thinking and land management ideas ring true. Powell can yet be our guide for navigating today's public land recreation challenges in the Colorado River Basin—overcrowding, lack of inclusiveness, and complaints about federal land management. To begin, as a geographer Powell saw the basin as a whole place, a space shaped by time and imbued with meaning, and from that vantage point he crafted a clear vision. He looked into the future and dreamt up systems to make his vision work, and now we must do the same, even if our vision for outdoor recreation in the basin—more about containing civilization than expanding it—differs in many ways from Powell's.

Loving Our Public Lands to Death

Overpopulation and crowding will increasingly strain the public lands supporting outdoor recreation in coming decades. The human population in and around the Colorado River Basin is expected to grow from about 40 million in 2015 to about 75 million by 2060 according to some projections,[22] and the global population is expected to grow from 7.6 billion today to 11–12 billion by 2100.[23] Meanwhile, expanding transportation gives people better access to public lands, while social media attracts hordes to places that otherwise might have seen few visitors.[24] At the same time, increasingly high-tech off-road vehicles, mountain bikes, backcountry skis, and other equipment mean recreationists access more miles of trail each day, venturing farther from trailheads than they could a generation ago.

Crowding has long been a concern in national parks and at trailheads, especially near urban centers. As Roderick Nash put it in his 1967 book *Wilderness and the American Mind,* outdoor recreationists—armed with improved equipment, transportation, and information about backcountry sites—are loving our public lands to death.[25] This problem has only exacerbated over the past few decades. Even remote backcountry destinations, such as Conundrum Hot Springs, 8.5 miles up a hiking trail in the Maroon Bells-Snowmass Wilderness Area above Aspen, Colorado, face issues with crowding. On summer nights, as many as 100 people visit the springs and camp nearby, some bringing cases of beer and speakers and leaving behind trash, unburied human waste, and abundant dog poop.[26] On some public lands, crowding threatens to permanently degrade special places and the experiences they offer.

Though expanding population and development on the arid lands was one of Powell's goals, he still has something to offer our thinking about this challenge. He was unique in his time for recognizing the finiteness of desirable resources as a defining feature of the region that would necessarily limit human habitation. Whereas Powell focused on the shortage of water, we now also recognize space and recreation infrastructure as limited resources on these lands. Powell argued time and again to the nation's boosters and leaders that this landscape would never support the agricultural production or population density of lands farther east. In the face of limited water, he spent extensive energy quantifying just how many people the land actually could support, and trying to convince the nation to constrain development to those limits.

We must take a similar view of outdoor recreation today. Allowing more and more visitors to flood limited recreation sites year after year degrades landscapes. Powell might have appreciated Garrett Hardin's 1968 paper "The Tragedy of the Commons," which reinforced the idea that limits are necessary for managing finite resources. That paper states it is impossible to provide the greatest good for the greatest number of people, because "[i]t is not mathematically possible to maximize for two (or more) variables at the same time."²⁷ If we want to maximize the "number"—in this case of people recreating on public lands—the result will be even more crowding at hot springs, scenic overlooks, and trailheads, which makes the experience less "good" for those participating.

With Powell's insights in mind, and by taking a landscape-scale view of recreation resources on the Colorado River Basin's public lands, it is time to limit human access to some of our most beloved destinations. This is already happening in some places. The Grand Canyon lottery system for river permits is an iconic example. Anyone can apply for the lottery. Applicants are not guaranteed a spot every year, but an elaborate point system gives those who apply a better chance of winning the longer they have waited. The National Park Service restricts the "number" of people who can boat through the canyon in any given year.²⁸ The result is a greater "good"—when you do draw that permit, you'll enjoy world-class campsites throughout your trip. And thanks to strict rules about waste removal and camping ethics, as well as rangers who enforce the rules, those sites will be clean even if 25,000 people have used them earlier in the season.²⁹

Public land managers are implementing similar systems at other destinations. Many popular lakes and canyons now require camping permits. The Forest Service now limits the number of overnight campers at Conundrum Hot Springs and plans to expand permitting systems to other sites in nearby wilderness areas.³⁰

Who Recreates on Public Lands

And yet, even as growing numbers recreate on public lands, those visitors do not represent society as a whole. Many public lands and recreation spaces remain inaccessible or unwelcoming to some members of society. For example, Rahawa Haile, a 30-something, queer, African American woman, through-hiked the Appalachian Trail in the summer of 2016. In a compelling piece for *Outside* magazine, she described the experience as "a 2,190-mile trek through Trump lawn signs," and talked about being afraid to enter communities where Confederate flags were flying. She described the feeling of not belonging in that outdoor recreation space.³¹

According to a Forest Service national survey, of the nearly 150 million visits made to national forestlands by citizens annually between 2012 and 2016, 95 percent were by white people.³² Another analysis of outdoor recreation trends on federal lands—including national forests, national parks, wildlife refuges, Bureau of Land Management lands, and other types of federal lands—found white people and Native Americans more likely than African Americans, Hispanic people, and Asians to participate in outdoor recreation.[33]

One of the most important considerations for public lands recreation today has to do with "who." Who do these lands benefit? What will the people who need these lands in coming generations look like? Who feels like these lands are there for them to enjoy, and who will advocate for these lands? And in what ways are our public lands, and the life-changing outdoor recreation opportunities they provide, falling short by leaving out the very people they were created to serve? We face something of a paradox in the need to address overcrowding at some public land recreation sites while at the same time needing to invite more—and more diverse—people to our public lands.

We need a substantial cultural shift. There is much progress to be made when it comes to welcoming diverse recreationists to public lands in the Colorado River Basin and elsewhere. Here, Powell's ethnocentric perspective seems to fall short since he saw the basin primarily as a place for white people. (Although, through the sacrifices he made in the Civil War, which brought an end to slavery in the United States, he and his generation arguably advanced equity among races more than any generation since.)

One way that Powell can serve as a guide in this endeavor is through his appreciation for the power of storytelling. Though he used it for much different purposes, he truly understood the power of vividly crafted narratives and images to shift the public's perception and draw stakeholders to a cause. This approach is proving useful to invite more diverse people to recreate on public lands. Whereas even just a decade ago, images of outdoor recreation portrayed almost exclusively fit, young, white men, today the federal land management agencies themselves, along with media, nonprofits, and the outdoor industry, increasingly depict imagery of more diverse constituents enjoying public lands recreation.

In 2016, the National Park Service began producing a series of videos as part of its 100th anniversary celebration, highlighting multicultural experiences and diversity in national parks.[34] One film in the series highlights the wedding of a Mexican American couple, one a park ranger, held in Grand Teton National Park. Another profiles a young Navajo girl learning about her family's culture in Canyon de Chelly National Monument. In 2013, a charismatic young leader named José González founded an organization called Latino Outdoors, which in part uses images and storytelling—as well as volunteer-led experiences—to invite

Latino families into the outdoors and welcome people who have so far been overlooked by the outdoor movement.[35] Catalogs from gear brands increasingly depict inspirational images of diverse recreationists, such as Ashima Shiraishi, a young female Japanese American bouldering champion from New York City.[36] Outdoor cooperative REI has led campaigns to get more women outdoors, including providing grants to programs that strive to increase diversity.[37]

We have a long way to go to achieve truly equitable access to public lands recreation, but shifting the perception of who these lands are for and telling a story of inclusion on these lands is an important step. Sustaining public lands recreation opportunities for future generations will require ensuring our public lands are as available to urban youth and underserved communities as they are to the whiter factions of our society who have claimed these lands since Powell's time.

How We Manage Recreation Resources

Finally, just as demands for improved access to recreation on public lands are coming to the fore, agencies that manage these places are facing budget cuts, hostility from stakeholders, and calls to divest public lands to the states. The National Park Service alone has a nearly $12 billion maintenance backlog,[38] and year after year the Forest Service spends an increasing portion of its budget fighting wildfire, leaving fewer funds for other important tasks, including recreation management. Wildfire spending, which surpassed $2 billion for the first time in 2017, is likely to increase even more in the face of widespread drought and longer fire seasons caused by climate change.[39] Budget appropriations for these agencies are not increasing apace with need. Funds for recreation programs are less available just when they are most critical. Activities like permitting, trail maintenance, and outreach fall short.

At the same time, other complaints, especially related to federal regulation of natural resource extraction, raise the ire of some stakeholders, partly triggering the political rallying cry for divesting public lands to state ownership. This call has been voiced in all the Colorado River Basin states, and perhaps most strongly in Utah where, in 2012, the state legislature passed and the governor signed the "Transfer of Public Lands Act" that purported to require the federal government to turn over select public lands to the state.[40] Many recreationists fear that public lands divestment would put places they love to visit off limits and replace priorities such as wildlife habitat, scenic vistas, and trailhead access with an emphasis on resource extraction, favoring corporations over citizen recreationists.

When it comes to the federal government's role in managing recreation on our public lands, Powell's ideas again offer guidance. Though he focused on utilitarian rather than non-consumptive uses of resources on public lands, he did advocate for national investments that would reap returns for citizens. Just as Powell urged spending $1 billion on irrigation infrastructure, promising a return to the nation of $5 billion,[41] we face a choice about investing in these lands versus leaving them to degrade, poorly managed by demoralized and underfunded public servants. As the outdoor recreation industry grows, the expected returns on investment are convincing. And as pressures increase on public lands, financial need will increase as well. Truly visionary leadership will see the value of such investments to our country's economic, physical, and spiritual health.

Further, to best serve citizens who would make their lives around public lands in the Colorado River Basin, Powell saw value in keeping some lands under federal ownership to ensure they would not be commandeered by wealthy corporations and monopolized. For example, of the lands that would be used for irrigation canals, he wrote, "these should be dedicated to public use, so that individuals may not acquire title to the lands for the purpose of selling them to the farmers when the irrigating works are to be constructed, and thus entailing upon agriculture an unnecessary expense."[42]

The same notion holds true for outdoor recreation. Common, hardworking citizens who stand to enjoy lands in the Colorado River Basin will most benefit when those lands remain in public ownership. As some parties in the West call for divestment to the states of federally managed public lands, outdoor recreationists have protested. After Utah passed its land transfer bill, followed by another resolution calling on federal officials to downsize Bear's Ears National Monument, the massive Outdoor Retailer trade show and its $45 million in annual spending moved, after twenty years in Salt Lake City, to Denver.[43] The move was a political protest against Utah leaders' disdain for public lands coveted by recreationists. In other Western states, hunters, hikers, mountain bikers, backpackers, and others—fearing that stripping federal authority from huge swaths of open, undeveloped public lands would start a process toward privatization or closure—have rallied at state legislative sessions and elsewhere.[44]

Thus, even today, during times dramatically different from those when Powell explored Arizona by horseback and pushed his wooden boats into the Colorado River's current, many of his ideas retain strength. We can look to him for a model of how to think about our way ahead.

A COURSE FORWARD

"Then on we ride through an open pine forest," Powell wrote, "until at last we come down to hills that are covered with piñons and cedars and rest for the night by a spring concealed among oak bushes. It has been a long ride, and we sleep well."[45]

Never again will a party explore northern Arizona by horseback for weeks on end without crossing paved roads or encountering others. Much has transformed in the Colorado River Basin over the past 150 years. And yet, thanks to some insightful programs initiated over that century-and-a-half, including our national park system, such opportunities are not totally lost to the world. It is possible, for example, to book a guided, week-long winter horse-packing trip along the north rim of Grand Canyon. You'll shelter from storms under rock ledges while typically dry pools fill with rainwater. You'll sleep under the stars in your bedroll, much as Powell did long ago. You'll wake up to the smell of sun on sage, feeling the bones of the earth under your back. And you'll carry that sense of adventure, the thrill of discovery, in a place relatively unshaped by human disruption.

To not only protect such experiences, but also to make them more accessible to future generations of diverse, urbanized citizens who will shortly become the ones deciding our public lands' future, we need to take action. Like Powell, we must see the basin as a whole landscape and recognize that its finite resources require us to set limits on our own consumption. We must use images and storytelling to shift public perception about who these lands are really meant to serve. As Powell suggested for irrigation infrastructure, we must invest both financial and human capital into public lands recreation management, expecting returns to our communities. And to ensure that the recreation we so greatly value continues to be accessible to common people on these lands, we must keep them in public ownership.

NOTES

1. John Wesley Powell, "The Non-Irrigable Lands of the Arid Region," *Century* 39 (1890): 915–22.
2. Ibid., 916.

3. John Wesley Powell, *Report on the Lands of the Arid Region of the United States with a More Detailed Account of the Lands of Utah with Maps* (Washington, DC: US Government Printing Office, 1879), 40.

4. John Wesley Powell, "Institutions for the Arid Lands," *Century* 40 (1890): 113.

5. Ibid., 115.

6. John Wesley Powell, *Exploration of the Colorado River and Its Canyons*, ed. Wallace Stegner (New York: Penguin Books, 1987), 127.

7. National Park Foundation, "A Sight Beyond Words: Grand Canyon National Park," accessed November 18, 2019, https://www.nationalparks.org/explore-parks/grand-canyon-national-park.

8. Donald Worster, *A River Running West: The Life of John Wesley Powell* (New York: Oxford University Press, 2000), 565–66.

9. Ibid., 566–69.

10. National Park Service, *A Survey of the Recreational Resources of the Colorado River Basin* (Washington, DC: US Government Printing Office, 1950), 21, https://www.nps.gov/parkhistory/online_books/colorado/index.htm.

11. Ibid., xxii.

12. Ibid., 17–21.

13. Outdoor Foundation, *Outdoor Recreation Participation Report* (2017), 1, outdoorindustry.org/wp-content/uploads/2017/05/2017-Outdoor-Recreation-Participation-Report_FINAL.pdf.

14. Christopher Leggett et al., Office of Policy Analysis, US Department of Interior, "Estimating Recreational Visitation to Federally Managed Lands," April 25, 2017, 1, https://www.doi.gov/sites/doi.gov/files/uploads/final.task1_.report.2017.04.25.pdf.

15. Ibid.

16. Bureau of Economic Analysis, "Gross-Domestic-Product-(GDP)-by-Industry Data, Gross Output," April 19, 2018, Excel sheet, www.bea.gov/industry/gdpbyind_data.htm.

17. Eric M. White et al., US Forest Service, "Federal Outdoor Recreation Trends: Effects on Economic Opportunities," November 2016, 1, https://www.fs.fed.us/pnw/pubs/pnw_gtr945.pdf.

18. Ibid.

19. Outdoor Industry Association, "The Outdoor Recreation Economy," 2017, 14, https://outdoorindustry.org/wp-content/uploads/2017/04/OIA_RecEconomy_FINAL_Single.pdf.

20. *Protected Areas Database of the United States (PAD-US)* shapefile, Version 1.4, US Geological Survey, 2016, gapanalysis.usgs.gov/padus/; "Colorado River Basin" shapefile, US Department of Agriculture, Natural Resource Conservation Service, 2014, www.nrcs.usda.gov/wps/portal/nrcs/detail/nh/home/?cid = stelprdb1254126.

21. Powell, *Exploration of the Colorado River*, 247.

22. US Department of Interior, Bureau of Reclamation, "Colorado River Basin Water Supply and Demand Study, Executive Summary" (2012), 8, https://www.usbr.gov/lc/region/programs/crbstudy/finalreport/Executive%20Summary/CRBS_Executive_Summary_FINAL.pdf.

23. United Nations Department of Economic and Social Affairs, "World population projected to reach 9.8 billion in 2050, and 11.2 billion in 2100," June 21, 2017, https://www.un.org/development/desa/en/news/population/world-population-prospects-2017.html.

24. Christopher Solomon, "Is Instagram Ruining the Great Outdoors?," *Outside*, March 29, 2017, https://www.outsideonline.com/2160416/instagram-ruining-great-outdoors.

25. Roderick Frazier Nash, *Wilderness and the American Mind*, 4th ed. (New Haven: Yale University Press, 2001), 316–19.

26. Rebecca Worby, "Forest Service confronts a popular hot springs' overuse," *High Country News*, August 17, 2017, https://www.hcn.org/articles/recreation-the-conundrum-of-loved-to-death-wilderness.

27. Garrett Hardin, "The Tragedy of the Commons," *Science* 162 (1968): 1243–48.

28. National Park Service, "Weighted Lottery—Non-Commercial River Permits," last updated March 15, 2019, https://www.nps.gov/grca/planyourvisit/weightedlottery.htm.

29. Steve Sullian, "2017 Backcountry and River Use Statistics," National Park Service Grand Canyon Backcountry Information Center, 2017, 23, https://www.nps.gov/grca/planyourvisit/upload/Backcountry_and_River_Use_Statistics_2017.pdf.

30. Worby, "Forest Service confronts a popular hot springs' overuse."

31. Rahawa Haile, "Going it Alone," Outside, 2017, www.outsideonline.com/2170266/solo-hiking-appalachian-trail-queer-black-woman.

32. US Forest Service, *National Visitor Use Monitoring Survey Results National Summary Report*, 2016, 12, https://www.fs.fed.us/recreation/programs/nvum/pdf/5082016NationalSummaryReport062217.pdf.

33. White et al., "Federal Outdoor Recreation Trends," 34–35.

34. "National Park Experience: NPX," accessed November 9, 2018, https://wildcities.org/project/national-park-experience-npx.

35. Latino Outdoors, *Latino Outdoors 2020: Connecting Cultura and Community with the Outdoors*, September 2017, 1, http://latinooutdoors.org/wp-content/uploads/2017/10/LO_Strategic_Plan_508.pdf.

36. The North Face, "She Moves Mountains," catalog and website, winter 2018, https://www.thenorthface.com/featured/she-moves-mountains.html.

37. REI, "Force of Nature" campaign, 2017, https://www.rei.com/h/force-of-nature.

38. Jake Bullinger, "Have 50 Years of Overcrowded Parks Taught Us Nothing?," *Outside*, March 2018, https://www.outsideonline.com/2292951/have-50-years-overcrowded-parks-taught-us-nothing.

39. US Forest Service, "Forest Service Wildfire Costs Exceed $2 Billion," news release, September 14, 2017, https://www.usda.gov/media/press-releases/2017/09/14/forest-service-wildland-fire-suppression-costs-exceed-2-billion.

40. Utah State Legislature, H.B. 148 "Transfer of Public Lands Act and Related Study" (2012), https://le.utah.gov/~2012/bills/static/HB0148.html.

41. Powell, "Institutions for the Arid Lands," 113.

42. Powell, "The Irrigable Lands of the Arid Region," *Century* 39 (1890): 770.

43. Jason Lee and Kristen Wyatt, "Salt Lake laments, Denver celebrates Outdoor Retailer move," *Deseret News*, July 6, 2017, https://www.deseretnews.com/article/865684343/Politics-citied-in-trade-shows-move-from-Utah-to-Colorado.html.

44. Laura Hancock, "Wyoming Senate President Kills Public Lands Transfer Bill," *Casper Star-Tribune*, January 20, 2017, http://trib.com/news/state-and-regional/govt-and-politics/wyoming-senate-president-kills-public-lands-transfer-bill/article_88bfb04b-6449-539d-8e70-081d781da35d.html.

45. Powell, "Non-Irrigable Lands," 916.

CHAPTER 8

Stewart Udall, John Wesley Powell, and the Emergence of a National American Commons

WILLIAM DEBUYS

Imagine you have been appointed secretary of interior. You step into the largest job of your life, one of the largest jobs in the nation, to oversee an imperial domain entailing hundreds of millions of acres and tens of thousands of employees. Your decisions affect the welfare of millions of citizens on every Native American reservation and in communities throughout the nation. The issues requiring your attention are beyond number. Many, perhaps most, involve matters with potential to entangle you, or the president for whom you work, in controversy. Urgency is normal. On Capitol Hill you must propitiate committee chairs, secure budgets, and advance programs. Within the department you must supervise bureau chiefs, loyal mainly to themselves, as well as fill key jobs, resolve feuds, and uncork bottlenecks. Lobbyists clamor for your time. More "friends" than you ever thought you had ask for favors. You must survive, but you must also lead, to influence the course of the nation. First, you must decide where to start.

If you are Stewart L. Udall, secretary of interior at the dawn of John F. Kennedy's New Frontier, you will do as none of your predecessors had done. You will write a book.

Stewart Udall coveted a place in history. He saw himself as descending from a long line of American conservationists, including John Wesley Powell, with whom he shared a personal connection to the Colorado River and intimate knowledge of the arid West. Udall saw his mission as Powell had seen his: to reconcile Americans to a more resilient, responsible, and democratic relationship with their land. For Udall, the path toward this lofty goal would require vast expansion of public parks, wildlife refuges, and other protected areas—enlargement of national conservation holdings that over the previous seventy years had become an American commons. Udall calculated that by writing the right kind of book, he might define the work that lay ahead and rally support for its execution.

Cabinet secretaries generally write books after they relinquish their responsibilities, not as they take them up. The press of duty hardly permits projects as time-consuming as book writing. But Udall charted his own path, and the eventual publication of *The Quiet Crisis,* months before JFK's assassination, would mark a turning point in American conservation history, when the lessons and themes of the past became refocused on an invigorated agenda. Udall invoked the diverse contributions of Powell and other historic conservation leaders to enlarge the federal mission to preserve America's natural beauty and landed heritage. He aimed to set aside parks, forests, seashores, and wildlife refuges sufficient to meet the needs of late-twentieth-century America.

The idealism of *The Quiet Crisis* soon collided with the realpolitik of Western water. At Interior, Udall commanded not just the National Park Service and the US Fish and Wildlife Service—heroes to supporters of a national commons—but also the Bureau of Reclamation—by the 1960s, a dam-building, canyon-flooding juggernaut. For many, Reclamation was the embodiment of anti-conservation evil. Udall could not avoid the contradictions inherent in his job, and the inevitable collision of values reached its crescendo in no less mythic a location than the depths of the Grand Canyon, where Udall, like Powell before him, met a turning point in life.

The Grand Canyon and the river running through it shaped both Powell's and Udall's contributions to the formation of a national American commons. Powell's vision of a Dryland Democracy took root during his first experiences in the canyon country and grew to fruition as he came to know the Colorado River Basin intimately. The canyon may have been less of a crucible for Udall—his commitment to a national commons wasn't formed there—but it tested his commitment, and the testing made it stronger.

Today, the testing continues at a national level. The idea of a shared heritage of remarkable lands, saved from private exploitation, faces challenges, not just within Grand Canyon National Park over such issues as uranium mining and river management, but even more heatedly on nearby lands, at such places as Bears Ears and Grand Staircase-Escalante national monuments. The story of a national American commons that Powell helped to start and that Udall grandly expanded remains unfinished.

GENESIS OF *THE QUIET CRISIS*

Only forty-one years old when he came to Interior, two and a half years younger than the president he served, Stewart Udall stormed into his job with grand ambitions. For three terms, he had represented Arizona's sparsely populated second congressional district, which included all of Arizona except metropolitan Phoenix. In 1959, Representative Udall worked hard for passage of a labor reform bill (the Landrum-Griffin Act), which Kennedy also supported. The crewcut southwesterner and the suave Massachusetts senator soon established a rapport. As Arizona prepared to select delegates for the 1960 Democratic presidential nominating convention, Carl Hayden, the state's powerful senior senator, indicated he would support Senator Lyndon B. Johnson of Texas. Udall brashly rebelled against Hayden, and organized a campaign for Kennedy. Improbably, Udall and his team narrowly prevailed, delivering all of Arizona's delegates for JFK. Interior was Udall's eventual reward.[1]

Shortly after Kennedy named Udall as secretary, a Stanford professor, Wallace Stegner, sent Udall a gift, a biography he had written some years earlier of John Wesley Powell entitled *Beyond the Hundredth Meridian*. Stegner thought "there might be something in it" that the secretary "could make use of."[2] Udall soon invited Stegner to visit. Both men were plain-speaking Westerners who knew well the geography of what Powell had called the "arid lands."[3] They were also deeply familiar with Mormonism, Udall by ancestry and Stegner through long residence in Utah. They struck up an instant friendship. As Stegner left their first meeting in Washington in January 1961, he gave Udall a copy of his recently drafted and now famous "Wilderness Letter."[4]

Udall was more than a little impressed. He read the letter publicly at a wilderness conference the following April, and he also asked Stegner to join his staff. Promising that Stegner would participate in high-level decisions, he especially entreated Stegner's assistance on a book he intended to write. He said he was otherwise "too busy to do a first-rate job" on the book, which he conceived, as his son Tom recalls, as a way to "learn his job."[5] Stegner approved the idea but demurred on leaving

Palo Alto for Washington. Still, Udall pressed him for ideas, and Stegner ultimately provided an outline that *The Quiet Crisis* largely follows.[6]

Initially, Udall brought in Henry Romney, an editor from *Field and Stream,* to guide the project. He also hired Sharon Francis, a recent graduate of Mount Holyoke College whose articles for *Living Wilderness,* the magazine of the Wilderness Society, had caught his attention. Romney told Francis that together they could help Udall knock out the book in a few months, an estimate that proved much too optimistic.[7] Nevertheless, Udall pressed ahead with impressive self-discipline.

Most mornings, he rose early and left his house in McLean, Virginia, by six-thirty, commencing work on the manuscript as soon as he settled into his chauffeured car. By seven, he was in his "back room," an antechamber adjacent to his big ceremonial office on the sixth floor of the Main Interior Building at 18th and C.[8] He continued work on the book until at least nine, when meetings and appointments took precedence.[9] Romney didn't last as the book's coordinator—he was unproductive, said some; others sensed he chafed under the secretary's staff structure and sometimes chaotic decision-making.[10] Stegner, meanwhile, had remained in contact with Udall and other team members. He took leave from Stanford during fall 1961 and moved into an office below Udall's on the fifth floor of the Interior Building.

Slowly *The Quiet Crisis* took shape. Alvin Josephy, the noted historian of Native America, helped for a while and wrote a first draft of "The Land Wisdom of the Indians," which begins the book. Sharon Francis took the lead on "The Stir of Conscience," discussing Thoreau and other naturalists. She also began "The Raid on Resources" (with generous advice from Stegner), as well as "The Beginning of Wisdom" about George Perkins Marsh, and other chapters. Udall reviewed drafts, providing comments and adding text, sometimes overhauling the drafts entirely. Francis remembers feeling crestfallen when the Marsh chapter, on which she had labored especially hard, came back from "the boss" with "eight pages of 'this is what I want to say.'" Seeing her distress at having her work undone, Udall said, "No, no. Add some of your things back in, too. I just want to make sure this is included."[11]

The writers followed no particular protocol. They shared drafts with Udall and each other. Francis, a young woman at a time when young women were routinely condescended to, swapped drafts and comments with Stegner, who, to her relief and pleasure, "treated me very much as a colleague, not as a junior."[12] And the team periodically changed, with others playing important roles. At the close of 1961, when Stegner returned to Palo Alto, Harold Gilliam and Donald Moser, both former students of Stegner, helped fill the void left by their mentor.

The question of who truly wrote *The Quiet Crisis* persists. Stegner deflected credit when he said, "Even when [Udall] would get a draft chapter from some helper, he tore it all apart and made it over again in his own way, so it's his book."[13] Sharon Francis doesn't contradict Stegner, but spreads the credit more broadly: "It was very much a collaboration. Stewart initiated, had initial thoughts about a chapter, and might toss the first draft to me or to Wally.... There was so much interaction I really can't say that there was one writer. It was kind of a brain trust, if you will, or a team that the secretary brought together, and he worked with us and we worked with each other and with him."[14]

The Quiet Crisis, with an introduction by President Kennedy (probably written by Ted Sorenson), appeared in early 1963. It sold well, and soon became viewed, like Rachel Carson's *Silent Spring,* published the previous year, as a core environmental text. As Carson probed the impacts of pesticides and herbicides, Udall examined American society's treatment of its lands and waters. Following Stegner's outline, he placed contemporary issues in the context of American history, sketching contributions from Thoreau, Emerson, Marsh, Powell, Schurz, Muir, Olmstead, Pinchot, the two Roosevelts, and many others, and linking them to an evolving consensus for conserving the nation's landed heritage. But Udall did not stop there. He tied the book to his political and programmatic agenda, questioning whether, despite the vastness of their patrimony, Americans had set aside enough parks, seashores, and wild places to satisfy the needs of future generations, and asking whether they were alert to the contamination and sprawl that threatened their inherited bounty:

> America today stands poised on a pinnacle of wealth and power, yet we live in a land of vanishing beauty, of increasing ugliness, and of an overall environment that is diminished daily by pollution and noise and blight.
> This, in brief, is the quiet conservation crisis of the 1960s.[15]

If Udall indeed meant to "learn his job" by writing *The Quiet Crisis,* he used the book even more to redefine the job the way he wanted it to be. Notwithstanding the many extractive activities occurring under the aegis of Interior, Udall cast himself as the nation's conservationist-in-chief. The choice suited his talents. Not even his most fervent admirers would have called him a skilled administrator. At best, his management style was "unorthodox"; more realistically, it was scattershot and turbulent. Udall had little patience for procedural details. His inclination was always to push ahead to the next big thing, the next big idea. And also to speak out. Udall had the energy and charisma to be effective on the largest stages, and he was naturally eloquent, both as a speaker and a writer (although his outspokenness also sometimes got him into trouble).[16]

But Udall was hardly satisfied with cheerleading. He aspired to the kind of impact that Gifford Pinchot had had in tandem with Teddy Roosevelt and that Harold Ickes had made with FDR. Under both Kennedy and Johnson, he persistently urged programs of "Rooseveltian proportions."[17] Although neither president responded with the enthusiasm he would have liked, during his eight years at Interior Udall oversaw the addition of nearly four million acres to the nation's protected holdings, including "four national parks . . . six national monuments, nine national recreation areas, twenty historic sites, fifty wildlife refuges and eight national seashores."[18] He also played a major role with such landmark legislation as the Wilderness Act and the Land and Water Conservation Fund Act, which President Johnson signed into law on the same day in 1964.

Udall's legacy, however, was ultimately less than he would have wished. He fervently hoped LBJ would conclude his administration with a great "gift to the American people" by conferring protection on an additional eight million acres of public land in Alaska, Utah, and Arizona. But Johnson, by then demoralized by Vietnam, balked at stretching his authority under the Antiquities Act as far as Udall would have him do. He was also outraged upon discovering Udall had misled him in reporting that Wayne Aspinall, the powerful chairman of the House Interior Committee, would acquiesce to the proposal. Johnson agreed to approve only a fraction (384,000 acres) of Udall's sprawling proposal. His denial of Udall's request for a final, sweeping, preservationist gesture may have been the greatest disappointment of Udall's government career.[19]

HIGH DAMS IN POWELL'S "GRAND CANYON"

Given Wallace Stegner's prominent role in outlining and writing *The Quiet Crisis*, one might expect the book to accord outsize emphasis to John Wesley Powell. This is not the case. Powell does not even get his own chapter. His story is paired with that of Carl Schurz, secretary of interior under Rutherford B. Hayes, in a chapter entitled, "The Beginning of Action." Udall presents Powell as a Cassandra, warning against misuse of the land and predicting suffering and loss if his cautions are ignored. This, of course, is also Udall's posture in *The Quiet Crisis,* that of the prophet calling on society to change course.

Udall, however, makes no mention of Powell's radical 1890 proposal to reorganize the West into a system of "watershed commonwealths."[20] Instead, he focuses on Powell's 1878 *Arid Lands Report,* holding up Powell as an apostle of science and land-use planning: "False estimates of fact and climate, [Powell] knew, would lead only to disaster, and the time to plan was before the patterns of settlement were fixed."[21]

The Quiet Crisis depicts Powell as out of step with the values of his day: the Major "used bear language in a bull market, and most of the Western leaders would have none of it."[22] Powell's example was not one that Udall wanted to follow. He sought not only to be *right,* like Powell, but also successful. Gifford Pinchot, the hero of the chapter following Powell's, was more to his liking, for Pinchot, through his relationship with Teddy Roosevelt, had access to executive power and got big things done.

Udall's trajectory through conservation history parallels Powell's in multiple ways. Both saw themselves as bearing a mission to reconcile American society to its land; both were accomplished writers who delivered messages not only to centers of power, but directly through popular publications to the general public; both were steeped in knowledge of the arid West and had absorbed its spirit. Even more specifically, the Colorado River and the Grand Canyon—the latter's name affixed by Powell during his 1869 Expedition—drew both to powerful reckonings.

More than any secretary of interior before or since, Stewart Udall was a river rat. In 1960, while still a congressman, he and his family rafted the Colorado River through Glen Canyon, which, although doomed, was then still intact. The dam that would drown it would not be completed until 1963, but plans for its construction had been in place since 1956, when the Colorado River Storage Project Act was enacted, long before Udall became secretary. (Nevertheless, Udall regarded Glen Canyon Dam's completion during his tenure at Interior as one of his greatest professional regrets.)[23] In 1961, now as secretary, Udall again floated the river, this time through the Green River confluence and Cataract Canyon, downstream of Moab, Utah. With him were Secretary of Agriculture Orville Freeman and chairman of the National Parks Advisory Board Frank Masland. The trip was part vacation and part reconnaissance, as Udall and his companions investigated possibilities for what would eventually become Canyonlands National

Park.[24] In 1967, he took to the river again as he wrestled with one of the greatest conflicts, not just of his tenure at Interior, but of his life.

In the 1950s and 1960s, the paramount duty of an Arizona congressman was simple: get water for Arizona. This meant promoting and supporting the Central Arizona Project (CAP)—the ultimate vehicle for realizing Arizona's entitlement to water from the Colorado River under the 1922 Colorado River Compact. The CAP was a colossally expensive, energy-consumptive scheme to lift water from the river at the California border, pump it over western Arizona's tablelands, and deliver it via tunnels, siphons, and aqueducts to Phoenix and Tucson, more than three hundred miles away. Never mind that the river's over-allocation had become clear and that the CAP would depend on potentially unreliable water supplies.[25] Never mind that California, by far the largest consumer of Colorado River water and possessing a much larger delegation in the House of Representatives, repeatedly blocked authorization of the CAP.[26] Congressman Stewart Udall and later his brother Morris, who succeeded him representing Arizona's second district, embraced the job of convincing all doubters that the CAP was vital to the rescue of agriculture in central Arizona, which had grown large and productive but depended on unsustainable groundwater pumping. Without the CAP, aquifers would run dry and Arizona's economy would collapse. So went the party line. Moreover, without the CAP, Arizona might never get the bonanza of pork-barrel public-works spending for which it had long waited and which, like every other basin state, it saw as its due.

In August 1963, Interior's Bureau of Reclamation released an outline of the Pacific Southwest Water Plan, with a more detailed exposition forthcoming the following January.[27] Udall's name was on the report's cover. The plan proposed that the CAP's gigantic liabilities—cost, energy consumption, and insufficient water—might be resolved through the expedient of equally gigantic dams.

The dams were to be sited on the Colorado River at either end of Grand Canyon National Park, which was then bounded by Grand Canyon National Monument and, overall, was much smaller than today. The sites were chosen to optimize hydropower, without "harming" the park. Marble Gorge Dam would be upstream of the park, and Bridge Canyon Dam, although its reservoir would drown much of the national monument, would cause only "minor" flooding at the park's downstream end. The projected flooding may have been "minor" in some eyes, but it would submerge the river's most spectacular surviving rapids, Lava Falls (other great rapids had been lost to Lake Mead), and also drown the turquoise pools at the mouth of Havasu Creek, one of the canyon's gems.

Marble Gorge and Bridge Canyon were envisioned to be "cash-register dams." They would generate power to meet the CAP's pumping needs, and their additional power sales would help defray the project's cost. Once the CAP was paid for, their revenues might finance still larger projects to import water from the Pacific Northwest or northern California, slaking the Southwest's thirst and "augmenting" the Colorado River's strained resources.[28] By generating money as well as electricity, they would enable re-plumbing of half of North America, the grandest hydraulic adventure in the history of humankind. Or so their advocates hoped.

Stewart Udall, intellectual descendant of Powell and advocate for America's natural heritage, soon found himself struggling to reconcile his conservation values with his advocacy for the most expensive manipulation of an American river ever—not to mention his imminent complicity in turning a revered national park into a "dam sandwich," with reservoirs and giant structures confining both ends.

In the early 1900s, conservationists had fought Hetch Hetchy Dam in Yosemite National Park—and lost. In mid-century, they had fought Echo Park Dam in Dinosaur National Monument—and won a pyrrhic victory, the price for protecting Dinosaur being acceptance of Glen Canyon Dam, which drowned the wonderland for which it was named. Now, led by David Brower, the Sierra Club's executive director, and Martin Litton, a powerhouse on the Sierra Club board, they resolved to accept nothing short of complete victory: there must be no Grand Canyon dams and no trade-offs.

The story of the ensuing, multi-year battle has been told many times; Marc Reisner's account in *Cadillac Desert* is classic. While the saga needs no repeating, it bears mentioning that the conflict was intensely personal for Udall. In 1966, the Sierra Club's famous full-page advertisements in the *New York Times* and *Washington Post* sometimes addressed him directly. One was an open letter from Brower that began, "Dear Mr. Udall, If Congress lets your Reclamation Bureau ruin Grand Canyon with two dams, can any national park be safe?" The letter continued with a personal, if covert, dig at the secretary: "You will remember what Theodore Roosevelt said about the Canyon in 1903: 'Leave it as it is. You cannot improve on it. The ages have been at work on it and man can only mar it.' We, and Arizonans (some of them secretly), know he was right."[29]

By then, Udall had supported the CAP for more than a decade, testifying before Congress many times in its favor. Now his brother Morris was the project's leading proponent in the House of Representatives, which meant that advocacy for the CAP touched on family loyalty. It also affected Udall's future political life after he departed Interior. Arizona, the heart of the Sunbelt, was growing thirstier—and more conservative. Udall may have had his eye on Carl Hayden's seat; Hayden had served in the Senate since the Coolidge administration, and his retirement was imminent. While Arizona voters might forgive Udall's liberality on conservation issues, a betrayal of the CAP would amount to political suicide.[30] Udall was in a fix: national public opinion was turning against the dams, and his reputation, historical legacy, and many close relationships were at stake in the decisions he would have to make.

Udall directed his staff to look for other ways to power the CAP. Ultimately, he selected an alternative that seemed nearly cost-free at the time but looks very different today. In February 1967, Udall's department recommended swapping Marble Gorge Dam for a new coal-fired power plant at Page, Arizona. (The department had already announced it would defer a decision on Bridge Canyon Dam.) Coal for the plant, soon dubbed the Navajo Generating Station (NGS), would be strip-mined from Navajo and Hopi lands. The NGS would supply the CAP's energy, and its revenues would help pay for the aqueducts and pumping stations.

Udall came to rue the NGS in many ways: the destruction caused by the strip-mining, the impairment of air quality by the plant's emissions, and the cynical betrayal, revealed years later, underlying agreements with the tribes. (Peabody Coal secretly employed John Boyden, attorney of record for the Hopi, who, in an ethical breach of the first magnitude, favored the coal company's interests over those of the tribe.)[31] Eventually, Udall also regretted the vast quantities of greenhouse gases released,[32] and, not least, the knock-on effects of the CAP itself, which he came to view as a massive betrayal. The project did not rescue Arizona agriculture— "[t]he farmers can't afford the water," he said—but rather catalyzed the metastasis of Phoenix. "It's an example of bad planning, an example of bad economics. I naturally have a lot of regrets about it. . . . I never in the 1960s thought of Phoenix becoming another Los Angeles, or Tucson becoming another Phoenix."[33]

These regrets, however, lay in the future. In 1967, Udall's change of tack on the Grand Canyon dams initiated new rounds of finger-pointing, as well as renewed political horse-trading. Plenty of Arizonans felt Udall had "double-crossed his own state"³⁴—they still wanted a cash-register dam on the Colorado to subsidize the CAP and finance future projects. To the surprise of many, however, Carl Hayden blessed the new approach, and Congress went into high gear reformulating a something-for-everybody Southwestern water bill, deleting the Grand Canyon dams and adding enough other projects to win over key figures like Aspinall and pass both houses.³⁵ The resulting Colorado River Basin Project Act of 1968 provided long-sought authorization for the CAP, for which construction began in 1973 and continued for more than two decades.

In the summer of 1967, with the storm over the Grand Canyon dams still raging, Stewart Udall ducked out of public view. Ethics rules were more relaxed then, and the secretary had directed the National Park Service to organize a raft trip that would allow him, as he informed President Johnson, to enjoy an "extended family vacation" and also "form some final opinions on the dams in the Grand Canyon controversy."³⁶

The Udall party put in at Lees Ferry, a legendary location named for Udall's great-grandfather (who was also the great-grandfather of his wife Lee). Under Brigham Young's instruction, John Doyle Lee operated a ferry in that "lonely dell" in the 1870s. The boat Lee used, at least initially, was probably the same vessel John Wesley Powell had ordered built there to carry his land expedition across the river in 1870.³⁷

At least some of Udall's deliberation, as he and his family descended the river, was orchestrated. A photographer had been brought along, and Udall's personal journal of the trip references the "article" that he intended to write, which would appear in *Venture*, a travel magazine, early in 1968. In addition, Tom Udall, then nineteen, remembers a helicopter whisking his father away one morning, perhaps to a meeting, perhaps to a press conference on the rim. If the latter, the purpose was not for Udall to announce a final position on Bridge Canyon Dam, the fate of which would remain in question into the next year. The dam, which had been renamed Hualapai Dam, after the tribe on whose land part of it would be anchored, was a focus of Udall's *Venture* article. He judged the recreational lake it would create to be inferior to Lakes Mead and Powell, and he described the scenery it would drown as "overpowering" and "sensational." In the article, Udall expresses skepticism about the wisdom of building the dam but withholds final judgment, concluding: "The burden of proof, I believe, rests on the dam builders. If they cannot make out a compelling case, the park should be enlarged [that is, Grand Canyon National Monument should be added to Grand Canyon National Park] and given permanent protection."³⁸

By contrast, the views Udall confessed to his journal are unambiguous. In these private, water-stained pages, he delivers "The verdict on Marble: As a recreation lake 4th rate as compared w/ Glen.... Increasingly am forced to the conclusion that the Grand Canyon N.P. is only half a park. The Bureau of Reclamation would never build half a dam, so why settle for half a park?" Days later, he notes Deer Creek, whose one-hundred-eighty-foot waterfall cascades into the river, is "a glorious stop," the canyon downstream from the Kanab Creek confluence "is magnificent," and Havasu canyon is "a Shangri-La." The approach to Havasu, he wrote, "is, for me, the most dramatic and overpowering part of the inner gorge. The Sierra Club is right once again. High Bridge [the high dam at Bridge Canyon] must never be built." And further, "No dam should ever be built that would inundate Havasu canyon and the upstream portion of the monument. This much is clear, if we are to take our conservation creed seriously."[39]

Indeed, the Sierra Club was doubly right. As David Brower had intimated, at least one Arizonan "secretly" agreed with Teddy Roosevelt that the Grand Canyon should be left alone.

Throughout his tenure at Interior, Udall maintained a guarded, mutually suspicious relationship with Floyd Dominy, the department's formidable commissioner of reclamation. Having cultivated favor with members of Congress since he first worked for the reclamation bureau in 1946, the commissioner operated largely independently of the secretary to whom he reported. Udall's misgivings about Dominy and the agency deepened as he journeyed through the Grand Canyon:

> I've been increasingly struck with the short term outlook of the Reclamation engineers. Mead and Lake Powell will both silt up in two hundred or so years, and the people of that age will garner our muddy legacy. And the reply of the Reclamationists, 'Well, two hundred years is a long time,' is as thoughtless and empty as 'Uncle Joe' Cannon's 'What do we owe posterity? What has posterity done for us?'[40]

Taking place a century after Powell's historic 1869 Expedition, Udall's 1967 Grand Canyon voyage consolidated the secretary's growing doubts about allowing big dams to flood the West's wonder places. In *Venture*, he admitted his original bias in favor of Reclamation: "I approached this problem with a less-than-open mind in early 1963, when we began our planning at Interior for the Lower Colorado Project." The trip down the river, however, underscored for him that "[t]he Secretary of the Interior should never make armchair judgments on national conservation issues."[41] Instead, he should see things firsthand. John Wesley Powell, an advocate for geographical empiricism if ever one existed, would have approved.[42]

THE EMERGENCE OF A NATIONAL AMERICAN COMMONS

Powell was on Udall's mind as he rafted the Grand Canyon. In his journal entry for day two, he quotes the explorer's description of the "giant architectural forms," now submerged, of Glen Canyon that "one could almost imagine . . . had been carved with a purpose." The loss of those marvels may have preyed on the secretary, especially as he inspected the proposed Marble Gorge Dam site, where exploratory tunnels had already been drilled into canyon walls. Powell's words had been shared with the entire group that night or the night before, for as Udall noted in his *Venture* article, "Powell's journal, read aloud around the campfire, helped us relive the fears and hopes of his team."[43]

Powell and Udall shared much—their chanticleer's desire to alert Americans to the dangers of misusing land, their skill as writers, their respect for Mormonism, their grasp of aridity's influence on the Intermountain West, and the constant pull of the Colorado River and its canyons on them. They also shared an experience that does not touch on the West: both served in the military and saw extensive combat. Powell's Civil War career, including his maiming at Shiloh, is well known; the fifty World War II bombing missions flown by Master Sergeant Udall, a waist gunner on B-24s operating out of Italy, are less so.

The strongest ties binding Powell and Udall, however, involve their contributions to a particular American project—the creation of a national commons. This unfinished enterprise was rarely couched in terms of "common land" or "ownership in commons" in the traditional sense. (After the Bolshevik Revolution of 1917, such terms invited criticism that the user was communistic or anti-American.) A separate vocabulary dominates discussion of public lands that became forest reserves and national forests, national parks and monuments, wildlife refuges, wilderness areas, and more. Labeling aside, lands placed under this range of designations have constituted a national commons, which has been mostly exempt from "enclosure" through privatization.

Henry Thoreau, had he lived long enough to observe the beginnings of this process, might have termed it, not a creation, but a restoration of a commons. Throughout his life, Thoreau rambled the *de facto* commons of New England—Walden Pond, the Maine Woods, Cape Cod, and along the Concord and Merrimack rivers. The free access he enjoyed to such places inspired all but his most explicitly political writing, while the diminishment of this commons—through degradation (logging and river damming especially) and enclosure (privatization of farmsteads and even berrying patches)—troubled him greatly in his final years.[44]

The apogee of Powell's career in the late 1880s marked a transition in American attitudes toward shared interest in land. The Homestead Act of 1862 had confirmed the small family farm as a national ideal and implicitly suggested the commons of the public domain might ultimately be converted to an agricultural empire of private 160-acre farms. Underlying the Homestead Act was the idea that ownership of freehold farms was reformative: irrespective of an individual's background, tilling one's own soil encouraged the kind of personal character that best suited a democracy and on which its perpetuation depended.

Idealistically, and in the event, cruelly, this notion was extended to Native American lands. In 1887, Congress passed the General Allotment Act, or Dawes Severalty Act, which ordered that Indian reservations be broken into small units and distributed to individual heads of household, who were expected to become farmers. Moreover, reservation land left over from allotment could be declared "surplus" and disposed of—a boon to many whites who coveted Indian land and a cause of the unholy alliance of greed and idealism that enabled the act's passage.

Private property ownership and extinguishment of the tribal commons, so the thinking went, would free reservation Natives from fealty to their chiefs, instill virtues of hard work and self-improvement, and speed their acculturation into mainstream society. In the words of historian T. H. Watkins, the allotment program was "[a] grand design, and quite possibly—next to Prohibition—the most thoroughly misguided and unworkable reform measure in American history."[45] Faith in private property's redemptive power would never be more widely shared—or more misplaced.

Powell's stance on Indian policy is revealing. He agreed that acculturation of Natives into American society should be the goal and that adoption of farming was a necessary first step. He further asserted that rupturing Native people's emotional bonds with traditional homelands would speed this process. In 1880, he elaborated his views for Senator Henry Teller of Colorado (soon to be President Chester A. Arthur's secretary of interior, 1882–85):

When an Indian clan or tribe gives up its land . . . its gods are abandoned . . . that is, everything most sacred to Indian society is yielded up.

Such a removal of the Indians is the first step to be taken in their civilization. . . .

The second great step in the civilization of the Indians consists in inducing them to take lands and property in severalty.[46]

In Powell's day, these were common normative views. As a leading expert on Indian society and culture—directing the Bureau of American Ethnology from its formation in 1879[47] to his death in 1902—Powell helped shape them. (Teller, to his credit, held contrary opinions.) Although often at odds with conventional thinking on other subjects, Powell reflected mainstream values on Indian policy. To be fair, he cautioned that allotment "should not be abruptly forced upon" Indians—but it was nevertheless necessary. He seemed to believe that, by speeding assimilation, such cruelty would be kindness in the end.[48] He appears to have concluded "not only that Indian tribes would vanish, but that they should."[49]

While urging privatization of the Indian commons, Powell was simultaneously—and inconsistently—beginning to think differently about land tenure among whites. As Donald Worster puts it, Powell "had a few doubts" about "economic individualism, rigid self-reliance, and competition . . . stirring in the back of his head, doubts that later grew into a critique of American ideology."[50]

Powell's ideas matured into a plan for Western settlement that he presented to Congress less than three years after the General Allotment Act's passage. Under his plan—which makes no mention of Indians—much of the Western landscape and nearly all its water would be secured as the common property of those who settled within watersheds to which those lands and waters belonged. Powell's chief ally in this effort was the strangest of political bedfellows, Senator John H. Reagan of Texas.

Powell had been a fervent abolitionist and supporter of the Union cause. By contrast, Reagan was possibly the highest-ranking Confederate official to serve in the postwar US Congress. Passionately in favor of secession, Reagan was the CSA's postmaster general in Jefferson Davis's cabinet. When Richmond fell, he fled with the Confederate president and was eventually captured with him in southern Georgia, thereafter being confined to a Union prison. Upon release, Reagan returned home to Palestine, Texas, and beginning in 1877 served five terms in the House of Representatives. In 1886, he won election to the Senate, where in due time he was appointed to the newly created Select Committee on Irrigation and Reclamation of Arid Lands, which brought him into close contact with Powell.[51]

In February 1890, Reagan introduced into the Senate the first of several bills written by Powell. S. 2837 intended "to provide for the irrigation of the arid lands of the United States and for other purposes." The bill would have reorganized Western lands as a system of "watershed commonwealths," following a plan that Powell described for a general audience in *Century* magazine a few months later. It called for individual ownership of town sites, irrigable farms no larger than eighty acres, and mineral and coal lands subject to existing law. But it also specified:

> [A]ll other lands in the irrigation districts are hereby declared to be public lands, to remain the property of the United States, and to be held for the use and benefit of the people of the irrigation districts as forest lands, and as pasturage lands, and as catchment areas or sources of supply for the waters to be used in the irrigation districts for irrigation and for other beneficial purposes.[52]

The plan embodied in S. 2837 differed significantly from the one Powell had advocated in his 1878 *Arid Lands Report*. Powell previously had called for settlement of "pasturage lands" by stock-raisers, who would settle in "colonies" of "nine or more persons" and manage—and own—their rangelands collectively. Further, Powell had been vague in 1878 about who should hold title to "timber lands," but gave no indication that the federal government should retain them.

The shift toward retained federal ownership in S. 2837, albeit with locally determined use of pasturage and timberlands, is arresting. Powell's motive is unclear. Possibly he was yielding to the growing political influence of Bernard Fernow and other forest protectionists who called for a federal system of forest reservations. Possibly Powell himself felt unease at the prospect of unrestrained local control over land and resources. In any event, by 1890 Powell changed course and advocated that the "General Government" should retain title to most of the arid region, save for irrigable lands and town sites. He thought the government should remain the owner of lands that its citizens would utilize as commons.[53]

Powell's vision for establishing a system of commons throughout the West died a tortured legislative death over the spring and summer of 1890. Powell's chief tormentor was Senator William Stewart of Nevada, who, some years earlier, had paradoxically instigated the formation of the

Irrigation Survey, an indispensable instrument for Powell's plan. (Stewart, who had previously made a fortune litigating mining claims in the Comstock Lode, thought speculation in Western irrigation projects might prove similarly lucrative.) The fight between Powell and Stewart grew personal, as well as ideological, ultimately precipitating the Irrigation Survey's termination and the decline of Powell's influence in Washington.[54] It also generated considerable newspaper interest, even to the point of compelling Reagan and Stewart to deny publicly, on June 20, 1890, that they had come to blows on the Senate floor.[55] Through part of the turmoil, Powell's famous multicolored map of Western watersheds hung in the chamber, "so that Senators who wanted to know more of the Major Powell irrigation problem might have opportunities to see how the plan appears on canvas." The *Washington Evening Star* unflatteringly described the map as "looking like an Easter-egg-dye advertisement."[56]

Even as Powell and Stewart battled, a different concept for a national commons was taking root. During the same congressional session that witnessed the Powell-Stewart-Reagan melee, a minor bill repealing the Timber Culture Act made its way through both chambers. The versions approved by the two houses being different, the bill was assigned to a conference, which proceeded slowly. The conference committee did not report back until February 1891. When it did, the bill reported featured a provision that neither original bill, going in, had possessed. This became known as the Forest Reserve Clause, which empowered the president to set aside "reservations" of forested land in the public domain. The legislation did not specify the purposes for which the reservations might be made, but advocates like Fernow and the American Forestry Association had repeatedly urged such a measure in the name of forest and watershed conservation.[57] The clause's text was brief and vague. It said that reservations might consist of "land wholly or in part covered with timber or undergrowth, whether of commercial value or not," and that the president should clearly declare their boundaries.[58] That was it.

Prior to this action, the government had taken steps to protect Yellowstone and Yosemite as national parks and had placed several Civil War battlefields under the War Department's protection. But authorizing the president to create forest reserves marks the true beginning of a national American commons. It differed from Powell's vision in that it was an entirely federal system, designated and controlled from Washington, whereas Powell's commons, although federally owned, would have been subject to local governance. Moreover, the impulse behind the forest reserves was resource protection, while Powell's agenda was broadly social and utopian. Powell saw his plan as essential not just to reconcile settlement with the realities of the land, but to foster the democratic values enshrined in the Homestead Act and related land laws.

The incipient national commons grew fast and initially enjoyed bipartisan support. President Benjamin Harrison, a Republican, set aside 13 million acres of forest reserves, and Grover Cleveland, a Democrat, 25 million. Although Cleveland's action generated heated opposition, William McKinley, a Republican, added seven million more acres. Then Teddy Roosevelt, aided by Gifford Pinchot, shifted the process into overdrive, renaming the reserves "national forests," transferring their management from the Department of the Interior to the Department of Agriculture, and more than tripling the protected area.[59]

A neglected conservation hero, Senator John Lacey of Iowa, meanwhile sponsored the eponymous Lacey Act (1900), which asserted a national interest in wildlife protection. He also steered the Antiquities Act into law in 1906, empowering the president to designate national monuments, with no explicit limit to their size. Later came the National Park Service Organic Act (1916), establishing the national park system, and the Taylor Grazing Act (1934), which attempted to protect the public's interest in the environmental health of the remaining unreserved public domain.

It is difficult to assess Powell's precise contribution to the construction of the national American commons. His warnings about land misuse, both in the halls of government and popular publications, certainly boosted the impetus toward conservation and lessened support for uniform privatization. His talk of commons, presented in his grand design for Western settlement, may also have reduced resistance to the idea of federal institutions holding land on a permanent basis.

INTO THE GREAT (NEW) UNKNOWN

By the time Stewart Udall became secretary of interior, almost six decades after Powell's death, the nation's courts had repeatedly examined and reaffirmed the federal government's constitutional authority to retain and administer an extensive system of lands (rather than simply divest its public domain).[60] The prevailing issue for Udall, and conservationists generally, was whether the system was adequate to the nation's needs, especially given the appetite of a growing population for outdoor recreation. Further, Udall and his allies questioned whether protections afforded to those lands were sufficient to defend their most valued qualities. These concerns lay at the core of *The Quiet Crisis*. They likewise impelled Udall's aggressive expansion of federal holdings within the national park and national wildlife refuge systems, and his commitment to such legislation as the Wilderness Act and the Land and Water Conservation Fund Act. During his tenure, popular sentiment shifted toward increasing support for expansion of the national American commons. The prosperity of the sixties contributed to a consensus that the nation was wealthy enough to forego economic opportunities that expansion of protected lands might jeopardize. *The Quiet Crisis* both embodied this new consensus and also helped to shape it.

The consensus, however, was hardly permanent, and the Colorado River Basin's public lands may be considered Exhibit A in the complicated story of its decline. The "Sagebrush Rebellion" of the Reagan years and the long-simmering dispute between federal land managers and the Cliven Bundy family of Laughlin, Nevada—which reached a boil in the armed takeover of Malheur National Wildlife Refuge in 2016—are symptomatic of a drive for diminished protections for public lands.

To state the obvious, the issue has become sharply partisan, with Republicans urging reduction of the national American commons, while Democrats continue to support expansion. Presidents Clinton and Obama acted decisively in favor of expansion when they set aside two large national monuments within the Colorado River Basin. Clinton created Grand Staircase/Escalante National Monument in 1996 (1.9 million acres), and Obama designated Bears Ears National Monument in 2016 (1.3 million acres, much of which had been included in Stewart Udall's original proposal for Canyonlands National Park, although later deleted).[61] In December 2017, however, Donald Trump dramatically sided with advocates of resource development and rescinded most of his predecessors' declarations, cutting Grand Staircase by almost half (to 1.1 million acres) and Bears Ears by 84 percent (to 220,000 acres). All three presidents claimed to have acted under authority conferred by the Antiquities Act of 1906.[62] Conservationists and Indian tribes subsequently filed lawsuits asserting that Trump's rescissions violated the law.[63] The suits, by pressing for clarification of presidential authority, have the potential to reshape the law of the national American commons, although if they are not resolved before January 2021, and if the 2020 election returns a Democrat to the White House, a reversal of the rescissions could render the suits moot.

Whatever the outcome, there can be little doubt that the Colorado River Basin, where both John Wesley Powell and Stewart Udall contributed materially to defining the goals of American conservation, will remain a battleground between the privatization of resources and the persistence of a national commons.

The "Lords of Yesterday"—to borrow Charles Wilkinson's term[64]—will continue to play dominant roles. Grazing, mining, forest management, and the operation of dams, if not the building of new ones, will spark furious argument, as they have for generations. Joined by the big business of (especially motorized) recreation, they will press hard against the shield of laws intended to protect wildlife and the land itself. Water allocation, or more particularly *re-allocation,* mainly from agriculture to municipal use, will top the basin's concerns, as surface water supplies dwindle from climate change. Owners of water rights will benefit mightily from the transfers; agricultural workers likely will not. Most at risk will be communities beyond the reach of the rivers and aqueducts that can distribute repurposed agricultural water. Cities and towns that depend on small watersheds and limited aquifers and that cannot tap large-scale infrastructure—Flagstaff, Arizona, is a good example—may eventually wither.[65]

John Wesley Powell was fond of saying, "With wisdom you may prosper, but with folly you must fail."[66] He was a scientific scold who never ceased admonishing his fellow Americans to respect the land's limits, lest they suffer the consequences of misuse. In writing *The Quiet Crisis,* Stewart Udall followed in Powell's tradition, while also arguing for a broadened vision of natural America, one with an extensive shared commons, prioritizing beauty and heritage over fevered development. Only forty-nine years old when he left Interior, Udall continued to speak out with a steady stream of newspaper opinion pieces, as well as such books as *The Energy Balloon* (1974) and *The Quiet Crisis and the Next Generation* (1988), a sequel to the original work.[67]

The two men might be imagined ensconced in the fictive choir loft of history, peering critically toward the future, as the arid lands, including the Colorado River Basin, grow hotter and drier. Both wisdom and folly will be much on display, and as much as one might hope the former will predominate, the so-called lessons of history provide little reassurance. Many sudden crises—earthquakes, floods, tornadoes, and the like—seem to draw people together, but drought often has an opposite effect.[68] One cannot know that a drought has truly begun until it is well advanced, and one never knows when it will end. Drought divides as often as it unites, for it gives its victims abundant time to contemplate their neighbors' deficiencies. The thirsty years ahead will be riven, no doubt, by desperate fights over land and water, and the basin may well prove a bellwether for the nation. Either its tradition as a national American commons will help to hold it together, or the commons itself, unendingly pressured to surrender what it protects, may give way.

In their shared love for the Colorado River Basin and the rest of the arid lands, Powell and Udall set an example that the rest of us would do well to follow. Love is the first ingredient of loyalty, and the basin's land still needs people, like them, who are loyal and willing to defend it. The basin also rewards its defenders. Those of us who love the basin are among the most fortunate people on the planet, for we know what it is to immerse ourselves in a kind of beauty duplicated nowhere else. The Colorado River Basin has rightly earned its place as a centerpiece of the national American commons, and the advantages to loving it don't stop there. The arid lands are on the march again, not, this time, because of overgrazing or other forms of land abuse, but because of what industrial society has done to the atmosphere. And so it is good to love the desert: there is going to be a lot more of it.

Acknowledgments

The author would like to express his sincere thanks to the John W. Kluge Center of the Library of Congress for the generous support that made much of the research underlying this chapter possible.

NOTES

1. Stewart L. Udall (hereafter SLU) to Charles T. Morrissey, March 15, 1979, Former Members of Congress, Inc., Oral History Interviews, Manuscript Division, Library of Congress, Part I: 10, pp. 17–22.

2. Philip L. Fradkin, *Wallace Stegner and the American West* (Berkeley: University of California Press, 2008), 197.

3. John Wesley Powell, *Report on the Lands of the Arid Region of the United States, with a More Detailed Account of the Lands of Utah,* Forty-fifth Congress, Second Session, H.R. Exec. Doc. 73, 1878.

4. Fradkin, *Wallace Stegner,* 197. The friendship between Udall and Stegner lasted decades. Stegner died in 1993 from injuries sustained in a car crash in Santa Fe, New Mexico, which occurred while he was returning to his hotel after a dinner with Udall.

5. Fradkin, *Wallace Stegner,* 206; Tom Udall to William deBuys, January 27, 2018, Santa Fe, New Mexico, and April 16, 2018, Washington, DC.

6. Thomas G. Smith, *Stewart L. Udall: Steward of the Land* (Albuquerque: University of New Mexico Press, 2017), 156–57; Fradkin, *Wallace Stegner,* 208–9, 213; Tom Udall, April 16, 2018.

7. Sharon Francis to William deBuys, May 8, 2018, by telephone.
8. After Udall's death in March 2010, Congress renamed the building the Stewart Lee Udall Department of the Interior Building.
9. Tom Udall, April 16, 2018; Sharon Francis, May 8, 2018.
10. Sharon Francis, May 8, 2018; Smith, *Stewart L. Udall*, 356n16.
11. Sharon Francis, May 8, 2018.
12. Ibid.
13. Fradkin, *Wallace Stegner*, 208.
14. Sharon Francis, May 8, 2018.
15. SLU, *The Quiet Crisis* (New York: Holt, Rinehart and Winston, 1963), viii.
16. Smith, *Stewart L. Udall*, 139–40, 150.
17. Ibid., 153, 186.
18. Keith Schneider and Cornelia Dean, "Stewart L. Udall, Conservationist in Kennedy and Johnson Cabinets, Dies at 90," *New York Times*, March 20, 2010.
19. Smith, *Stewart L. Udall*, 286–91; Wayne Norviel Aspinall to Nancy Whistler, February 15, 1979, Former Members of Congress, Inc., Oral History Interviews, Manuscript Division, Library of Congress. Also archived with the Former Members of Congress material, see Aspinall to David McComb, June 11, 1974, Oral History of Colorado Project. In Tom Udall's opinion, Johnson lacked the heart for a final political fight, least of all with Aspinall (Tom Udall, April 16, 2018).
20. See John Wesley Powell, "Institutions for the Arid Lands," *Century* 40 (1890): 111–16. This article is collected in John Wesley Powell, *Seeing Things Whole: The Essential John Wesley Powell* (Washington, DC: Island Press, 2001), 299–313.
21. SLU, *Quiet Crisis*, 91.
22. Ibid., 94.
23. Charles Wilkinson, *Fire on the Plateau* (Washington, DC: Island Press, 1999), 216ff. See also SLU to Peter Steere, October 24–25, 1996, The Morris K. Udall Oral History Project, Special Collections, University of Arizona, Interview with Stewart L. Udall (part 3, tape 2, side A).
24. Smith, *Stewart L. Udall*, 146. See also Thomas G. Smith, "The Canyonlands National Park Controversy, 1961–64," *Utah Historical Quarterly* 59 (1991): 216–42.
25. William deBuys, *A Great Aridness* (New York: Oxford, 2011), 141, 164–72.
26. California sent thirty representatives to the House and Arizona sent two through the 1950s. After reapportionment following the 1960 census, the margin was thirty-eight to three. *Biographical Directory of the United States Congress, 1774–2005* (Washington, DC: Government Printing Office, 2005), 400–27.
27. Smith, *Stewart L. Udall*, 233. The January release can be found at https://www.usbr.gov/lc/region/programs/crbstudy/PSWPRptJan64.pdf.
28. US Bureau of Reclamation, "Pacific Southwest Water Plan" (Washington, DC: Government Printing Office, 1964); Marc Reisner, *Cadillac Desert: The American West and Its Disappearing Water* (New York: Viking Penguin, 1986), 281–93; Smith, *Stewart L. Udall*, 229ff.

29. *New York Times*, June 9, 1966, C35.
30. Floyd Dominy to Jack Loeffler, August 16, 2001 (author's personal collection).
31. Wilkinson, *Fire on the Plateau*, 298–304.
32. Personal communication. SLU and the author were friends for the last twenty years of Udall's life. They discussed climate change and the Southwest's development on numerous occasions.
33. SLU to Peter Steere, October 24–25, 1996, part 3, tape 2, side A.
34. Smith, *Stewart L. Udall*, 246.
35. Ibid., 245–47.
36. Ibid., 248; Tom Udall, April 16, 2018.
37. Powell, *Seeing Things Whole*, 115.
38. SLU, "Wilderness Rivers: Shooting the Wild Colorado," *Venture*, February 1968, 70.
39. SLU, untitled [notes on Grand Canyon raft trip, June 1967], SLU Papers, University of Arizona Libraries, Tucson, Arizona, Special Collections, Box 136, Folder 15.
40. Joseph "Uncle Joe" Cannon was the famously tyrannical speaker of the House of Representatives from 1903 to 1911.
41. SLU, "Wilderness Rivers," 70.
42. Marble Canyon National Monument was created by presidential decree in January 1969 as part of the much-reduced final package of land protections Udall had urged on President Johnson. The Grand Canyon National Park Enlargement Act of 1975 conferred further protection by absorbing both Grand Canyon and Marble Canyon national monuments, along with adjacent lands, into the park, nearly doubling its size to 1.2 million acres. See Michael F. Anderson, *Polishing the Jewel: An Administrative History of Grand Canyon National Park* (Grand Canyon, Arizona: Grand Canyon Association, 2000), 67.
43. SLU, untitled [notes on Grand Canyon raft trip], n40, quoting Powell's entry for July 30, 1869; SLU, "Wilderness Rivers," 70.
44. Laura Dassau Walls, *Henry David Thoreau* (Chicago: University of Chicago Press, 2017), 423–44.
45. T. H. Watkins, *Righteous Pilgrim: The Life and Times of Harold L. Ickes, 1874–1952* (Lexington, MA: Plunkett Lake Press, 1990), 532. Ickes and his commissioner of Indian Affairs, John Collier, implemented the Indian Reorganization Act of 1934, which largely reversed the General Allotment Act.
46. Donald Worster, *A River Running West* (New York: Oxford, 2001), 270–71.
47. Originally, "The Bureau of Ethnology." "American" was added to the name in 1897.
48. Worster, *A River Running West*, 271; see also "Statement of Major J. W. Powell made before The Committee on Indian Affairs as to the condition of the Indian tribes west of the Rocky Mountains," House of Representatives, Misc. Doc. No. 86, 43rd Congress, 1st Sess., January 13, 1874.
49. Charles Wilkinson, "Filling in the Blank Spots on Powell's and Stegner's Maps: The Role of Modern Indian Tribes in Western Watersheds," *Journal of Land Resources and Environmental Law* 23 (2003): 43.

50. Worster, *A River Running West*, 272.

51. Ben Proctor, *Not Without Honor: The Life of John H. Reagan* (Austin: University of Texas Press, 1962).

52. 51st Congress S. 2837. For Powell's *Century* article, see *Seeing Things Whole*, 299–313.

53. Powell, *Seeing Things Whole*, Selections 8 and 14, and more particularly 195–99 and 310n11.

54. Worster, *A River Running West*, 494–522.

55. Congressional Record—Senate, June 20, 1890, 6288–6289.

56. *Washington Evening Star*, Washington, DC, July 15, 1890, 5.

57. E.g., Congressional Record—House, March 22, 1890, 2537–2538.

58. Record of the 51st Congress, Sess. II, Chap. 561 (Approved, March 3, 1891), Sec. 18.

59. Samuel Trask Dana and Sally K. Fairfax, *Forest and Range Policy*, 2nd ed. (New York: McGraw Hill, 1980), 56–67; deBuys, *A Great Aridness*, 255–58.

60. John D. Leshy, "Are US Public Lands Unconstitutional?" *Hastings Law Journal* 69 (2018): 499–581.

61. Tom Udall, April 16, 2018.

62. Julie Turkewitz, "Trump Slashes Size of Bears Ears and Grand Staircase Monuments," *New York Times*, December 4, 2017; Eric Lipton and Lisa Friedman, "Oil Was Central in Decision to Shrink Bears Ears Monument, Emails Show," *New York Times*, March 2, 2018.

63. Thomas Burr, "Judge Consolidates Lawsuits over Bears Ears, Grand Staircase Monument Changes," *Salt Lake Tribune*, February 1, 2018.

64. Charles Wilkinson, *Crossing the Next Meridian: Land, Water, and the Future of the West* (Washington, DC: Island Press, 1992), chapter 1.

65. Climate change's probable effects on the American Southwest are discussed in deBuys, *A Great Aridness*.

66. Powell, *Seeing Things Whole*, 311.

67. Smith, *Stewart L. Udall*, 385; SLU et al., *The Energy Balloon* (New York, McGraw-Hill, 1974); SLU, *The Quiet Crisis and the Next Generation* (Salt Lake City: Peregrine Smith, 1988); SLU and Lee Udall, "A Message to Our Grandchildren," *High Country News*, March 31, 2008.

68. deBuys, *A Great Aridness*, 312.

PART THREE

Native Americans

Parts I and II of this volume speak to water and land, respectively, all of which was once Native estate. Euro-Americans' wresting of those resources from North America's Indigenous Peoples entailed justifying why a "civilized" society could steal a continent. The "Manifest Destiny" framework of conquest became deeply embedded within the nation's psyche. From Chief Justice John Marshall's incorporation of the "Doctrine of Discovery" into US law, to military campaigns and settler efforts reflecting genocidal impulses, the United States was prepared to do whatever it took to realize imperial ambition.

John Wesley Powell's arid region was no exception—the Colorado River Basin included. Native connections to this portion of North America are inexpressibly deep, tracing back millennia, or perhaps forever, in many instances. Having inhabited the landscape for this long, Native peoples know how to live *with* it, not just *on* it. It is instructive that the Hopi Villages, dating back nearly a millennium, are some of the oldest continuously inhabited settlements in North America. Many Ancestral Puebloan ruins lie across the Colorado Plateau, a homeland for seamless generations of Native peoples. Today, tribes hold title to a significant portion of the basin's lands and water rights.

Native Americans fascinated Powell from an early age—an interest that flourished later in life but was not widely shared across US society. Yet this aspect of Powell's character was firmly moored in his historical context, confined by an inability to escape the prevailing ethnocentrism that rationalized Euro-American conquest. Although Powell could be extremely imaginative with water and land policy, he was spectacularly uncreative in his thinking about relations between Native and Euro-American peoples. That dichotomy complicates Powell's legacy. It also raises important questions about what lies ahead for Colorado River Basin tribes, and the relative value of Powell's legacy to this ancient, living piece of the basin's future.

Authored by Weston McCool and Daniel McCool, chapter 9 introduces Powell's unilinear evolutionary theory in anthropology, and debunks the purported stages of savagery/barbarism/civilization through which all human cultures supposedly evolved. This theory underpinned Powell's advocacy for assimilation of Native Americans into mainstream US society. Distinguishing Powell's assimilationist viewpoint from an "annihilationist" counterpart, the authors describe Powell's belief that "he could save the lives of Indians by forcibly converting them into facsimiles of white people." The rejection of unilinear evolutionary theory was the first step in a more enlightened policy toward Native peoples that would eventually stress tribal sovereignty and self-determination. The chapter thus explains how tribes went from a powerless condition to one of autonomy and strength. However, the future holds many perils for tribes as the basin goes through convulsive changes. They face their own "Great Unknown," and the chapter offers ideas about how tribes can not only survive, but thrive in an age of increasing scarcity.

Indeed, "Indians are still kicking around the Colorado River Basin in the twenty-first century," explains Autumn Bernhardt in chapter 10, despite the dim prognosis of the "vanishing Indian" myth and considerable extermination and assimilation efforts. Bernhardt's chapter focuses on the deep-rooted Euro-American bias for "pastoral and civilized" land, water, and people, and how that bias impacts both nature and tribes in common. Ironically, the bias has created advantages to basin tribes in modern times involving tribal sovereignty, solidarity, and water rights. These are critical assets given the dangers of a "new Manifest Destiny" mindset pervading communities in and around the basin. A host of cultural, ethical, legal, and policy changes are in order to avoid the callous mistakes of an earlier era. Acknowledgement of basin tribes' permanence should dovetail with embrace of their knowledge and wisdom.

Daniel Cordalis and Amy Cordalis turn to the Colorado River Basin's sacred places in chapter 11. "The basin's sacred places defined the very existence of its Indian people," describe the authors, discussing Powell's historical awareness of this fact through his extensive work with tribes. Yet policies supported by Powell and others resulted in basin tribes being separated from ancestral homelands and sacred sites. This separation was not inadvertent. Flipping Powell's cultural-stages theory on its head, the authors suggest that tribal-federal cooperative management of public lands in the basin may be "the most civilized progression modern American society can make." The chapter considers Bears Ears National Monument as a model for how tribal-federal collaborative governance might be structured in the "Great Unknown."

William Gribb concludes this part with a proverbial bounty in chapter 12, examining tribal agricultural development in the Colorado River Basin from historical, contemporary, and prospective angles. Which tribes inhabited the basin at the time of the 1869 Expedition, and how engaged were they in agriculture? The chapter sheds light on this important historical context. Yet nothing about the discussion is stationary. It delves into the prevalence and modes of agriculture within basin reservations in modern times, and also touches on the status of tribal water rights, in both recognized and unrecognized forms. Eventually setting his sights on the "Great Unknown," Gribb steers the chapter toward an intractable truth: "Colorado River Basin tribes' agricultural activities will be directly impacted by climate change" as the twenty-first century unfolds. Powell's legacy re-enters the picture at this juncture. Four of his strategies for land and water management may prove fruitful for tribes' future agricultural plans.

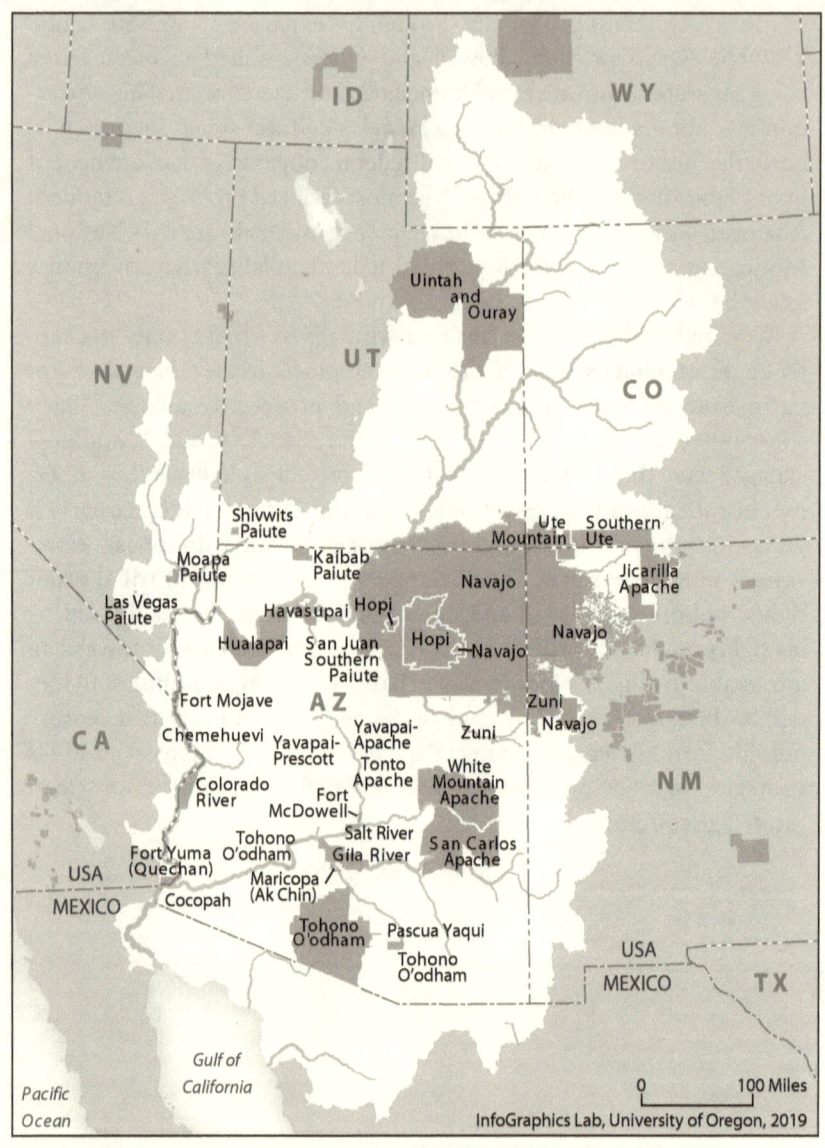

MAP 4. Native American Reservations, Colorado River Basin. Cartography: P. William Limpisathian and James Meacham, InfoGraphics Lab, University of Oregon, 2019.

FIGURE 14. Chip Thomas, *free yo mind + yo ass will follow* (large format toner print on regular bond paper, acrylic gel medium, installed at a Little Colorado River Gorge overlook vendor stand, highway 64, 2013). This image helps us remember that possibilities are infinite. As with all struggles, it takes teamwork to make the dream work.

FIGURE 15. Will Wilson, *Auto Immune Response: Confluence of 3 Generations* (archival pigment print on paper, 44" × 86," 2015). The *Auto Immune Response* series takes as its subject the quixotic relationship between a post-apocalyptic Diné man and the devastatingly beautiful yet toxic environment he inhabits. The series is an allegorical investigation of the extraordinarily rapid transformation of Indigenous lifeways, the disease it has caused, and the strategies of response that enable cultural survival. In this image, the protagonist of the series (left) has discovered other Indigenous survivors (right) at the confluence of the Colorado River and Little Colorado River canyons—a powerful, sacred site.

FIGURE 16. Will Wilson, *Melissa Pochoema, Insurgent Hopi Maiden* (talking tintype, CIPX Santa Fe, 50" × 40," 2015). This image references George Lucas's appropriation of the Hopi maiden hairstyle for the *Star Wars* character Princess Leia. By downloading the free Talking Tintype app from Apple's AppStore, readers can scan the image and access a counter-appropriation in which the portrait's subject, Melissa Pochoema, rewrites Princess Leia's secret message to Obi-Wan Kenobi, casting it as a message to Popé, the leader of the Pueblo Revolt of 1680.

FIGURE 17. Chip Thomas, *step in cow springs, navajo nation on the colorado plateau* (large format toner print on regular bond paper, acrylic gel medium, photographed by Ben Knight, installed August 2014). In 2011, it was still undecided whether Snowbowl ski resort outside Flagstaff, Arizona, would be allowed to desecrate a mountain sacred to thirteen area tribes by making snow from reclaimed wastewater. I asked several friends their feelings about this possibility. Whatever they said was written on their faces and then photographed. These photos were wheatpasted to make murals in Flagstaff and elsewhere of citizens speaking out against the reclaimed-wastewater snow.

FIGURE 18. Patrick Kikut, *Dream Catcher* (oil on canvas, 60" × 72," 2017). In Arizona, off Interstate 40 next to abandoned plywood curio shops, there is a large, wind-damaged "dream catcher" reflecting the contemporary reality of Manifest Destiny.

CHAPTER 9

"We Must Either Protect Him or Destroy Him"

WESTON C. MCCOOL AND DANIEL C. MCCOOL

In 1869, the year John Wesley Powell first ran the Colorado River, justice was not an option for American Indians. It is difficult to imagine today the level of racism and hatred for Native peoples during that era.[1] We should avoid applying today's moral standards to people of another era, but we must never shirk from accurate description. With the advantage of 150 years of hindsight, we can outline the impact of Powell's thinking on American Indians in the Colorado River Basin during that troublesome time. The goal of this chapter is to trace Powell's legacy in the basin as it relates to the rights of American Indians, the changing relationship between the "dominant" culture and Native cultures, and the development of Powell's anthropological theories that depict and attempt to explain that relationship. We explore the dangers of the new "Great Unknown" as the basin enters an era of scarcity and faces unprecedented problems that challenge our commitment to justice for Native peoples. Lastly, we discuss the future of the basin and its people, and advocate for fair and inclusive collaboration, increased Native American political involvement, science-based sustainability strategies, and continued anthropological research to protect the basin's cultural resources.

NATIVE AMERICA IN AN ERA OF CULTURAL MANIFEST DESTINY

In the nineteenth century, there were two prevailing schools of thought regarding American Indians. We label one of them the "assimilationist" approach, which was endorsed by Powell. It assumed that Native peoples had only two choices: conform to Euro-American culture, or be destroyed.[2] Politically it was dominated by organizations such as the Indian Rights Association, and reflected in President Grant's church-heavy "peace policy." These Anglo "protectors" of Native peoples were humanitarians by impulse, but white Christian capitalists by predilection, which biased their work in the same way that cultural biases shaped Powell's thinking.[3] The second approach is best described as "annihilationist," and argued for complete destruction of Native peoples.[4]

Powell recognized the contrast between these two approaches when he declared in 1874 that the US faced a stark choice regarding Native Americans: "we must either protect him or destroy him."[5] Compared to the annihilationist approach, the assimilationist view appears downright humane. Both views were *prima facie* racist, and much of Powell's writing is decidedly cringe-worthy. For example, he argued that the government's mission was to secure "the ascendency of the Anglo-Saxon branch of the Aryan family, and the ultimate spread of Anglo-Saxon civilization over the globe."[6] But among his peers Powell was something of a visionary, one who could see value in Native languages and cultures, and he sought to protect Indian people from those who would murder them to the last man, woman, and child. He was convinced that he could save the lives of Indians by forcibly converting them into facsimiles of white people. In short, Powell was a progressive do-gooder in an era when doing good, especially in regard to Native Americans, was often considered an absurdity.

For many decades, "Indian policy"[7] was a mixture of these two approaches, with the annihilationist view taking precedence initially but gradually losing out to the assimilationist view. This view, in turn, has been largely, but not completely, supplanted by a third approach that emphasizes self-determination. But that third approach did not emerge until the latter half of the twentieth century. It followed centuries of war and conquest that decimated American Indians. In the last decade of the nineteenth century, when Powell was near the height of his career, the population of Native Americans reached its nadir at slightly more than a quarter-million—down from millions and perhaps tens of millions prior to European invasion.[8]

Many nineteenth-century Americans simply assumed that the "inferior" Indians would eventually die off. It was this mistaken assumption that compelled Powell and others to attempt to save the last remnants of Native cultures and languages. It also spurred ethnologists—including

Powell—to both study Native cultures and attempt to build theories that explained the differences between Native and Anglo societies.

Ethnology in Powell's Era

Before discussing Powell's specific contributions to American Indian policy, ethnology, and anthropology, we must first provide historical context, without which Powell's ideas sound backward and outright prejudiced.

In the seventeenth century, Western Europe was emerging as one of the world's economic and intellectual centers. Concomitant with economic growth was increasing commitment to the sciences and a moral philosophy based on self-determination.[9] Europeans became enamored with the concepts of progress, rationality, and common sense, which culminated in the Enlightenment philosophy. Enlightenment-era thinkers believed a European had the "God-ordained, intelligent self-sufficiency . . . to work out his own way in his common sense, his analytical reason, and his specific moral sense."[10] Europe's economic and intellectual progress was therefore viewed as self-generated and exponential.

By the mid-nineteenth century, a camp was emerging that sought to connect Enlightenment-era philosophy with the emerging field of Darwinian evolution.[11] These scholars saw the development of societies as analogous to the evolution of biological systems. Anglo scholars argued that human cultures could be categorized into pseudo-taxonomic hierarchies from simple to complex. This "evolutionist" school proposed that cultures evolve linearly, through self-generated advancement in economic, intellectual, and moral domains. This line of thought buttressed the arguments of assimilationists such as Powell.

Evolutionist scholars began to investigate human social processes through the lens of the natural sciences to build a general theory of social change.[12] Central to this theory were the ideas that "[a]ll human groups . . . possess essentially the same kind and level of intelligence and the same basic emotions . . ."[13] and that human biology does not impede any race or culture from progressing. Thus, all peoples were considered capable of progressing entirely through natural, self-generated processes. From these central tenets, evolutionists proposed that Indigenous Peoples had failed to progress out of the "primitive" state and thus could benefit from European civilization. This assimilationist program was contrary to the annihilationists' argument that Native peoples were inferior and unworthy of continued existence. The assimilationists, on the other hand, could argue that "civilizing" efforts would redeem Indian people by forcing them up through successive cultural stages.

As these ideas were being formalized, a new science of human culture—ethnology—was being developed. Many of its earliest practitioners used Enlightenment-era philosophy to frame theories of culture change. European Enlightenment was brought to American ethnology through the work of Lewis Henry Morgan (1818–81). Basing his work on Edward B. Tylor's *Primitive Culture* (1871),[14] Morgan developed the most cogent version of cultural evolution with his book *Ancient Society* (1877).[15] Morgan proposed a theory of cultural change in which all human cultures evolve linearly through a series of three stages: from savagery to barbarism to civilization. These stages represented Morgan's conceptualization of progress along technological, economic, and humanistic lines. In reality, his framework placed European elite society at the evolutionary apex, and worked to classify other cultures' "progress" by how closely they resembled contemporary Anglo society. Today we can clearly see this formula as raw jingoism and an overt justification for European imperialism, but in Powell's day the theory was considered innovative and rational. As a result, unilinear evolution theory came to dominate anthropological thought for decades, and had a profound influence on Powell and fellow assimilationists.

Powell and the Ethnology of American Indians

Powell's work in ethnology began with his 1873 commission by the federal government to complete several reports on Indian affairs in the Great Basin and surrounding country.[16] Over the next several years, Powell conducted informal ethnography focused on recording Indian customs, politics, languages, and beliefs, as well as the economic conditions of various tribes.

Powell's ethnological accounts reveal profound contradictions in his attitude towards American Indians. Powell's descriptions of the "savage condition" unflinchingly tack between praise of Indian knowledge—"they know every rock and ledge, every gulch and canyon—just where to wind among these to find a pass, and their knowledge is unerring"[17]—and condescension about their beliefs: "Indian theology is a degeneracy from some higher type ... ethically a hideous monster of lies ... a system which beautifully reveals the mental condition of savagery."[18] Powell's reports focus on the "whipped" and destitute condition of the Ute, Paiute, and Shoshone tribes, and advocate for forced economic intervention and relocation to reservations in order to enable "them to become self-sustaining, and [convert] . . . from vicious, dangerous savages to civilized people."[19] Powell saw Indian resistance to Euro-American incursions as futile and recommended strong authoritarian prescriptions that were "[t]he only course left by which these Indians can be saved. . . ."[20]

Powell, like many Anglos before him, saw a future where Indians would either be protected or utterly destroyed.[21] Powell advocated strongly for the protection and assimilation of Indian tribes amid a loud audience calling for land-theft and genocide. Thus, Powell's ethnological interests in American Indians turned into advocacy for authoritarian protection and eventual assimilation into Anglo society.

To a great extent, such conceptualizations were part of a larger effort to justify the near-total dispossession of Native lands—the racial correlative of Manifest Destiny. American Indians were virtually powerless to stop their loss of land, water, and identity. For example, the Pimas in central Arizona were granted a small reservation, but it was rendered virtually useless because nearly the entire flow of the Gila River above the reservation was diverted by settlers, leading the Indian Commissioner to remark in 1880 that in Arizona there was a "prevailing opinion . . . that Indians have no water rights which white men are bound to respect."[22] The Bureau of Indian Affairs (BIA) began an irrigation project on the Colorado River Indian Reservation in 1867 but failed to complete it—a shortcoming so common that BIA employees had a saying: "We began our first irrigation project in 1867 and we've never finished one yet."[23]

In Western states with the water law doctrine of prior appropriation, the failure to build projects and divert water for beneficial use meant the loss of that water. The first glimmer of hope for Native American water rights came with the Supreme Court's momentous 1908 decision in *Winters v. United States*, which recognized reserved water rights for Indian reservations and (unlike prior appropriation) did not hinge the existence of these water rights on beneficial use.[24] But the prevailing political environment ensured that the decision would have little impact. The only basinwide recognition of Indian water rights would come as a slight during negotiations over the 1922 Colorado River Compact; Herbert Hoover inserted a disclaimer that he crudely referred to as the "wild Indian article."[25] What became known as the "Law of the River" was a complex system to deliver water to powerful Western interests; Native people, without power, were almost completely excluded.

In regard to land tenure, the first reservation in the Colorado River Basin was established in 1859 on the Gila River. By the 1920s, the current system of reservation lands and boundaries was firmly established, with the exception of the Navajo Reservation, which did not acquire its current boundaries until 1933. The current reservation system in the basin includes twenty-nine reservations (see map 4).[26]

As reservations were being established, and American Indians began to adjust to their new reality, ethnological concepts regarding Native peoples began to change. While Powell's thoughts on Indian policy were coalescing, he was becoming increasingly interested in exploring theories on cultural development and diversification. In 1876, Powell formalized his adherence to Morgan's theory of unilinear evolution and began using it to characterize Native tribes. Powell accepted as given that all societies pass through a linear set of cultural stages, stating: "Some tribes are yet savages; other tribes are yet barbarians; and some peoples have attained civilization."[27]

Powell's particular contribution to cultural evolution theory was to characterize the political, religious, and humanistic characteristics of tribes. To Powell, "savage" societies did not distinguish man from beast, religious from secular life, public from private property, natural from man-made, and peace from justice.[28] These distinctions made clear that Powell believed "savagery" to involve the absence of particular distinctions and institutions that he considered critical to Anglo progress.

In each domain of society, Powell defined what progress consisted of, with the implication that Native societies were missing some or all of these characteristics. Economically, Powell saw progress as the development of irrigated agriculture, animal domestication, private property, industrialization, commerce, explicit division of labor, and specialization.[29] Politically, advancement was attained through a centralized tripartite government that exerts authority over its people, regulates its institutions, and formalizes principles of law that work towards "peace, authority, and justice."[30] Further, Powell asserted a gendered hierarchy into the cultural stages, with savage societies worshiping maternal kinship, barbarous cultures praising paternal kinship, and civilization praising territorial boundaries and nationalism.[31] In regard to religion, Powell saw a natural progression from polytheism to monotheism, with attainment of Judeo-Christian religion as the most evolved state.[32] Finally, Powell saw advancement in the sciences as "the greatest intellectual achievement of civilization."[33] In each domain, Powell sought to characterize contemporary Anglo institutions as hallmarks of civilization and thus progress. The further a non-Western society was from the Anglo system, the lower it was placed in the evolutionary schema.

By placing emphasis on the fixed characteristics of "savage" societies, Powell and his contemporaries provided little understanding of how or why Indian institutions came to be, let alone their functions. Instead, Powell and other cultural evolutionists preferred to create pseudo-taxonomic orders of Indian practices and beliefs that espoused the tautological notion that Indian institutions both produce "savagery" and are the product of it. What made Indian lifeways "savage" was, of course, their non-conformity to contemporary Anglo society.

The Shift to Cultural Anthropology

Powell's and his contemporaries' failure to examine *why* Native societies adopted certain practices or beliefs, or *how* Native institutions functioned in society, assured a limited shelf life for unilinear evolution theory. Indeed, a new era of anthropology was emerging by the early 1900s under the auspices of Franz Boas and other practitioners involving what is today called cultural anthropology.[34] Boas and his contemporaries developed a distinct understanding of human culture that emphasized the diversity and validity of Anglo and Indigenous peoples alike and sought to understand non-Western cultures on their own terms. The Boasian school did away with cultural stages and unilinear evolution, instead seeking to explain why certain practices and beliefs arise among different cultures, and what those institutions mean to those practicing them. Boasian "relativism" explicitly rejected attachment of ethnocentric morality to sociocultural forms.[35] This new approach meant a parting of ways between the assimilationists and anthropologists; the former still clung to the idea of Indian cultures as an impediment, while the latter could see the value of preserving rather than displacing them.

After the first few decades of the twentieth century, unilinear evolution theory had been explicitly falsified by long-term ethnographic and archaeological investigations.[36] Critics of the theory emphasized the moral myopia of Powell and his colleagues, who had characterized non-civilized societies as brutish and cruel while ignoring the vast catalog of atrocities perpetrated by Anglo states. In addition, Enlightenment-era scholars failed to recognize the egalitarian social structure of many non-Western societies that permitted far more personal freedom and mobility than Europe's classist societies. Finally, unilinear theorists failed to understand that organisms—including humans—do not evolve along a linear track from simple to complex, nor does natural selection favor a social system simply because it aligns with subjective notions of "progress." Thus, by the mid-twentieth century, Powell's ideas and those of other cultural evolutionists were relegated to the footnotes of history. Parallel to the anthropological developments that characterized Anglo and Native societies as cultural equals was dramatic progress in Native self-determination.

NATIVE AMERICA DEVELOPS ITS OWN VOICE

All American Indians—within the Colorado River Basin and elsewhere—became citizens with the 1924 Indian Citizenship Act.[37] This did not automatically lead to political power, but it created opportunities for Native Americans and their allies to begin building a social and political infrastructure that would require decades of struggle to bear fruit.

The next step forward came during the Depression when tribes, the poorest of the poor, suffered greatly. In 1934, Congress passed the Indian Reorganization Act, setting up a process for the creation of tribal governments.[38] The Act firmly put to rest the notion that Native peoples were going to simply vanish into the great cement-mixer of American culture. They, and their reservations with attendant land and water rights, were here to stay.

It took a world war to propel things further. Many Native Americans fought in World War II against totalitarianism and for democracy. But they came home to a country that did not permit many of them to vote. Returning Native veterans helped form the National Congress of American Indians (NCAI) in 1944, dedicated to advocating for Indian rights. The NCAI immediately became involved in an effort to challenge Arizona's prohibition on Indian voting, which paid off in 1948 with a victory in the Arizona Supreme Court.[39] The same year Native veterans in New Mexico challenged that state's law prohibiting Indians who did not pay state taxes from voting; they too succeeded.[40] The last state in the Colorado River Basin to grant Indians the right to vote, albeit grudgingly and under imminent threat of a lawsuit, was Utah, which finally allowed all Native people to vote in 1957.[41] These advances in voting rights were later strengthened by the 1965 Voting Rights Act and its 1975 and 1982 amendments.

Native political power in the basin continued to build as a result of the tumultuous 1960s and 1970s and the focus on civil rights and equality. The Native American Rights Fund (NARF) was established in Boulder, Colorado in 1971 to litigate on behalf of American Indian tribes. Militant groups such as the American Indian Movement began to demand justice for Native people. Native sovereignty was enhanced in 1975 with the Indian Self-Determination and Education Assistance Act.[42] The combined effect of these developments assisted Native peoples in becoming their own most effective advocates. Basin state politicians could no longer ignore their demands.

As Native advocacy organizations and tribes developed political skills, Indian policy gradually shifted to a more progressive and tolerant approach that ultimately led to the ascendency of tribes as major players in policymaking, especially in regard to water and land rights and sovereignty issues. By the 1970s and 1980s, advocacy for Native rights had shifted from the all-white organizations of Powell's era that stressed assimilation, to Indian-led activism that focused on sovereignty, self-government, and the protection of Native land, water, and cultural resources. At the same time, Native people began demanding equal voting rights, and then using their newfound power to elect candidates with favorable attitudes. Thus, a state such as Arizona, with a long and sordid history of oppressing Native people, would elect candidates in the 1970s who acknowledged they won because of the Indian vote.[43] And in Utah—again, the last basin state to allow American Indians to vote—Navajos and Utes would use the Voting Rights Act to gain an equal opportunity to elect candidates of their choice in a county election.[44]

JUSTICE IN THE AGE OF SCARCITY

The Colorado River Basin today is struggling with a burgeoning population, an insufficient and declining level of water in the Colorado River system, and an increasing need for all parties to confront scarcity and shared use in new and innovative ways. And today, unlike the past, Native Americans constitute a major power in the basin, with enormous claims to land, water, and political autonomy. We suggest four modes of action that will contribute to solving the myriad problems facing basin tribes.

Collaboration

Advocacy on behalf of Native Americans did not really develop into a positive, truly pro-Native force until American Indians formed their own organizations and began leading from the front, rather than having well-meaning Anglos, such as Powell, attempt to interpret their needs and preferences. In addition to the NCAI and NARF, several Native coalitions in the basin have proven to be effective advocates. Examples include the Ten Tribes Partnership, formed to protect reserved Indian water rights to the Colorado River, and the Inter Tribal Council of Arizona.[45] In addition, individual tribes have become their own best advocates; the Navajo Nation Human Rights Commission exemplifies how tribes are developing increased capacity to protect themselves.[46]

Tribes have been quite successful in negotiating settlements to their water claims; those settlements set an example of what can be accomplished through respectful dialogue. Collaboration, as equal partners with other stakeholders, is essential to addressing threats to tribal sovereignty and land and water rights in the basin.

Powell, 150 years ago, saw the value of engaging with Native Americans—of listening rather than talking—in stark contrast to the shrill calls for genocide by other leading voices of the time. In this respect, he set a standard that should be emulated today. We must ensure that, this time around, Native Americans are not given the short end of the stick.

Beyond Consultation

When the concept of government-to-government consultation was first promulgated, it was seen as a step forward in the dialogue between tribes and federal agencies.[47] But it soon became apparent that "consultation" simply meant that federal agencies would consider tribal interests but make all decisions on their own and then inform tribes. In other words, consultation did not give tribes real power. However, the protection of tribal water, land, and sovereignty requires that tribes have not just a voice, but a determinative role in deciding how resources are allocated when it affects their interests. In a modern, increasingly crowded West, what happens *off* reservation often has an enormous impact *on* reservation, and *vice versa*.

A case in point is Bears Ears National Monument in southeastern Utah. When it was created in 2016, one of the biggest issues was whether tribes would have a meaningful role in the management of the monument, which is located on traditional lands of several tribes and contains literally thousands of archaeological sites. The original monument proclamation created an advisory commission consisting of tribal leaders, and required the relevant federal agencies to "meaningfully engage" with the commission, providing that when "developing or revising the management plan, the Secretaries [of Agriculture and Interior] shall carefully and fully consider integrating the traditional and historical knowledge and special expertise of the Commission...."[48] As described later in this volume, this approach established a model for an increased role for tribes in collaboratively managing public lands that affect tribal resources and well-being.

This same model could be applied to water resources, especially given the fact that tribes now have rights to 2.9 million acre-feet of the Colorado River system's flows, and still have large, unquantified claims to additional water.[49] Resolving such issues requires more than mere consultation; it requires a direct role in decision-making processes. This comports directly with Powell's vision of a basinwide, communitarian approach to managing water resources, but without Powell's Eurocentric biases.

Facing Reality and Utilizing Science

Unreality is a theme that runs through the entire history of the West, from Joseph Ives's myopic declaration that the Grand Canyon was a "profitless locality" that no one would visit,[50] to William Gilpin's "blaze of mystical fervor" and the "sunburst dazzle of Manifest Destiny,"[51] to fanciful notions of irrigated empires and grandiose plans to "put the landless man on the manless land"—land that in fact had been inhabited by Native peoples for millennia.[52] Powell's greatest feat of bravery, after his Civil War service, was not leading the 1869 Expedition, but rather standing up to Western politicians who staked their careers on a fantastical vision of desert farmers wallowing in an irrigated cornucopia wrested from murderous savages and a cruel desert.

In the last quarter of the twentieth century, science (and thus Powell) was again under attack by politicians who preferred fantasy to facts; the West of today faces the same standoff. Powell's "heritage of conflict" (arguably his most famous quote)[53] is an apt description of the overallocated Colorado River that now dies in the sands of Baja long before it reaches the sea. Our commitment to justice for all peoples, including Native Americans, requires that we face the facts, even though that requires difficult choices that must be made with all major stakeholders, including tribes, at the table. Science can help us understand the realities of hydrology, climate change, culture, and infrastructure, but it must be combined with a commitment to justice if we are to have a just and sustainable future in the basin.

The Role of Anthropology in the Age of Scarcity

As described above, Powell committed much of his professional life to the paternalistic protection of tribes in the West. He feared that without direct intervention it was possible the tribes could become "extinct."[54] Powell firmly believed that the loss of the Native component of America would not only be immoral, but also diminish the splendor of the West. He therefore committed to protecting the tribes with the means he felt most appropriate—colonization and assimilation. Today we can see these processes as extensions of imperialism, and we need not expound on the terrible repercussions assimilationist programs have had, and continue to have, on Native peoples. As we have stated, Native peoples themselves have become effective self-advocates for tribal sovereignty, identity, and justice. In tandem with the great strides made in this area, we believe a program of expanded anthropological research would continue to advance mutual Native and Anglo interests in a number of ways.

To reiterate, ethnology in Powell's day focused on description rather than understanding peoples considered foreign or exotic from a Western perspective. Modern ethnology is much broader in scope and forms an important component of numerous disciplines, including anthropology, sociology, demography, economics, women's studies, and more. Ethnology provides a bottom-up perspective that highlights issues of cultural and economic context and variation on individual and community scales.[55] Modern ethnographies utilize formal and informal interviews, surveys, recorded statements, and observation to provide rich context while permitting the voices of local peoples to be heard.[56] Contemporary ethnology also looks at modern Western society to provide a more comprehensive examination of humanity from a cross-cultural perspective. In this way, ethnology can provide a bridge between Native and Anglo peoples by gaining and sharing an understanding of what it means to belong to a tribe, to grow up Anglo in the West, or to struggle with multiple cultural identities in a globalized world.[57] Ethnology has the potential to create cross-cultural connections that emphasize mutual interests and commonalities. These connections can mitigate conflict and engender cooperation within the heady political milieu that is the modern Colorado River Basin.

To prescribe the exact ethnographic work that should be conducted in the basin is difficult, even counterproductive. Numerous Colorado River Basin research programs have employed ethnology to explore topics as broad as traditional Navajo medicines,[58] Navajo fire collection strategies,[59] the nature of Hopi and Zuni cultural affiliations,[60] foraging strategies of the Numic Ute,[61] Native notions of cultural resource management,[62] and much more. Clearly, the ethnological epistemology of Powell's day has been replaced by ethnology as a fieldwork methodology, and its current use spans numerous research domains. We advocate for continued ethnological research to be carried out in the basin so that mutual understanding between Native and Anglo cultures can deepen, cooperation can be enhanced, and we can gain better comprehension of humanity today and in our shared past.[63]

Along similar lines, while the continued survival of Native tribes in the Colorado River Basin is no longer an issue, due in large part to Native political activism, many of the region's cultural resources face an uncertain future. Archaeological remains that provide tangible history of Native American life in the basin and adjoining regions are under threat. Bears Ears National Monument alone contains 8,480 known sites spanning 13,000 years.[64] The nonprofit organization Archaeology Southwest notes that only 10 percent of the monument has been surveyed, and estimates the entire monument may contain as many as 100,000 sites.[65] Nevertheless, the Trump Administration's recent proclamation purports to reduce the monument to a fraction of its former size.[66] The dramatically reduced monument remarkably does *not* include most of the best-known and most-visited archaeological sites.[67] Nor does the new proclamation recognize the monument's significance to local tribes, who see Bears Ears as a place of critical importance to their cultures and long-term existence.[68]

Clearly, Trump's proclamation and other actions by local Anglo politicians have diminished tribal authority over the land and ancient sites that are such key pieces of history and tribal identity. Tribal reactions to the proclamation have been overwhelmingly pro-monument. Indeed, a coalition of the Hopi, Navajo, Ute Indian, Ute Mountain Ute, and Zuni tribes are suing Trump and members of his administration, claiming the Antiquities Act provides no legal authority to rescind or revise a national monument designation.[69] In addition, experts on the archaeology of the Bears Ears region are unanimous in their declaration that the attempted reduction of the monument will lead to the loss of critical protections for, and the resultant destruction of, archaeological sites.[70]

The threats to Bears Ears National Monument do not stand in isolation. The Trump Administration, with the avid support of local Anglo politicians, has also attempted to dramatically reduce Grand Staircase-

Escalante National Monument.[71] If these reductions withstand legal challenge, both monuments will be vulnerable to increased damage from extractive industries and motorized recreation. In each case, the reduced dimensions will exclude thousands of archaeological sites, including some areas with the greatest density. Thus, we also advocate for an expanded archaeology program to inventory sites in threatened regions of the Colorado River Basin, and joint Anglo-Native prerogatives that work towards conserving these areas so crucial to Native identity and our understanding of the American and pre-American past.

CONCLUSION

John Wesley Powell had an enormous and influential role in two government-led initiatives: the protection of American Indians from annihilation, and the preservation of Native cultures and languages. He was the first to make ethnology a national goal and recognized that preserving language, art, and ceremony was essential to understanding the history of the land and its peoples. He truly helped start the trend of ethnologists studying Native ways, and built an initial firewall between Native peoples and total cultural destruction. We must give him credit for these efforts, which have led to an impressive body of research on Native cultures, languages, archaeology, and contemporary socio-political trends.

Powell's theories of race and civilization, on the other hand, are no more than a footnote in introductory textbooks that describe the history of misguided ideas. Indeed, Powell's name is scarcely mentioned, pushed to the margins by his more famous contemporaries Edward Tylor, Lewis Henry Morgan, and Herbert Spencer. In line with his 1869 Expedition, Powell's most enduring legacy is as an explorer of the Colorado River Basin and broader arid region, and as a visionary of future land and water management policies in the West.

In sum, Powell's legacy is a complex mixture of contradictions. He correctly noted that "[i]njustice is a strange monster," but did not always recognize when he was practicing it.[72] That may be merely a reflection of the fundamental contradictions in American culture and politics. The world's leading democracy embraced slavery for a half-century, practiced ethnic genocide against its Native inhabitants, and to this day does not always live up to its creed. Some of these enduring contradictions are reflected in Powell's thinking. He concurrently loved and disparaged Native cultures; he was at times sympathetic and at turns fiercely oppressive; he broke free of many of the dogmas of his era, yet was constrained by those same dogmas. In many ways, these contradictions are reflections of the nation's collective attitude toward Native peoples. We cannot understand the role of American Indians in the Colorado River Basin today without exploring these complex and often troubling assumptions and stereotypes, which were clearly apparent in early ethnological work. How Native peoples managed to not only survive in such a milieu, but to establish themselves as a political force in the basin is a story of amazing perseverance in the face of seemingly insurmountable opposition.

Even today some cultural beliefs and assumptions are leftovers from Powell's era. The basin must adapt and commit itself to a new vision of egalitarianism for all basin residents. This project requires recognizing that tribes are not "vanishing" as Powell and others thought, but instead are a permanent part of the basin's political and cultural fabric. They have inhabited it for millennia; there is much we can learn from them in regard to long-term, sustainable land and water practices.

Powell's concepts for dramatically reforming land and water policy in the arid West were, as Wallace Steger put it, "[t]hree quarters of a century ahead of their possible fulfillment,"[73] and today are widely admired. Indeed, some of them have become policy. Powell's anthropological concepts, in contrast, have been dutifully swept out the idea scupper. In the final analysis, Powell's thinking on "civilization" is reminiscent of Hannah Arendt's "banality of evil"—an example of the crude, humdrum ethos of his day that was deeply embedded in white privilege. He can be excused for being so human, but his limited ability to see beyond the confines of the scientific establishment of his time begs the question: how many "thinkers" today have nestled too comfortably into that easy chair of privileged complacency?

NOTES

1. This discrimination did not end with that era. For a recent analysis, see Harvard School of Public Health and NPR, "Discrimination In America: Experiences and Views of Native Americans," 2017, https://www.rwjf.org/content/dam/farm/reports/surveys_and_polls/2017/rwjf441678.

2. Frederick Hoxie, *A Final Promise: The Campaign to Assimilate the Indians, 1880–1920* (Lincoln: University of Nebraska Press, 2001).

3. In this chapter, we use the term "Anglo" rather than "non-Indian" as a shorthand to describe non-Native peoples, principally but not exclusively Caucasians from Europe or of European ancestry.

4. Laughlin McDonald, *American Indians and the Fight for Equal Voting Rights* (Norman: University of Oklahoma Press, 2010), 154.

5. John W. Powell and G.W. Ingalls, *Report of Special Commissioners JW Powell and GW Ingalls on the Condition of the Ute Indians of Utah: The Pai-Utes of Utah, Northern Arizona, Southern Nevada, and Southeastern California; the Go-si Utes of Utah and Nevada; the Northwestern Shoshones of Idaho and Utah; and the Western Shoshones of Nevada; and Report Concerning Claims of Settlers in the Mo-a-pa Valley (southeastern Nevada)* (Washington, DC: Government Printing Office, 1874), 25; Donald Worster, *A River Running West: The Life of John Wesley Powell* (New York: Oxford University Press, 2001), 273.

6. Worster, *A River Running West*, 96.

7. This term is of course a misnomer for most of our history. A more accurate term would be "Anglo policy imposed upon Indians." It is only in recent years that Native peoples have become major drivers of policies affecting them.

8. Russell Thornton, "Population History of Native North Americans," in *A Population History of North America*, ed. Michael Haines and Richard H. Steckel (Cambridge: Cambridge University Press, 2000), 9–50; Thomas Mann, *1491: New Revelations of the Americas Before Columbus* (New York: Vintage Books, 2006); David Stannard, *American Holocaust: The Conquest of the New World* (New York: Oxford University Press, 1993).

9. Bruce Trigger, *A History of Archaeological Thought* (Cambridge: Cambridge University Press, 2006).

10. Roy Pearce, *The Savages of America, A Study of the Indians and the Idea of Civilization* (Baltimore: John Hopkins Press, 1956), 82.

11. Trigger, *A History of Archaeological Thought*, 100–3.

12. Ibid.

13. Ibid., 100.

14. Edward Burnett Tylor, *Primitive Culture: Researches into the Development of Mythology, Philosophy, Religion, Art, and Custom*, Vol. 2 (London: J. Murray, 1871).

15. Lewis H. Morgan, *Ancient Society; or, Researches in the Lines of Human Progress from Savagery, through Barbarism to Civilization* (New York: H. Holt, 1877).

16. Powell and Ingalls, *Report of Special Commissioners*.

17. John Wesley Powell, "An Overland Trip to the Grand Canyon," *Scribner's Monthly* 10 (1875): 665.

18. John Wesley Powell, "A Discourse on the Philosophy of the North American Indians," *Journal of the American Geographical Society of New York* 8 (1876): 261–62.

19. John Wesley Powell, *Indians West of the Rocky Mountains. Statement made before the Committee on Indian Affairs as to the Condition of the Indian Tribes West of the Rocky Mountains*. 43rd Cong, 1st Sess., H. Misc. 86 Serial 1618. (Washington, DC: Government Printing Office, 1874), 16.

20. Powell and Ingalls, *Report of Special Commissioners*, 25.

21. Ibid.

22. Alvin Josephy, *500 Nations: An Illustrated History of North American Indians* (New York: Alfred A. Knopf, 1994), 4.

23. Daniel C. McCool, *Command of the Waters: Iron Triangles, Federal Water Development, and Indian Water* (Berkeley: University of California Press, 1987), 112.

24. Winters v. U.S., 207 U.S. 564 (1908); John Shurts, *Indian Reserved Water Rights: The Winters Doctrine in Social and Legal Context, 1880s–1930s* (Norman: University of Oklahoma Press, 2003).

25. Norris Hundley, Jr., *Water and the West: The Colorado River Compact and the Politics of Water in the American West* (Berkeley: University of California Press, 2009), 211–12.

26. US Bureau of Reclamation and Ten Tribes Partnership, Colorado River Basin Ten Tribes Partnership Tribal Water Study, Study Report (2018), 1–2.

27. John Wesley Powell, "From Savagery to Barbarism," *Transactions of the Anthropological Society of Washington* 3 (1885): 191.

28. John Wesley Powell, "Human evolution. Annual address of the president, J. W. Powell, delivered November 6, 1883," *Transactions of the Anthropological Society of Washington* 2 (1882): 176–208.

29. Powell, "Certain Principles of Primitive Law," *Science* 92 (1884): 436–37.

30. Ibid., 437.

31. John Wesley Powell, "From Barbarism to Civilization," *American Anthropologist* 1, no. 2 (1888): 121.

32. Ibid., 102.

33. Ibid., 123.

34. Trigger, *A History of Archaeological Thought*.

35. Franz Boas, "The Methods of Ethnology," *American Anthropologist* 22, no. 4 (1920): 311–21.

36. R. J. McGee, *Anthropological Theory: An Introductory History* (New York: McGraw Hill, 2003).

37. Indian Citizenship Act, 43 Stat. 253 (1924).

38. Indian Reorganization Act, 48 Stat. 984 (1934).

39. Harrison v. Laveen, 196 P.2d 456 (Ariz. 1948); 67 Ariz. 337.

40. Trujillo v. Garley, Civ. No. 1353 (D.N.M. 1948).

41. Daniel C. McCool, Susan M. Olson, and Jennifer L. Robinson, *Native Vote: American Indians, the Voting Rights Act, and the Right to Vote* (Cambridge: Cambridge University Press, 2007), 95–97.

42. P.L. 98-638 (1975).

43. McCool, Olson, and Robinson, *Native Vote*, 20.

44. *Navajo Nation v. San Juan County, UT*, "Memorandum Decision and Order," Case No. 2:12-cv-00039-RJS-SPB. See also Julie Turkewitz, "For Native Americans, A 'Historic Moment' on a Path to Power at the Ballot Box," *The New York Times*, January 4, 2018, https://www.nytimes.com/2018/01/04/us/native-american-voting-rights.html.

45. "Ten Tribes Partnership," Colorado River Water Users Association, accessed March 19, 2020, https://www.crwua.org/ten-tribes.html; "Inter Tribal Council of Arizona," accessed October 16, 2019, http://itcaonline.com.

46. "Navajo Nation Human Rights Commission," accessed October 16, 2019, http://www.nnhrc.navajo-nsn.gov.

47. US Department of the Interior, Office of Collaborative Action and Dispute Resolution, "Why Do We Consult Tribes? A Legal and Policy Perspective," accessed October 16, 2019, https://www.doi.gov/pmb/cadr/programs/native/gtgworkshop/Implementing-the-Government-to-Government-Relationship.

48. President Barack Obama, "Presidential Proclamation—Establishment of the Bears Ears National Monument," December 28, 2016, https://obamawhitehouse.archives.gov/the-press-office/2016/12/28/proclamation-establishment-bears-ears-national-monument.

49. "Ten Tribes Partnership"; US Bureau of Reclamation, Colorado River Basin Water Supply and Demand Study, Appendix C9, Tribal Water Demand, Scenario Quantification (2012).

50. Worster, *A River Running West*, 130.

51. Wallace Stegner, *Beyond the Hundredth Meridian: John Wesley Power and the Second Opening of the West* (Boston: Houghton Mifflin, 1954), 16, 19.

52. McCool, *Command of the Waters*, 33.

53. John W. Powell, Remarks before the Second International Irrigation Congress, Los Angeles, CA (Official Report of the International Irrigation Congress, 1893), 109–11.

54. John W. Powell, "Are Our Indians Becoming Extinct?," *Forum* 15 (1993): 343–54.

55. J. H. Bodley, *Cultural Anthropology: Tribes, States, and the Global System* (Lanham, MD: Rowman Altamira, 2011), 10–13.

56. Ibid.

57. Alexandra Harmon, *Indians in the Making: Ethnic Relations and Indian Identities around Puget Sound* (Berkeley: University of California Press, 1998).

58. Kurt W. Deuschle, "Cross-Cultural Medicine: The Navajo Indians as Case Exemplar," *Daedalus* (1986): 175–84.

59. Brian Codding and Kate Magargal, "Dynamic Impacts of Environmental Change and Biomass Harvesting on Woodland Ecosystems and Traditional Livelihoods," 2017, https://nsf.gov/awardsearch/showAward?AWD_ID = 1714972.

60. Kurt E. Dongoske et al., "Archaeological Cultures and Cultural Affiliation: Hopi and Zuni Perspectives in the American Southwest," *American Antiquity* 62, no. 4 (1997): 600–8.

61. Lynda D. McNeil, "Recurrence of Bear Restoration Symbolism: Minusinsk Basin Evenki and Basin-Plateau Ute," *Journal of Cognition and Culture* 8, no. 1 (2008): 71–98.

62. Richard W. Stoffle et al., "Cultural Landscapes and Traditional Cultural Properties: A Southern Paiute View of the Grand Canyon and Colorado River," *American Indian Quarterly* 21, no. 2 (1997): 229–49.

63. Ibid.

64. Archaeology Southwest and Friends of Bears Ears, Bears Ears Archaeological Experts Gathering (2017), https://www.archaeologysouthwest.org/pdf/Bears_Ears_Report.pdf.

65. Ibid.

66. Cally Carswell, "Archaeologists Uneasy as Trump Shrinks Bears Ears Monument Lands," *Nature* 552 (2017): 13–14.

67. William D. Lipe, "Bears Ears Controversy: Some Monumental Issues" (2018), https://research.libraries.wsu.edu:8443/xmlui/bitstream/handle/2376/12883/Lipe_post.pdf.

68. Ibid.

69. Courtney Tanner, "Five American Indian tribes, furious over Trump shrinking Bears Ears on his trip to Utah, sue the president," *Salt Lake Tribune*, December 4, 2017, https://www.sltrib.com/news/politics/2017/12/04/five-american-indian-tribes-furious-over-trump-shrinking-bears-ears-sue-the-president.

70. Lipe, "Bears Ears Controversy: Some Monumental Issues"; "Archaeologists push for Bears Ears National Monument," *Crow Canyon News Letter*, 2016, https://www.crowcanyon.org/e-newsletter/2016/June/2016_June_Bears_Ears.html; Carswell, "Archaeologists Uneasy."

71. Julie Turkewitz, "Trump Slashes Size of Bears Ears and Grand Staircase Monuments," *New York Times,* December 4, 2017, https://www.nytimes.com/2017/12/04/us/trump-bears-ears.html.

72. William deBuys, *Seeing Things Whole: The Essential John Wesley Powell* (Washington, DC: Island Press, 2004), 355.

73. Stegner, *Beyond the Hundredth Meridian,* 49.

CHAPTER 10

"Pastoral and Civilized"

*Water, Land, and Tribes in the
Colorado River Basin*

AUTUMN L. BERNHARDT

John Wesley Powell has a complicated legacy with respect to tribes and Indian people. Although Powell believed he was doing a great service, he burdened Indians by promoting imperial westward expansion and undermined the environmental resiliency of the country by denying the value of Native cultures. During the period of early westward expansion, certain Euro-Americans sought to exterminate Indians completely while others made persistent efforts to "civilize" Indians with the plow and the Bible. The quest to make good Christian farmers out of Indians is reflected in Powell's writings and embodied in laws, both past and present. Populating the Colorado River Basin and other parts of the arid West without proper respect for either Native peoples or the necessary workings of nature has overwhelmed environmental resources and perpetuated injustices yet to be resolved—or even fully addressed.[1]

Lessons learned from Powell's writings, as well as the nation's past growth and expansion into the arid West, are particularly relevant today because the Colorado River Basin is undergoing another surge in growth and expansion.[2] For purposes of this chapter, I use the term "Manifest Destiny" broadly to refer to a mindset that perceives growth and expansion into the arid West, and particularly the Colorado River Basin, as beneficial and inevitable. In this sense, Manifest Destiny is not confined to a particular time frame within American history.[3] It is instead an ongoing belief system that overemphasizes the brilliance of human endeavor in the face of ecological limits. It is a belief system that tends to do things *to* Indigenous people and *to* the natural environment rather than doing things *with* them. This new era of Manifest Destiny is less agricultural and more suburban and metropolitan in nature. It is also less overtly racist. That being said, the contemporary version of Manifest Destiny still heralds rapid expansion in and around the Colorado River Basin with insufficient regard for Indigenous people and the natural world.

The exact future of the Colorado River Basin is uncertain to a degree, but American history has taken a well-established and predictable course when there has been competition for land and water. When human communities do not "honorably harvest"[4] resources in the arid West, certain members of creation, namely Indians and the larger natural environment, are called upon to make sacrifices so dominant society can progress along what is rationalized as a predetermined, glorious path. Tribes have considerable water rights in the basin due to past assimilationist efforts aimed at making them "pastoral and civilized,"[5] but many of these water rights are still being ignored while cities proliferate in and around the basin's deserts.

Population growth, a new round of westward expansion, and the perpetual aridity of the region offer fresh opportunities to finally do the right thing in areas characterized by environmental injustice. The good news is that principles of Indigenous environmental stewardship can be integrated into culture and law to guide Colorado River Basin policy down a more sensible course than it took in the past. The basin is on the precipice of another great change that invites reexamination of American law and culture—a precipice captured by this volume's "Great Unknown" theme. Following Indigenous environmental stewardship principles, and making a clear commitment to avoid new versions of old Manifest Destiny thinking, will help human communities across and beyond the basin to live in peace with each other and to live respectfully within the limits of nature.

POWELL'S RACIAL AND CULTURAL POLITICS

Powell was decidedly a child of his time. He spoke to and about Indians as if they were inane curiosities, yet did not always appreciate the wisdom of Native cultures. He thought the best way to "protect" Indians of the Colorado River Basin from extinction was to force them to assimilate into "civilized" American society. Predictably, "civilization" looked a lot like Powell. It was characterized by a hostility toward wilderness, hierarchical and male-dominated political institutions, and a religious freedom whose outer limit extended only to Christianity. From a broad perspective, Powell's cultural politics certainly could have been better, but they also could have been worse. The more positive and less problematic aspects of Powell's work should be acknowledged from the outset. Powell never became swept up in Social Darwinism, he disagreed with other Euro-Americans who wished to exterminate Indians outright, and his studies of Indians made him aware of actual cultural differences among tribes.

Slightly Better Than Other Alternatives

Like many people in his generation, Powell did not believe in true social equality between races. Unlike many people of his generation, Powell did acknowledge some degree of humanity in people not of European descent. Powell was an abolitionist and an opponent of what came to be known as Social Darwinism, which over time pervaded American intellectualism.[6] He specifically noted: "I have denied that man has progressed by the survival of the fittest in the struggle for existence, and I have affirmed that old philosophy that human progress is by human endeavor."[7] Although Powell still presumed Native Americans were inferior to Euro-Americans based on cultural differences, he did not believe their inferiority was an inherent condition of biology.

Powell made more of an effort to interact with Native Americans than most Euro-Americans involved in Indian policy at the time. His visits with tribes while traveling through the Colorado River Basin and other parts of the arid region made him an authority on Indian affairs—at least according to the judgment of the dominant culture and those in government.[8] On one noteworthy instance, when testifying before Congress about how the government should handle the Utes of western Colorado, Powell argued for restraint in troop placement and removal to reservations.[9] Powell's message to Congress seems well-intentioned and designed to spare atrocities routinely visited upon subjugated Indians. His approach was at least distinguishable from violent tactics taken by the federal government against other "non-compliant" Indians that predictably ended in massacres like those at Wounded Knee and Sand Creek.[10]

Lastly, Powell acknowledged the diversity of tribes. He noted that "the white man did not know that he was dealing with hundreds of distinct governments" or know that "Indians were not a homogenous people."[11] Although Powell never supported tribal sovereignty as currently understood, he did concede that there were inherent cultural differences among tribes and recommended that the government deal with tribes as distinct entities.

A Civilization Based on Homogeneity and Hierarchy

According to Powell, human cultures inherently progressed from "savagery" exemplified by many North American tribes to "barbarism" and then eventually to true "civilization" exemplified by Euro-American culture.[12]

Powell argued that "savagery" was characterized by animistic religion, which he more or less understood as polytheism and nature worship. In his understanding of savagery, there was female leadership of clans, kinship based on affinity as well as blood relations, and communal ownership of property by either clans or tribes.[13] Nature remained largely unaltered, and people subsisted by hunting and gathering, along with limited incidences of what he considered lower agriculture. Powell claimed savages were "denizens of forest and wold without the skill necessary to clear away the forests and establish higher agriculture and domesticate herds of animals."[14] Powell also noted that multiple languages were spoken in a state of savagery.

On the opposite end of the spectrum, civilization was characterized by patriarchy, private property, Christianity, hierarchical and irrigated agriculture and industry that treated other parts of the natural world as subservient to man, and the speaking of a single language.[15]

Barbarism represented the transitional stage between savagery and civilization, and Powell described what he thought the transition from savagery to barbarism would look like. Presumably, America's many tribes would take this course.

> With the acquisition of herds, farming lands and store of grain, wealth is accumulated, and this wealth is controlled by the gentile patriarchs. It is no longer clan property, but gentile property in the possession and under the control of the patriarch, who wields a power never known in savagery.[16]

Most of Powell's distinctions between these cultural stages concerned the degree of authority over people as well as the natural world. Greater homogeneity in religion, language, and overall land use was perceived as progress. It is also notable that "civilization," by Powell's definition, was significantly less democratic in terms of social organization.

Killing the Indian to Save the Man

Powell departed from contemporaries who believed that all Indians are the same and that "the only good Indian is a dead Indian."[17] Instead, he remained steadfast in his assimilationist convictions. Powell spoke highly of government boarding schools and complimented the work of Carlisle Indian School founder Captain Richard H. Pratt, who is given credit for the phrase "kill the Indian in him, and save the man."[18]

Powell did countenance cultural genocide, though. Deliberate slaughter of game that Indians depended upon for survival,[19] forced confinement of Indians to reservations, and governmental repression of Indian cultures were presumed both good for the country and good for the Indians. Taming Indians as well as the wildness of the West was supposedly part of an inevitable national destiny. Powell knew assimilation was painful for Native people yet noted:

> The conquering race, impelled by motives of humanity, has ever endeavored to raise the savage in culture. It has been a difficult task, because the things which we most desired to do for them they scorned with contempt. That for which they prayed, that for which they fought, could not be yielded. They wanted a wilderness for bounding game and blushing fruits; they wanted the primeval condition of savagery; they wanted beast-gods, scalp dances, and Terpsichorean worship. The conquering race wanted the continent for higher and holier purposes,—for a transcendent state of culture, for homes and cities and temples in which to worship God.[20]

LAWS THAT WHISTLE THE TUNE OF MANIFEST DESTINY: REDEEMING NATURE FROM SIN AND COINCIDENTALLY MAKING IT PROPERTY

Land, water, and Indian laws were infused with the ideology shared by Powell and other immigrant Americans who saw domination of nature and irrigated agriculture as necessary means to "civilize" the Colorado River Basin and the West as a whole. As law is based upon precedent and gives deference to what has happened before, understanding the broader context that created early land and water laws is essential. Cherokee legal historian Rennard Strickland once observed that "law is part of a time and a place, the product of a specific time and an actual place."[21] The West still lives with the legacy of laws conceived during the fervor of Manifest Destiny and early westward expansion.

Powell did not create the laws that prevailed during westward expansion, and on multiple occasions he publicly challenged the reckless mentality propelling these laws. He did not want the Colorado River Basin and other parts of the arid region settled in a "mad, unplanned rush," but rather wanted the region "settled slowly, cautiously, in a manner that would work."[22] Powell certainly had a plan for settlement, but imperialistic expansion was the wrong plan overall.

The same ethnocentric and anthropocentric presumptions that Powell made in his writing are embodied in prior appropriation laws. "Prior appropriation" refers here not just to existing laws that allocate water in Colorado River Basin states, but also to a broader classification of laws. Early land distribution laws that share foundational principles of prior appropriation, such as Homestead Acts, the Swamp Lands Act, the Desert Land Act, and even the Doctrine of Discovery, all fall within a similar vein of thought. These varied laws operate differently but share two main currents. The first is that resources should be awarded based upon "first in time, first in right." The second is that property rights vest only if land or water is changed from its natural state.

According to Powell, Christianity[23] and control of the natural environment[24] were characteristics of the highest state of civilization. Christian interpretations of the Bible, at least the kind that prevailed during westward expansion and that are still very salient for a large segment of Americans, convey a hierarchical land ethic with deep hostility toward wilderness and deep bias toward cultivated landscapes.[25] In Genesis, God instructs humans to "be fruitful, and multiply, and replenish the earth, and subdue it: and have dominion over the fish of the sea, and over the fowl of the air, and over every living thing that moveth upon the earth."[26] This passage has been consistently used to argue that humankind is not only separate from, but also *above* nature, and has a divine entitlement to do whatever it chooses.

According to many doctrinal interpretations of the Garden of Eden story, humanity as well as nature itself had become fallen and in need of redemption.[27] Early Euro-Americans found redemption for nature and themselves by instituting laws that rewarded the cutting down of forests, the draining of wetlands, the irrigation of deserts, and the conversion of wilderness into farms and towns. Even after the first wave of westward expansion, the influence of religious doctrine on law continued with the Reclamation Act and the era of large-scale dam building.

Controlling the flow of once wild rivers in reservoirs was in many ways an effort to redeem deserts and create a virtual Garden of Eden in an area Powell referred to as the "arid region."[28]

Despite notable references in the Bible to wilderness as a sanctuary for both Jesus and John the Baptist,[29] the Garden of Eden story, along with numerous Old Testament disparagements of wilderness, sent the message that wilderness was a type of hell on earth. Perhaps ignoring certain biblical passages that spoke favorably of deserts and other uncultivated wilds, and emphasizing passages that stigmatized these lands, had less to do with official religious dogma than with the fact that most Euro-Americans practiced not only Christianity, but also capitalism.

John Locke's writings inspired American law and concepts of private property. Locke's *Second Treatise of Government* propounded that if a man removed something from its natural state and mixed his labor with it, it must become his property.[30] Although Powell embraced communitarian concepts and public works in certain contexts, private property was a fundamental element of his ideal civilization, as well as tied through prior appropriation to the domination of nature. Echoing language within Genesis that was consistent with the sentiments of Powell, Locke noted that "subduing or cultivating the earth, and having dominion, we see are joined together." Wilderness did not have any inherent value unless changed by man into property.

As applied to the Colorado River Basin's coveted flows, the State of Colorado's prior appropriation law insisted water be taken from its natural state and applied to a "beneficial use" such as agriculture, mining, or municipal use.[31] After a storied history of litigation and legislative battles, recreational in-channel uses, instream flow rights for fisheries, and storage rights for wildlife and fish habitat can now meet the elements of prior appropriation, but these outlying water rights are still modest exceptions to the consumptive requirements of the doctrine.[32] Beneficial use of privately owned, direct flow rights in Colorado is still bound by history and excludes any use that would keep water in the stream for fish or for the aesthetic beauty of a wild, flowing river or landscape.[33]

Prior appropriation principally awards water rights when river flow is transformed into irrigation diversions or diversions for towns and cities. A similar picture emerges in relation to land. Not only have Americans found spiritual redemption in transforming wilderness into agricultural land, they have also found private property.[34]

AN UNINTENDED LEGACY: TRIBAL SOVEREIGNTY AND WATER RIGHTS

Powell's clearest gifts to the tribes that he studied in the Colorado River Basin and elsewhere were unintentional. While he sought to save Indians by assimilation, perhaps what has saved Indians more than anything else has been collective resistance to assimilation. Fighting colonization tied together tribes' futures and created solidarity out of which several successions of the tribal sovereignty movement have been born and reborn. Furthermore, the *Winters* decision tried to reconcile the federal government's assimilation efforts with the practical reality of farming in a desert region, and created water rights with considerable use volumes and early priority dates.

Resistance Makes Us Stronger

Despite considerable extermination and assimilation efforts, Indians are still kicking around the Colorado River Basin in the twenty-first century. Powell stated that "civilization overwhelms savagery, not so much by spilling blood as by mixing blood."[35] At present, tribal populations are growing, and many mixed-blood people still identify as Indian. Although Indians have adapted to new forms of culture, as a matter of both choice and survival, the reservation system advocated by Powell actually insulated tribal cultures and aided in the preservation of environmental stewardship practices that are a gift to the nation.

After removal to the reservations, Powell sought the eventual diminution of reservation lands, which would acculturate tribes to private property ownership and conveniently free up more land for settlers.[36] Efforts to divest tribes of land, such as allotment, treaty renegotiations to reduce reservation boundaries, etc., became common experiences within Indian country. The Bureau of Indian Affairs (BIA), which was tasked with making good Christian farmers out of reservation Indians, often used its authority to hurt Indian people and to exploit tribal resources in order to benefit non-tribal interests. The shared pain of resisting dominant society and enduring governmental exploitation and ineptitude motivated Indian people to fight not only for their own reservation homelands, but also for the homelands of other tribes and the dignity of Indigenous ways of being.[37]

The legacy of being forcibly "civilized" has brought considerable intergenerational trauma to Native people, and many battles are still yet to be won, particularly with respect to sacred lands, environmental justice, and language revitalization. That being said, Charles Wilkinson observed: "[I]t says a great deal about the staying power of tribes, for virtually no one, Powell or Stegner included, expected them to emerge at the beginning of the twenty-first century as viable governments and productive participants in the modern West."[38] The assimilation efforts supported by Powell ultimately prompted Indian people to form alliances and to secure laws that afford greater protection to themselves and their beliefs.

The Water Rights Legacy of Compelling Indians to be Pastoral and Civilized

Tribes have a legal advantage with water rights precisely because the federal government intended to make the West as well as the Indians "pastoral and civilized." From his expeditions, Powell knew viscerally that the Colorado River Basin was arid and contained many areas where it was impractical to farm without irrigation—or at all.[39] However, Powell's biases toward farming as a "civilized" practice still compelled him to advocate that Indians become farmers in the desert, rather than live off game and conduct small-scale agriculture as many tribes had been doing successfully since time immemorial.

According to the Indian reserved water rights doctrine set forth in *Winters v. United States,* tribes have a priority date to water rights determined by the creation date of their reservations, with a quantity of water use determined by what is necessary to "fulfill the purposes of the reservation."[40] In *Winters,* the Supreme Court reasoned that tribes and the federal government had reserved water rights when reservations were created because "it was the policy of the government and it was the desire of the Indians ... to become a pastoral and civilized people."[41] Echoing sentiments that irrigation "improves" land, which again underlie John Locke's writings as well as prior appropriation doctrine, *Winters* stated that reserved water rights for reservations were essential because the "lands were arid, and, without irrigation, were practically valueless."[42] In *Arizona v. California,* the Supreme Court created a "practically irrigable acreage" (PIA) standard to quantify how much water is necessary to make a particular reservation farmable.[43] Given the large land mass of some reservations, Indian tribes now have water rights of "potentially enormous magnitude"[44] with early priority dates.

NAVIGATING THE GREAT UNKNOWN: THE COLORADO RIVER BASIN CANNOT SOLVE PROBLEMS WITH THE SAME THINKING THAT CREATED THEM

Reexamining mainstream beliefs is necessary to avoid replicating behaviors that have made the Colorado River Basin vulnerable today. Indians in the basin and the broader West share the same fate as the natural environment, and Indian cultures more readily acknowledge their dependence upon nature than mainstream society. Charles Wilkinson has described how Indians have a worldview "at once ecological and spiritual," expressing his associated belief that "of all the societies in the West, none can put forth a voice for the land in more articulate, knowledgeable, and authentic terms than the American Indian tribes."[45] Yet, speaking in legal terms, there is ongoing discrimination toward Indian religions in matters pertaining to sacred lands and waters, such that the National Environmental Policy Act (NEPA) and Religious Freedom Restoration Act (RFRA) need to be properly applied for basin tribes to exercise religious freedom. Traditional ecological knowledge, as embodied in Indigenous stewardship and languages, likewise should be given increasing formal recognition as a source of knowledge for environmental decision-making.[46] In a similar vein, states, municipalities, and counties in and around the basin need to limit their incessant ambitions for growth, and make decisions about land and water use planning that are in line with environmental justice. In particular, Indian water rights throughout the basin need to be respected, and certain aspects of prior appropriation should be modified to more fully respect all of creation, including the fish and the rivers themselves.

The Misunderstood Beauty of Indian Religions and Cultures

Powell acknowledged that "the whole of daily life of an Indian is religious life."[47] However, he also went on to disparage what he termed "Indian theology" as "absurd prohibitions," "a mass of nonsense, a mass of incoherent folly," and "ethically a hideous monster of lies."[48] Although Powell's critiques seem outdated by some contemporary standards and increasing respect has been extended, Indian religions are often still treated as childish romanticism and disregarded when land and water use decisions are made.

For the most part, Indigenous belief systems are animistic and presume that rivers, mountains, and meadows are alive and have spirits.[49]

The Indian way of being is based upon a relational land ethic, a kinship with nature, and an acknowledgement of the interconnectedness of life.[50] Rather than emphasizing the "intellectual superiority of man"[51] and man's ability to master the "wonders of the universe,"[52] as Powell did, tribal religions emphasize humility and humanity's dependence on nature and other creatures. In many Indigenous belief systems, when any resource is harvested by hunting, gathering, or agricultural cultivation, the principles of an "honorable harvest"[53] are followed: prayer is offered; permission to harvest is requested and the answer is heeded; the first deer, leek plant, or whatever it may be is not usually taken; no more than half is taken; the resource is known intimately so it can be taken care of; thanksgiving and an offering are given; and the harvest is shared.

Place-based, animistic religions also treat wilderness as a highly regarded aesthetic.[54] Wilderness, deserts, and free-flowing rivers do not need to be redeemed from a fallen state or made economically productive by dam construction or housing subdivisions. In stark contrast to American views of nature embodied in past and current laws, humanity's highest purpose is not to try to dominate nature, but rather to live in harmony with all of creation. Nature leaves little for humanity to do other than to try to understand, respect, and learn to live in balance with it.

Wholesale conversion to Indigenous religions by those in mainstream society would be inauthentic, and is not prescribed as the exclusive means for approaching the natural world in the Colorado River Basin or elsewhere. Mainstream society does, however, need to acknowledge the role that certain interpretations of the Judeo-Christian tradition have played and continue to play in shaping both the culture and laws that prey upon Native belief systems and undercut human beings' ability to live in and around the basin with continuing longevity.[55] All cultural movements, including the civil rights movement, women's movement, and environmental movement, have been accompanied by reforms to dominant American interpretations of religious texts. In the not-so-distant past, religion was used to justify slavery, bans on interracial marriage, and laws precluding women from owning property, yet those religious arguments today are largely dismissed as contrived.[56] Increasingly, people raised in the Christian tradition are feeling "God's presence in the gliding riffles and silent pools"[57] of rivers, and "are recognizing that destruction of creation is a moral issue."[58] Thankfully, mainstream Christian doctrine and modern beliefs are becoming less at odds with nature and by extension less antagonistic to Indigenous religions rooted in the natural world.

Rather than trying to educate Indians on being Christian farmers as Powell and the federal government attempted, mainstream US society and its governmental institutions should learn from tribal ways of being and look to them as a source of wisdom.[59] This goes beyond just checking the "tribal consultation box" because a government-to-government relationship with tribes is legally mandated. Certainly not all aspects of tribal cultures are worthy of preservation, but incorporating aspects of Indigenous stewardship practices would not conflict with the dominant society's adherence to science, Christianity, or democracy, and in some ways would offer a more authentic expression of these ideologies than currently exists. Acknowledging humanity's role as a steward rather than a master, applying the principles of an honorable harvest to resource management, and acknowledging kinship with the rest of creation should be part of the Colorado River Basin's collective ethos.

True Religious Freedom for Tribes and Indian People

Tribal religions deserve cultural acceptance, but they also deserve legal protection. In *Navajo Nation v. USFS* ("Snowbowl"), thirteen Colorado River Basin tribes, including the White Mountain Apache, Navajo, Hopi, Hualapai, and several others, sued the Forest Service for issuing a permit to Snowbowl Ski Resort to use reclaimed water for snowmaking on a sacred site.[60] Snowbowl is located on Humphrey's Peak and, along with other peaks, forms a single, larger mountain known as the San Francisco Peaks. The tribes opposed the use of reclaimed water because the San Francisco Peaks represents one of the four holy mountains between which creation arose, they are a site of ceremonies central to tribal religions, and they are a place for gathering plants as well as spring water used for healing the sick.[61]

RFRA was designed to "protect the exercise of all religions, including the religions of American Indians,"[62] from substantial burden. Rather than determining that there was a substantial burden on tribal religion, the Ninth Circuit Court of Appeals minimized the spraying of treated effluent on the San Francisco Peaks as upsetting "subjective, emotional religious experience" and "sensibilities."[63] In the context of animistic religion, a substantial burden on religion is a disrespect for the aliveness of a place, which is often dependent upon the continuation of the landscape's natural state.[64] If a substantial burden is shown under RFRA, the government must prove a compelling interest underlies its action, and it is using the least restrictive means to effectuate that action.[65] The Ninth Circuit refused to consider whether the Forest Service had used the least restrictive means or whether the government had a compelling interest in letting Snowbowl put treated effluent on a place of fundamental religious importance to tribes.

Religious discrimination under US law impacts not just Colorado River Basin tribes, but all of Indian Country. Although Standing Rock[66] and Snowbowl are different in important ways, there are relevant comparisons because similar issues were raised. To state it even more directly, legal disputes concerning tribal religions are not going to go away anytime soon, and it is important that the law be properly applied. Unfortunately, some federal appellate courts' interpretations of RFRA, including the *Navajo Nation v. USFS* decision, are not in line with either the spirit or letter of the law. In a country ostensibly founded on free religious expression, the current state of the law is troublesome. If tribes are to succeed in protecting sacred places and eliminating discrimination against animistic religions, RFRA must be applied as it was intended, and NEPA must consider actual environmental impacts rather than being treated as a procedural rubber stamp on whatever course of action the federal government aims to pursue.[67] The history of suppressing tribal religions is repeating itself not through BIA regulations, but through narrow-minded interpretations of RFRA and NEPA.

Better Environmental Decision-Making Through Traditional Ecological Knowledge

Traditional ecological knowledge should be regarded as a relevant authority in guiding land and water use decisions in the Colorado River Basin and beyond. Powell obviously did not care much for Indian religions, but nonetheless observed, "there is not a trail they did not know; every gulch and every rock seemed familiar."[68] Science, even with its technological sophistication, cannot replace the intimacy of knowledge gathered over generations by people living upon the land. Traditional ecological knowledge is rooted in the belief that all things in nature are connected, so the field of ecology was somewhat late to the party when it finally acknowledged the interconnectedness of ecosystems. There might be a benefit to employing both science and traditional ecological knowledge when considering the effects of an action upon a river or landscape. Potawatomi botanist Robin Wall Kimmerer once wrote:

When I stare too long at the world with science eyes, I see an afterimage of traditional knowledge. Might science and traditional knowledge be purple and yellow to one another, might they be goldenrod and asters? We see the world more fully when we use both.[69]

Powell remarked that the number of languages "diminish in number with the progress of culture."[70] Unfortunately, many Indigenous languages are imperiled due to assimilationist policies favored by Powell. Although Powell did study Indigenous languages, he failed to recognize they are living libraries of ecological knowledge. Languages are site-specific and act as a record of biodiversity and environmental changes that predate Euro-American contact. They are meant to be spoken by the descendants of the culture that created them, not merely housed in books like relics.

Evaluating ethnobotany preserved in tribal languages in combination with science when making land and water use decisions in the Colorado River Basin may prove invaluable. Science constitutes a limited construct. In contrast, tribal languages and traditional ecological knowledge speak the "grammar of animacy" and remind humans that there are intelligences beyond our own.[71] When approaching complicated decisions about the Colorado River Basin, it makes sense to consult science as well as ways of knowing that consider a broader time frame and value more than just human interests.

Indigenous Environmental Stewardship Lighting the Path

Traditional ecological knowledge and Indigenous environmental stewardship practices also make sense practically. Tribal land and water management programs, inspired by belief systems that emphasize kinship and respect for nature, have often been able to achieve environmental standards much higher than those of the federal or state governments.

One classic story of tribal stewardship concerns the White Mountain Apache Tribe's preservation of the Apache Trout. Although the tribe has still not received full recognition for the gift of biodiversity it gave the American Southwest, its "early and visionary action is primarily responsible for preventing the extinction of Apache trout."[72] In the not-so-distant past, Apache Trout had been an abundant species, but their numbers were decimated over time by policies reflective of Powell's historical thinking—namely, policies that disregarded Indians as being of lower culture and adhered to a hierarchical view of nature.

In line with the assimilationist policy advocated by Powell, the BIA opened up Fort Apache Indian Reservation to aggressive farming, ranching, and timber harvesting. As was typical of this era of BIA paternalism, federal management of tribal resources served to benefit non-natives and was done without the tribe's consent. Overgrazing, soil tillage, and timber cuts eroded the land and streambanks and caused sedimentation to pervade rivers during runoff.[73] High sedimentation not only impacted fish health and habitat, it also interfered with Apache Trout spawning.[74]

To add to the troubles that the Apache Trout were experiencing from land misuse, state and federal wildlife agencies encouraged overfishing and then tried to compensate for population declines by stocking streams with non-native fish. Apache Trout were out-competed for habitat, preyed upon by German brown trout, and ended up hybridizing with rainbow trout. As early as the 1940s, the tribe recognized that the Apache Trout was suffering and started closing streams to fishing. At the Apache Trout's lowest point, overall habitat had been reduced to thirty miles of stream within the reservation. By 1955, the tribe closed a large area around Mount Baldy, one of its sacred mountains, to preserve the mountain in its wilderness state for cultural and religious reasons, and to protect a pure strain of Apache Trout that remained in Mount Baldy's waters.[75]

In the 1960s, the tribe's efforts to manage natural resources according to their own belief systems took yet another interesting turn. Under BIA management, large stands of tribal forest were being clear-cut and even non-commercial phreatophytes like cottonwoods were being removed.[76] Considering that reservation forests contribute a significant amount of downstream river flow, tribal suspicions of BIA motives were high.[77] Although collusion between the BIA and Arizona cities was never addressed by a court, "outraged tribal council members were convinced that the BIA jacked up the timber yield to send more water downstream to the Salt River Project, which supplied water to the fast-growing Phoenix metropolitan area."[78] The tribe moved swiftly to advocate for a sharply reduced timber yield, declined to renew milling and logging contracts, and exercised increased self-determination over its own forests.[79]

More sustainable forest management advocated by the tribe prevented erosion and had a positive impact on river habitat. The tribe has not stopped there, however. Riparian areas have been actively restored and cattle are fenced out of certain sections of water.[80] The tribe has erected fish barriers on many creeks to prevent encroachment by the descendants of non-native fish that were introduced generations ago, and the tribal wildlife agency invests time and resources into electroshocking and removing non-native fish. Apache youth are educated about the fish, and a tribal hatchery program was implemented to take pressure off the wilder strain.[81] Years before the Endangered Species Act was put into place in the 1970s,[82] Apache Trout were relocated from compromised waters in old-time, metal milk containers. Now, the tribe has a vibrant ecotourism industry that is based upon its management of trophy elk as well as its management of the little golden fish.[83] Tribal land and water management founded on kinship and relational principles benefits not only tribal lands, but also interconnected ecosystems on private, state, and federal lands. Tribal practices of this sort should not just be celebrated, but emulated within the broader Colorado River Basin.

Respecting Indian Water Rights and All Our Relations

The truism that "justice delayed is justice denied" can certainly be applied to Indian water rights based upon the *Winters* Doctrine. Indian water rights still have not been quantified for a significant number of Colorado River Basin tribes, despite these water rights typically having senior priority dates that go back to the establishment of reservations. The fact that the earliest Americans still struggle with access to clean, readily available water in a modern, first-world country is an environmental justice concern. Additional federal funding, staffing, focus, and planning are just a few methods to expedite recognition of these water rights.[84]

In recent years, the cloud of uncertainty surrounding tribal water rights has become even more troubling. Tribal water rights are included in state general stream adjudications,[85] but there is ongoing conflict in the law concerning the quantification and use of *Winters* rights. Strong authority suggests that tribes can change the uses made of *Winters* rights into non-consumptive uses more in line with traditional kinship values.[86] But there is also divergent authority that has prevented tribes from changing *Winters* rights from agricultural use.[87] To add to the complexity, Colorado River Basin states are being settled by a new wave of immigrants that augment inherent pressure placed upon water resources in an arid climate. The bonanza attitude of Manifest Destiny that overwhelms nature and naively ignores, at best, and callously disrespects, at worse, Indians' access to water is repeating in modern times. Cities are swelling inside and outside the basin. Water rights historically applied to agricultural use are increasingly being gobbled up by these metastasizing cities.

They are becoming entrenched as water monopolies and oligopolies within and adjacent to the basin.

Given the new stresses of population growth and climate change, as well as the familiar stresses of drought and aridity recognized by Powell, upstream states in the basin need to be even more mindful of their Colorado River Compact obligations.[88] They should do this not only as a matter of comity, but as a matter of peace and environmental justice. Failure to deliver compact water potentially will be felt by many water users, but it may be felt most acutely by those with large volumes of senior water rights within downstream states, namely tribes.

Although Colorado River Basin states bear the legal burden of complying with the compact, land- and water-use planning in cities is paramount because these are the places where considerable portions of state water rights are used and will continue to be used in the future. Instead of costly and environmentally destructive transbasin diversions, pipelines, and reservoirs, commonsense conservation and environmental stewardship should be the first option in planning processes.

At present, many Colorado River Basin states and cities still find it unfathomable to consider restrictions on future reservoirs or transbasin diversions. However, as a matter of ethics and practicality, states and cities should consider policies that steer society away from additional reservoir construction and transbasin diversions such as those which fueled unsustainable growth in the past. As just one example, moving more Colorado River system water out-of-basin to cities like those springing up or burgeoning along Colorado's Front Range will destroy ecosystems within native basins and ensure growth continues in areas where water is already heavily appropriated, subject to compact limitations, or otherwise hydrologically unavailable. It is a tragic cycle of absurdity that repeats the mistakes of American history. As the book *Cadillac Desert* chronicles, the costly and improvident era of large-scale dam building took place partly because efforts to irrigate pastoral lands in a desert were failing.[89] Continuing to foster breakneck development in Powell's arid region is the latest wave of delusional thinking. Extensive pipelines and reservoirs should be repudiated as an option to bail out unsustainable urban and suburban growth, particularly when conservation is readily available, cheaper, and more respectful to all of creation.

Despite the many things Powell got wrong about Indians, he at least understood the Colorado River Basin's aridity. Instead of trying to recreate the Garden of Eden as was done during several early incarnations of Manifest Destiny, the basin may be repeating its history by building fountain-spewing Babylons if it does not realistically address population growth and associated water demands. Absent unprecedented efforts to honor Indian water rights, to bolster instream flow rights, and to conserve water, the new wave of growth in and around the basin will be built on the backs of Indians as well as nature.

CONCLUSION

If John Wesley Powell and contemporary proponents of Manifest Destiny had made more of an effort to learn from Indians, rather than seeking to "educate" them about proper religion, language, and land and water use, many of the uncomfortable realities now facing the Colorado River Basin could have been avoided. As is true of the human condition, however—and particularly true of individuals with great privilege—Powell simply could not get out of his own way, even though he wanted to do good. Powell understood the basin's aridity, and it is a shame his Euro-American counterparts in government did not heed some of his warnings about building a "civilization" in an arid region. Despite his acknowledgment of aridity and emphasis on methodical expansion, however, Powell still believed in imperialism, domination of nature, and the cultural inferiority of Indians. The biases of Powell and those similar to him for "pastoral and civilized" land, water, and people ran roughshod over nature and the tribes whose cultures and religions were well adapted to living in an arid landscape. The current pressures on water and other natural resources in and around the basin are similarly attributable to deluded cultural beliefs and laws that overstate human ingenuity in relation to nature.

To promote a peaceful future in the "Great Unknown"—a future where dominant society, tribal peoples, and the rest of creation can endure—communities throughout and beyond the Colorado River Basin need to incorporate principles of Indigenous environmental stewardship into law and culture and to learn from the mistakes of the Manifest Destiny mindset. According to that mindset, "the sense of destiny replaces the sense of place, replaces the sense of wonder, replaces common sense."[90] Growth and overconsumption in the Colorado River Basin are not inevitable or beneficial. The tribes, rivers, and landscapes of the basin deserve more than someone else's "sense of destiny."

NOTES

1. Charles Wilkinson, *Blood Struggle: The Rise of Modern Indian Nations* (New York: Norton, 2005), 3–56.
2. Colorado Statewide Supply Initiative, accessed October 19, 2018, http://cwcbweblink.state.co.us/WebLink/ElectronicFile.aspx?docid = 144066&searchid = 2c16c041-d0b2-4ec5-ac42-8b95aa0c04e3&dbid = 0.
3. Autumn Bernhardt, "Manifest Destiny this week and Night Nostalgia," *The MOON Magazine*, March 4, 2017, http://moonmagazine.org/autumn-bernhardt-manifest-destiny-this-week-and-night-nostalgia-2017-03-04.
4. Robin Wall Kimmerer, *Braiding Sweetgrass: Indigenous Wisdom, Scientific Knowledge, and the Teachings of Plants* (Minneapolis: Milkweed Editions, 2013), 175–201.
5. Winters v. United States, 207 U.S. 564, 576 (1908).
6. William deBuys, *Seeing Things Whole: The Essential John Wesley Powell* (Washington, DC: Island Press, 2004), 8, 338n8.
7. John Wesley Powell, "From Barbarism to Civilization," *The American Anthropologist* 1, no. 2 (1888): 121.
8. As described by Charles Wilkinson, "Powell was widely regarded as the most knowledgeable person about Native Americans, at least in the non-Indian society." "Filling in the Blank Spots on Powell's and Stegner's Maps: The Role of Modern Indian Tribes in Western Watersheds," *Journal of Land Resources & Environmental Law* 23 [2003]: 43.
9. *The Condition of the Indian Tribes West of the Rocky Mountains: Before the Committee on Indian Affairs*, 43rd Cong. 8–9 (1874) (statement of Major J. W. Powell).
10. Dee Brown, *Bury My Heart at Wounded Knee: An Indian History of the American West* (New York: Henry Holt and Company, 1970); Mari Sandoz, *Cheyenne Autumn* (New York: McGraw-Hill, 1953).
11. John Wesley Powell, "Proper Training and the Future of the Indians," *The Forum* 18 (September 1894-February 1895): 627.
12. John Wesley Powell, "From Savagery to Barbarism" (Annual Address of the President, Anthropological Society, February 3, 1885); Powell, "From Barbarism to Civilization."
13. John Wesley Powell, *On Primitive Institutions* (Saratoga, NY: Report of the Nineteenth Annual Meeting of the American Bar Association, 1896), 577–80.
14. Powell, *On Primitive Institutions*, 586.
15. Powell, "From Barbarism to Civilization," 97–123.
16. Powell, *On Primitive Institutions*, 587.
17. Although variations of this sentiment were typically expressed during the time frame, some popular accounts attribute the origin of the aphorism to Phillip Sheridan, who fought in the Indian Wars of the Great Plains. See Dee Brown, *Bury My Heart At Wounded Knee*, 170–72.
18. *Official Report of the Nineteenth Annual Conference of Charities and Correction* (1892), 46–59. Reprinted in Richard H. Pratt, "The Advantages of Mingling Indians with Whites," in *Americanizing the American Indians: Writ-*

ings by the *"Friends of the Indian," 1880–1900*, ed. Francis Paul Prucha (Cambridge, MA: Harvard University Press, 1973), 260–71.

19. *The Condition of the Indian Tribes West of the Rocky Mountains: Before the Committee on Indian Affairs*, 43rd Cong. 7 (1874) (statement of Major J.W. Powell).

20. John Wesley Powell, "Are Our Indians Becoming Extinct?," *Forum* 15 (1893): 352.

21. Charles Wilkinson, *Fire on the Plateau: Conflict and Endurance in the American Southwest* (Washington, DC: Island Press, 1999), 81.

22. Marc Reisner, *Cadillac Desert: The American West and Its Disappearing Water* (New York: Penguin Press, 1993), 48.

23. Powell, "Proper Training and the Future of the Indians," 629.

24. John Wesley Powell, "Human Evolution," *Transactions of the Anthropological Society of Washington* 2 (1883): 190.

25. Roderick Nash, *Wilderness and the American Mind* (New Haven: Yale University Press, 2014), 1–43.

26. Genesis 1:28 (KJV); see also 1:26 (KJV).

27. Vine Deloria, *God is Red* (Golden, CO: Fulcrum Publishing, 1994), 78–97.

28. Reisner, *Cadillac Desert*, 477–95.

29. Mark 1:12–13 (NIV); Mark 1:1–7 (NIV).

30. John Locke, *Of Civil Government: Second Treatise* (Chicago: Henry Regnery Company, 1971).

31. Andrew Jones and Tom Cech, *Colorado Water Law for Non-Lawyers* (Boulder: University of Colorado Press, 2009), 60–61.

32. Rebecca Abelyn, "Instream Flow, Recreation as Beneficial Use, and the Public Interest in Colorado Water Law," *University of Denver Water Law Review* 9 (2004): 520–24.

33. Empire Water & Power v. Cascade Town, 205 Fed. 123 (8th Cir. 1913).

34. Reisner, *Cadillac Desert*, 43–44.

35. Powell, "From Savagery to Barbarism," 193–94.

36. Wilkinson, "Filling in the Blank Spots," 43, 45.

37. Wilkinson, *Blood Struggle*.

38. Wilkinson, "Filling in the Blank Spots," 42.

39. John Wesley Powell, *Report on the Lands of the Arid Region of the United States* (Washington, DC: Government Printing Office, 1979).

40. Winters v. United States, 207 U.S. 564 (1908).

41. Ibid., 576.

42. Ibid.

43. Arizona v. California, 373 U.S. 546, 600–601 (1963).

44. James S. Lochhead, "An Upper Basin's Perspective on California's Claims to Water from the Colorado River: Part I, The Law of the River," *University of Denver Water Law Review* 4, no. 2 (2001): 321.

45. Wilkinson, "Filling in the Blank Spots," 55.

46. 50 C.F.R. § 11(b)(6)(2017) (traditional knowledge).

47. John Wesley Powell, "A Discourse on the Philosophy of the North American Indians," *Journal of the American Geographical Society of New York* 8 (1876): 265.

48. Ibid., 261.
49. Rebecca Tsosie, "Tribal Environmental Policy in an Era of Self-Determination: The Role of Ethics, Economics, and Traditional Ecological Knowledge," *Vermont Law Review* 21 (1996): 225–333.
50. Ibid., 272.
51. Powell, "From Barbarism to Civilization," 123.
52. Ibid.
53. Wall Kimmerer, *Braiding Sweetgrass*, 175–201.
54. Luther Standing Bear, *Land of the Spotted Eagle* (Lincoln, NE: Bison Books, 2006), 38.
55. Deloria, *God is Red*, 78–97.
56. Autumn L. Bernhardt, "The Profound and Intimate Power of the Obergefell Decision: Equal Dignity as a Suspect Class," *Tulane Journal of Law & Sexuality* 25 (2016): 11–15.
57. Jeff Debellis, "The Holiness of Nature," *The Drake* (Fall 2015): 57.
58. Sally Bingham, "John 5:1–9," in *The Global Warming Reader*, ed. Bill McKibben (New York: Penguin Books, 2012), 301.
59. David H. Getches, "A Philosophy of Permanence: The Indians' Legacy for the West," *Journal of the West* 29, no. 3 (July 1990): 54–68.
60. Navajo Nation v. USFS, 408 F. Supp. 2d 866 (D. Ariz. 2006).
61. Navajo Nation v. USFS, 479 F.3d 1024, 1034–39 (9th Cir. 2007).
62. Navajo Nation v. USFS, 535 F.3d 1058, 1113 (9th Cir. 2008).
63. Ibid.
64. Jessica Wiles, "Have American Indians Been Written Out of the Religious Freedom Restoration Act?," *Montana Law Review* 71 (2010): 471–502.
65. Navajo Nation v. USFS, 535 F.3d 1058, 1106–07 (9th Cir. 2008) (Fletcher, J., dissenting).
66. Standing Rock Sioux v. USACE, 16 CV 1534 (2016).
67. Raymond Laws, "NEPA and the Northern Integration Supply Project: Wielding the 'Paper Tiger' in the Tenth Circuit," *Colorado Natural Resources, Energy & Environmental Law Review* 27 (2016): 101–31.
68. John Wesley Powell, "An Overland Trip to the Grand Cañon," *Scribner's Monthly* 10 (1875): 665.
69. Wall Kimmerer, *Braiding Sweetgrass*, 46
70. Powell, *Relation of Primitive Peoples to Environment*, 635.
71. Wall Kimmerer, *Braiding Sweetgrass*, 48–59.
72. Randy Scholfield, "In a Native Place," *Trout Magazine* (Winter 2017): 49.
73. Craig Springer, "Blue Lines and Yellow Trout," *Trout Magazine* (Summer 2017): 16–17.
74. Scholfield, "In a Native Place," 48.
75. Ibid.
76. Wilkinson, *Blood Struggle*, 315–16.
77. Wilkinson, "Filling in the Blank Spots," 53.
78. Wilkinson, *Blood Struggle*, 316.
79. Ibid., 317.
80. Springer, "Blue Lines and Yellow Trout," 17.

81. Scholfield, "In a Native Place," 49–50.

82. Ibid., 48.

83. "White Mountain Apache Tribe Game and Fish," White Mountain Apache Tribe, accessed October 23, 2018, https://www.wmatoutdoor.org; "White Mountain Apache Tribe History/Culture," White Mountain Apache Tribe, accessed July 28, 2018, http://www.wmat.nsn.us.

84. Amy Cordalis and Dan Cordalis, "Indian Water Rights: How *Arizona v. California* Left an Unwanted Cloud Over the Colorado River Basin," *Arizona Journal of Environmental. Law & Policy* 5 (2014): 333–62.

85. Arizona v. San Carlos Apache, 463 U.S. 545, 549 (1983).

86. In re Gila River Adjudication, 35 P.3d 68, 315–19 (Az. 2002); U.S. v. Adair, 723 F.2d 1394, 1414 (9th Cir. 1984); Colville Confederated Tribes v. Walton, 647 F.2d 4249 (9th Cir. 1981).

87. In re Big Horn Adjudication, 835 P.2d 273, 275 (Wyo. 1992).

88. Colo. Rev. Stat. § 37-61-101 (2018); Colo. Rev. Stat. §37-62-101 (2018).

89. Reisner, *Cadillac Desert*.

90. Bernhardt, "Manifest Destiny this week and Night Nostalgia."

CHAPTER 11

Civilizing Public Land Management in the Colorado River Basin

DANIEL CORDALIS AND AMY CORDALIS

The Colorado River Basin is home to twenty-nine American Indian tribes who at one time were the only human inhabitants of the basin's roughly 242,000 square miles. Its canyons, arches, buttes, towering peaks, and other unique natural features—the same features that drew John Wesley Powell's interest and admiration—played central roles in the tribes' cultural and spiritual identities. These sacred sites were home to spiritual figures, provided ceremonial materials, and constituted a source of strength and religion for tribes. Prominent peaks around Navajo ancestral lands in Arizona, Colorado, and New Mexico are the homes of important deities; the Hualapai and Havasupai hold springs in side canyons of the Grand Canyon to be sacred places; and the Ute consider sacred the rock formations of the Garden of the Gods in Colorado. During aboriginal times, the tribes managed the basin's lands to their benefit—clearing with fire to diversify habitat, encourage wildlife, and improve hunting prospects—and created water diversions to store water in the semi-arid climate.[1] Let there be no mistake, tribes were active managers that took from and gave back to the land. In doing so, the tribes strove to live in harmony and balance with it.

Today, the basin's lands are managed by handfuls of federal, state, local, and tribal agencies, and Indian tribes have primary jurisdiction over only a fraction of the land base (see maps 3 and 4). Many, if not most, of the tribal sacred sites are now under federal ownership on public lands. Management priorities for these public lands are often at odds with each other—grazing, timber, mineral extraction, recreation, agriculture, and preservation—while the states simultaneously vie for economic benefits from those differing uses. For much of the basin's population, this management tension can be frustrating and even cause-worthy. For basin tribes, however, the impacts of federal land management where sacred sites are located may be existential: the priorities of non-Indian federal land managers can cause the destruction of irreplaceable tribal cultural and spiritual resources. Because tribal spiritual practices are rooted in the connection Native people have with the earth, including at specific locations, this makes tribes vulnerable to multiple land uses and extractive activities. Exacerbating the problem, these land management decisions are typically made without tribal input and even in the face of significant tribal opposition, as in the Arizona Snowbowl decision discussed below.

Looking back to understand how we got here, we can see that federal Indian policy, not public land policy, is to blame. The divestment of land from tribal control in the 1800s was accomplished through federal policies initially pushing Indians onto reservations and then cutting up and allotting those reservations in severalty. The goals of these policies were to shrink tribal landholdings to open the rest of the land for non-Indian settlement, and to assimilate the Indians into the "civilized," non-Indian world by imposing on them Christianity, private property, and agriculture. These policies were intended to break the tribes' connection with the land such that they could be swept into the new nation and the land could be conquered.

A sympathetic purveyor of this vision, John Wesley Powell supported the goals and motivations of the Indian policies. Yet Powell's correspondence back to Washington, DC showed deep respect for Native people and cultures, particularly regarding their connection to land. But while Powell used his understanding of Indian people to both educate and inform federal policy, that understanding was ultimately harnessed to hurt tribes. Powell's advocacy for reservation and allotment policies, advocacy he determined was in tribes' best interests, supported the tearing of Indians from the land and the erosion of tribal cultures. Although we cannot blame Powell alone for these policies—each had been tested at least a decade before by Commissioner of Indian Affairs George Manypenny[2]—no doubt Powell's advocacy lent weight to Congress's support of them. The result was catastrophic to Native people in the Colorado River Basin and elsewhere for many reasons, but one, specifically, is discussed here.

Through treaty negotiations and allotment, Indian tribes first physically lost a significant part of their lands. Longer term, including up to the present, the reservation and allotment policies have strained tribes' spiritual relationships with their homelands by separating them from sacred places and restricting their ability to protect and preserve cultural resources. It cannot be argued that the policies were ignorant of this type of future harm to tribes—the policies' effectiveness was actually predicated on it. The result is that for over a century and a half, tribes in the Colorado River Basin have had limited success in protecting sacred sites on public lands from overuse or misuse. This is even in the face of the current self-determination and tribal sovereignty movements. Still standing in the way is a federal land management philosophy that treats land as a commodity, not as a connected landscape to be respected.

We should not accept this. Thankfully, the Eurocentric land-management approach of the past is showing cracks. Moral and legal obligations owed to tribes are seeping into those cracks, forcing them open wider. Within these cracks lies the "Great Unknown"—a path forward to right the basin's historical wrongs, a path lit by a legal framework that can support tribal involvement in land planning and cultural resource preservation on public lands. This vision was recently realized in President Obama's 2016 proclamation creating Bears Ears National Monument in southeastern Utah, where five tribes collaborated and secured direct management roles and an opportunity to protect important cultural and natural resources in an area sacred to each of them. Powell may not have been able to foresee this reality 150 years ago. But if he were alive today, his understanding of tribal spirituality, coupled with the present erratic management of the public lands, may have enabled him to push beyond his own Eurocentric beliefs and advocate for tribal-federal collaborative management as the most civilized progression modern American society can make.

POWELL'S INTEREST IN INDIAN PEOPLE AND CULTURES TAKES SHAPE

Indian people fascinated John Wesley Powell from an early age. He first encountered Indians during the early 1840s. A group of Winnebago came through the Powell family farm in Wisconsin on their way back from a trip to Chicago,[3] staying a week and feasting and dancing each night. Powell, his mother, and two sisters visited the camp during that week, not to complain about the Indians' presence, which was uninvited, but to meet and talk with them. In fact, they learned that the Winnebago's camp was located on a traditional hunting and camping ground used to catch rabbit, obtain spring water, and snag fish in the creek.[4] A young Powell soaked in this experience, and his interest in Indian people took root.

Decades later, when Powell explored the West, that interest found space to grow. Powell's writings in the 1870s demonstrate an understanding of Native people that did not then exist outside tribal communities. Federal officials in Washington, DC took notice of Powell's expertise and appointed him and G. W. Ingalls as Special Commissioners of Indian Affairs in the greater Nevada-Utah area in 1873. Their reports to Congress and in public journals advocated for separation and "civilization" of tribes through reservations, a policy discussed below, but the reports also offered a vivid look into the lives and knowledge of Indian people, even as compared to Powell himself:

> It was curious now to observe the knowledge of our Indians; there was not a trail they did not know; every gulch and every rock seemed familiar. I have prided myself on being able to grasp and retain in my mind the topography of a country, but these Indians put me to shame. My knowledge is only general, embracing the more important features of a region which remains as a map engraved on my mind; theirs is specific; they know every rock and ledge, every gulch and cañon—just where to wind among these to find a pass, and their knowledge is unerring; they cannot describe a country to you, but they can tell you all the details of a route.[5]

The land's spiritual importance to Native people hit Powell squarely; he wrote, "the whole of daily life of an Indian is religious life."[6] Powell's ability to listen to, and gain the trust of, Native people, allowed that insight:

> [Indian] lore consists in a mass of traditions or mythology. It is very difficult to induce them to tell it to white men. . . . But in a confidential way, when you are alone, or when you are admitted to their camp-fire on a winter night, you will hear the stories of their mythology. I believe that the greatest mark of friendship or confidence that an Indian can give, is to tell you his religion.[7]

Through his travels in the Colorado River Basin, Powell came to appreciate that "every spring, creek and river, every valley, hill and mountain as well as the trees that grow upon the soil are made sacred by the inherited traditions of [Indian] religion. These are the homes of their gods."[8] Powell was right. The basin's sacred places defined the very existence of its Native people.

THE "CIVILIZATION" OF INDIAN PEOPLE

Powell's understanding of Indian spirituality and tribes' reliance on the land and its resources nonetheless did not discourage his belief that tribes would be better off on reservations and assimilated into western civilization. Powell saw the Indians of the Colorado River Basin as savages, even as the "most primitive" people he had ever seen. If the Indians were to survive, Powell believed they had to progress and learn the arts of "civilized" people—land ownership and accompanying agriculture. But the question of how to accomplish this change was harder, and one of degree.

Powell believed reservations where Indians could be separated from non-Indians and cared for and managed by the federal government were the best approach. As he described:

> Where the Indians are now scattered about the country there seems to be no way by which justice can be secured to the Indians.... It seems to me that the only way to secure justice to these Indians is to gather them on reservations, where they can be under the supervision of men who have a care for their rights. In this way many of the evils which grow out of the present relations of the Indians to the white men can be avoided.[9]

But actually moving Indian people was difficult. Powell argued that the way to do so was to force tribal people off the land, "the locus of religion." Powell wrote that "[w]hen an Indian clan or tribe gives up its land it not only surrenders its home as understood by civilized people but its gods are abandoned and all religion connected therewith, and connected with the worship of ancestors buried in the soil; that is, everything most sacred to Indian society is yielded up."[10] Once that bond was broken, Indian people could see the land as a resource to be used, not revered. Civilization could then follow.

Powell might not have advocated so clearly for the push of tribes into "civilization" but for what he saw on the ground—the tsunami of non-Indian settlement into Western tribal lands and prevailing ideas about Indian policy after the Civil War. "There is now no great uninhabited and unknown region to which the Indian can be sent," described Powell, "[h]e is among us, and we must either protect him or destroy him."[11]. As the press of "civilization" bore down on the West, Powell saw only one path forward:

> [T]he march of humanity cannot be stayed; fields must be made, and gardens planted in the little valleys among the mountains of that Western land, as they have been in the broader valleys and plains of the East, and the moun-

tains must yield their treasure of ore to the miner, and, whether we desire it or not, the ancient inhabitants of the country must be lost; and we may comfort ourselves with the reflection that they are not destroyed, but are gradually absorbed, and become a part of more civilized communities.[12]

By the time Powell set off on his westward travels, it was clear that Indians in the Colorado River Basin and other parts of the West would not be able to continue their traditional ways of life and that the US government would have to address their future treatment to allow non-Indian settlement. In his seminal biography *A River Running West,* Donald Worster described the situation Powell found himself in with Indian people: "The Indians were afraid, worried, uncertain, despairing, and demoralized. They needed friends to help them make a transition. Powell saw himself as such a friend but one whose job it was to bring bad news where necessary and insist that the Indians accept and adapt."[13]

THE DISMANTLING OF NATIVE AMERICA:
RESERVATIONS AND ALLOTMENT

By the time Powell had returned East from his 1869 Expedition, federal Indian policy was focused on obtaining more Indian land for white settlement, and Powell helped sharpen that focus. The early nineteenth century treaty-making era, followed by the allotment policy at the end of the century, remade both America and Native America.

The Promise of Treaties

During the early 1800s, the federal government entered into treaties with tribes as a way to terminate Indian title to land, settle disputes, and separate tribes from non-Indian settlers. These treaties embodied grants of rights from Indian people to the United States—for example, land cessions, reservations of aboriginal hunting and fishing rights—in exchange for varying programs and goods, including health and education services, federal protection over newly created reservations, even cattle and steel. Treaties preserved the "unique and most cherished rights of America Indians," to be protected "forever" or "permanent[ly]."[14] But the US government regularly succumbed to pressures from settlers to encroach on treaty-secured Indian lands and resources, and the hard-fought treaties were not honored as the supreme law of the land that the Constitution declared them to be. Tribal leaders' requests to uphold treaties were often ignored, and Indians witnessed desecration of their lands and the plants and animals relied upon for survival. Post-treaty conflicts between Indians and non-Indians over land and resources resulted in Indian wars throughout the 1800s. New treaties were signed following these wars, stripping tribes of even more land. Treaty negotiations were not balanced: fraud, coercion, threats, and bribery ensured that the United States would get the bargain—and land—it desired.

The rapid growth of the nation in the early 1800s, especially in the East, coupled with the United States flexing its authority after victory over the British in the War of 1812, created pressure to use treaties to move tribes westward off their ancestral lands. Andrew Jackson's successful 1828 presidential election set off the formal policy of Indian removal, a policy codified two years later when Congress passed the Indian Removal Act. In 1838, when many Cherokee refused to leave their homelands in the southeast, federal troops forced them into camps and drove them west; over 4,000 died on the "Trail of Tears." By 1850, the majority of tribes in the East had been removed west of the Mississippi.[15]

In the Colorado River Basin, tribes faced similar land hunger. Following the end of the Mexican-American War and the 1848 Treaty of Guadalupe Hidalgo, which gave the United States control of much of the West, gold rushes and westward expansion devastated the basin tribes' land base. This story is displayed vividly in the histories of the Ute bands—whose aboriginal territory ranged from most of present-day Utah through western and central Colorado, with hunting territory radiating south into New Mexico, north into Wyoming, and east into Kansas, Oklahoma, and Texas—and the Navajo—whose aboriginal territory ranged through present-day Arizona, southern Colorado, southern Utah, and New Mexico.

In Utah, where Ute bands claimed the entire territory, conflict between the tribes and the Mormons was rife in the 1850s. At the urging of the growing Mormon population, President Lincoln established by executive order the Uintah Reservation in northeastern Utah in 1861—a single reservation for all the Utah bands.[16]

In the Colorado Territory to the east, Utes signed a treaty in 1868 creating a reservation covering roughly the western third of Colorado, cutting the tribe's territory from fifty-six million to eighteen million acres, including all lands west of the continental divide.[17] But only six years later, in 1874, the mineral-rich San Juan Mountains were removed from the reservation to accommodate a mining boom, leaving approximately twelve million acres, and by 1881, only the southern portion of that diminished reservation remained.[18]

During that time, in the northern part of the Colorado Ute reservation, particularly after Colorado statehood in 1876, there was a push to remove Utes from western Colorado lands, which would enable those lands to be mined, farmed, or otherwise ranched by settlers. When Nathan Meeker was named White River Ute Indian Agent in 1878, his paternalistic brand of management reflected this outlook.[19] Meeker set up his Indian agency in a grassy park along the White River at a site traditionally used for rearing and racing horses, angering the Utes. Ten years prior, Powell had camped among the Utes at this same location, and the site took the informal name of "Powell Park." Powell had spent the winter days and nights in the Ute camp, making use of his first extended opportunity to study Native people. Powell remarked that his party "have had fair success" in understanding the Utes, and his experience with the Utes would blossom to later make Native people his chief intellectual interest.[20]

Meeker's relationship with the White River Utes did not go as well. He stubbornly pushed Christianity and farming as civilizing mechanisms upon the Utes, who refused both, holding tight to their hunting and gathering lifestyle, and thus angering Meeker. Like Powell, Meeker tied his vision of civilization to control over the earth—farming—which conflicted with a Ute culture that valued hunting and horse racing over farming, a practice reserved for women, slaves, or lower classes. The two ideologies would not find common ground. Meeker responded by withholding rations and continuing to preach the value of the plow and hard labor. In perhaps the last straw, in his quest to attack Ute horse culture, Meeker ordered a tribal member's horse pasture plowed over. As soon as Meeker's men started to plow, Utes shot at them. Meeker telegraphed Governor Pitkin, requesting the cavalry to intervene. After a decade of withheld rations, relentless imposition of religious and farming practices, broken promises, and an encroaching cavalry, the White River Utes physically fought back. In the end, Meeker and nine other men were killed at the agency, and women and children were held hostage for twenty-nine days.[21]

The response to the so-called "Meeker Massacre" was devastating to the Utes. Coloradans demanded their removal from the state, and the federal government responded. In 1880, the Ute Removal Act was signed, revoking the remaining twelve-million-acre Colorado reservation and removing the White River Utes to Utah. The Uncompahgre Band was removed to Utah in 1881 and settled on the Ouray Reservation, named after Chief Ouray who had died the previous year.[22] The Act also created new reservations for the Southern Ute and Ute

Mountain Ute along the southwestern flanks of Colorado, the only remaining Ute lands within the state. In a matter of two decades, the Utes lost nearly all their land in Utah and Colorado, including some of their best hunting and gathering grounds.

To the south, the Navajo tribe's experience was different in process, but not in result. By the time the Navajo encountered English-speaking Americans, they had already adopted some forms of farming and ranching.[23] Navajos had frequently traded with the Spanish and had become expert weavers, relying on sheep and goats the Spanish brought. Navajos traded for metal tools and other manufactured articles, and rode horses as far as western Nebraska to trade with the Pawnee. In some ways, Navajos had already realized the Powell/Meeker vision of civilization. But the Navajo realization was more complex than this vision allowed, and it had to be reined in.

After the end of the Mexican-American War, the United States guaranteed protection to non-Indians against raiding Indian tribes. The United States had the Navajo in mind, as the Navajos' preferred method of depredation was not war, but carefully planned raids. In the winter of 1846–47, the first military expedition against the Navajo commenced, sparking fifteen years of conflict. In 1862, during the Civil War, Navajos stepped up their raids on Rio Grande settlements. The government responded by ordering Kit Carson to Navajo country in June 1863 to destroy all crops and livestock. All Navajo males were to surrender or be shot. Carson and his troops killed Navajo people in their homes, burned their crops and hogans, took prisoners, killed livestock, and destroyed anything that Navajos could use to survive. Carson's scorched-earth campaign worked, and in early 1864 many Navajos surrendered at Fort Defiance. What followed is commonly known as "The Long Walk," which was four separate 300-mile military-led marches to the Bosque Redondo Reservation in Fort Sumner, New Mexico. By the end of April 1864, nearly 6,000 Navajos had endured the same march, and eventually that number totaled 8,000.[24] The United States forced its brand of farming on the captured Navajo, but the land was of such poor quality that it would not take, and the funding was completely inadequate to sustain the projects.[25]

In 1868, treaty negotiations between the Navajo and United States proceeded at Bosque Redondo. The United States sought removal of the Navajos to the Oklahoma Indian Territory, where many tribes in the East and Midwest had been relocated. Navajo leader Barboncito replied to the US position:

Our Grandfathers had no idea of living in any other place except our own land, and I don't think it is right for us to do what we were taught not to do. When the Navajo were first made, First Woman pointed out four mountains and four rivers that was to be our land. Our grandfathers told us to never move east of the Rio Grande River or west of the San Juan River. . . . I hope to God you will not ask me to go anywhere except my own country.[26]

The Treaty of 1868 allowed the Navajo to return to the sacred mountains. The four years at Bosque Redondo claimed 2,000 Navajo lives and was culturally catastrophic to the Navajo people.[27] Nevertheless, they fought off removal and returned to their home.

Like the Ute and other basin tribes, the Navajo lost a large amount of ancestral land during treaty negotiations. The tribes stood as strong as they could, but the unyielding drive of the United States for more land was too much to withstand.

Allotment: The Pulverizing Machine

Once the treaty-making era ended in 1871, federal Indian policy morphed to prioritize assimilation of Indian people—or, as Powell called it, "civilization." While Powell was careful to stay out of direct policy decisions involving tribes' land rights, his feelings about assimilating and civilizing Native people were clear in Washington, DC: put the land in individual Indians' hands and they will evolve for their own betterment and that of the United States. But the assimilation policy was motivated not purely by a moral charge. It was meant to acquire Indian land. If Indians adopted civilized practices, the theory went, they would need less land, and the surplus could be taken for non-Indian settlement.[28]

The General Allotment Act of 1887, commonly known as the "Dawes Act" after its main sponsor, Massachusetts Senator Henry Dawes, codified the assimilation charge, which lasted until 1934.[29] The Dawes Act authorized the division of tribal land into allotments 40 to 160 acres in size for individual Indians and families. Individuals were either given permission to select allotments for themselves and their children, or the Indian agency superintendent would assign parcels. When the amount of reservation land exceeded the amount needed to provide allotments, the United States could negotiate to purchase the surplus land from the tribes in order to convey it to non-Indian settlers. Thus, once the reservation lands were allotted in severalty, the surplus lands would be opened to non-Indian settlement. Title to allotments would be held in trust for individual Indians by the federal government for twenty-five years, at which time the individual would receive a fee patent.

Ten years after the Dawes Act's passage, over 50 million acres of Indian land was lost through allotment. By 1900, half of the Indian land—78 million of the 156 million acres in 1881—was lost. By the time the policy was revoked in 1934, only 48 million of the 156 million acres remained.[30]

In the end, the Dawes Act took the most from the Ute tribes of the Colorado River Basin. The Southern Ute lost 33,473 acres, and the Uintah and Ouray Reservation lost nearly 30,000 acres.[31] Many other basin tribes had their reservations allotted, but some were able to retain lands in tribal members' hands. In Arizona, the Gila River Tribe had over 97,000 acres allotted and retained; the Salt River Tribe, over 25,000 acres; and the Tohono O'odham Tribe, nearly 42,000 acres.

Thus, although allotment did not meet its purported goal of civilizing and assimilating Indians, it did break up Indian Country by providing millions of acres of Indian land for non-Indian settlement. The rapid succession of allotment on the heels of the reservation policy was an abrupt about-face. Regardless of whether more time adjusting to reservation life would have softened the transition to allotment, the motivation to separate tribal people from their land and resources would have had the same harmful effect. Altogether, the reservation and allotment policies spanned nearly seventy years, severing ties between Indians and traditional lands in many cases, and leaving behind a legacy of perplexing tribal land ownership patterns, vulnerable tribal sacred sites, and desecrated hunting and gathering grounds and associated life ways within the Colorado River Basin.

BREAKING THE BOND: BASIN TRIBES AND SACRED SITES

At its core, the Indian worldview places humankind as part of the natural world, not separate from it. In *God is Red,* Vine Deloria writes that in the Indian religious format, "the natural physical world is regarded as integral to human ambitions and activities," and "Indians virtually eliminate the human element in their religious ceremonies and concentrate on representing the physical universe."[32] The earth, therefore, is not an entity separate from Native spirituality and personality; they are one and the same. Heaven, as a concept to Indian people, is this earth. This philosophy stands in stark contrast to "Near Eastern" religions that "seek and guarantee *salvation,* which is conceived as an escape from this planet to a place where loyal followers can enjoy eternal life."[33] Heaven, as understood here, is not this earth, but somewhere else, somewhere better. But the land, to Indian people, is the embodiment of life and afterlife, and fear of losing the land has always been present:

> It is quite possible, therefore, that as we look for the origin of peoples, we must discover religious experiences; as we look for the origins of religions, we must discover nations of people, and whichever way we look, it is to the lands on which the people reside and in which the religions arise that is important. This possibility is what has dominated the concerns of American [Indian] peoples from the very beginnings. The chance that lands would be lost meant that religious communities would be destroyed and individual identities forsaken. As sacred mountains became secularized, as tribal burial grounds became cornfields, as tribes no longer lived on the dust of their ancestors' bones, the people knew that they could not survive.[34]

The devastating reservation and allotment policies of the 1800s and 1900s tore Colorado River Basin tribes from most of their sacred homelands. The Ute lost access to Pike's Peak, the nearby waters of Manitou Springs, and the canyon country of southeastern Utah. While the Navajo continue to live within their four sacred mountains, all of them, as well as other important sacred sites, now lie outside the Navajo Reservation. The survival of the basin's Indian peoples, being dependent on the exercise of tribal spiritual practices, were jeopardized by those policies.

Indian tribes are place-based peoples whose spiritual centers lie in specific geographic locations, such as a mountain or rock formation. This rich, distinct aspect of tribal cultures is pervasive and readily apparent in the Colorado River Basin. Sacred sites are central to the religious and cultural practices of tribes and are the foundation of many tribal beliefs and practices.[35] Indians travel to these sites to communicate with the spirits, experience revelations, or gather important cultural materials such as plants, medicines, or other objects. The protection of these sites, therefore, is vitally important to ensure that tribes maintain a relationship with the land and their spirits.

Today, many Indian people hold these religious principles and strive to reconnect to the land lost over the past two centuries. The primary obstacle for tribes in protecting sacred sites is that they are often located off-reservation on public lands. Because the federal government and judiciary have had difficulty understanding the importance of sacred sites, they have done a poor job protecting them.³⁶ US law doesn't reflect the Indian worldview, and in most cases supports land management contrary to it. Nonetheless, tribes have been forced to fight in court for sacred site protection through judicial review of federal agency decisions, an effort that has thus far largely failed. Two cases, in particular, illustrate these difficulties.

In 1982, a group representing the interests of the Yurok, Karuk, and Tolowa tribes of northern California challenged a Forest Service decision approving a project to construct logging roads and allow timber harvesting in a sacred area of the Six Rivers National Forest in Yurok ancestral territory, the High Country. It is a beautiful, raw forest, full of majesty and power, revered by all of the area tribes. Nevertheless, despite federally commissioned cultural reports describing the project's significant impacts on the tribes' spiritual practices, the Forest Service pushed forward and allowed the project to proceed. In the Supreme Court case that resulted, *Lyng v. Northwest Indian Cemetery Protection Association*,³⁷ tribal plaintiffs argued that development would degrade sacred lands and erode the area's religious significance, violating the Free Exercise Clause of the Constitution. The Supreme Court disagreed, upholding the agency decision. Writing for the Court, Justice O'Connor stated that, while the project would "virtually destroy" the Indians' ability to practice their religion, "[w]hatever rights the Indians may have to the use of the area, . . . those rights do not divest the government of its right to use what is, after all, its land."³⁸ Tribal scholar and legal practitioner Walter Echo-Hawk thus concluded: "After *Lyng*, no constitutional principles exist to protect Native worship on holy ground located on public lands. . . . Under this loophole in religious freedom, there is no enforceable legal protection for this universal form of worship at holy places in the American legal system."³⁹

Within the Colorado River Basin, tribes have been similarly unable to rely on litigation to protect sacred sites. The Snowbowl Ski Area outside Flagstaff in Arizona's Coconino National Forest has been a source of tension since its inception in 1937. The ski area is located on the San Francisco Peaks (*Dook'o'oosłííd*, in Navajo, meaning "shining on top"), the most important sacred site to the Navajo and Hopi people, and sacred to eleven other tribes. Deities live in the Peaks and tribal members gather ceremonial items on the mountains' flanks. Their purity is essential to maintain the power of these spirits and cultural items. The Forest Service, however, has continually approved ski resort expansions, including the recent use of reclaimed water—treated industrial and residential water—for snowmaking. The Navajo and other tribes challenged this decision, asserting that because some of the reclaimed water comes from hospitals and domestic waste, it contains elements of death and disease, and its use for snowmaking desecrates the Peaks and severely impairs spiritual practices that require purity of place.[40] The tribes lost the challenge. In his dissent, Ninth Circuit Judge William Fletcher remarked, "in [holding for the Forest Service], the majority misstates the evidence below, misstates the law . . . , and misunderstands the very nature of religion."[41]

Coming back to *Lyng,* Justice O'Connor stated in that opinion: "the Government's rights to the use of its own land . . . need not and should not discourage it from *accommodating* religious practices like those engaged in by the Indian respondents."[42] O'Connor's "accommodation" language showed that federal agencies could, at their discretion, find ways to protect tribal sacred sites without running afoul of the law, a practice that is making headway. An example of such collaboration is Cave Rock—a sacred site of the Washoe on the shore of Lake Tahoe—which was closed to climbers to protect its cultural heritage, including its importance to the area tribes.[43] And in the Lewis and Clark National Forest, a Forest Service travel plan prohibited motorized use in most of the Badger-Two Medicine area, a sacred area to the Blackfeet, which a Montana district court upheld.[44] Federal public land agencies have broad discretion, and they can rely on policy directives such as the American Indian Religious Freedom Act and Executive Order 13007 for greater security in making sacred site protections.

RECLAIMING SACREDNESS IN THE GREAT UNKNOWN:
TRIBAL-FEDERAL PUBLIC LAND MANAGEMENT

The modern consequences of the reservation and allotment policies advocated by Powell and instituted by the federal government in the mid/late-1800s have left the protection of many tribal sacred sites at the mercy of federal agencies and courts. Regrettably, this has not worked out well for tribes in the Colorado River Basin and elsewhere. Can we do better? Of course. As mentioned above, the law supports agency decisions to provide sacred site accommodations. The next step is to ensure tribes are provided practical, on-the-ground opportunities to participate meaningfully in federal land management and planning processes so that cultural resources are protected and incorporated into management plans for public lands. Tribal sacred sites should be treated as national sacred sites, and cultural natural resources should be valued as a national priority. The law should protect both. Tribes are in the best position to cooperatively manage with federal agencies to ensure proper protection. The most promising model comes from the heart of the Colorado Plateau: the tribally envisioned Bears Ears National Monument management structure.

Bears Ears National Monument

In December 2016, President Obama created Bears Ears National Monument by proclamation in southeastern Utah. The 1.35 million-acre monument was the product of years of advocacy by the Bears Ears Inter-Tribal Coalition, an unprecedented collaboration of five Colorado Plateau tribes—the Navajo Nation, Ute Mountain Ute Tribe, Ute Indian Tribe, Hopi Tribe, and Zuni Tribe.[45] Together, the five tribes—relying heavily on the work of the Native-led grassroots nonprofit Utah Diné Bikéyah—submitted a proposal to President Obama in October 2015 for the creation of a 1.9-million-acre national monument to protect important spiritual and cultural lands that were targeted for future energy development and whose tribal artifacts had been extensively looted.[46]

The October 2015 Coalition proposal to President Obama took years to create and represented more than just mere ideology. It represented hard data, GIS mapping, tribal historical research, and ecosystem science. To define the 1.9 million-acre boundary, the Coalition examined tribal uses on the Bears Ears landscape, including "land valued by Tribal members for gathering of medicines and herbs, worshipping at sacred areas, holding ceremonies, protecting archaeological sites, gathering firewood, hunting, protecting wildlife habitat for deer, elk, and bighorn sheep, and maintaining natural beauty and solitude."[47]

The Coalition knew a national monument alone would be insufficient to garner the land use protections that the tribes needed, so the proposal's other critical component was collaborative management—actual on-the-ground tribal input to shape the monument's day-to-day and long-term management. The proposal asserted that, while "the tribes have no legal right to expansive management responsibility," it was a matter of good public policy for the tribes to be involved.[48] Citing examples of other monuments where prescriptive management directives had been issued and upheld in court, the proposal offered a detailed collaborative management arrangement that would empower a newly created Bears Ears Inter-Tribal Management Commission—comprised of representatives chosen by each tribe and a representative from each federal land agency—to supervise and direct the monument's federal managers. And while the proposal described the nuts and bolts of how collaborative management would work, the true thrust and uniqueness of it—tribal engagement in public land management—rang clearly:

> Collaborative Management at Bears Ears offers a first-ever opportunity to truly infuse Native values into public lands administration by pulling upon both indigenous knowledge and Western science. Both have great value. The enterprise of honoring and using both bodies of thought and experience, and thus mediating across knowledge systems, can be a unique contribution of this monument. As such, their work can both enrich on-the-ground conditions and produce cutting-edge research for land managers everywhere.[49]

A year and two months after receiving the Coalition's proposal, President Obama issued a proclamation under the Antiquities Act establishing Bears Ears National Monument.[50] The Obama Proclamation did not mirror the proposal, however, and chopped the monument's size down nearly 600,000 acres. The Proclamation did retain the collaborative management framework, albeit tweaked slightly. The Bears Ears Commission would comprise one representative from each tribe, chosen by that tribe, and work with the interior and agriculture secretaries directly "in the development of the management plan and to inform subsequent management of the monument."[51] The Commission was given great authority to define management, with the Proclamation providing that the "Secretaries shall carefully and fully consider integrating the traditional and historical knowledge and special expertise of the Commission."[52] When the secretaries chose not to incorporate the Commission's input, they were required to report the reasons to the Commission in writing. Through the Proclamation, the tribes could manage their cultural resources and protect their sacred sites in a way never accomplished before.

Institutionalizing Tribal-Federal Collaborative Management

The process of achieving the Bears Ears collaborative management structure is not very instructive writ large, unfortunately. It is impractical to replicate this lengthy and resource-heavy advocacy effort on the scale necessary to provide requisite protections throughout the public lands. That being so, in other parts of the Colorado River Basin and elsewhere, the management structure—with tribal and federal land managers side-by-side on a decision-making tree—can be accomplished through congressional legislation accompanied by federal regulations that reflect the Inter-Tribal Coalition proposal's framework.

This is not as big a leap as it may seem. The principles of collaborative management and partnership between tribes and the federal government did not first arise with Bears Ears. In the Northwest, tribes have worked with federal agencies for decades in managing fishery harvests, and they also work with the Bureau of Land Management, Park Service, Bureau of Reclamation, and other agencies to share expertise and resources to manage public lands. These partnerships are successes, both for the partners and for the lands and waters. Recently, former Interior Secretary Jewell endorsed greater tribal-federal partnerships through Secretarial Order 3342 in October 2016.[53] The Order was issued to "encourage cooperative management agreements and other collaborative partnerships" between tribes and the Interior Department, and to create a process to ensure that federal land managers develop opportunities to create partnerships to benefit both tribes and federal agencies.[54] Providing legal authority for the partnerships, the order made clear that existing statutes support more tribal-federal collaboration. In the context of the Colorado River Basin and more broadly, what the effort needs is greater federal agency support, and more guidance. This is where Congress can step in to effectuate the Order's intent through statute, requiring the interior and agriculture departments to enter into collaborative agreements with tribes. The agencies can then promulgate regulations to guide the process, crafting these regulations to accomplish several goals.

First, local federal agency bodies must include a high-level management entity that receives direct input from tribal leadership, chosen by tribes with historical and cultural ties to the particular land. The agency should support the tribal leaders' participation both financially and with staffing. The Bears Ears Inter-Tribal Management Commission leadership was to be supported by dedicated staff that would coordinate with the five tribes to put forth proposals to the agencies. The most important element is that tribal representatives who provide management input are selected by the interested tribes, not by Congress, the state, or the agency.

Second, federal agencies must fully consider tribal recommendations and be held accountable if these recommendations are not implemented. In the Bears Ears model, the Commission leadership would make recommendations directly to the interior and agriculture secretaries. If the secretaries chose not to implement these recommendations, they were required to report to the Commission and explain their refusal. A new regulation should not be so demanding on the secretaries, but it should require that tribal-leader input be considered directly by the regional superintendent, who would have to report to the secretary why any recommendation was not implemented. Two things are important here: (1) tribal input is considered by the highest-level agency staff involved in decision-making, and (2) the agency is held accountable to fully consider the tribal input. This approach will ensure that tribal recommendations are not treated like input in a tribal consultation meeting—that is, input that can be ignored at will or addressed in a comment matrix on page 497, Appendix X of a management plan.

Third, federal agencies must work with tribal representatives during on-the-ground management after the planning process is complete. Tribes would designate their management representatives—likely the tribal historic preservation officer, range manager, or forester—to work through management issues with agency staff.

Fourth, there must be a dispute resolution system through which tribal and federal agency leadership are capable of discussing conflicts that arise and seeking resolution. Should the parties be unable to find resolution, the agency supervisor must present the particular issue to the appropriate secretary, who will then report to a congressional committee for final determination. This process can balance the decision of the agency against the decision of the political body to reach an outcome in the public's best interest, hopefully avoiding local politics or pressures to suppress tribal input or to limit the tribes' role.

Fifth, there must be funding. Any successful endeavor requires time, effort, and intent. To show intent on the federal side, financial assistance must be available to support the collaboration and tribal involvement. So where is the source of authority for this financial assistance? We need to look no further than the federal trust responsibility that arises from treaties and treaty equivalents establishing reservations in the Colorado River Basin and elsewhere, promising tribes the ability to continue their sovereign status into the future in exchange for the millions of relinquished acres.[55] As we know from sacred site issues, there is nothing more basic to tribal existence than the spiritual connection Indian people have to the land: protect the land, save the Indian people. The federal government has an obligation to assist Indian tribes in managing ancestral lands and sacred sites that are now on public lands.

These prescriptions offer a workable framework for tribal-federal collaborations for public land management. But there should also be more collaboration between tribes and federal agencies, such as considering the location of agency offices and how they are organized, agency superintendent hiring decisions, and contractor selections—true collaborative management. There are plenty of examples that show the legal underpinnings for this framework exist and that collaborative management can be successful. We just need the federal government to be brave.

CONCLUSION: COLLABORATION AND OUR CIVILIZATION IN THE GREAT UNKNOWN

Loosely based on Powell's interpretation of it, the path to "civilization" means controlling and manipulating the land for the benefit of people. Arguably, we have approached public land management in an *uncivilized* manner for over one hundred years in the Colorado River Basin and broader West, considering how our management has yielded diminishing benefits over time while increasing the need to restore the land and its resources. Federal agencies have inconsistently applied legal mandates to benefit only extractive interests, treating the public and the landscape as disconnected entities. But they are interconnected, and this management practice, which regularly oscillates between preferred methods, has hurt the land and the communities that depend on the ecosystems. Intensive land use practices, including agriculture and energy development, have decimated fish runs on the West Coast; fire suppression and logging have turned our national forests into even-aged tinder boxes; and the popularity of national parks has skyrocketed and threatened the wilderness values of those lands. We cannot forget that these are tribal ancestral lands, and their degradation includes harm to tribal cultural resources and sacred places.

Powell's vision was for Indian people to come off their lands and gently fold into American society. But what Powell had learned about Indian people—that their spiritual connections and understandings of the land were deeper than even he could grasp—made his goal impossible and rendered impractical the policies that attempted to achieve it. In its wake, Indian tribes were left with comparatively small land bases and little ability to manage those lands as necessary to protect the resources. Still, Indian people persist and are reclaiming their ability to protect their most important cultural resource—land. Relying, again, on Vine Deloria's words:

> Sacred places are the foundation of all other practices and beliefs because they represent the presence of the sacred in our lives. They properly inform us that we are not larger than nature and that we have responsibilities to the

rest of the natural world that transcend our own personal desires and wishes.... There probably is not sufficient time for the non-Indian population to understand the meaning of sacred lands and incorporate the idea into their lives and practices. We can but hope that some protection can be afforded these sacred places before the world becomes wholly secular and is destroyed.[56]

Looking forward, as we should, the Colorado River Basin has incredible tribal knowledge to draw from to help guide public land management. Tribes should be encouraged and supported to be cooperative managers alongside the federal government on ancestral lands now under federal ownership. This is important for so many reasons, but the most important is practical: tribes have an unmatched interest in the land's health and diversity that will create holistic management practices to improve the viability of ecosystems. For tribes, having the ability and right to get back on the sacred landscapes within the basin in order to protect and manage sacred places is profoundly important, both for the spiritual aspect of this practice and the recognition of sovereignty that tribes fight each day to preserve.

The way we choose to interact with and treat public lands in coming decades is a key aspect of the "Great Unknown." We can choose to compartmentalize objectives and continue to satisfy the highest bidder, or we can choose to view the land as an extension of ourselves, correlating our own wellbeing with its. Our survival depends on choosing the latter path. If we are to restore balance within and between our communities in the Colorado River Basin and elsewhere, we need to heal our connections with the land. We need tribes to guide this effort, and we need to empower tribes to collaboratively manage our public lands.

NOTES

1. Gary Paul Nabhan, *Growing Food in a Hotter, Drier Land—Lessons from Desert Farmers on Adapting to Climate Uncertainty* (Hartford, CT: Chelsea Green, 2013).

2. See *Cohen's Handbook of Federal Indian Law* (New York: LexisNexis, 2005), §1.03[6][b].

3. Donald Worster, *A River Running West: The Life of John Wesley Powell* (Oxford: Oxford University Press, 2000), 44.

4. John Wesley Powell, "Proper Training and the Future of the Indians," *Forum* 18 (1895): 623.

5. John Wesley Powell, "An Overland Trip to the Grand Cañon," *Scribner's Monthly* 10 (1875): 665.

6. John Wesley Powell, "A Discourse on the Philosophy of the North American Indians," *Journal of the American Geographical Society of New York* 8 (1876): 256.

7. Powell, "An Overland Trip," 676.

8. Worster, *A River Running West*, 270.

9. *Indians West of the Rocky Mountains: Statement of Major J. W. Powell Made Before the Committee on Indian Affairs as to the Condition of the Indian Tribes West of the Rocky Mountains*, 43rd Cong, 1st Sess., H. Misc. Doc. 86 Serial 1618 (Washington, DC: Government Printing Office, 1874), 9.

10. Worster, *A River Running West*, 270.

11. *Report of Special Commissioners J. W. Powell and G. W. Ingalls on the Condition of the Ute Indians of Utah; the Paiutes of Utah, Northern Arizona, Southern Nevada, and Southeastern California; the Go-Si-Utes of Utah and Nevada; the Northwestern Shoshones of Idaho and Utah; and the Western Shoshones of Nevada; and Report Concerning Claims of Settlers in the Mo-a-Pa Valley, Southeastern Nevada* (Washington, DC: Government Printing Office, 1874), 25.

12. Powell, "An Overland Trip," 677.

13. Worster, *A River Running West*, 270.

14. Charles F. Wilkinson and John M. Volkman, "Judicial Review of Indian Treaty Abrogation: 'As Long as Water Flows, or Grass Grows Upon the Earth'—How Long a Time Is That?," *California Law Review* 63 (1975): 602.

15. *Cohen's Handbook*, 54.

16. President Abraham Lincoln, Executive Order, October 3, 1861.

17. Treaty of March 2, 1868, https://collections.lib.utah.edu/details?id = 361671.

18. "History," Southern Ute Indian Tribe, accessed October 15, 2019, https://www.southernute-nsn.gov/history.

19. On Meeker, see Brandi Denison, *Ute Land Religion in the American West, 1879–2009* (Lincoln: University of Nebraska Press, 2017), 47–62.

20. Worster, *A River Running West*, 150.

21. Denison, *Ute Land Religion*, 60.

22. "History: The Northern Utes," Utah American Indian Digital Archive, accessed October 15, 2019, https://utahindians.org/archives/ute/history.html.

23. Clyde Kluckhorn and Dorothea Leighton, *The Navaho* (Cambridge, MA: Harvard University Press, 1951), 6.

24. Ibid., 9.

25. Raymond D. Austin, *Navajo Courts and Navajo Common Law: A Tradition of Tribal Self-Governance* (Minneapolis: University of Minnesota Press, 2009), 5.

26. "Barboncito's Speech to General Sherman at Fort Sumner," Southwest Crossroads, accessed October 15, 2019, http://www.southwestcrossroads.org/record.php?num = 391.

27. John Burnett, "The Navajo Nation's Own 'Trail of Tears,'" *National Public Radio*, June 15, 2005, https://www.npr.org/2005/06/15/4703136/the-navajo-nation-s-own-trail-of-tears.

28. *Cohen's Handbook*, 77.

29. Ibid., 71–79.
30. Ibid., 78–79.
31. The figures in this paragraph are drawn from reservation- and state-specific data available in the Tribe/Reservation Allotment Legislation section of "Land Tenure History," Indian Land Tenure Foundation, accessed November 7, 2019, https://iltf.org/land-issues/history.
32. Vine Deloria, Jr., *God Is Red: A Native View of Religion* (New York: Putnam, 1973), 142–53.
33. Ibid.
34. Ibid., 142.
35. Ibid., 285.
36. See Michelle Kay Albert, "Obligations and Opportunities to Protect Native American Sacred Sites on Public Lands," *Columbia Human Rights Law Review* 40 (2009): 479–521.
37. 485 U.S. 439 (1988); Amy Bowers and Kristen Carpenter, "Challenging the Narrative of Conquest: The Story of *Lyng v. Northwest Indian Cemetery Protective Association*," in *Indian Law Stories*, ed. Carole Goldberg et al. (New York: Foundation Press, 2011).
38. Lyng v. Northwest Indian Cemetery Protective Association, 485 U.S. 439, 453 (1988).
39. Walter R. Echo-Hawk, *In the Courts of the Conqueror: The 10 Worst Indian Law Cases Ever Decided* (Golden, CO: Fulcrum Press, 2010), 349.
40. See Maria Glowacks, Dorothy Washburn, and Justin Richland, "Nuvatukya'ovi, San Francisco Peaks: Balancing Western Economies with Native American Spiritualities," *Current Anthropology* 50 (2009): 553.
41. Navajo Nation v. US Forest Service, 535 F.3d 1058, 1081 (9th Cir. 2008).
42. Lyng v. Northwest Indian Cemetery Protective Association, 485 U.S. 439, 453–454 (1988).
43. Access Fund v. USDA, 499 F.3d 1030 (9th Cir. 2007).
44. Fortune v. Thompson, 2011 WL 206164 (D. Mont., 2011).
45. Bears Ears Inter-Tribal Coalition, "Who We Are," accessed October 15, 2019, https://bearsearscoalition.org/about-the-coalition.
46. Bears Ears Inter-Tribal Coalition, "Proposal to President Barack Obama for the Creation of Bears Ears National Monument (2015), http://www.bearsearscoalition.org/wp-content/uploads/2015/10/Bears-Ears-Inter-Tribal-Coalition-Proposal-10-15-15.pdf.
47. Ibid., 20.
48. Ibid., 22.
49. Ibid., 33.
50. President Barack Obama, "Presidential Proclamation—Establishment of the Bears Ears National Monument," December 28, 2016, https://obamawhitehouse.archives.gov/the-press-office/2016/12/28/proclamation-establishment-bears-ears-national-monument.
51. Ibid.
52. Ibid.
53. Secretarial Order 3342, "Identifying Opportunities for Cooperative and Collaborative Partnerships with Federally Recognized Indian Tribes in the

Management of Federal Lands and Resources," October 21, 2016, https://www.doi.gov/sites/doi.gov/files/uploads/so3342_partnerships.pdf.
    54. Ibid.
    55. *Cohen's Handbook*, 418–23.
    56. Deloria, *God is Red*, 285.

CHAPTER 12

John Wesley Powell's Land and Water Policies and Southwestern Native American Agricultural Practices

WILLIAM J. GRIBB

John Wesley Powell's 1869 exploration of the Green and Colorado rivers provided the impetus to pioneer more settlements within the Colorado Basin. However, Powell was not the first explorer into the region, as almost three hundred years before the Spanish had ventured into this area in search of riches, glory, and the pretext of spreading Christianity.[1] Further, over ten thousand years before the Spanish, Native Americans were cyclically inhabiting dwelling places based on seasonal resources and eventually establishing permanent communities. Over the ensuing centuries, a wide range of colonists, frontiersmen, missionaries, surveyors, and settlers came to the Southwest to identify its natural resources, exploit them, and use the land for their economic benefit. The mystical story of the Native Americans that have inhabited this region for thousands of years is lost in the Euro-American story of discovery, exploration, and settlement. This chapter represents a short timeframe, approximately two hundred years, beginning with the early settlement of the Southwest; through Powell's 1869 Expedition, followed by his ideas of arid land and water management; then one hundred years of water development, allocation, and adjudication; and, finally, into the future about fifty years.

The focus is on Powell's proposed land and water policies relative to southwestern agricultural practices of Native Americans and the policy challenges they will face in the coming half century. Powell's 1869 Expedition initially yielded scientific information about the "Great

Unknown," but also provided him with knowledge to expound revolutionary visions of how to settle the West. His ideas and policies had a rollercoaster effect on southwestern Native Americans, providing some hope while still diminishing their cultures.

THE SOUTHWEST EXPLORED BY POWELL

By the time Powell's 1869 Expedition ventured into this region, there had been three phases of human activity and occupation.[2] Native Americans were the first to settle in the Colorado River Basin. The earliest human inhabitants came to the Southwest approximately 11,500 BP.[3] These were nomadic hunters, but over time the Paleo-Indians started to settle into farming areas about 3,000 BCE.[4] The semi-established settlements would change over time according to different climatic conditions, with agriculture becoming the main subsistence activity around 2,000 BCE, and permanent settlements appearing around 1,400 BCE.[5] With the wanderings of de Vaca[6] and the exploration by de Coronado[7] in the mid-1500s, the first Europeans began coming into the Southwest, later to be followed by missionaries and Spanish pioneers. Overall, the Spanish colonized this region for over 350 years.[8] They established missions, settlements, and mining areas as part of northwestern Mexico. Spanish and Mexican settlements and towns were concentrated along major river courses in the southern portion of the region and adjacent to the Rio Grande, with scattered rancheros into the hinterlands. The estimated population was small, ranging from 30,000–50,000 people.[9] Two major events in the mid-1800s brought a new round of immigrants: the treaty negotiations to establish the southwestern US–Mexican border and the California Gold Rush. The Treaty of Guadalupe Hidalgo in 1848, followed by the Treaty of Mesilla and the Gadsden Purchase in 1854, opened the southwestern US to a wide range of explorers, surveyors, pioneers, settlers, and military posts.[10] At the same time, the lure of the California gold fields brought thousands of fortune-seekers across the Southwest.

These explorations, political events, and mining discoveries overshadowed the presence of the original inhabitants. Native Americans were not participants in the explorations, discoveries, or treaties; rather, they happened to be in the area and had to be dealt with one way or another. The opening of the Southwest by Euro-Americans began a critical series of interactions between Native Americans, the United States, Spanish and Mexican governments, the military, and commercial entities.

Native American Agricultural Practices | 267

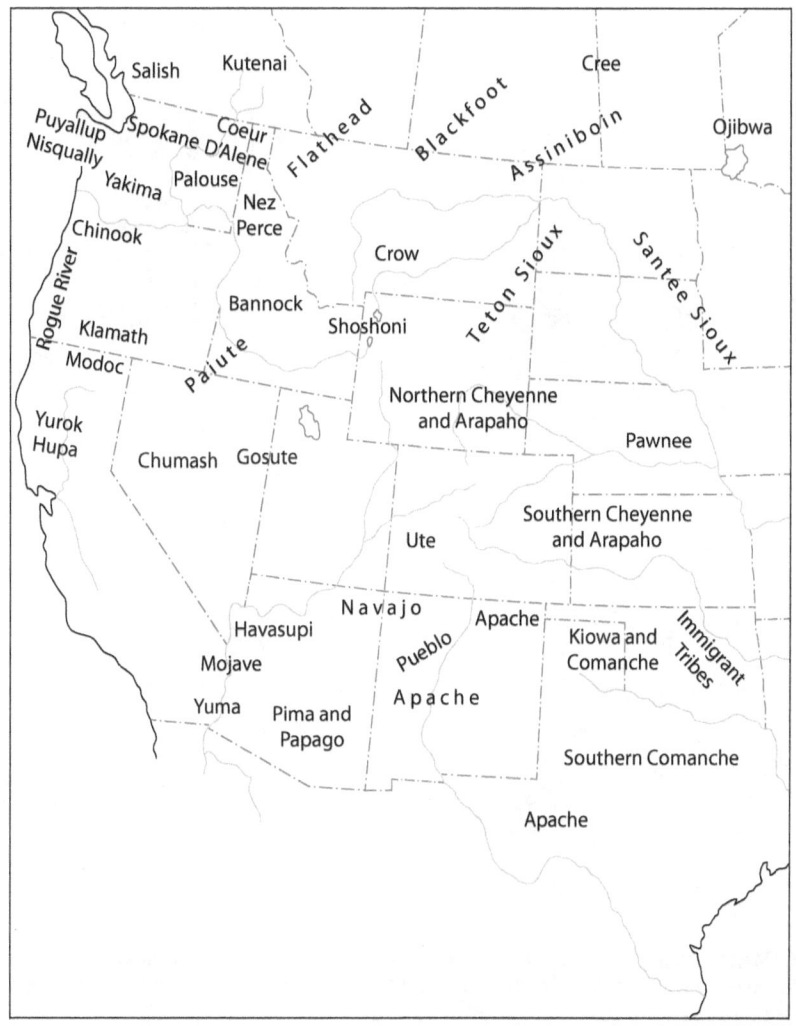

MAP 5. Distribution of Major Tribes in and around Colorado River Basin, circa 1860. Source: William Gribb, 2019.

Map 5 provides a basic illustration of the distribution of Native American tribes in the southwestern US around 1860.[11] Map 6, in turn, depicts regional military posts during this period.[12] The posts were positioned to assist Euro-American migrants across the Southwest on their way to California and the gold fields or newly developing agricultural lands. At approximately the same time, the search for a southern

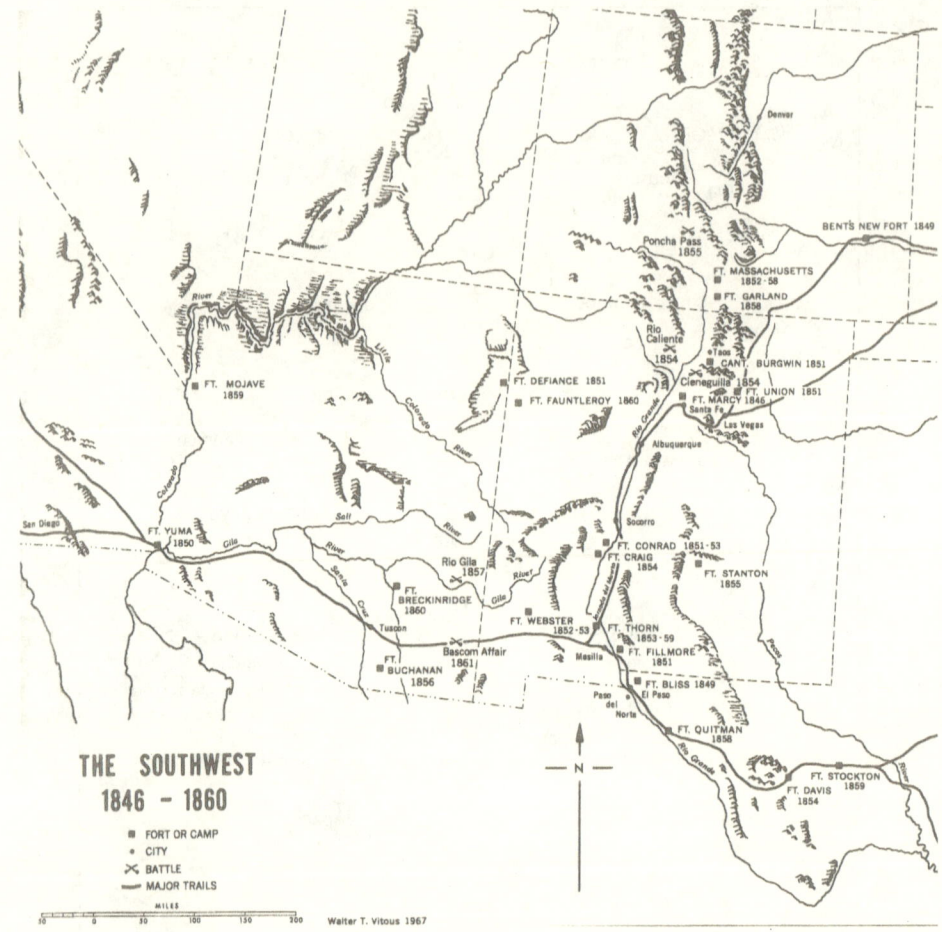

MAP 6. Major Military Posts and Transportation Networks in the Southwest. Source: Robert M. Utley, *Frontiersmen in Blue: The United States Army and the Indian, 1848–1865* (Lincoln: University of Nebraska Press, 1981).

railroad route was being conducted, which would exacerbate the problem by bringing more migrants at a faster rate.[13]

In the 1870s, the distribution of southwestern Native Americans was a mix of sedentary agriculturalist, semi-nomadic, and nomadic groups. It is important to understand the differences between these groups during their initial contacts with John Wesley Powell. They differed in settlement patterns and types, population size, and economic activity. The

Native American Agricultural Practices | 269

population of the tribal groups and bands was never very large; most of the tribes had 500–5,000 members. The largest group was the Navajo in the Arizona, New Mexico, and Utah territories, while the smallest groups were the more nomadic Goshute Ute in the Utah Territory, who practiced subsistence hunting and gathering. Overall, there were approximately 55,000 Native Americans in the southwestern US in 1875, according to the Commissioner of Indian Affairs.[14] By the mid-1870s, most of the tribal groups lived on reservations or in their vicinity. Some members of the roving bands were not inclined to occupy a reservation and opposed the restrictions and subservient role forced on them by the federal government.

The tribal groups that John Wesley Powell had direct contact with were only a small subset of the overall Native American population, consisting mainly of those who were adjacent to the Colorado River or about whom he had heard. In the first part of *The Exploration of the Colorado River and Its Canyons,* Powell discussed the tribal groups' distribution and distinguished between the desert valley and plateau regions.[15] Near the headwaters of some of the Colorado River's eastern tributaries were the Apaches and Navajos, while in the Gila River valley were the Pimas, Maricopas, and Papagos. In the southern floodplain of the Colorado River could be found the Mojave and Yuma Indians, while north of them were the Chemehuevas, who occupied an area encompassing the river floodplain and adjacent western mountains. In the Little Colorado River valley, two groups dominated: the Zuni Pueblo and the pueblos of the Tusayan (Hopi). The plateau created by the Little Colorado River and the San Juan River was home to the Navajo among the mountains and small valleys. Just to the northwest of the Navajo were several southern Paiute people who lived on the Kaibab Plateau in small groups: the Shivwits, Uinkarets, and Unkakaniguts. To the far north near the headwaters of the Colorado River, the northern Ute tribes occupied the valleys dissected by the Green, Yampa, Grand, Uintah, and White rivers. Map 5 illustrates the distribution of tribes that Powell had, or could have had, contact with during the 1869 Expedition.

In *The Exploration of the Colorado River and Its Canyons,* Powell also provided basic descriptions of economic activities of tribal groups he encountered along the river and on side trips.[16] On July 2, 1869, almost six weeks into the expedition, Powell traveled up the Uinta River to the Uintah Reservation, describing the farms as being in a "very beautiful district where many fine streams of water meander across alluvial plains and meadows." He went on to explain that the Indian farms were patches of ground two or three acres in size raising "wheat, potatoes, turnips, pumpkins, melons, and other vegetables." However, Powell did state that it would take irrigation for "successful farming" in this arid region.[17]

Yet not all tribal groups were solely dependent on agriculture at this time. For example, living on a plateau adjacent to the Colorado River, a typical sequence of economic activities for the Havasupai and the Walapais (Hualapais) has been described as spending spring planting corn, beans, and squash along simple irrigation networks in the canyons, and moving to the plateaus in winter to hunt and gather other foodstuffs.[18]

Powell observed that in the more southern stretches of the Colorado River traversed by the expedition, tribal groups generally were up on plateaus beside the river. His crew found little or "no evidence that the tribe of Indians ... come down to the river."[19] However, on August 26, 1869, during an episode when the expedition was on minimal rations, Powell and his crew were fortunate to come across a small area planted with corn and squash and irrigated from springs along the cliffs. The expedition helped themselves to the squash, as the corn was not ripe. In contrast, in other portions of the Colorado River Basin, there was intensive agricultural production. For example, tribes along the Gila River had an intricate irrigation and farming system that supplied crops to a large, sedentary group of people,[20] though this area was not visited by the expedition.

Overall, farming occurred on only small portions of southwestern reservations during this period. According to federal records, the amount of tillable acreage on major reservations varied from less than 1,000 acres to as much as 500,000 acres, if it existed at all.[21] On average, approximately 18 percent of any reservation had tillable acreage, as most reservation lands were not suited for agriculture. The Ute bands at the Los Pinos Agency had a large number of tillable acres (500,000), but the lands were noncontiguous and scattered across an enormous area. Only two other reservations had sizeable tillable acreage—the Colorado River (50,000) and the Pima and Maricopa (8,000)—but they also had access to historical sources of irrigation water and a larger portion of their lands were contiguous in adjacent floodplains to their settlements.

LAND AND WATER IN THE SOUTHWEST

Land rights for Native American tribes in the West are based on governmental policy that has changed considerably through space and time. Initially, the Spanish and Mexican political systems set aside historical

Native American settlements by providing them with Spanish or Mexican land grants measured in leagues (one square league is equivalent to 4,340.3 acres or 17.6 square kilometers).[22] A land grant would be measured either as a radius of one league from the center of the village or as four square leagues, depending upon topography.[23] Overall, there were twenty-one Spanish and Mexican land grants to Native American groups in the Colorado River Basin totaling 364,434 acres (1,474.8 square kilometers).[24] After the Mexican-American War, the Treaty of Guadalupe Hidalgo protected the Spanish land grants in the southwestern US, including lands for Pueblos and other tribal communities.[25]

As early as 1850, the Commissioner of Indian Affairs thought "[a] square, each side of which shall measure fifty miles in length, if properly selected, would be ample . . . and they could be instructed in agricultural pursuits."[26] Early treaties with the Utes and Navajos were signed in the 1860s establishing their base reservations. In the 1868 Treaty with the Ute, a new element was apparent.[27] Article 7 stated that if "an individual belonging to said tribe . . . being head of a family, shall desire to commence farming, he shall have the privilege to select . . . a tract of land within said reservation not exceeding one hundred and sixty acres." This element changed the dynamics of Western treaties and eventually created major land problems for Native Americans.

The 1870s was also the time most tribes in the West were being moved onto reservations created mainly by executive orders. These orders were used to set aside lands for different tribal groups, because they did not require congressional approval. Executive orders were straightforward in text and would state the area in which particular tribes would be settled; they almost always closed with the statement "for their use and occupancy." The reservation system of the 1870s and 1880s limited the area of tribal occupation and forced Native Americans to acculturate into mainstream US society through (among other institutions) Euro-American agricultural practices.[28] Unfortunately, at roughly the same time, the federal government was encouraging settlement of the West. The problem still remained, as earlier, that Native Americans were in the way, and their lands were considered part of the new settlement, mainly areas in the floodplain and with access to water.

In some cases, a treaty, statute, or executive order would set aside land for a single tribe (for example, the Navajo), while in other situations the lands were shared between either several bands of the same tribe (for example, the Tabeguache, Muache, Capote, Weeminuche, Yampa, Grand River, and Uintah bands of Utes) or several different

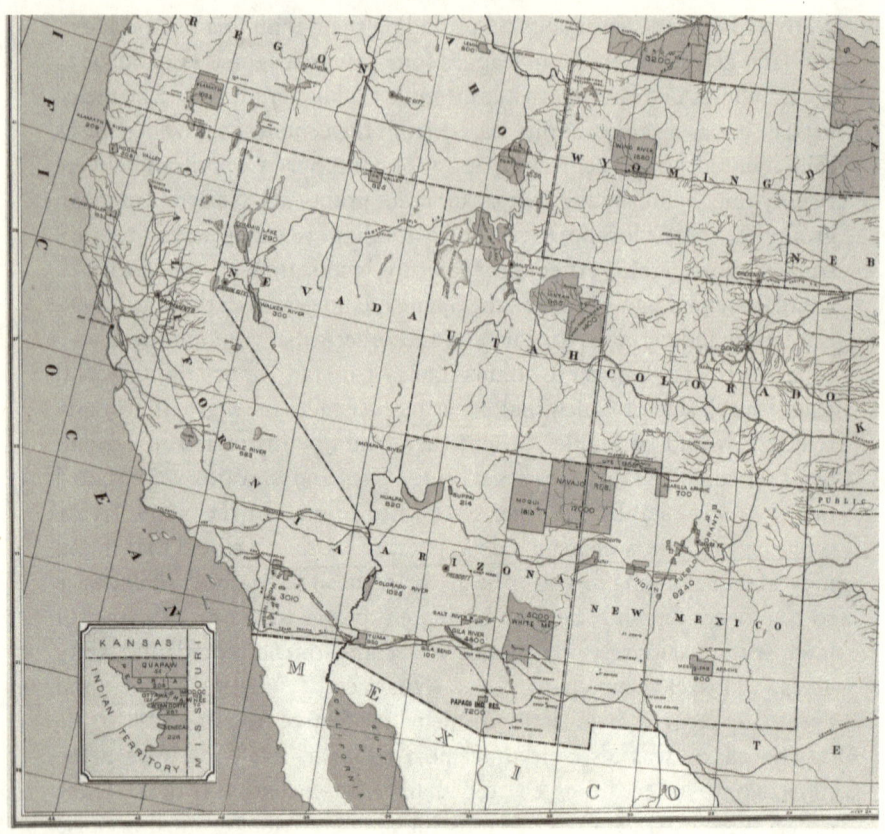

MAP 7. Southwestern Reservations, 1880s. Source: P. T. Brodie and H. Price, *Map of the Indian Reservations Within the Limits of the United States* (Smithsonian Institution: s.n., 1883).

tribes (for example, the Mojave, Chemehuevi, Hualapais, and Cocopah). Overall, as shown in map 7, approximately 17,682,095.1 acres (71,556.9 square kilometers) were designated as reservation lands in the Colorado River Basin by the late 1880s . However, these lands were not entirely held in trust for the tribal groups. As described above, the treaties provided that individuals or families could identify tracts of land and be allotted up to 160 acres (0.647 square kilometers) to start farms. Again, the intent was to acculturate Native Americans into Euro-American agrarian capitalist society. However, this policy also separated allotted parcels from trust status and thereby subjected them to taxation, land sales, and forfeiture. Allotment provisions in treaties continued until the end of the treaty-making era in 1871. More broadly, Powell and some of his contemporaries believed that reservations were essential to educate Native Americans so that they could be absorbed into American society and "lost."[29] As much of an ethnographer as Powell claimed to be, he did not recognize the cultural aspects of Native Americans' sense of place, even though he understood what the sense of place meant.[30]

Native Americans' trust land holdings changed radically further with passage of the General Allotment or Dawes Act in 1887, which opened up reservation lands to allotment and provided that any surplus lands could be transferred by the federal government to non-Indians under public land laws. In 1886, reservations encompassed a total of 138 million acres (558,464 square kilometers), yet by the end of the allotment era—with passage of the Indian Reorganization Act of 1934—reservations were reduced to only 40.8 million acres (165,305 square kilometers)—a reduction of 70.4 percent.[31] This dramatic land loss impacted agricultural lands the most, because the primary lands lost were the most productive lands, the lands in floodplains that had rich soils and access to water.

CURRENT TRIBAL LAND AND WATER MANAGEMENT

Moving from past to present, land and water management are critical to effective and efficient use of Colorado River Basin water. As Powell stated many times, the land has no worth without water.[32] This observation warrants an examination of basin tribes' existing land and water management systems. What is their status? In short, land and water issues have proven to be an area of continuing conflict between basin tribes and the federal and state governments.

There are twenty-nine reservations within the Colorado River Basin (see table 1).[33] Overall, the reservations account for 21.2 percent of the basin's lands—encompassing 33,362,944.9 acres (135,015.2 square kilometers)—with the Navajo Nation being the largest and the Yavapai-Apache Nation the smallest. Although there are not accurate calculations of the amount of agricultural lands on reservations, it is possible to extrapolate from the USDA Agricultural Census of 2017.[34] According to survey information from the reservation-specific Agricultural Census, an average of 33.4 percent of reservation lands are placed into irrigated agriculture, which would represent approximately 11,143,217 acres (45,095 square kilometers). However, this value is misleading because it reflects the overall reservation estimate based on survey

TABLE 1. COLORADO RIVER BASIN RESERVATIONS, 2018

Reservation	Sq. Km.	Acres
Ak-Chin	86.1	21,276.9
Chemehuevi	124.8	30,847.4
Cocopah	26.1	6,457.3
Colorado River	1,004.6	248,249.9
Fort Apache-White Mountain	6,814.6	1,683,922.3
Fort McDowell	100.7	24,885.3
Fort Mojave	108.7	26,860.4
Fort Yuma	182.5	45,089.7
Gila River	1,512.2	373,666.6
Havasupai	714.5	176,568.2
Hopi	6,561.3	1,621,320.0
Hualapai	4,154.9	1,026,708.8
Jicarilla Apache	3,558.2	879,238.9
Kaibab	489.5	120,952.0
Las Vegas Paiute	15.9	3,924.8
Moapa River	2,871.6	709,589.2
Navajo	62,564.6	15,460,029.8
Paiute (UT)	131.1	32,387.6
Pascua Pueblo Yaqui	9.1	2,240.3
Salt River	220.9	54,574.6
San Carlos	7,580.9	1,873,278.5
Southern Ute	2,754.3	680,592.2
Tohono O'odham	11,533.5	2,849,976.7
Tonto Apache	1.5	370.6
Uintah and Ouray	17,673.3	4,367,171.8
Ute Mountain Ute	2,332.1	576,273.8
Yavapai-Apache	2.6	650.9
Yavapai-Prescott	5.7	1,411.2
Zuni	1,879.5	464,429.2
Total	135,015.2	33,362,944.9

SOURCE: US Census Bureau, *Cartographic Boundary Shapefiles* (2018).

responses. When solely considering agricultural lands operated by Native Americans, only 3.4 percent of the land is irrigated, equivalent to 1,134,337.3 acres (4,590.5 square kilometers).

An agricultural system has many components and takes many forms as a viable economic activity. American agriculture has been described as involving one of two scenarios: (1) the industrial food system with large farms or networks of farmers that produce food and fiber in response to consumer demands, and (2) the small farms that produce for local markets, with goods that are fairly traded, humanely processed, and may have historical, traditional, or cultural value.³⁵ The second scenario fits existing models for agroecology and principles of traditional ecological knowledge historically practiced by Native Americans in their agricultural activities.³⁶ Unfortunately, agriculture on reservation lands is in a "quagmire" because of water and land management rights, land tenure issues, lack of economic agricultural knowledge, and inadequate infrastructure.³⁷

In the context of the Colorado River Basin and more broadly, currently land ownership on reservations is generally a mix of tribal trust lands, Native American allotted lands, and fee simple lands. Trust and allotted lands are managed by tribal councils or the Bureau of Indian Affairs, while fee simple lands are owned by private individuals and are under the jurisdiction of county governments. The agricultural management strategy of a tribe varies depending on the jurisdiction. For instance, the Navajo Nation Department of Agriculture's vision statement aspires to "[a]ttain sustainability of land, people, water and agricultural resources through conservation, protection and preservation."³⁸ This vision is complemented by a mission statement that calls for the agency to "provide guidance [to] the Diné people in the stewardship of Mother Earth by providing leadership, knowledge and technological assistance in the management and conservation of her resources, for the inheritance of generations to come."³⁹ Thus, agricultural purpose is blended with cultural characteristics.

One potential form of tribal economic development on reservations is land and natural resource development, which includes agriculture, extractive industries, forestry, and recreation. However, the specific focus here is on agricultural development, which in the arid region requires irrigation and water infrastructure. According to the Bureau of Reclamation, basin tribes collectively hold annual diversion rights of 2.9 million acre-feet (maf), representing approximately 18.1 percent of the overall water whose use was apportioned by the Colorado River Compact.⁴⁰

The Supreme Court's *Winters* doctrine and *Arizona v. California* decision set fundamental parameters on tribal water rights within the Colorado River Basin.⁴¹ To assist in their collective bargaining and management of water rights established by adjudications or negotiated settlements, a coalition of ten basin tribes joined together in 1992 to advocate their positions regarding management of the Colorado River and its tributaries.⁴² The partnership consists of the Chemehuevi Indian

Tribe, Cocopah Indian Community, Colorado River Indian Tribes, Fort Mojave Indian Tribe, Jicarilla Apache Tribe, Navajo Nation, Northern Ute Tribe, Quechan Indian Tribe, Southern Ute Indian Tribe, and Ute Mountain Ute Indian Tribe. Their main objectives are to have equal representation at the water-bargaining table, to maximize reservation water use, and to manage water as a commodity. To accomplish these objectives, the organization has articulated several goals for the next ten years: (1) each tribe has settled or otherwise resolved its reserved water rights claims; (2) each tribe has the ability to maximize its on-reservation use of water and the flexibility to explore, facilitate, and implement off-reservation use and transfers; (3) each tribe benefits from water infrastructure projects promised or obtained through settlements or negotiations with state and federal governments and partners in a timely fashion; and (4) the federal government firmly asserts and exercises its trust responsibility to protect the tribes' reserved water rights in all of its management actions related to the Colorado River.

Land resources of Colorado River Basin tribes vary from high-mountain forests to bottomlands along the river system.[43] However, this discussion is concerned with land and water management on reservations as advocated by Powell. As described throughout this volume, Powell proposed that land and water rights should be conjoined and watersheds should be established as the basic unit of water districts. Each district would manage their own land and water through cooperatives. This premise holds true for reservations, where land and water rights cannot be sold and are linked through the *Arizona v. California* decision's practicably irrigable acreage (PIA) standard.[44] Tribes' water rights are quantified under the PIA standard based on the irrigable acreage contained on their reservations. For instance, the Utes have several reservations and population centers, but a very small percent of their land is irrigated (4.3 percent). Thus, their water rights are not proportional to the overall area or the size of their settlements. Currently, there are thirteen basin tribes whose water allocations have not been recognized or quantified: Navajo Nation, Ute Indian Tribe, and Ute Mountain Ute Tribe in the Upper Basin, and Havasupai Tribe, Hopi Tribe, Hualapai Tribe, Kaibab Band of Paiute Indians, Navajo Nation, Pascua Yaqui Tribe, San Carlos Apache Tribe, San Juan Southern Paiute Tribe, Tohono O'odham Nation, Tonto Apache Tribe, and Yavapai Apache Nation in the Lower Basin.[45]

The structure of tribal farming is important to understand. According to the Special Reservation Agricultural Census of 2017, fourteen tribes in the Colorado River Basin provided information on agricultural activities on their reservations.[46] The majority of farms (62.7 percent) are small acreage (.1–9 acres), and almost 80 percent are under 180 acres. Farming on the surveyed reservations is generally a small business or family business and not part of a major agricultural industrial complex. Further, these small farms do not generate large incomes, with almost 80 percent deriving less than $5,000 from agricultural sales.

Tribal water demands are directly related to agricultural land use. Agriculture consumes approximately 80 percent of available water throughout the West.[47] Powell made the statement that Western agriculture would be possible with 1 cubic feet second (cfs) of water per 80–100 acres or 7.24 acre-feet per acre.[48] This is almost the exact amount adjudicated in the Supreme Court's *Arizona v. California* decision, which allocated approximately 1,000,000 acre-feet for 135,000 acres of land, or 7.4 acre-feet per acre, for the five tribes addressed in the judicial decree.[49] This precedent allows other reservations to use the same PIA standard and possibly receive a proportional amount of water for irrigable lands. As mentioned previously, there are possibly 1.134 million acres (4,489.1 square kilometers) of irrigated lands operated by Native Americans on the twenty-nine reservations within the Colorado River Basin. At the rate of 7.4 acre-feet per acre, this could translate to approximately 8.32 maf allocated to reservations over the entire basin, which is roughly 52 percent of the total Colorado River Compact apportionment.

NATIVE AMERICAN AGRICULTURAL
POTENTIAL IN THE FUTURE

How do John Wesley Powell's water policies relate to climate variability in the southwestern US, and what strategies can tribes use to manage and adjust their water resources and demands over the next fifty years? In addition, given that the southwestern US is predicted to have one of the highest population growth rates in the next century, what role could tribal water management play in this prediction?[50] Three elements will be considered to address these questions: (1) climate change predictions extending to 2060, (2) future water management policy, and (3) Native American policy options for the next fifty years. Taken together, this material aims to assess how Powell's policies on land and water use are impacted by climate change, a factor that he may have mentioned, but did not anticipate in its full effects. Specifically, in Powell's *Arid Lands Report* (1878), G.K. Gilbert expressed concern over climate change, indicating that he believed it is part of the larger global climate system and that at that point in time "the greater cycles of change are still beyond our reach. Although withdrawn from the domain of the unknowable, they remain within that of the unknown."[51]

Climate Change Predictions for the Southwestern United States

The challenges to arid region development that Powell's policies addressed were mainly physical conditions. The physiography of the region had been built through the evolution of the geosphere, biosphere, hydrosphere, and atmosphere. However, increased human activities have accelerated the evolutionary rate of change, and it is the resulting impacts that we have to manage. Global warming will increase the capacity of the atmosphere to hold moisture, leading to more precipitation in some locations and less in others. Although overall global precipitation will increase, regional variations are more difficult to estimate.[52]

The southwestern US has experienced severe climatic conditions in the past. Archaeological and other methods have revealed several historical drought periods, with some lasting more than fifty years.[53] Using different climatic models and a combination of historical and derived data, the National Climate Assessment was able to project climatic trends for the next eighty years. The models forecast a continued trend in increasing temperatures and a shift in the type and amount of precipitation. They indicate that precipitation totals will decrease slightly, but more importantly, snowfall and corresponding snow water equivalent totals in higher elevations will decrease significantly. This change from snow to rain will mean that there will be a reduction in runoff and soil moisture, leading to a severe decrease in streamflow.[54]

In addition, a lower amount of available moisture at higher elevations will decrease snow accumulation and soil moisture while increasing the potential fire hazard, both lengthening the fire season and increasing fire temperatures. Forests at higher elevations provide a multitude of ecosystem services, particularly related to hydrology. They act as a storage region for moisture that is typically released during spring and early summer snowmelt. The spring melt corresponds with the beginning of a plant's phenology, when moisture and nutrients are needed for growth.[55]

Water availability is critical in the Southwest because of the defining regional characteristic emphasized so emphatically by Powell: aridity. As historical and contemporary climatic records show, there has always been a cyclical pattern of drought in the region.[56] The National Climate Assessment indicates that from 1901 to 2015 average annual precipitation in the United States increased by almost 4 percent, except in the Southwest, where it decreased by almost the same amount.[57] This pattern is projected to continue into the future, with the Southwest experiencing decreases close to 40 percent in available water through snow, runoff, and soil moisture.[58] The region's mountain areas will no longer be the water towers they were during Powell's time or earlier.

Changes in moisture availability have impacted the timing of peak streamflow and the amount of water in the Colorado River system. In the Southwest, peak flows are coming earlier in the year, and annual flow levels are decreasing.[59] Overall, the Southwest will experience only slight flow decreases in the winter, while spring and summer flow decreases will be more significant.[60] Thus, the coupling of higher temperatures, less precipitation, and decreased streamflow will lead to long-term drought conditions over multiple seasons, increasing plant and soil moisture depletions and exacerbating arid conditions.

The effects of these conditions will be amplified because of concurrent increasing population projections and growing water demands of municipalities and industry.[61] The Bureau of Reclamation has estimated that by 2060 an additional 36.5 million new residents could be living in the Colorado River Basin states, an increase of more than 91 percent over the current estimated population of 40 million.[62] Commensurate with that growth, overall water demands may increase 34 percent by 2060 and from 42 percent to 82 percent by 2090, depending on the emissions scenario.[63]

Climatic changes currently being experienced in the Southwest, along with the predicted future population changes, will have a tremendous impact on Native American populations, economies, and cultures.[64] The changes will be direct and indirect. Direct changes will manifest in terms of population, employment, and revenues generated from resource extraction (agriculture, mining, oil/gas, water development, and forestry). Indirect consequences relate to relying on outdated or nonexistent infrastructure to distribute water efficiently and effectively. Changes will be evident in Native American cultural and environmental heritage. Cultural heritage is composed of many elements, including traditional ecological knowledge, spiritual values, religious ceremonies, and traditional material culture. Environmental heritage includes land and water rights and place-based practices and activities.[65] In conjunction with past cycles of climatic change, basin tribes' traditional ecological knowledge has enabled several coping strategies.[66] Historically, during times of extended drought, tribes would concentrate around the most productive lands and areas after suffering population declines. Will some of these strategies be feasible in the future?

Climate change will directly impact Colorado River Basin tribes' agricultural activities. Though irrigated agriculture is only a small part of southwestern reservation land economics, the effects will be felt in all sectors of the reservations. Adjustments will have to be made to crop types and yields, seed selection (drought resistance), livestock size, and local and global market availability.[67] Where applicable, agriculture from traditional ecological knowledge could buffer tribes from some impacts, but markets would be needed for products. However, uncertainty in production due to increased temperatures, less available water, and extreme weather events will change future agricultural development, limiting growth or even declining this sector of the southwestern economy.

Management Strategies for Southwestern Native Americans

To address the impacts of climate change, a revision of Powell's strategies may have to occur for the benefit of Colorado River Basin tribes and the survival of their lands. There are three key elements to Powell's strategies for water development in the basin and other parts of the West: (1) planning and decision-making should be done at the watershed level, (2) water rights should be linked to land rights, and (3) farm and ranch sizes should be a function of landscape characteristics. Each of these elements can be viewed as a catalyst for Native American land and water management policies in the future.

Turning to the first element, Powell's previously described settlement proposals called for water and land being managed in watershed commonwealths, and these ideas are still viewed as best practices for local or regional planning processes.[68] Care of the watershed and riparian areas requires knowledge of upstream and downstream conditions, tributaries entering the drainage system, and understanding and managing from the watershed's headwaters to its outlet or delta.[69]

Powell believed that water and land knowledge was a key factor in water management and that there should be a quantification of water resources and an identification of lands that can be irrigated.[70] In the twenty-first century, this information is available in forms that can be incorporated into a geographic information system. It is now possible to integrate historical data, field observations and measurements, and remotely sensed data (satellite and electronic field sensors) into models for climate prediction and agricultural production so that a decision support system can assist decision-makers in implementing informed policies for future water and agricultural development.[71]

At the basin or national scale, mismanagement of water is evident in the iron-triangle concept.[72] In this model, the benefits of water development are distributed among stakeholders and may not necessarily be manifested within the water system. The controlling entity (Congress) creates legislation to assist local parties within a basin by creating a project; a bureaucratic entity such as the Bureau of Reclamation administers the project; and local stakeholders receive the project benefits. For Native Americans, a fourth dimension to the "iron triangle" is the Bureau of Indian Affairs, which could possibly oversee project management on reservations. Thus, local control of the watershed is lost in the politics of the "iron triangle." In contrast, Powell's water management at the watershed level allows partnerships between federal, state, and local stakeholders for place-based planning instead of a "stovepipe" approach coming down from the federal government.[73]

In line with Powell's thinking, a broader management structure for Western lands needs to be underpinned by a full understanding of different landscape elements.[74] This concept follows an ecosystem management scheme being used by water resource teams in the West. The Columbia River Basin integrated management plan is an example of how this model can be used in large basin management.[75] For Native Americans, an additional factor is traditional ecological knowledge manifested by a community-based "sense of place" that incorporates major cultural elements into tribal perspectives of place and the ecosystem.[76] The cultural aspects of religion, history, language, social and political organization, ceremonies, and material components (art and music) go beyond just knowing an area's physical and environmental facets.[77] Native Americans' culturally rooted knowledge provides an understanding deeper than the environmental and economic properties of the area, knowledge that embraces the totality of available ecosystem services. It is this whole that needs to be integrated into basin and watershed management strategies.[78]

For Western reservations, tribal authorities act as the central control, with the whole reservation community as the local emphasis. Tribal councils determine "beneficial uses" of water and build them into water codes. A common conception, exemplified by the Navajo Water Code, is that all natural resources are interconnected and that water resources have "cultural, spiritual and economic values that guide the appropriate use."[79] As this provision illustrates, it is imperative not only to know the cultural significance of water and other natural resources, but to allow the tribal community to practice that significance in management decisions.[80]

Moving to the second element, the Native American reservation system is the one example in which Powell's concept that water rights should be tied to land rights (appurtenance) can be correctly applied.[81] The *Winters* doctrine provides that water was implicitly reserved upon the creation of reservations.[82] In this manner, reservation trust lands are a single block to which reserved rights adhere based upon the date of the treaty, statute, or executive order creating the reservation, and thus reserved rights cannot be sold or transferred on a permanent basis.[83] This binds the water to the land. The amount and type of water use permitted by a reserved right is determined by two factors: the purpose of the reservation per *Winters* and, for agricultural reservations, the reservation's PIA per *Arizona v. California*. Generally, the purpose of reservations was to acculturate tribes to farming so they could be self-sufficient and eventually assimilate into mainstream US society.[84] As tribes defined their water rights in court, they would have to negotiate the amount of water use permitted by classifying their lands as irrigable or non-irrigable and determining the amount of water needed to sustain typical crops for the area.[85] This calculation would provide the amount of water possibly available to a reservation. As discussed earlier, Colorado River Basin tribes currently hold 2.9 maf of annual diversion rights, although further negotiations and litigation may increase this value.[86] The important aspect to consider, however, is that water on reservations is not just for irrigation, but rather should also include religious, ceremonial, ecological, and other beneficial uses. An additional beneficial use can be for economic development, financed by utilizing water as a commodity to be leased off-reservation. The Ten Tribes Partnership has developed a water management strategy of this sort.[87]

Regarding the third element, as the Colorado River Basin and other parts of the West were being settled, the balance between the land offered to Euro-Americans by public land laws (such as the Homestead, Desert Lands, and Timber Culture acts) and the efficient use of water was becoming dubious. Powell proposed that smaller parcels for irrigation would use water more efficiently than the larger parcels provided for by the acts. He thought parcels for irrigation of about 80 acres with pasturage were necessary to make livestock raising worthwhile—a total of 2,560 acres.[88] Thus, eight to ten landholders in a single watershed would possess about 25,600 acres (102.6 square kilometers). Powell's community area compares remarkably to the average size of watersheds within the Upper Basin and Lower Basin, which are calculated to be 22,819 acres (92.35 square kilometers) and 23,945 acres (96.91 square kilometers), respectively.[89]

Powell's theme in the *Arid Lands Report* and elsewhere of smaller parcels being managed in hydrographic basins corresponds to the Mormon pattern of settlement during the mid-1800s. Fradkin reiterates a statement by a religious leader that under the Mormon agrarian doctrine, "[a] little farm well cultivated near homes, I know, is your doctrine and it is mine and ever was."[90] Smaller well-organized farms provide a more efficient use of the irrigable land and water, both of which are limited in the arid region, as Powell well understood. According to the USDA Agricultural Census, average farms on the surveyed reservations are generally family-operated and, depending on the reservation, smaller than 80 acres.[91] Thus, Powell's proposal actually follows the reality of Native American farm size.

Adjudications and water rights settlements predicated on *Winters* and *Arizona v. California* provide Colorado River Basin tribes with the natural resource to manage and the amount of that resource. In turn, the American Indian Agricultural Resource Management Act of 1993 furnishes tribes with the means to plan and manage the resource for agriculture.[92] The Act provides the following with regard to tribal agricultural resource management plans:

- Tribes will have broad discretion in designing and carrying out the community-based agricultural management planning process.
- Plans will identify available agricultural resources, including lands and infrastructure for crops and range development.
- Plans will state specific tribal agricultural resource goals and objectives.
- Plans will establish agricultural management structures and objectives.
- Plans will identify action strategies to be implemented to obtain identified agricultural goals and objectives.
- The Secretary of the Interior will conduct all management activities on Indian agricultural land in accordance with the goals and objectives set forth in the approved plan.

This Act thus affords tribes in the Colorado River Basin and elsewhere the ability to integrate their agricultural land resources with their water resources as stated in self-determined goals, objectives, and actions (policies) for irrigated lands. Thus, basin tribes can control their land and water within a plan that they themselves construct.

VENTURING INTO THE UNKNOWN . . . FUTURE

Native Americans existed in the Colorado River Basin and broader Southwest for centuries before Euro-Americans infiltrated the region. During this time, they farmed and lived off the land through cyclical changes in the climate. Their ability to adapt to the environmental changes allowed their cultures to survive and at times thrive. With the political, economic, and social constraints imposed on them by Euro-American governments over the last four hundred years, basin tribes' capacity to cope with the changing environmental and economic landscape has been diminished. Powell's concept of localized watershed management offers a mechanism by which these tribes can manage their own land and water resources. The reservation system provides the sovereignty structure for the tribes to administer their lands, and the *Winters* doctrine and *Arizona v. California* set the framework for water management. As basin tribes develop their land/water management plans, they can prioritize beneficial water uses that best fit their future cultural and economic needs in the Great Unknown. To accomplish this task, it will take a collaboration among all major stakeholders: the citizens on the reservations, the tribal councils, and the layers of local, state, and federal agencies. Tribal development of land and water resources for agricultural purposes will need to be flexible in coming decades.[93] Climate change predictions forecast warmer temperatures and a decrease in precipitation and streamflow for the Southwest. A potential strategy for Native Americans is to use traditional ecological knowledge and to adjust agricultural priorities to the land capabilities demonstrated by their ancestors—that is, limiting agriculture to prime and concentrated areas. This may lessen the scope of basin tribes' agricultural lands, but will possibly provide higher yields and make more water available for other uses. With modern computer and satellite technologies to monitor weather/climate patterns coupled with water characteristics, soil conditions, and land use changes, tribal leadership has the tools to make informed decisions—both short- and long-term.

NOTES

1. Edward H. Spicer, *Cycles of Conquest: The Impact of Spain, Mexico, and the United States on the Indians of the Southwest, 1533–1960* (Tucson: University of Arizona Press, 1962).

2. Edward Dolnick, *Down the Great Unknown: John Wesley Powell's 1869 Journey of Discovery and Tragedy Through the Grand Canyon* (New York: Harper-Collins, 2001).

3. James M. Adovasio and David Pedler, "Peopling of North America," in *North American Archaeology*, ed. Timothy R. Pauketat and Diana DiPaolo Loren (Malden, MA: Blackwell, 2005), 30–55.

4. John C. McGregor, *Southwestern Archaeology*, 2nd ed. (Urbana: University of Illinois Press, 1965).

5. Harry J. Shafer, "Prehistoric Agricultural Climax in Southwestern New Mexico: The Classic Mimbres Phase," in *Southwestern Agriculture: Pre-Columbian to Modern*, ed. Henry C. Dethloff and Irvin M. May (College Station: Texas A&M University Press, 1982), 3–15; Richard B. Woodbury and Ezra B. W. Zubrow, "Agricultural Beginnings, 2000 B.C.-500 A.D.," in *Handbook of North American Indians: Southwest*, vol. 9, ed. Alfonso Ortiz (Washington, DC: Smithsonian, 1979).

6. Adolf F. Bandelier, "Alvar Nunez Cabeza De Vaca," in *The Classic Southwest: Readings in Archaeology, Ethnohistory, and Ethnology*, ed. Basil C. Hedrick, et al. (Carbondale: Southern Illinois University Press, 1973), 42–50.

7. Ibid., 45.

8. Jay J. Wagoner, *Early Arizona: Prehistory to Civil War* (Tucson: University of Arizona Press, 1975); Richard L. Nostrand, *The Hispano Homeland* (Norman: University of Oklahoma Press, 1992).

9. John L. Kessell, *Spain in the Southwest: A Narrative History of Colonial New Mexico, Arizona, Texas, and California* (Norman: University of Oklahoma Press, 2002). John F. Bannon, *The Spanish Borderlands Frontier, 1513–1821* (Albuquerque: University of New Mexico Press, 1974).

10. Wallace Stegner, *Beyond the Hundredth Meridian: John Wesley Powell and the Second Opening of the American West* (Boston: Houghton Mifflin, 1954).

11. Robert M. Utley, *The Indian Frontier of the American West, 1846–1890* (Albuquerque: University of New Mexico Press, 1984).

12. Robert M. Utley, *Frontiersmen in Blue: The United States Army and the Indian, 1848–1865* (Lincoln: University of Nebraska Press, 1981).

13. Gouverneur Kemble Warren, et al., *Map of the Territory of the United States from the Mississippi River to the Pacific Ocean: ordered by Jeff Davis, Secretary of War to accompany the reports of the explorations for a railroad route.* (Washington, DC: War Department, 1863).

14. Commissioner of Indian Affairs, *Annual Report of the Commissioner of Indian Affairs to the Secretary of Interior, 1875* (Washington, DC: Government Printing Office, 1875).

15. John Wesley Powell, *The Exploration of the Colorado River and Its Canyons* (New York: Penguin Books, 1875).

16. Ibid., 181, 184.

17. Ibid., 184.

18. Douglas W. Schwartz, "Havasupai," in *Handbook of North American Indians: Southwest*, vol. 10, ed. Alfonso Ortiz (Washington, DC: Government Printing Office, 1983), 15.

19. Powell, *Exploration*, 274.

20. Wagoner, *Early Arizona*, 87; Thomas Sheridan, *Arizona: A History* (Tucson: University of Arizona Press, 1995), 43.

21. Commissioner of Indian Affairs, *1875 Annual Report*.

22. Roland Chardon, "The Elusive Spanish League: A Problem of Measurement in Sixteenth-Century New Spain," *The Hispanic American Historical Review* 60, no.2 (1980): 294–302.

23. Ray H. Mattison, "Early Spanish and Mexican Settlements in Arizona," *New Mexico Historical Review* 21, no. 4 (1946): 273–327.

24. J.J. Bowden, "Spanish and Mexican Land Grants in the Southwest," *Land & Water Law Review* 8, no. 2 (1975): 467–512; W.A. Keleher, "Law of the New Mexico Land Grant," *New Mexico Historical Review* 4, no. 4 (1929): 350–71.

25. Stephen L. Pevar, *The Rights of Indians and Tribes*, 4th ed. (Oxford: Oxford University Press, 2012), 259.

26. Commissioner of Indian Affairs, *Annual Report of the Commissioner of Indian Affairs to the Secretary of Interior, 1850* (Washington, DC: Government Printing Office, 1850).

27. Treaty with the Ute Indians, March 2, 1868, 15 Stat. 619.

28. Francis Paul Prucha, *American Indian Policy in the Formative Years: The Indian Trade and Intercourse Acts, 1790–1834* (Lincoln: University of Nebraska Press, 1983).

29. William deBuys, ed., *Seeing Things Whole: The Essential John Wesley Powell* (Washington, DC: Island Press, 2001), 106.

30. Donald Worster, *A River Running West: The Life of John Wesley Powell* (New York: Oxford University Press, 2001), 270–71.

31. Kirke Kickingbird and Karen Ducheneaux, *One Hundred Million Acres* (New York: Macmillan, 1973); Janet A. McDonnell, *The Dispossession of the American Indian, 1887–1934* (Bloomington: Indiana University Press, 1991).

32. John Wesley Powell, *Report on the Lands of the Arid Region of the United States: With a More Detailed Account of the Lands of Utah, 1878*, in *The Arid Lands*, ed. Wallace Stegner (Lincoln: University of Nebraska Press, 1962), 50.

33. US Census Bureau, "Cartographic Boundary Shapefiles," accessed October 30, 2018, https://www.census.gov/geo/maps-data/data/cbf/cbf_aiannh.html.

34. US Department of Agriculture, *2017 Census of Agriculture: American Indian Reservations*, vol. 2, Subject Series, Part 5, AC-17-S5, National Agricultural Statistics Service (Washington, DC: Government Printing Office, 2019).

35. Paul B. Thompson, *The Agrarian Vision: Sustainability and Environmental Ethics* (Lexington: University Press of Kentucky, 2010).

36. Keith Douglass Warner, *Agroecology in Action: Extending Alternative Agriculture Through Social Networks* (Cambridge, MA: MIT Press, 2007); R. Douglas Hurt, *Indian Agriculture in America: Prehistory to the Present* (Lawrence: University Press of Kansas, 1987).

37. Hurt, *Indian Agriculture*, 214–27.

38. Navajo Nation Department of Agriculture, "Vision Statement," accessed October 30, 2018, http://www.agriculture.navajo-nsn.gov/nnda.html.

39. "Welcome," Navajo Nation Department of Agriculture, accessed October 30, 2018, www.agriculture.navajo-nsn.gov.

40. US Bureau of Reclamation, *Colorado River Basin Water Supply and Demand Study: Appendix C9* (2012), 29, http://www.usbr.gov/lc/region/programs/crbstudy/finalreport/Study%20Report/CRBS_Study_Report_AppendixC.pdf.

41. Charles Meyers, "The Colorado River," *Stanford Law Review* 19, no. 1 (1966): 1–75; Jason Anthony Robison, "The Colorado River Revisited," *University of Colorado Law Review* 88, no. 3 (2017): 475–569.

42. Colorado River Water Users Association, "Ten Tribes Partnership," accessed October 30, 2018, https://www.crwua.org/colorado-river/ten-tribes.

43. US Bureau of Reclamation, *Colorado River Basin Water Supply and Demand Study, Study Report* (2012), http://www.usbr.gov/lc/region/programs/crbstudy/finalreport/Study%20Report/CRBS_Study_Report_Final.pdf (hereafter, *CRBWSDS*).

44. Monroe Price, *Law and the American Indian: Readings, Notes and Cases* (Indianapolis: Bobbs-Merrill Company, 1973), 365–66.

45. Bureau of Reclamation, *CRBWSDS, Appendix C9*.

46. US Department of Agriculture, *2017 Census*, Table 1, Land in Farms, Farms by Size, Farms by Value of Sales.

47. National Research Council, *Water Management: Evaluating and Adjusting to Hydroclimatic Variability* (Washington, DC: National Academies Press, 2007).

48. Powell, *Exploration*, 18.

49. Amy Cordalis and Daniel Cordalis, "Indian Water Rights: How *Arizona v. California* Left an Unwanted Cloud over the Colorado River Basin," *Arizona Journal of Environmental Law & Policy* 5 (2014): 333–62.

50. Bureau of Reclamation, *CRBWSDS*.

51. Powell, *Arid Lands Report*, 82–84.

52. K. Hayhoe, et al., "Our Changing Climate," in *Impacts, Risks, and Adaptation in the United States: Fourth National Climate Assessment, Volume II*, ed. D.R. Reidmiller, et al., US Global Change Research Program, (Washington, DC, 2018), 72–144.

53. P. Gonzalez, et al., "Southwest," in *Impacts, Risks, and Adaptation*, 1101–84.

54. Ibid., 1109.

55. Charles L. Walthall, et al., "Climate Change and Agriculture in the United States: Effects and Adaptation," *Geological and Atmospheric Sciences Reports* 1 (2013), http://lib.dr.iastate.edu/ge_at_reports; Stephen R. Gliessman,

Agroecology: Ecological Processes in Sustainable Agriculture (Chelsea: Ann Arbor Press, 1998), 82.

56. D.R. Easterling, et al., "Precipitation change in the United States," in *Climate Science Special Report: Fourth National Climate Assessment, Volume I*, ed. D.J. Wuebbles, et al., US Global Change Research Progam (Washington, DC, 2017), 207–230, https://science2017.globalchange.gov/downloads/CSSR2017_FullReport.pdf.

57. Hayhoe, *Our Changing Climate*, 91.

58. Gonzalez, *Southwest*, 1112.

59. Ibid.

60. Ibid., 1137.

61. US Bureau of Reclamation, *Colorado River Basin Water Supply and Demand Study, Executive Summary* (2012), 8, https://www.usbr.gov/lc/region/programs/crbstudy/finalreport/Executive%20Summary/CRBS_Executive_Summary_FINAL.pdf.

62. Bureau of Reclamation, *CRBWSDS*, 84.

63. Ibid., 298.

64. L.C. Jantarasami, et al., "Tribes and Indigenous Peoples," in *Impacts, Risks, and Adaptation*, 572–603.

65. Ibid., 579.

66. Ibid., 584.

67. Ibid.

68. Mark K. Briggs, *Riparian Ecosystem Recovery in Arid Lands: Strategies and References* (Tucson: University of Arizona Press, 1996); K.N. Brooks, et al., *Hydrology and the Management of Watersheds*, 2nd ed. (Ames: Iowa State University Press, 1997), 269–85.

69. Takashi Gomi, et al., "Understanding Processes and Downstream Linkages of Headwater Systems," *BioScience* 52, no. 10 (2002): 905–16.

70. deBuys, *Seeing Things Whole*, 3.

71. Lynn E. Johnson, *Geographic Information Systems in Water Resources Engineering* (Boca Raton, FL: CRC Press, 2009); C. Giupponi and P.E.V. Van-Walsum, "3.6 Integrated assessment tools and decision support systems," in *The Adaptive Water Resource Management Handbook*, ed. J. Mysiak, et al. (London: Earthscan, 2010), 57–62.

72. Daniel McCool, *Command of the Waters: Iron Triangles, Federal Water Development, and Indian Water* (Berkeley: University of California Press, 1987); Jantarasami, "Tribes and Indigenous Peoples," 583.

73. Andrea K. Gerlak, "Federalism and US water policy," in *Federal Rivers: Managing Water in Multi-Layered Political Systems*, ed. D. Garrick et al. (Cheltenham, UK: IWA Publishing, 2014), 41–56.

74. deBuys, *Seeing Things Whole*, 5.

75. Thomas M. Quigley, et al. eds., *Integrated Scientific Assessment for Ecosystem Management in the Interior Columbia Basin: And Portions of the Klamath and Great Basins* (Portland, OR: US Department of Agriculture, 1996).

76. Yi-Fu Tuan, *Topophilia: A Study of Environmental Perception, Attitudes, and Values* (Englewood Cliffs, NJ: Prentice-Hall, 1974); Jay Johnson and

Soren Larsen, "Introduction: A Deeper Sense of Place," in *A Deeper Sense of Place: Stories and Journeys of Collaboration in Indigenous Research*, ed. Jay T. Johnson and Soren C. Larsen (Corvallis: Oregon State University Press, 2013), 7–18.

77. Imre Sutton, *Indian Land Tenure: Bibliographical Essays and a Guide to the Literature* (New York: Clearwater Publishing, 1975).

78. Ian Convery, et al., eds., *Making Sense of Place: Multidisciplinary Perspectives* (Woodbridge, UK: Boydell Press, 2012).

79. Navajo Water Code (Window Rock, AZ: unpublished document, 1984).

80. C. Flanagan and M. Laituri, "Local Cultural Knowledge and Water Resource Management: The Wind River Indian Reservation," *Environmental Management* 33, no. 2 (2004): 262–70.

81. Powell, *Arid Lands Report*, 187.

82. Felix S. Cohen, *Handbook of Federal Indian Law* (Albuquerque: University of New Mexico Press, 1942), 316–19; Price, *Law and the American Indian*, 310–29.

83. Monique C. Shay, "Promises of a Viable Homeland, Reality of Selective Reclamation: A Study of the Relationship Between the *Winters* Doctrine and Federal Water Development in the Western United States," *Ecology Law Quarterly* 19, no. 547 (1992): 579–83; Justin Nyberg, "The Promise of Indian Water Leasing: An Examination of One Tribe's Success at Brokering Its Surplus Water Rights," *Natural Resources Journal* 55, no. 181 (2014): 181–203.

84. Hurt, *Indian Agriculture*, 118.

85. Shay, "Promises of a Viable Homeland," 580.

86. Bureau of Reclamation, *CRBWSDS, Appendix C9*.

87. "The Ten Tribes Partnership and Water Marketing in the Colorado River Basin," *Tribal Water Uses in the Colorado River Basin*, accessed October 30, 2018, http://www.tribalwateruse.org/?page_id = 682.

88. Powell, *Arid Lands Report*, 28.

89. "National Hydrography, Watershed Boundary Dataset," accessed July 30, 2018, https://www.usgs.gov/core-science-systems/ngp/national-hydrography/watershed-boundary-dataset?qt-science_support_page_related_con = 4#qt-science_support_page_related_con.

90. Philip L. Fradkin, *A River No More: The Colorado River and the West* (Berkeley: University of California Press, 1996), 133.

91. US Department of Agriculture, *2017 Census*, Table 1.5–129.

92. American Indian Agricultural Resource Management Act of 1993 (P.L. 103-177; 107 Stat. 2011).

93. Jantarsami, "Tribes and Indigenous Peoples," 574.

Afterword

JOHN C. SCHMIDT

There is no doubt that John Wesley Powell eloquently described the *place* that is the Colorado River Basin, and that description endures today. But what about Powell's *vision* for the river and its watershed; does it also endure? The contributors to *Vision & Place* have pursued that very question.

Powell's 1875 *Exploration of the Colorado River of the West* is a poetic drama that celebrates the Colorado River and its canyons. The book launched Powell's career and made him famous, and he continued to give talks about the 1869 Expedition into his last years of life. Powell's descriptions of the canyon-bound river and the surrounding landscape, first published as a report for the Smithsonian Institution, have stood the test of time. Today, passengers on commercial river trips learn about Powell when their guides read from *Exploration*, including the "Down the Great Unknown" entry that is perhaps Powell's most celebrated. That gives them a sense of the adventure of the 1869 trip—the thrill, fear, dissension, and drama—as well as the sublime beauty of the river and its canyons.

But the legacy of John Wesley Powell is also derived from his vision for the arid lands. As described in the chapters of *Vision & Place,* Powell challenged the know-nothing boosterism of the late 1800s and argued for scientifically-based comprehensive settlement and development of scarce water resources. Powell understood clearly that there were limits to the amount of irrigable land and population growth in the Colorado River Basin and the arid West as a whole. In his Foreword, Charles Wilkinson summarized some of Powell's lasting concepts explored throughout the volume: watershed governance, dryland democracy, collaboration, and traditional ecological knowledge. The chapters of *Vision & Place,* in turn, have asked whether Powell's historic ideas have shaped the region in contemporary times, and whether those ideas should do so in the future. As these chapters reveal, modern citizens of the arid West do not universally share all aspects of Powell's vision.

On a modern Colorado River trip through Grand Canyon, inconsistencies in Powell's vision become apparent. Approximately forty miles downstream from Lees Ferry, most boating parties stop at the Marble Canyon Dam site. Adits were excavated here in the 1950s to evaluate the integrity of the bedrock for a dam. This stop is an unexpected moment when river runners confront technological civilization in what they otherwise perceive as a wilderness reminiscent of Powell's day. From reading and listening to passages in *Exploration,* passengers might even consider the differences between their safe and comfortable boating and abundant food supply, and the fear, apprehension, and hunger of the 1869 Expedition, brought on by poorly designed boats and dwindling supplies of bacon, flour, and coffee.

At the Marble Canyon Dam site, passengers learn about a 310-foot-tall dam once planned at this narrow spot, and hear about David Brower and Martin Litton. Passengers who only know Powell from *Exploration* might be surprised that his subsequent writings about full development of rivers can be logically linked to the proposal to build Marble Canyon Dam. Few passengers appreciate the paradox that Powell's early writing about Marble Canyon's beauty would later be quoted in coffee table books published to stop that very dam. How could Powell have described so eloquently the beauty of the Colorado River's canyons yet also advocated so fervently for dams and diversions—even for complete dewatering of rivers?

Vision & Place brings this paradox to the fore. It is animated by our ongoing struggle to understand the full measure of Powell's vision for water, public lands, and Native Americans within the Colorado River Basin and the arid West.

Today, society struggles to define its goal for the Colorado River. On the one hand, the Colorado River is the most extensively developed large river in the United States, and the basin states, the federal governments of the United States and Mexico, tribes, and agricultural and municipal interests debate and negotiate how the available water supply should be shared. But others have a vision for the river inspired by Powell's eloquent writing in *Exploration,* and some go so far as to argue for decommissioning existing dams. Powell paradoxically inspires both sides of the modern debate.

It is easy to think of the Colorado River only as a source of water. The reservoirs of the river and its headwater tributaries are the largest in relation to natural stream flow of any large watershed in North America. Lake Mead and Lake Powell are the two biggest reservoirs in the United States by storage capacity, and they occur in series, separated only by a beautiful bedrock ditch—the Grand Canyon. Half of the entire length of the "Colorado" as originally named—the watercourse beginning at the confluence of the Green and Grand rivers and ending at the Sea of Cortez—has been transformed into reservoirs, and other parts of the river downstream from Hoover Dam have been channelized and lined by levees. Downstream from Morelos Dam near Yuma, the river is usually dry, and the largest city on the banks of the river, San Luis Rio Colorado, looks out on a dry, sandy bed.

From this perspective, modern society has achieved Powell's vision, articulated in the 1878 *Arid Lands Report,* that "[a]ll the waters of all the arid lands will eventually be taken from their natural channels." As described in this volume, Powell's vision reflects his conception of the arid region as "a land of small farm communities and desiccated, empty riverbeds." The *Arid Lands Report* and related articles such as "The Lesson of Conemaugh" and "Institutions for the Arid Lands" envision a region where rivers are typically dry and perhaps only carry occasional runoff from unusually large storms. Today, anyone seeking to reach the Sea of Cortez via the river must *walk* the last sixty miles.

But there are other visions for the Colorado River and its watershed beyond mere water supply. The Colorado River is perhaps the United States' most spectacular river. The Grand Canyon is one of Earth's greatest celebrations of geology and topography. The southern Colorado Plateau has the densest concentration of National Park Service units in the United States. The entire 500-mile length of the Colorado River between the Grand/Green river confluence and Grand Wash Cliffs, where the namesake river leaves the Colorado Plateau, is managed by the National Park Service.

In these dramatic landscapes that Powell described so elegantly, the National Park Service celebrates John Wesley Powell's legacy, and the park visitor is encouraged to connect landscape spectacle with Powell. A monument to Powell, at Powell Point near Grand Canyon Village, was built in 1912 to honor him and the crews of his 1869 and 1871/1872 expeditions. The landscape and the view are incomparable. Far to the northwest is the Powell Plateau on the opposite side of the Colorado River. Would Powell have felt honored by this effort to associate him with landscape?

Landscape spectacle is also evident where Glen Canyon Dam impounds the Colorado River to form Lake Powell. Here, the National Park Service manages recreation on what is arguably the most beautiful reservoir in the world—a reservoir that inundates one of the most beautiful canyons in the world named by Powell for its many "glens" of tiny springs covered by ferns and mosses. Some of those who swim, water ski, explore, and sleep in houseboats on Lake Powell may have no idea who Powell was. It is easy to repeatedly enjoy Lake Powell's waters without knowing much about the reservoir's namesake or the paradox between the Powell of sublime landscapes and the Powell of utilitarian water development. The chapters of *Vision & Place* attest to how the Colorado River's future essentially revolves around the challenge of reconciling these two visions.

Reconciliation is now forced by progressively declining watershed runoff. As described in the volume, the watershed's stakeholders debate how to share the pain of declining available water supply while also maintaining ecosystem values and endangered species. Powell's historical call for watershed governance certainly is a modern inspiration for negotiating how to divide the Colorado River system's declining water supplies. Even water managers in the most politically conservative parts of the watershed accept the truth of declining watershed runoff caused by climate change.

The Colorado River Basin is the water supply for 40 million people, but the river is also spiritual and recreational sustenance for the nation and even the world. Planning for the river's future requires precise articulation of both water supply and natural values, and ultimately an integrated vision that will be as complex and potentially contradictory as Powell's vision in the late 1800s. Implicit in contemporary molding of the Law of the River to the reality of climate change is the question of how much water should be used by agriculture and growing cities, and how much to invest in making consumptive water uses more efficient. There are no "right" answers when addressing these issues, but the watershed's citizens and governments must reach consensus on a common vision—a point well emphasized in this volume's chapters addressing collaborative water governance.

Declining water supplies and a growing population bring society to the brink of fundamental decisions about our vision of the future. No approach is inherently "right." Instead, there are competing visions of very different futures. Should the emphasis be on sustaining agriculture, growing ever-larger cities, or protecting the natural environment? The native river ecosystems explored by Powell have been profoundly transformed, and no part of the river can ever be completely restored to the conditions that existed in 1869. The demands placed on the modern river have fundamentally changed all of the drivers of natural ecosystems, and scores of non-native species have been introduced. The interplay between the societal good provided by water-supply development and the inevitable ecosystem change caused by dams and diversions means that society must decide what balance between utilitarian and natural ecosystem processes should exist in the river network moving forward.

Today, only a small proportion of the Colorado River at its most downstream end in Mexico is entirely dry except for occasional floods. As noted, only in the river delta does the river realize that part of Powell's vision that stream flow be entirely diverted for utilitarian use. And even here scientists and environmental groups seek to find a way to "waste" a tiny bit of the Colorado River so that flow can reach the sea, thereby sustaining a narrow strip of riparian vegetation. In March 2014, history was made when a month-long pulse of water bypassed Morelos Dam and a small part of the river reached saltwater. But today, that river bed is again dry, and it is unclear if such pulse flows will ever be repeated.

Upstream from Morelos Dam and the Delta, the Colorado River is extensively fragmented by Hoover, Davis, Parker, Painted Rock, and Imperial dams. Here, the river is progressively depleted by distribution to southern Nevada, southern California, central and southern Arizona, riverside irrigation districts, and the Imperial Valley, while the last bit of water is diverted to the Mexicali Valley at Morelos Dam. Powell's vision for the Lower Colorado River surely included its depletion by channel-side irrigation districts, but he may not have envisioned long aqueducts snaking across the Mojave and Sonoran deserts to distant cities. And the Imperial Valley's massive Imperial Irrigation District, with its corporate agriculture, may not comport with Powell's vision for watershed democracy.

Many other questions loom about Powell's vision for the Lower Colorado River. He might have been inspired by the Lower Basin states' recent efforts to write a drought contingency plan, but it is hard to imagine what he might think about the Lower Colorado River Multi-Species Conservation Program. Likewise, we cannot know what Powell would think of the significant water rights held by Native American tribes today. As described in the chapters of *Vision & Place,* Powell imagined that these tribes would not even exist in the distant future. Thus, Powell's vision of Native Americans was perhaps as paradoxical as his perceptions of nature, and does not provide an enlightened path toward postcolonialism.

Upstream from Lake Mead, the Grand Canyon appears wild to the casual eye, but not to the observant river ecologist. The river's daily flow is wholly controlled by releases from Glen Canyon Dam that are determined by allocation agreements and the production of hydroelectricity. Today's river has little fine sediment, and the river temperature is unusually cool where released from full reservoirs. Often, the river is gin clear—an eerie phenomenon for a river once described as "colorado." Many of the fish species are non-native, and some native species have been extirpated. The river ecologist understands that the Grand Canyon ecosystem is "novel" and not "native," and only vaguely resembles the ecosystem that Powell and his crew survived in 1869. Nevertheless, virtually every contemporary visitor to the Grand Canyon is renewed by the beauty and adventure that still abound.

Today's watershed democracy for the Colorado River in Grand Canyon is complex and robust, and organized as the Glen Canyon Dam Adaptive Management Program. Powell undoubtedly would be surprised that several tribes with direct or spiritual connections to the Grand Canyon—Hopi, Hualapai, Navajo, Southern Paiute, and Zuni—still exist and participate in the program. Conversely, Powell would consider it entirely appropriate that each of the basin's seven state governments participate in, and strongly influence, this program.

In the Grand Canyon, the conflict among contrasting visions for the river is starkly evident. Modern stakeholders have struggled to agree on a common vision for this iconic waterscape. The contrasting visions include a river that provides water supply, hydroelectricity, recreational opportunities, and a mix of native and non-native ecosystem elements. There is also disagreement about which ecosystem elements, which ecosystem services, and which utilitarian benefits should be emphasized. The only agreement is that there is no going back to the ecosystem experienced by Powell and his crew.

Upstream from Lake Powell, much of the channel network remains riverine and has not been transformed into reservoir. Nevertheless, the assemblage of fish species is mostly non-native, and there are dense stands of tamarisk lining the banks. Today's river runners have an opportunity to feel small, alone, perhaps to even imagine themselves on the river in 1869. Nevertheless, the observant ecologist recognizes that only a few segments of the channel network function as they did 150 years ago—the Yampa being the largest. And some tributaries have been dewatered, including stretches of the Duchesne, Price, and San Rafael rivers.

The diversity of impacts caused by dams and diversions in different parts of the basin remind us that there is no universal blueprint for river restoration. In fact, the word "restoration" is inappropriate in defining a vision for the river of the future and plotting that course. There is no obvious answer to what kind of river is desirable. Stakeholders must impose their values to shape a vision of what kinds of novel ecosystems ought to exist in different parts of the Colorado River watershed. Such a conversation is one that Powell might have imagined—and assuredly this is the seed *Vision & Place* aspires to plant. The basin's future will be determined by negotiations on where and how much water should be allocated in various locales. Different strategies for allocating and managing water supply will unavoidably create, destroy, or change novel ecosystems in each part of the watershed. We will have to decide what kinds of novel ecosystems should be created or maintained in different parts of the basin.

In this sense, Powell did not realize that "use" of the Colorado River system does not require that every river go dry and every ecosystem be transformed. Today, "full consumption" of the Colorado River system includes ecosystem services, opportunities for spiritual renewal, and recreation. Society must decide the degree to which each part of the river system is to be transformed, and which parts should be protected. Because so many senior water rights exist in the Lower Basin, large parts of the upstream river network will always have significant water flow to fulfill these downstream rights. Only in the Delta is there a fundamental, and perhaps insurmountable, challenge to provide sufficient water to the wetlands and marshes of an area Aldo Leopold once dubbed the "Green Lagoons." In this sense, the geography of consumptive water use guarantees that much of the Colorado River system will always remain a "river," not a dry channel bed.

How should society make decisions about future climate change, declining runoff, water consumption, mitigation strategies for novel ecosystems, and possibly decommissioning dams? As proposed by the chapters of *Vision & Place*, perhaps John Wesley Powell's vision of watershed democracy can guide us. Although today's policy debates about the Colorado River are typically led by lawyers and engineers, scientists, with an ever-growing body of evidence on ecosystem requirements, can influence future negotiations regarding when and where to store water for consumptive water use.

John Wesley Powell knew that science proceeds by proposing, testing, analyzing, rejecting, and revising hypotheses. Paradigms arise, persist, founder, and are sometimes discarded. River science will inevitably change and evolve as new measurements are made, monitoring results interpreted, and alternative paradigms proposed. Public policy for the Colorado River Basin's future must be guided by robust river science that is rich, modern, comprehensive, and predictive. This science must continually assess the impacts of water supply allocation and hydropower production, and re-evaluate strategies to achieve desired outcomes for ecosystems, regional/local/tribal economies, tribal spiritual and cultural values, and democratic distribution of access to water supply, recreation, and ecosystem services. Perhaps this is John Wesley Powell's long-lasting legacy in the "Great Unknown"—the commitment to establish and maintain a science infrastructure that can help inform decisions by the watershed's citizens about the future of the river and its basin. In this way, vision will continue to shape place.

References

John Wesley Powell's ideas offer a complex lens through which to examine Euro-American settlement of the Colorado River Basin and the broader West. Powell lived during a period when single individuals—particularly, those of privileged ethnicity and gender—could exercise inordinate influence on the United States' development as it expanded into the arid region. Powell identified issues that have vexed the region continuously since the 1869 Expedition and even earlier. To promote dialogue about these issues, this volume has relied on the foundational topics of water, public lands, and Native Americans. Extensive bibliographic references to Powell's writings and statements on these topics appear in Marcia L. Thomas, *John Wesley Powell: An Annotated Bibliography* (Westport, CT: ABC-CLIO/Greenwood, 2004), and William deBuys, ed., *Seeing Things Whole: The Essential John Wesley Powell* (Washington, DC: Island Press, 2001). The list below identifies Powell's key writings and statements in these areas. It aims not only to invite readers to explore Powell's ideas—prescient, outdated, or otherwise—but also to encourage readers to push their own thoughts into the future. The latter goal has animated *Vision & Place* for the collaborating authors, artists, cartographers, and editors.

POPULAR

"An Overland Trip to the Grand Cañon." *Scribner's Monthly* 10 (1875): 659–78.
Exploration of the Colorado River of the West and Its Tributaries. Washington, DC: Government Printing Office, 1875.
"The Ancient Province of Tusayan." *Scribner's Monthly* 11 (1875): 193–213.
First Through the Grand Canyon: Being the Record of the Pioneer Exploration of the Colorado River in 1869–70. New York: Nelson Doubleday, 1915.
Canyons of the Colorado. Meadville, PA: Flood and Vincent, 1895.

WATER & PUBLIC LANDS

Geographical and Geological Surveys West of the Mississippi. 43rd Cong., 1st Sess., H. Rept. 612 Serial 1626, 9–10, 46–56. Washington, DC: Government Printing Office, 1874.

Report on the Lands of the Arid Region of the United States: With a More Detailed Account of the Lands of Utah, With Maps. Washington, DC: Government Printing Office, 1878.

"The Administration of the Scientific Work of the General Government." *Science* 5 (1885): 51–55.

The Geological Survey, Statement of J.W. Powell. In *Statements Before Subcommittee on the Sundry Civil Bill.* 50th Cong., 1st Sess., S. Rept. 1814, Serial 2525, 63–72, 111–26. Washington, DC: Government Printing Office, 1888.

Letter From the Secretary of the Interior, Transmitting, in Response to Senate Resolution of Feb. 13, 1888, Report Concerning the Irrigation of Certain Lands. 50th Cong., 1st Sess., S. Ex. Doc. 134, Serial 2513. Washington, DC: Government Printing Office, 1888.

Letter From the Secretary of the Interior, Transmitting, in Response to Senate Resolution of March 27, 1888, Report Relative to the Reservoirs for the Storage of Water in the Arid Regions of the United States. 50th Cong., 1st Sess., S. Ex. Doc. 163, Serial 2513, 2–6. Washington, DC: Government Printing Office, 1888.

"Trees on Arid Lands." *Science* 12 (1888): 170–71.

Address to the Montana Constitutional Convention, August 9, 1889. In *Proceedings and Debates of the Constitutional Convention*, 820–23. Helena: State Publishing Company, 1921.

Address to the North Dakota Constitutional Convention, August 5, 1889. *Reclamation Era* 26, no. 9 (1936): 201–2.

Letter From the Secretary of the Interior, Transmitting, in Pursuance of Law, Report of the Geological Survey on the Subject of Irrigation, 50th Cong., 2nd Sess., S. Ex. Doc. 43, Serial 2610, 3–12. Washington, DC: Government Printing Office, 1889.

"The Lesson of Conemaugh." *North American Review* 149 (1889): 150–56.

Report of the Special Committee of the United States Senate on the Irrigation and Reclamation of Arid Lands. 51st Cong., 1st Sess., S. Rept. 928, Serial 2708, Pt. 5, vol. 4, 5–95, 151–204. Washington, DC: Government Printing Office, 1890.

"Institutions for the Arid Lands." *Century* 40 (1890): 111–116.

"The Irrigable Lands of the Arid Region." *Century* 39 (1890): 766–76.

"The Non-Irrigable Lands of the Arid Region." *Century* 39 (1890): 915–22.

Statement of Maj. J.W. Powell, Director of the Geological Survey, on *Ceding the Arid Lands to the States and Territories.* 51st Cong., 2nd Sess., H. Rept. 3767, Serial 2888, 11–202. Washington, DC: Government Printing Office, 1891.

"The New Lake in the Desert." *Scribner's Monthly* 10 (1891): 463–68.

"Address and Comments." *Official Report of the International Irrigation Congress*, vol. 2, 107–16. Los Angeles: Los Angeles Chamber of Commerce, 1893.

"The Water Supplies in the Arid Region." *Irrigation Age* 6 (1894): 54–65.
"Ownership of Lands in the Arid Region." *Irrigation Age* 6 (1894): 143–49.

NATIVE AMERICANS

Indians West of the Rocky Mountains: Statement of Major J. W. Powell Made Before the Committee on Indian Affairs as to the Condition of the Indian Tribes West of the Rocky Mountains. 43rd Cong, 1st Sess., H. Misc. Doc. 86, Serial 1618. Washington, DC: Government Printing Office, 1874.

Report of Special Commissioners J. W. Powell and G. W. Ingalls on the Condition of the Ute Indians of Utah; the Paiutes of Utah, Northern Arizona, Southern Nevada, and Southeastern California; the Go-Si-Utes of Utah and Nevada; the Northwestern Shoshones of Idaho and Utah; and the Western Shoshones of Nevada; and Report Concerning Claims of Settlers in the Moa-Pa Valley, Southeastern Nevada. Washington, DC: Government Printing Office, 1874.

"A Discourse on the Philosophy of the North American Indians." *Journal of the American Geographical Society of New York* 8 (1876): 251–68.

"Human Evolution." *Transactions of the Anthropological Society of Washington* 2 (1883): 176–208.

"Certain Principles of Primitive Law." *Science* 4 (1884): 436–37.

"From Savagery to Barbarism." *Transactions of the Anthropological Society of Washington* 3 (1885): 173–96.

"From Barbarism to Civilization." *American Anthropologist* 1 (1888): 97–123.

"Are Our Indians Becoming Extinct?" *Forum* 15 (1893): 343–54.

"Proper Training and the Future of the Indians." *Forum* 18 (1895): 622–29.

"Relation of Primitive Peoples to Environment, Illustrated by American Examples." In *Annual Report of the Board of Regents of the Smithsonian Institution*, 625–37. Washington, DC: Government Printing Office, 1896.

"On Primitive Institutions." In *Report of the 19th Annual Meeting of the American Bar Association*, 573–93. Philadelphia: Dando, 1896.

Contributors

AUTHORS

ROBERT W. ADLER, Distinguished Professor, S.J. Quinney College of Law, University of Utah

AUTUMN L. BERNHARDT, Instructor, College of Liberal Arts, Colorado State University; Non-citizen, Lakota Nation

AMY CORDALIS, General Counsel, Yurok Tribe; Yurok Tribal Member

DANIEL CORDALIS, Attorney; Navajo Nation Tribal Member

WILLIAM DEBUYS, Author and Conservationist, El Valle, New Mexico

ROBERT GLENNON, Regents' Professor & Morris K. Udall Professor of Law & Public Policy, James E. Rogers College of Law, University of Arizona

WILLIAM J. GRIBB, Professor Emeritus, Department of Geography, University of Wyoming

PAUL HIRT, Professor of History, Senior Sustainability Scholar, Arizona State University

ROBERT B. KEITER, Distinguished Professor & Wallace Stegner Professor of Law, S.J. Quinney College of Law, University of Utah

AMORINA LEE-MARTINEZ, Ph.D. Candidate, Environmental Studies Program, University of Colorado, Boulder

PATRICIA LIMERICK, Professor of History, Faculty Director & Chair of the Board, Center of the American West, University of Colorado, Boulder

DANIEL C. MCCOOL, Professor Emeritus, Department of Political Science, University of Utah

WESTON C. MCCOOL, Postdoctoral Researcher, Department of Anthropology, University of California, Santa Barbara

EMILENE OSTLIND, Editor & Communications Coordinator, Haub School of Environment & Natural Resources, University of Wyoming

JOHN C. SCHMIDT, Professor, Janet Quinney Lawson Chair in Colorado River Studies, Department of Watershed Sciences, Utah State University

RACHEL ST. JOHN, Associate Professor, Department of History, University of California, Davis

LOUIS S. WARREN, W. Turrentine Jackson Professor of US Western History, Department of History, University of California, Davis

CHARLES F. WILKINSON, Distinguished Professor & Moses Lasky Professor of Law Emeritus, University of Colorado, Boulder

ARTISTS

KATE AITCHISON, Instructor, Rhode Island School of Design; Lecturer in Fine Arts, Brandeis University

BRANDON GELLIS, Assistant Professor of Graphic Design & Emergent Technology, Department of Visual & Literary Arts, University of Wyoming

DAVID JONES, Instructional Art Technician & Research Scientist, Department of Visual & Literary Arts, University of Wyoming

PATRICK KIKUT, Senior Associate Lecturer, Painting, Department of Visual & Literary Arts, University of Wyoming

ERIKA OSBORNE, Associate Professor, Department of Art & Art History, Colorado State University

BAILEY RUSSEL, Associate Academic Professional, Photography, Department of Visual & Literary Arts, University of Wyoming

CHIP THOMAS (AKA "JETSONORAMA"), Photographer, Public Artist, Activist, Physician, Navajo Nation

WILL WILSON, Photography Program Head, School of Arts, Design and Media Arts, Santa Fe Community College; Navajo Nation Tribal Member

CARTOGRAPHERS

P. WILLIAM LIMPISATHIAN, Ph.D. Candidate, Department of Geography, University of Oregon; Graduate Employee, InfoGraphics Lab, University of Oregon

JAMES E. MEACHAM, Executive Director, InfoGraphics Lab, University of Oregon; Senior Research Associate, Department of Geography, University of Oregon

Index

acequia systems of Hispanic communities, xiii, 30, 36, 57. *See also* Spanish exploration and land governance
Agricultural Census (USDA, 2017), 273, 276–277, 283
agriculture: Bureau of Reclamation's diversion projects for, 77; in Dolores River Basin, 55, 57, 59–61, 65; future water use and management for, 43, 90, 277–284; legislation on, 283–284; livestock grazing, 114, 138, 150, 234, 250, 280, 282; pasturage districts for, Powell on, 30–31, 35, 76–77, 106, 139, 149, 182; PIA standard, 228, 276, 277, 282; Powell's descriptions of Ute farms, 269–270; statistics on water use by, 87–88; water transfer programs in, 88. *See also* land governance; water rights; watershed governance
Aitchison, Kate, 8*fig.*, 100–101*fig.*
Ak-Chin Tribe, 269, 270
Albuquerque, New Mexico, 86, 111
All-American Canal, 79
allocation of water resources: *vs.* appropriation, 33, 186; current system of, 77–78. *See also* water rights; watershed governance
allotment program, xvi, 180–181, 251–252, 181, 272–273. *See also* reservations
American Anthropological Association, xx

American Forestry Association, 183
American Indian Agricultural Resource Management Act (1993), 283–284
American Indian Religious Freedom Act (1978), 255. *See also* religious freedom and discrimination; Religious Freedom Restoration Act (RFRA)
American Indians. *See* Native Americans
Ancestral Puebloans, 59, 191. *See also* Native Americans
Ancient Society (Morgan), 204
animal protection. *See* endangered species protection; fish habitat and species protection; wildlife protection
animism, 223, 229–230, 231, 232. *See also* religious freedom and discrimination
annihilation *vs.* assimilation, 202, 214, 224, 238n17. *See also* assimilation
Anthropological Society of Washington, xx
anthropology: as discipline, xx, 207–208; Powell's work in, xxi, 192–193, 212; role in modern resource management, 212–214. *See also* archaeological sites; cultural-stages theory; ethnology
anti-Communist movement, 14–15
Antiquities Act (1906), xxii, 109–110, 184, 185, 213
Apache Tribe, 233–234, 269, 273, 276
Apache Trout, 233–235
Appalachian Trail, 159

appropriation *vs.* allocation of water, 33, 186. *See also* water rights; watershed governance

archaeological sites, 138, 153, 210, 213–214, 256. *See also* anthropology; sacred site protection

Archaeology Southwest, 213

Arches National Park, 111, 115, 117, 118, 154

Arendt, Hannah, 215

aridification *vs.* drought, planning for, 44–45, 56, 83–85. *See also* climate change

Arid Lands Report (Powell): on boundaries and hydrographic districts, 76–77, 95; on climate change, 277–278; on communitarianism, xiii, xiv, 22–23, 28, 67, 130, 150; on federal role in water management, 39; on forest management, 20; land classification scheme in, 130, 149–150; on planned governance, 128–129; reviews of, xxi, 13; Stegner on, 14, 19; Udall on, 173; on water diversions, 17, 19, 291–292. *See also* Powell, John Wesley

Arizona: Arizona Water Settlements Act, 89; Boulder Canyon Project Act and, 79–80; Central Arizona Project (CAP), 77, 80, 88–89, 174, 175; Colorado River Compact and, 79; Firescape program, 143; Native voting rights in, 208; *Navajo Nation v. USFS*, 199, 231–232, 243, 254; Phoenix, 86, 88, 111, 174, 176, 234; Powell's description of, 148, 163; public lands of, 155; Tucson, 86, 111, 174, 176; Yuma, 79. *See also under* Grand Canyon; *names of specific places*; Native Americans

Arizona v. California (1963), 41–42, 79, 80, 228, 275, 276, 282

Arkansas River, 41

Army Corps of Engineers, 136

Aspinall, Wayne, 61, 172, 177

assimilation, 201–207; Powell on, 181, 192, 201–202, 214, 221–222, 224, 246–247; reservation system and, 272–273. *See also* cultural-stages theory; reservations

Auto Immune Response: Confluence of 3 Generations (Wilson), 196–197*fig.*

Babbitt, Bruce, xi

"barbarism." *See* cultural-stages theory

Barboncito, 250–251

Basin Study. See *Colorado River Basin Water Supply and Demand Study* (2012)

Bears Ears Inter-Tribal Coalition, xvii, 112, 213, 244, 256–258

Bears Ears Inter-Tribal Management Commission, 210–211, 256–258

Bears Ears National Monument: cultural resources in, 213; establishment and co-management of, xvi–xviii, 112, 185, 210–211, 244, 256–258; recreation in, 154; reduction of, xxii, xvi–xvii, 112, 119, 162, 185

Beyond the Hundredth Meridian (Stegner), xi, 2, 14–21, 91, 169. *See also* Stegner, Wallace

BIA. *See* Bureau of Indian Affairs (BIA)

biblical interpretation, 225, 226. *See also* Christianity

Black Canyon of the Gunnison, 111

Blackfeet Tribe, 255

BLM. *See* Bureau of Land Management (BLM)

bluehead sucker fish, 62, 63

Boas, Franz, xx, 207. *See also* anthropology

boating. *See* recreation and tourism industry; whitewater recreation

Bosque Redondo, 250–251

Boulder Canyon Project Act (1928), 41, 79–80

Boyden, John, 176

Bridge Canyon Dam (proposed), 174–175, 176, 177, 178

Brower, David, 175, 178, 291. *See also* Sierra Club

brown trout, 62, 63, 234

Bryan, Todd, 70–71

Bryce Canyon National Park, 111, 115, 117

Bundy family, 185

Bureau of American Ethnology (Smithsonian Institution), xiv, xx, 11, 22, 68, 181

Bureau of Forestry, 20. *See also* national forest system and US Forest Service

Bureau of Indian Affairs (BIA), 205, 227, 232, 234, 269, 275

Bureau of Land Management (BLM), xvii, 62, 110, 111, 137

Bureau of Reclamation: Basin Study by, 82–83, 83*fig.*; Colorado River management and, 15; Dolores River Project and McPhee Dam by, 59, 61; establishment of, 40, 77, 136; future projections by, 279; on Powell's legacy, 11, 13; Udall and, 178

Index | 305

Cadillac Desert (Reisner), 175, 236
California: *Arizona v. California* on water rights of, 41–42, 79–80; Boulder Canyon Project Act on, 79; CAP and, 77, 80, 174; forest management in, 136; history of water rights in, 21, 32, 34, 174; Imperial Valley, 38, 79, 293; Interim Surplus Guidelines, 44; reuse water program in, 86. See also *names of specific places*
California Oregon Power v. Beaver Portland Cement (1935), 32
Canyon de Chelly National Monument, 160
Canyonlands National Park, 154, 173–174, 185
CAP. See Central Arizona Project (CAP)
capitalism: *vs.* communalism, 35–36; economic depression and, 136; Powell on, 28, 29. See also corporate power
Capote Ute Band, 271. See also Ute Indian Tribe and reservation
Carson, Kit, 250
Carson, Rachel, xi, 171
Cave Rock sacred site, 255
Central Arizona Project (CAP), 77, 80, 88–89, 174–177
Central Valley Project, 77
Century (publication), 22
Chemehuevi Tribe, 269, 272, 275–276
Cherokee Tribe, 248
Chesapeake Bay Program, 44, 46
Christianity: Indian assimilation and, 202, 220, 223, 227, 243; Meeker and, 249; missionary work, 265; on nature and wilderness, 225–226, 230–231; in Powell's cultural-stages theory, 206, 222. See also religious freedom and discrimination
chub, 62, 63
Churchill, Winston, 127
Civilian Conservation Corps, 136
"civilization." See assimilation; cultural-stages theory
Civil War (1861–1865), 22, 28, 127, 135, 160
Clean Air Act (1963), 110
Clean Water Act (1972), 110
Cleveland, Grover, administration, 129, 184
climate change, xxiii, 1; causes and effects of, 70; deniers of, 24; future watershed governance and, 43, 277–284, 292. See also drought; ecology and preservation of ecosystems; science, as tool for resource management

Clinton, Bill, administration, 185
coal mining, 112, 176. See also mining industry
Cocopah Tribe, 272, 276
Coffin v. Left Hand Ditch (1882), 32
collaborative land and water management, 141, 144; of Colorado River restoration projects, 43–46; between federal–tribal entities, xvii–xviii, 112, 209–211, 213, 231, 255–260; Firescape program, 143; at Glen Canyon Dam, 143; history of, xiii–xiv. See also communitarianism; land governance; watershed governance
colonial land governance, 30, 36, 266, 270–271. See also land governance
Colorado (state): Cortez, 60–61; Denver, 81, 111, 162; Dolores River Basin, 54–55, 59–67, 71–72; future dam projects in, 85; legal cases on water rights, 32; public lands of, 137, 155. See also *names of specific places*
Colorado River Basin, 109–112, 290–295; current water allocation system of, 77–78; dendrochronology and annual flows of, 77, 80–81, 83; future of, 140–144, 186–187, 291; increased recreation and tourism in, 114–116; interstate compact in, 41–42, 43, 79; maps, 5*map*, 98*map*, 194*map*, 267*map*; phases of human activity and exploration of, 266–270, 284; Powell's description of Grand Canyon, xxiii, 18, 108, 148, 156; Powell's description of Northern Arizona, 148, 163; Powell's river expeditions in, xiii, xix–xx, xxi, xxv*map*, 11, 73, 156, 266; public land estate of, 111–112, 114, 137–138, 140; recreation on public lands in, 152–156; restoration projects in, 43–44. See also dams; Grand Canyon; land governance; *names of specific parks and tributaries*; Native Americans; Powell, John Wesley; watershed governance
Colorado River Basin Project Act (1968), 80, 177
Colorado River Basin Water Supply and Demand Study (2012), 82–83, 83*fig*.
Colorado River Commission, 44–45
Colorado River Compact (1922), 41–42, 43, 79, 83, 143, 236
Colorado River Exploring Expedition (1869), xiii, xix–xx, xxv*map*, xxi, 28
Colorado River Indian Tribes, 276

Colorado River Storage Project Act (1956), 173
commons. *See* public lands
communitarianism, 28–29, 47; *vs.* capitalism, 35–36; in forest management, 20; historical perspective on, 32–42; nonprofit and user-controlled institutions, 36–38; Powell on, xiv, 20, 22–23, 28, 67, 130, 150; Powell proposal for watershed governance, 29–32, 57. *See also* collaborative land and water management; watershed governance
Compact Clause of the US Constitution, 41
conservation movement, overview, xi–xiii, 96, 109–110, 116. *See also* ecology and preservation of ecosystems; national park system and National Park Service; public lands
conservation projects, 86, 87. *See also* ecology and preservation of ecosystems; restoration projects
Conundrum Hot Springs, 158, 159
corporate power: *vs.* federal control, 134–135; Powell on, 23, 24, 35–36; public land management and, 162; of water and land resources, 30. *See also* capitalism
Cortez, Colorado, 60–61
Cortez Bootstraps, 61
Cortez Land and Investment Company, 60
Cosmos Club, xx, 22
Culp, Peter, 90
cultural anthropology. *See* anthropology
cultural heritage, defined, 279
cultural-stages theory, 192, 193, 203–204, 206–207, 214, 223–224. *See also* anthropology; assimilation
cultural survival, 196–197*fig.*, 227–228, 260–261. *See also* Native Americans; sacred site protection; self-determination; traditional ecological knowledge
Cuvier Prize, xxi

dams, 5*map*, 132; hydroelectric power from, 79, 85, 175, 294; interbasin projects, 59–61; Muir on, 108; Powell on, 2, 16–17, 19, 29, 32, 40, 55; proposed projects, 85, 174–175; Reclamation Act on, 40, 225–226. *See also* Bureau of Reclamation; irrigation infrastructure; *names of specific projects*; watershed governance; wild rivers
Darrah, William Culp, 13
Davis, Jefferson, administration, 181
Davis Dam, 293
Dawes Act. *See* General Allotment Act (1887)
DCP. *See* Lower Basin Drought Contingency Plan (DCP)
deBuys, William, 28, 44, 97
deficit irrigation, 88
Deloria, Vine, 252, 260–261
Delta Stewardship Program, 44
dendrochronology, 77, 80–81
Denver, Colorado, 81, 111, 162
Depression, 136
desalination projects, 86–87
Desert Land Act (1877), 39, 225, 282
DeVoto, Bernard, 23, 47
Dinosaur National Monument, 15–16, 154, 175
diversions. *See* dams; irrigation infrastructure
Doctrine of Discovery, 225
Dolores River Basin: boating industry of, 62–63; competing interests and disputes in, 63–65; conflict resolution in, 65–67, 71–72; description of, 54, 59; history of water diversions in, 59–60; McPhee Dam and Reservoir, 59, 61–63; National Conservation Area (NCA), 66; paradoxes of, 54–55
Dolores Water Conservancy District (DWCD), 61–63, 65, 67
Dominy, Floyd, 178
Dream Catcher (Kikut), 200*fig.*
drought, 81; *vs.* aridification, planning for, 44–45, 56, 83–85. *See also* climate change
"dryland democracy," as term, 28. *See also* communitarianism; watershed governance
Duchesne River, 294
Dust Bowl, 14
Dutton, Clarence, xxi

Echo-Hawk, Walter, 254
Echo Park Dam (proposed), 15, 175
ecology and preservation of ecosystems, 294–295; as concept and discipline, xvii, 18; for fish, 62, 63, 66, 233–235, 258, 294; Muir on, 96, 110, 111, 113; national park management and, 113–114; restoration projects, 43–45, 293; traditional ecological knowledge, xvii–xviii, 95, 212–213, 229, 232–233, 256, 275, 279–280; tribal environmental stewardship, 221, 227, 233–235, 242,

Index | 307

256; wildlife protection, 114, 184, 256.
  See also Colorado River Basin;
  endangered species protection; science,
  as tool for resource management;
  wilderness
economic statistics: on mining industry,
  154; on recreation industry, 115,
  153–154
Ecotopia (Callenbach), 134
ejidos. See Mexican land governance
El Paso, Texas, 86
Endangered Species Act (1973), 43, 65,
  110, 138, 235
endangered species protection: of fish, 62,
  63, 66, 233–235, 258, 294; planning
  for, 45; Powell's lack of concern for, 18.
  See also ecology and preservation of
  ecosystems; restoration projects;
  riparian areas; wildlife protection
The Energy Balloon (Stewart Udall), 186
environmental heritage, defined, 279
ethnobotany, 233. *See also* traditional
  ecological knowledge
ethnology, 202–203, 204–207, 212. *See
  also* anthropology
Everglades Restoration Program, 44
evolutionary theories of culture. *See*
  cultural-stages theory
*The Exploration of the Colorado River and
  Its Canyons* (Powell), 97, 151, 269–270,
  290. *See also* Powell, John Wesley
extractive industries. *See* mining industry;
  oil and gas exploration

farming. *See* agriculture
federalism, defined, 58, 132–133
federal land estate. *See* public lands
Federal Land Policy and Management Act
  (1976), 110, 137, 141
federal–tribal collaborative management,
  209–211, 231, 255–260
federal *vs.* state water jurisdiction, 38–42,
  57–58, 69
Fernow, Bernard, 182
fires. *See* wildfire management
Firescape program, 143
"first in time, first in right" water rights, 30,
  34, 225. *See also* water rights
fish habitat and species protection, 62, 63,
  66, 233–235, 258, 294. *See also* wildlife
  protection
Flagstaff, Arizona, xi, 148, 154, 186. *See
  also* Snowbowl Ski Area
Flaming Gorge Country, 7*fig.*, 154

Flaming Gorge Dam, 114
flannelmouth sucker fish, 62, 63
Fleck, John, 44
flood irrigation method, 87–88, 90. *See also*
  agriculture; irrigation infrastructure
folly. *See* wisdom *vs.* folly
forced relocation program, 247–251, 271.
  See also assimilation; reservations
Forest Reserve Clause (General Revision
  Act), 109, 129, 183–184
forests. *See* national forest system and US
  Forest Service
Fort Apache Tribe and reservation, 234
Fort Mojave Tribe, 276
Francis, Sharon, 170–171
Freeman, Orville, 173
free yo mind + yo ass will follow (mural by
  Thomas), 195*fig.*

Gadsden Purchase (1853), 126, 266
Garden of the Gods, 242
Gellis, Brandon, 102*fig.*, 103*fig.*
General Allotment Act (1887), xvi,
  180–181, 251–252, 273
General Revision Act (1891), 109, 128–129,
  142, 183–184
Getches, David, 44
Gila River, 205, 206, 269, 270
Gila River Indian Community (GRIC) and
  reservation, 89, 252
Gilbert, Grove Karl, xxi, 277–278
Gilliam, Harold, 171
Gilpin, William, 211
Gleick, Peter, 70
Glen Canyon Dam, 8*fig.*, 76, 114; building
  of, 77; Interim Shortage Guidelines and,
  81–82; management of, 292, 294; Udall
  on, 173, 175. *See also* Lake Powell
Glen Canyon Dam (monotype by
  Aitchison), 8*fig.*
Glen Canyon Dam Adaptive Management
  Program, 143, 294
God is Red (Deloria), 252
gold, 59. *See also* mining industry
Gold Rush, 21, 32, 248, 266
González, José, 160
Goshute Tribe, 269
government-to-government consultation
  (federal–tribal), 209–211, 231,
  255–260. *See also* collaborative land
  and water management
Grand Canyon, 111–112, 292; images and
  paintings of, 9*fig.*, 102*fig.*, 104*fig.*; Ives
  on, 211; modern ecosystem and future

308 | Index

Grand Canyon *(continued)*
of, 294; Powell's description of, xxiii, 18, 108, 148; recreation and tourism development in, 153, 154. *See also* Colorado River Basin

Grand Canyon National Park: Powell on, 108–109; Powell Point, 104*fig.*, 292; protection and enlargement of, 43, 112, 115, 122n38, 143, 177, 189n42; river lottery system of, 159; Udall and proposals for, 168–169, 174–175, 177–178

The Grand Canyon of Arizona (Powell), 152–153. *See also* Powell, John Wesley

Grand Canyon Protection Act (1992), 43, 143

Grand Coulee Dam, 13

Grand River, 269, 271, 291

Grand River Ute Band, 269, 271. *See also* Ute Indian Tribe and reservation

Grand Staircase-Escalante National Monument, xxii, 118, 119, 154, 169, 185, 213–214

Grand Teton National Park, 160

Grand Wash Cliffs, 292

Grant, Ulysses, administration, 202

Great Lakes Program, 44, 47

"The Great Unknown," Powell on, xix, xxiii, 156, 290. *See also* Colorado River Basin

Green River, 6*fig.*, 7*fig.*, 291; dam proposals and, 15; management of, 132; oil and gas extraction in basin, 99; Powell's 1869 Expedition, xix–xx, xxi, 11, 73, 151, 265; Powell's governance plan for, 132; recreation on, 21; tribes of, 269. *See also* Colorado River Basin

GRIC. *See* Gila River Indian Community (GRIC)

Hague, Arnold, 109
Haile, Rahawa, 159
Hanna, James W., 60
Harrison, Benjamin, administration, 129, 184
Havasu Creek, 174–175, 178
Havasupai Tribe and reservation, 122n38, 242, 270, 276
Hayden, Carl, 169, 176, 177
Hayden, Ferdinand, xxi
Herbert, Hilary, xxi
"heritage of conflict," Powell on, 1, 3, 85, 211
Hetch Hetchy Dam, 175

Hispanic water management (historical). *See acequia* systems of Hispanic communities
Holmes, Oliver Wendell, Jr., 22
Homestead Act (1862), 13, 76, 95, 128–129, 180, 225, 282
homesteading program, xiv, xv, 150. *See also* westward expansion
Hoover, Herbert, administration, 12, 205
Hoover Dam, 10*fig.*, 114, 291, 293; Boulder Canyon Project Act on, 79; building of, 13, 77; Interim Shortage Guidelines on, 81–82. *See also* Lake Mead
Hoover Gates (painting by Osborne), 10*fig.*
Hopi Tribe and reservation: Bears Ears and, xvii, 112, 210–211, 213, 256–258; coal mining on, 176; cultural appropriation of, 198*fig.*; legal case by, 231–232; prehistory of, 191; sacred sites of, 199, 231–232, 243, 254–255, 294; traditional ecological knowledge of, 213; traditional lands of, 269; water and agricultural systems of, 59, 276
Hualapai Dam. *See* Bridge Canyon Dam (proposed)
Hualapai Tribe and reservation, 112, 231, 242, 270, 272, 294
The Hull 1 (Aitchison), 100–101*fig.*
The Hull 2 (Aitchison), 100–101*fig.*
hydroelectric power, 79, 85, 175, 294. *See also* dams
Hyperion Water Treatment Plant, Los Angeles, 86

Ickes, Harold, 172
Imperial Dam, 293
Imperial Irrigation District, 38, 79, 293
Imperial Valley, California, 38, 79, 293
Indian Citizenship Act (1924), 208
"Indian policy," as term, 202, 216n7
Indian Removal Act (1830), 248
Indian Reorganization Act (1934), 189n45, 208, 273
Indian Rights Association, 202
Indians. *See* Native Americans
Indian Self-Determination and Education Assistance Act (1975), 209
Indigenous belief systems. *See* animism; religious freedom and discrimination; traditional ecological knowledge
Indigenous environmental stewardship, 221, 227, 233–235, 242. *See also* Native Americans; sacred site protection; traditional ecological knowledge
Indigenous Peoples. *See* Native Americans

Index | 309

individualism, 12, 28. *See also* communitarianism; personal liberty *vs.* public good, debates on
industrialization, 34–35, 132–133
Ingalls, G. W., 245
"Institutions for the Arid Lands" (Powell), 56, 65, 78, 106–107, 130–132, 140, 292. *See also* Powell, John Wesley
Interim Shortage Guidelines (2007), 44, 81–82. *See also* Law of the River
Interim Surplus Guidelines, 44
International Boundary and Water Commission, 42
International Irrigation Congress, 17, 23, 129
Inter Tribal Council of Arizona, 210
iron triangle, 281
irrigation infrastructure: *acequia* systems, xiii, 30, 36, 57; federal role in, 39, 77, 126; flood method, 87–88, 90; nonprofit and user-controlled governance of, 37–38; Powell on, 2, 16–17, 29–32, 40, 57, 131, 150, 162, 270, 291–292; Pueblo community irrigation system, 30, 59. *See also* dams; *names of specific projects;* watershed governance
Irrigation Survey, 182–183
island-community model, 132–135, 139
Ives, Joseph, 211

Jackson, Andrew, administration, 248
James, William, 22
Jewell, Sally, xviii, 258
Jicarilla Apache Tribe, 276
Johnson, Lyndon B., administration, 169, 172, 189n42
Jones, David, 99*fig.*
Josephy, Alvin, 170

Kaibab Paiute Band, 276
Karuk Tribe, 254
Katie Lee (Aitchison), 100*fig.*
Keiter, Robert, 96
Kennedy, John F., 168, 169, 171
Kikut, Patrick, 104*fig.*, 200*fig.*
Kimmerer, Robin Wall, 232–233
King, Clarence, xxi, 34

Lacey Act (1900), 109, 184
Lake Mead, 31, 44, 84–85, 291. *See also* Hoover Dam
Lake Powell, 31, 44, 76, 84–85, 291, 292. *See also* Glen Canyon Dam
land allotment program. *See* allotment program

Land and Water Conservation Fund Act (1965), 110, 172, 185
land governance: colonial-era, 30, 36, 266, 270–271; federal homesteading program, xiv, xv, 150; tribal, 273–277; tribal environmental stewardship, 221, 227, 233–235, 242. *See also* agriculture; collaborative land and water management; public lands; reservations; watershed governance
Landrum-Griffin Act (1959), 169
language preservation, 202, 204, 214, 229, 233, 281
Las Vegas, Nevada, 86
Latino Outdoors, 160–161
Law of the River: 2007 Interim Shortage Guidelines, 44, 81–82; Basin Study on, 82–83, 83*fig.*; as term, 78, 205. *See also* legal history of early western settlement; water rights
Lee, John Doyle, 177
Lees Ferry, Arizona, 177
legal history of early western settlement, 224–226. *See also* Homestead Act (1862); Law of the River; *names of specific legislation*
Leopold, Aldo, xii, xvii, 295
"The Lesson of Conemaugh" (Powell), 292. *See also* Powell, John Wesley
Lewis and Clark National Forest, 255
Libecap, Gary, 90
Lincoln, Abraham, administration, 248
Little Colorado River, 23, 156, 195*fig.*, 196–197*fig.*, 269
Litton, Martin, 175, 291
livestock grazing, 114, 138, 150, 234, 250, 280, 282. *See also* agriculture
local *vs.* outsider, debates on, 139
Locke, John, 226, 228
Long Walk, 250–251
Looking for Moran (Osborne), 102*fig.*
Los Angeles, California, 86, 111
Louisiana Purchase (1803), 126
Lower Basin Drought Contingency Plan (DCP), 89
Lower Colorado River. *See* Colorado River Basin
Lower Colorado River Multi-Species Conservation Program, 293
Lower Dolores Plan Working Group (LDPWG), 65–67
Lower Dolores River. *See* Dolores River Basin
Lux v. Haggin (1886), 32, 37

Lyng v. Northwest Indian Cemetery Protection Association (1988), 254, 255

Malheur National Wildlife Refuge, 185
Manifest Destiny: historical framework of, 191, 205, 211; modern versions of, 221, 224–225, 235–237; as term and concept, 220–221; visualization of, 102*fig.*, 200*fig.*
Manypenny, George, 243
Marble Canyon, 9*fig.*
Marble Canyon National Monument, 189n42
Marble Gorge Dam (proposed), 174–175, 176, 178, 179, 291
Maricopa Tribe, 269, 270
Maroon Bells-Snowmass Wilderness Area, 158
Marshall, John, 191
Masland, Frank, 173
McGee, W. J., xxi
McKinley, William, 184
McPhee Dam and Reservoir, 59, 61–63, 67–68. *See also* Dolores River Basin
Meeker, Nathan, 249
Meeker Massacre (1879), 249
Melissa Pochoema, Insurgent Hopi Maiden (image by Wilson), 198*fig.*
Menand, Louis, 22
Mexican–American War (1846–1848), 125, 126, 135, 248. *See also* Treaty of Guadalupe Hidalgo (1848)
Mexican land governance, xiii, 30, 36, 265–271
Mexico, Colorado River Compact and, 42, 43, 79
military reservations, 126, 129, 137, 249, 266–267, 268*map*
military service: of Native Americans, 208; of Powell, xi, 28, 179; of Udall, 179
mineral rights, 39, 139
mining industry: economic statistics on, 154; effects on national parks, 114; Gold Rush era water management for, 21; on Navajo Nation, 112, 176; in San Juan Mountains, 59–60, 248; in Utah, 138
Mississippi River, 18, 126
Missouri River, 17
Moab, Utah, 115
mobility, 139, 146n37, 157
modernization, 133. *See also* cultural-stages theory; industrialization
Mojave Tribe, 269, 272, 276

Montana Constitutional Convention, 131
Montezuma Valley, 59–61, 63, 65–67. *See also* Dolores River Basin
Montezuma Valley Irrigation Company (MVIC), 60–61
Montezuma Valley Water Supply Company, 60
Morelos Dam, 291, 293
Morgan, Lewis Henry, 204, 206, 214
Mormons: conflict with Ute Tribe, 248; water rights system of, xiii, 30, 36, 57, 283
Moser, Donald, 171
Mount Baldy, 234
Muache Ute Band, 271. *See also* Ute Indian Tribe and reservation
Muir, John: on interconnection and preservation of ecosystems, 96, 110, 111, 113, 140; on national park system, 105–106, 108–109; on wilderness, 117
Multiple-Use Sustained-Yield Act (1960), 146n34

NARF. *See* Native American Rights Fund (NARF)
Nash, Roderick, 158
National Climate Assessment, 278, 279
National Congress of American Indians (NCAI), 208, 210
National Environmental Policy Act (1969), 110, 141, 229, 232
National Forest Management Act (1976), 110, 141
national forest system and US Forest Service, xvii; Colorado River Basin administration by, 111; ecological assessments of, 114, 128; establishment of, 96, 110, 126, 129; Forest Reserve Clause, 109, 129, 183–184; Powell on, 19–20, 130–131, 145n21; recreation and, 154; tribal cases against, 231–232, 254; values and uses of, 137, 138; wildfire management, 143, 161. See also *names of specific forests*; public lands
National Geographic Society, xx, 22
national monuments. See *names of specific monuments*
National Park Service Organic Act (1916), 113, 184
national park system and National Park Service: ecological policies of, 113–114; establishment of, 96, 109, 110, 113, 126, 184; future challenges and reforms of, 116–120, 142; increased recreation

Index | 311

and tourism, 114–116; legislation on, 113, 184; list of Colorado River Basin parks, 111–112, 292; modern experience of, 152; Muir on, 108–109; Powell on, 105, 108–109; reservations and, 112; revenue generated by, 115, 123n54; statistics on, 115, 153; *A Survey of the Recreational Resources of the Colorado River Basin*, 153; use of storytelling by, 160–161; use restrictions and permit systems of, 159. See also *names of specific parks*; public lands; recreation and tourism industry
national recreation areas, 138
National Wild and Scenic Rivers System, 62, 65–66. See also Wild and Scenic Rivers Act (1968); wild rivers
national wildlife refuge system: establishment of, 96, 126, 129, 137, 185; management of, 110, 111, 137–138. See also *names of specific refuges*; US Fish and Wildlife Service; wildlife protection
Native American reservations. *See* reservations
Native American Rights Fund (NARF), 208–209, 210
Native Americans, xv–xvi, xxxiii, 191–193, 214–215, 220–221; annihilationist arguments against, 192, 202, 203, 238n17; anthropological work on, 202–203, 204–207, 212–214; assimilation program for, 181, 192, 201–207, 214, 221–222, 224, 246–247, 272–273; Bears Ears Inter-Tribal Coalition, xvii, 112, 213, 244, 256–258; Bears Ears Inter-Tribal Management Commission, 210–211, 256–258; colonial land governance and, 266, 270–271; community irrigation of Pueblo tribes, 30, 59; environmental stewardship of, 221, 227, 233–235, 242, 256; history of regional groups, 266–269, 267*map*; land dispossession of, 122n38, 126, 180–181, 247–252; language preservation of, 202, 204, 214, 229, 233, 281; massacres of, 222; military service of, 208; modern land and water management by, 273–277; religious freedom of, 222, 229–230, 231–232, 252–255; sacred site protection, 196*fig*., 242–244, 252–257, 259, 260–261; self-determination of, 202, 208–210, 216n7, 227; traditional ecological knowledge of, xvii–xviii, 95,

212–213, 229, 232–233, 256, 275, 279–280; tribal diversity of, Powell on, 222–223; tribal sovereignty, 227–228; voting rights of, 208, 209; water rights of, 35, 59, 62, 68, 89, 210–211, 228, 235–237, 275–276. See also *names of specific tribes*; reservations
Navajo Generating Station (NGS), 112, 176
Navajo Nation: agricultural system and water management of, 275–276, 282; Bears Ears and, xvii, 112, 210–211, 213, 256–258; Canyon de Chelly National Monument, 160; coal mining on, 112, 176; forced relocation and assimilation of, 250–251; *Navajo Nation v. USFS*, 199, 231–232, 243, 254–255; recreation users of, 160; reservation lands of, 126, 155, 206, 248, 271, 273; sacred sites of, 242, 253, 294; traditional ecological knowledge of, 212–213; traditional lands of, 269; on tram proposal, 112; voting rights of, 209
Navajo Nation Human Rights Commission, 210
Navajo Nation v. USFS (2007), 199, 231–232, 243, 254
Navajo Water Code, 281–282
NCAI. *See* National Congress of American Indians (NCAI)
Nevada, 79, 86
Newberry, John Strong, xxi
New Deal era, 12–13
Newlands Reclamation Act (1902), 132
New Mexico, 39, 41, 57, 86, 111, 208
Noble, John, 19
"The Non-Irrigable Lands of the Arid Region" (Powell), 130. See also Powell, John Wesley
nonprofit water management institutions, 36–37
Northern Ute Tribe, 276. See also Ute Indian Tribe and reservation

Obama, Barack, administration, xvi–xvii, 112, 185, 244, 256–257
O'Connor, Sandra Day, 254, 255
oil and gas exploration, 114
Orange County Water District, water reuse program, 86
Oregon Treaty (1846), 126
Organic Administration Act, "Pettigrew Act" (1897), 109, 129
Osborne, Erika, 10*fig*., 102*fig*.

312 | Index

Ouray Reservation. *See* Uintah Ute Band and reservation
Outdoor Industry Association, 115, 154–155
outdoor recreation. *See* recreation and tourism industry
Outdoor Retailer trade show, 162
outsider *vs.* local, debates on, 139
overgrazing, 234. *See also* agriculture; livestock grazing

Pacific Northwest, 13, 136, 175, 258
Pacific Railway Acts, 128
Pacific Southwest Water Plan (1963), 174
Painted Rock Dam, 293
Paiute Tribe, 204, 269, 276, 294
Palo Verde Nuclear Generating Station, 86
Papago Tribe. *See* Tohono O'odham Tribe and reservation
paradox, as concept, 1, 3, 55, 63, 69, 70–72, 160, 291–292. *See also* wisdom *vs.* folly
Paradox Valley, 54, 59. *See also* Dolores River Basin
Parker Dam, 293
parks. *See names of specific parks*; national park system and National Park Service
partisanship, 185
Pascua Yaqui Tribe, 276
pasturage districts, 30–31, 35, 76–77, 106, 139, 149, 182. *See also* agriculture; watershed governance
Peabody Coal, 112, 176
Pecos River, 41
personal liberty *vs.* public good, debates on, 126–127. *See also* individualism
Pettigrew Act. *See* Organic Administration Act (1897)
Phoenix, Arizona, 86, 88, 111, 174, 176, 234. *See also* Central Arizona Project (CAP)
PIA. *See* practicably irrigable acreage (PIA) standard
Pima Tribe, 205, 269, 270
Pinchot, Gifford, 131, 134, 171, 172, 173, 184
Pochoema, Melissa, 198*fig.*
Popé, 198
population growth, 2; future projections of, 279; public land use and, 156–159; statistics on, xxiii
Powell, John Wesley, 11–13; academic awards of, xx–xxi; authoritarian leadership style of, 28; biographies about, xi, xiii, 13–21; death of, 11, 12; description of Northern Arizona by, 148, 163; on "heritage of conflict," 1, 3, 85, 211; military service and injury of, xi, 28, 179; modern relevance of, xiii–xv, xxi–xxii, xix, 21–25, 47, 67–70, 139, 290–295; paradoxical philosophies of, 55; river expeditions by, xiii, xix–xx, xxi, xxv*map,* 28, 151, 156, 265; Stegner on, 14, 16–21, 23–24, 77, 215; use of storytelling, 148–149, 151, 160–161, 163; as USGS director, xiv, xx, 31, 76, 149–150; on wisdom *vs.* folly, 57, 69, 72, 131, 151, 186. *See also* Colorado River Basin
– Native Americans and: anthropological work by Powell, xxi, 192–193, 212; assimilation of, 181, 192, 201–202, 214, 221–222, 224, 246–247; Bureau of American Ethnology and, xiv, xx, 11, 22, 68, 181; cultural-stages theory and, 192, 193, 203–204, 206–207, 214, 223–224; ethnological work by Powell, 202–203, 204–207, 212; Powell as Special Commissioner of Indian Affairs, 245; Powell on diversity of tribal groups, 222–223; Powell on "Indian theology," 229, 245–246; Powell on reservation and allotment policies, 180–181, 243–244, 246–252; Ute Tribe descriptions by Powell, 249, 269–270; Winnebago Tribe and Powell, 244–245
– public lands and, 106–107, 127; on forest management, 130–131, 145n21, 150; on homesteading program, xiv–xv, 150, 224–225; land survey work by, 149–150; on national parks, 105, 108–109; S. 2837 bill by, 182; Stewart and, 182–183; Udall and, 172–173, 179, 186
– water and, 78; on communitarianism, xiii, xiii–xiv, xiv, 20, 22–23, 28, 67, 130, 150–151, 157; on dams, 2, 16–17, 19, 29, 32, 40, 55; on diversions and irrigation infrastructure, 2, 16–17, 29–32, 40, 57, 131, 150, 162, 270, 291–292; on federal role in water management, 39–41; on forest management, 19–20; on hydrographic districts, 56–58, 76, 107; watershed governance, 29–32, 42, 46, 113, 131, 134, 281–283
– writings, xx, 297–299; *The Exploration of the Colorado River and Its Canyons,*

97, 151, 269–270, 290; *The Grand Canyon of Arizona*, 152–153; "Institutions for the Arid Lands," 56, 65, 78, 106–107, 130–132, 140, 292; "The Lesson of Conemaugh," 292; "The Non-Irrigable Lands of the Arid Region," 130; on "The Great Unknown," xix, xxiii, 156, 290. *See also* Arid Lands Report (Powell)
Powell of the Colorado (book by Darrah), 13
Powell Point (painting by Kikut), 104*fig.*
Powell Point, Grand Canyon National Park, 104*fig.*, 292
practicably irrigable acreage (PIA) standard, 228, 276, 277, 282. *See also* agriculture
Pratt, Richard H., 224
preservationism, 96, 113. *See also* conservation movement, overview; ecology and preservation of ecosystems
Price River, 294
Primitive Culture (Tylor), 204
prior appropriation, 30, 34, 225. *See also* water rights
private property: Christian ethos on, 225–226; *vs.* public land, debates on, 96, 125–127. *See also* public lands
Progressive Conservation movement, 133–135
public lands, 95–97; acquisition of, 125–126; challenges and future management of, 138–144, 155, 260–261; divestment of, 43, 161–163, 184; early 19th c. federal policy on, 127–128; federal–tribal collaborative management of, xvii, 112, 209–211, 213, 231, 255–260; General Revision Act, 109, 128–129, 142, 183–184; Homestead Act, 13, 76, 95, 128, 180, 225, 282; map, 98*map;* Powell's management plan for, 131–132, 140; *vs.* private property, debates on, 96, 125–127; Progressive Conservation movement on, 133–135; Thoreau and, 179–180; wars, economy, and public opinion on, 135–136. *See also* land governance; national forest system and US Forest Service; national park system and National Park Service; national wildlife refuge system; recreation and tourism industry
public trust doctrine, 33
Pueblo tribal water management systems, 30, 59

Quechan Tribe, 276
The Quiet Crisis (Stewart Udall), xi, 97, 167–172, 185, 186. *See also* Udall, Stewart
The Quiet Crisis and the Next Generation (Stewart Udall), 186

racism, 159, 202, 214. *See also* assimilation; Manifest Destiny; Native Americans
rafting. *See* recreation and tourism industry; whitewater recreation
railroad, 128, 133, 153, 267–268
rainbow trout, 62
rational governance, Powell on, 55–56, 57. *See also* watershed governance
Reagan, John H., 181–182
Reclamation Act (1902), 40, 225–226
reclamation projects. *See* Bureau of Reclamation; dams
recreation and tourism industry, xxiii; on Colorado River Basin public lands, 152–153; in Dolores River Basin, 55, 62–63, 65; future of, 115–116, 163; lack of diversity of users in, 159–161; national park management and, 110; Navajo Nation *vs.* USFS and, 199, 231–232, 243, 254; population growth and, 114–115, 156–159; Powell and, 97, 148–149, 152; resource management by, 161–163; statistics on, 115, 153–154; Udall's rafting trips, 173–174, 177–179. *See also* national park system and National Park Service; public lands
Red Scare, 14–15
REI, 161
religious freedom and discrimination, 222, 229–230, 231–232, 252–255. *See also* animism; Christianity; sacred site protection
Religious Freedom Restoration Act (RFRA), 229, 231–232. *See also* American Indian Religious Freedom Act (1978)
relocation programs. *See* forced relocation program; reservations
reservations: 19th c. populations on and off, 269; allotment program, xvi, 180–181, 251–252, 272–273; establishment of, xvi, 204–205, 206, 247–251, 271–272; Indian Reorganization Act on, 189n45, 208, 273; land statistics of, xvi, 248, 249, 252, 270, 273, 274*table;* maps, 194*map,* 272*map;* national parks and, 112; Powell on, 180–181, 243–244, 246–247; public land policy and, 126;

reservations *(continued)*
   recreation on, 155; water rights on, 35, 59, 62, 68, 89, 205, 228, 235–237. *See also* assimilation; *names of specific reservations;* Native Americans
Resettlement Administration, 13
resource management. *See* communitarianism; land governance; public lands; watershed governance
restoration, as term, 294
restoration projects, 43–45, 293. *See also* endangered species protection
reuse water programs, 86
RFRA. *See* Religious Freedom Restoration Act (RFRA)
Rio Grande River Basin, 39, 41, 57
riparian areas: restoration of, 234, 280, 293; water rights in, 32, 33–34, 39. *See also* ecology and preservation of ecosystems; endangered species protection; restoration projects; watershed governance
river permit systems, 159
A River Running West (Worster), 247
rivers. *See names of specific rivers;* watershed governance; wild rivers
Rocky Mountain National Park, 137
Romney, Henry, 170
Roosevelt, Franklin, administration, 12–13
Roosevelt, Theodore, administration, 108, 129, 134, 175
roundtail chub, 62, 63
rugged individualism, 12
Russel, Bailey, 6*fig.*, 7*fig.*, 9*fig.*

S. 2837 (proposed bill), 182. *See also* watershed governance
sacred site protection, 196*fig.*, 242–244, 252–257, 259, 260–261. *See also* archaeological sites; Indigenous environmental stewardship; religious freedom and discrimination; traditional ecological knowledge
Sagebrush Rebellion, 185
Salt Lake City, Utah, 81, 110, 162
Salt River Project, 89, 132, 234
Salt River Tribe and reservation, 252
San Carlos Apache Tribe, 276
Sand Creek Massacre (1864), 222
San Francisco Peaks, 199, 231–232, 243, 254–255
San Juan Mountains, 59–60, 248
San Juan River Basin, 59, 269
San Juan Southern Paiute Tribe, 276

San Luis Rio Colorado, Mexico, 291
San Rafael River, 294
"savagery." *See* cultural-stages theory
Schurz, Carl, 172
science, as tool for resource management, xvii, 18, 113–114, 211, 232–233, 257, 290, 295. *See also* climate change; ecology and preservation of ecosystems; traditional ecological knowledge
Sea of Cortez, 42, 291, 292, 293
The Search for Order–1877–1920 (Wiebe), 132
Second Treatise of Government (Locke), 226
Secretarial Order 3342, 258
Seeing Things Whole (deBuys), 97
Select Committee on Irrigation and Reclamation of Arid Lands, 182
self-determination, 202, 208–210, 216n7, 227. *See also* cultural survival; Native Americans
Senate Special Committee on Irrigation and Reclamation of Arid Lands, 40–41
Sequoia National Park, 109
Shiraishi, Ashima, 161
Shivwits Paiute Band, 269
Shoshone Tribe, 204
Sierra Club, 15, 109, 175, 178
Sigl, Patrick, 89
Silent Spring (Carson), xi, 171
silver, 59. *See also* mining industry
Six Rivers National Forest, 254
slavery, 127, 160, 214, 222, 230
smallmouth bass, 63
Smithsonian Institution, Bureau of American Ethnology, xiv, xx, 11, 22, 68, 181
Smythe, William, xxi
Snowbowl Ski Area, 199, 231–232, 243, 254–255
social capital, as term, 44
Social Darwinism, 222
Soil Conservation Service, 13
Sorenson, Ted, 171
Southern Paiute Tribe, 294
Southern Ute Tribe and reservation, 249, 252, 269, 276. *See also* Ute Indian Tribe and reservation
Spanish exploration and land governance, 30, 36, 250, 265–271. *See also acequia* systems of Hispanic communities
Spencer, Herbert, 214
spirituality. *See* animism; Christianity; religious freedom and discrimination

stakeholder legitimacy, 139, 142–143
Standing Rock Sioux, 232
Star Wars, 198*fig.*
state *vs.* federal water jurisdiction, 38–42, 57–58, 69
Stegner, Wallace: *Beyond the Hundredth Meridian*, xi, 2, 14–21, 91, 169; on "dryland democracy," 28; on Powell, 14, 16–21, 23–24, 77, 215; *This is Dinosaur*, 15–16; on understanding the West, xii; "Wilderness Letter," 169; writing support of *The Quiet Crisis* by, 169–171
step in cow springs, navajo nation on the colorado plateau (mural by Thomas), 199*fig.*
Stewart, William "Big Bill," xiv, xxi, 182–183
storytelling, Powell's use of, 148–149, 151, 160–161, 163
Strickland, Rennard, 224–225
subsurface drip irrigation method, 90
Subterranean BTUs (Jones), 99*fig.*
sucker fish, 62, 63
A Survey of the Recreational Resources of the Colorado River Basin (National Park Service), 153
Swamp Lands Act (1850), 225

Tabeguache Ute Band, 271. *See also* Ute Indian Tribe and reservation
tamarisk, 63, 114
Taylor Grazing Act (1934), 13, 184
Teller, Henry, 180
Tennessee Valley Authority, 13
Ten Tribes Partnership, 210, 282
terra incognita. See "The Great Unknown," Powell on
This is Dinosaur (Stegner), 15–16
Thomas, Chip, 195*fig.*, 196–197*fig.*, 199*fig.*
Thoreau, Henry David, xii, 170, 171, 179–180
timber. *See* national forest system and US Forest Service
Timber Culture Act (1873), 128, 183, 282
Tohono O'odham Tribe and reservation, 252, 269, 276
Tolowa Tribe, 254
Tonto Apache Tribe, 276
tourism. *See* recreation and tourism industry
Towaoc, Ute Mountain Ute Reservation, 62
traditional ecological knowledge, xvii–xviii, 95, 212–213, 229, 232–233, 256, 275, 279–280. *See also* cultural survival;
Indigenous environmental stewardship; Native Americans; sacred site protection
"The Tragedy of the Commons" (Hardin), 158–159
Trail of Tears, 248
transcontinental railway system. *See* railroad
Transfer of Public Lands Act (2012), 161
treaties, 247–251, 266, 271. *See also* Native Americans; reservations
Treaty of Guadalupe Hidalgo (1848), 248, 266, 271. *See also* Mexican-American War (1846–1848)
Treaty of Mesilla (1854), 266
tree-rings. *See* dendrochronology
tribal environmental stewardship, 221, 227, 233–235, 242, 256
tribal governance: –federal collaboration, 209–211, 231, 257–260; maps, 98*map*, 267*map*; Powell on, xv–xvi, 222–223; sovereignty rule, 227–228. *See also* Bears Ears Inter-Tribal Management Commission; self-determination
tribal water rights, 35, 59, 62, 68, 89, 228, 235–237, 275–276. *See also* Native Americans
trout, 62, 233–234
Trump, Donald, administration, xvi–xvii, 112, 119, 185, 213
Tucson, Arizona, 86, 111, 174, 176. *See also* Central Arizona Project (CAP)
Tucson/Phoenix CAP Exchange, 88. *See also* Central Arizona Project (CAP)
Turner, Frederick Jackson, 109
Twain, Mark, 1
Tylor, Edward, 204, 214

Udall, Morris, 176
Udall, Stewart, 167–168; on CAP and dam proposals, 174–177; *The Energy Balloon*, 186; posthumous recognition of, 188n8; Powell and, xi, 172–173, 186; *The Quiet Crisis*, xi, 97, 167–172, 185, 186; *The Quiet Crisis and the Next Generation*, 186; Stegner and, 169; whitewater rafting by, 173–174, 177; "Wilderness Rivers: Shooting the Wild Colorado," 177, 178–179
Udall, Tom, 177
Uinkarets Paiute Band, 269
Uintah River, 269
Uintah Ute Band and reservation, 194, 248, 249, 252, 269–270, 271, 274. *See also* Ute Indian Tribe and reservation

Uncharted 1–3 (Osborne), 102–103*fig.*
Uncompahgre (Gunnison) reclamation project, 132
Uncompahgre Ute Band, 249. *See also* Ute Indian Tribe and reservation
United States–Mexico Treaty (1944), 42, 44–45, 79, 80, 83
University of Arizona, Tree-Ring Laboratory, 80–81, 83
Unkakaniguts Paiute Band, 269
Upper Colorado River Basin Compact, 43. *See also* Colorado River Compact (1922)
Upper Colorado River Commission, 43
uranium mining, 114, 138. *See also* mining industry
USDA Agricultural Census (2017), 228, 276, 277, 282
US Department of the Interior, xiv, 41, 188n8, 258. *See also* Udall, Stewart
US Fish and Wildlife Service, 110, 111, 138–139. *See also* national wildlife refuge system
US Forest Service. *See* national forest system and US Forest Service
US Geological Survey, 109; award for, xxi; Powell as director of, xiv, xx, 31, 76, 149–150
US Postal Service, 16
Utah: future dam projects of, 85; mining industry in, 138; Moab, 115; Native voting rights in, 208, 209; public lands of, 111, 112, 115, 155, 161; Salt Lake City, 81, 110, 162; Ute Removal Act, 249–250. *See also* Bears Ears National Monument; *names of specific places*
Utah Diné Bikéyah, 256. *See also* Bears Ears Inter-Tribal Coalition
Ute Indian Tribe and reservation: Bears Ears and, xvii, 112, 210–211, 213, 256–258; Powell on, 204, 269–270; regional groups of, 249, 252, 269, 270, 271, 276; reservation lands of, 137, 248–250, 252, 253, 271; sacred sites of, 242; traditional ecological knowledge of, 213; voting rights of, 209; water management systems of, 59
Ute Mountain Ute Tribe and reservation: Bears Ears and, xvii, 112, 210–211, 213, 256–258; coalition on water rights of, 276; McPhee Dam and water diversions to, 59, 62, 68; Powell on conflict among, 222; reservation lands of, 248–250

Ute Removal Act (1880), 249–250

View of Flaming Gorge (Russel), 7*fig.*
View of Green River Lakes (Russel), 6*fig.*
View of Marble Canyon at Soap Creek (Russel), 9*fig.*
voting rights, 38, 208, 209
Voting Rights Act (1965), 208, 209

Walapai. *See* Hualapai Tribe and reservation
Walt Disney Corporation, 16
Ward, Lester Frank, xx
Washoe Tribe, 255
waste regulations on water use, 33, 64–65, 69. *See also* irrigation infrastructure; watershed governance
water companies, 20–21
water diversions. *See* dams; irrigation infrastructure
water exchanges, 87–89, 186. *See also* Central Arizona Project (CAP)
water marketing, 87–89
water rights, 1–3; allocation *vs.* appropriation, 33, 186; *Arizona v. California*, 41–42, 79, 80, 228, 275, 276, 282; current system of, 77–78, 81–82; history of, xiii, 21, 30, 32, 34, 57, 224–226; land-tied *vs.* severed, 33–35; of tribal groups, 35, 59, 62, 68, 89, 210–211, 275–276; *Winters v. United States*, 41, 68, 205, 227, 228, 235, 275, 282. *See also* collaborative land and water management; Law of the River
watershed governance: based on hydrographic districts, 56–58, 76, 107; competing interests in, 45–47, 63–65; "dryland democracy," as term, 28; iron triangle and, 281; modern tribal methods of, 273–277; nonprofit institutions of, 36–37; Powell on, 29–32, 42, 46, 113, 131, 134, 281–283; proposed future system of, 42–47; state and federal roles in, 38–42. *See also* collaborative land and water management; communitarianism; dams; irrigation infrastructure; land governance; water rights
water sustainability, defined, 70
water transfers, 88–89
Watkins, T.H., 180
Weeminuche Ute Band, 271. *See also* Ute Indian Tribe and reservation
westward expansion, xiv, xv, 150, 224–226, 267–268. *See also* colonial land

governance; homesteading program; Manifest Destiny
Wheeler, George, xxi
White Mountain Apache Tribe, 231
White River, 269
White River Ute Band and Agency, 249, 269. *See also* Ute Indian Tribe and reservation
whitewater recreation: in Dolores River Basin, 62–63; in Grand Canyon, 115, 173–174, 177–179. *See also* recreation and tourism industry
Wiebe, Robert, 132
Wild and Scenic Rivers Act (1968), 110. *See also* National Wild and Scenic Rivers System; wild rivers
wilderness: as concept, xvi, 15, 18, 225–226; federally designated areas of, 96, 138; legislative protection of, 110, 172, 185; Worster on, 107. *See also* ecology and preservation of ecosystems
Wilderness Act (1964), 172, 185
Wilderness and the American Mind (Nash), 158
"Wilderness Letter" (Stegner), 169
"Wilderness Rivers: Shooting the Wild Colorado" (Stewart Udall), 177, 178–179
wildfire management, 143, 161, 212, 242. *See also* national forest system and US Forest Service
wildlife protection, 114, 184, 256. *See also* ecology and preservation of ecosystems; fish habitat and species protection; Indigenous environmental stewardship; national wildlife refuge system

wild rivers, 2, 15–18, 55, 62, 65–66, 110, 226. *See also* dams; ecology and preservation of ecosystems; irrigation infrastructure; *names of specific rivers*
Wilkinson, Charles, 186, 228
Wilson, Will, 198*fig.*
Winnebago Tribe, 244
Winters v. United States (1908), 41, 68, 205, 227, 228, 235, 275, 282
wisdom *vs.* folly: Powell on, 57, 69, 72, 131, 151, 186; in water rights disputes, 70–73. *See also* paradox, as concept
World War I, 12, 135–136
World War II, 13, 135–136, 179, 208
Worster, Donald, 11, 12, 47, 107, 181, 247
Wounded Knee Massacre (1890), 222
Wright Act (1887), 37
Wyoming, 85, 154

Yampa River, 15, 21, 269, 294
Yampa Ute Band, 271. *See also* Ute Indian Tribe and reservation
Yaqui Tribe, 276
Yavapai Apache Nation, 273, 276
Yellowstone National Park, 107, 108, 109, 126, 183
Yosemite National Park, 108, 109, 175, 183
Yuma, Arizona, 79
Yuma Tribe, 269
Yurok Tribe, 254

Zion National Park, 111, 115, 117, 118
Zuni Tribe: Bears Ears and, xvii, 112, 210–211, 213, 256–258; Grand Canyon and, 294; traditional lands of, 269

Founded in 1893,
UNIVERSITY OF CALIFORNIA PRESS
publishes bold, progressive books and journals
on topics in the arts, humanities, social sciences,
and natural sciences—with a focus on social
justice issues—that inspire thought and action
among readers worldwide.

The UC PRESS FOUNDATION
raises funds to uphold the press's vital role
as an independent, nonprofit publisher, and
receives philanthropic support from a wide
range of individuals and institutions—and from
committed readers like you. To learn more, visit
ucpress.edu/supportus.

www.ingramcontent.com/pod-product-compliance
Lightning Source LLC
Chambersburg PA
CBHW030520230426
43665CB00010B/703